Technology Enhanced Learning:
Best Practices

Miltiadis D. Lytras
University of Patras, Greece

Dragan Gašević
Athabasca University, Canada

Patricia Ordóñez de Pablos
University of Oviedo, Spain

Weihong Huang
Kingston University, UK

IGI PUBLISHING

Hershey • New York

Acquisition Editor:	Kristin Klinger
Development Editor:	Kristin Roth
Senior Managing Editor:	Jennifer Neidig
Managing Editor:	Jamie Snavely
Assistant Managing Editor:	Carole Coulson
Copy Editor:	Jeannie Porter
Typesetter:	Jeff Ash
Cover Design:	Lisa Tosheff
Printed at:	Yurchak Printing Inc.

Published in the United States of America by
  IGI Publishing (an imprint of IGI Global)
  701 E. Chocolate Avenue
  Hershey PA 17033
  Tel: 717-533-8845
  Fax: 717-533-8661
  E-mail: cust@igi-global.com
  Web site: http://www.igi-global.com

and in the United Kingdom by
  IGI Publishing (an imprint of IGI Global)
  3 Henrietta Street
  Covent Garden
  London WC2E 8LU
  Tel: 44 20 7240 0856
  Fax: 44 20 7379 0609
  Web site: http:/www.eurospanbookstore.com

Library of Congress Cataloging-in-Publication Data

Technology enhanced learning : best practices / Miltiadis Lytras ... [et al.], editors.
  p. cm. -- (Knowledge and Learning Society book series ; 4)
 Summary: "This book goes beyond traditional discussion on technology enhanced learning provides research and insights on increasing the efficiency of learning for individuals and groups, facilitating the transfer and sharing of knowledge in organizations, and understanding of the learning process by exploring links among human learning, cognition, and technologies. "--Provided by publisher.
 Includes bibliographical references and index.
 ISBN-13: 978-1-59904-600-6 (hardcover)
 ISBN-13: 978-1-59904-602-0 (e-book)
 1. Education--Effect of technological innovations on. 2. Educational technology. 3. Computer-assisted instruction. 4. Organizational learning. I. Lytras, Miltiadis D., 1973-
 LB1028.3.T39683 2008
 371.33--dc22
        2007037716

British Cataloguing in Publication Data
A Cataloguing in Publication record for this book is available from the British Library.

All work contributed to this book is new, previously-unpublished material. The views expressed in this book are those of the authors, but not necessarily of the publisher.

Technology Enhanced Learning:

Best Practices

Table of Contents

Foreword

It is my pleasure to write some words for this edited volume. Technology is being used in rather innovative ways in the learning process, and it now takes very little time in which it moves from "unusual use" mode to commonly known practice! It is interesting to see the shift of focus from teaching to learning and recognition of the important role informal and non-formal learning plays in the so-called knowledge society. I would not discount the role of formal learning either, but technology has certainly widened the access to education for those who, in increasingly global and competitive environment, are unable to pursue formal educational avenues or simply want to cross over the boundaries of formal education for further achievements.

With emerging technologies come discussions about change of instructional paradigms. I believe that it is important to look at this issue with open mind and ensure that we can make the best of the changes that technology is bringing to serve the changing needs of younger generations. While traditional educational system has produced good results, and those of us who are products of that system did not turn out to be failures, lot of research is out there that clearly indicates that a lot is also left to be desired. Technology has continued to make difference for long time, but the rate of change has become rather significant in recent years.

While changes bring new perspectives and a fresh look at the ways learning is facilitated and how the process could be improved, the absence of any benchmarks make it difficult to assess if the changes are actually happening in the right direction. The first step towards creating such benchmarks is to look at the ways adopters of technology are using it and identify best practice examples. I am pleased to see this book as a timely step in that direction.

The book contains a right balance between the uses of technology, effects on and implications of theories, a critical look at wider strategies, along with sophisticated "intelligent" systems that have emerged in recent times. It concludes with an interesting proposal for roadmap of future technology enhanced learning. Not only that various chapters would serve as guide for practitioners in deciding better ways to implement technology enhanced learning, but the whole book would also serve as a referential archive for future educational technology researchers.

Kinshuk

Athabasca University, Canada

Kinshuk is professor and director of School of Computing and Information Systems at Athabasca University, Canada since August 2006. Before moving to Canada, Kinshuk worked at German National Research Centre for Information Technology as Postdoctoral Fellow, and at Massey University, New Zealand as associate professor of Information Systems and director of Advanced Learning Technology Research Centre. He also holds Docent position with University of Joensuu, Finland. He has been involved in large-scale research projects for adaptive and mobile learning environments and by 2007, he has published over 200 research papers in international refereed journals, conferences and book chapters. He is Chair of IEEE Technical Committee on Learning Technology and editor of the SSCI indexed Journal of Educational Technology & Society.

Preface

Technology Enhanced Learning: Best Practices is the fourth book in the *Knowledge and Learning Society Book Series*. Three titles are already available in the bookstores:

- *Intelligent Learning Infrastructure for Knowledge Intensive Organizations: A Semantic Web Perspective*
- *Open Source for Knowledge and Learning Management: Strategies Beyond Tools*
- *Ubiquitous and Pervasive Knowledge and Learning Management: Semantics, Social Networking and New Media to their Full Potential*

This book is complementary and is published together with the 5th book of the series entitled:

- *Knowledge Management Strategies: A Handbook of Applied Technologies* (Editors: Miltiadis D. Lytras, Meir Russ, Ronald Maier, and Ambjörn Naeve)

For mid-2008, two more edited volumes which contribute further to our vision for the knowledge society are planned.

- *Knowledge and Networks: A Social Networks Perspective* (Editors: Miltiadis D. Lytras, Robert Tennyson, and Patricia Ordonez De Pablos)
- *Semantic Web Engineering for the Knowledge Society* (Editors: Jorge Cardoso and Miltiadis D. Lytras)

Technology Enhanced Learning is the best term to describe the domain of Knowledge Society Technologies as applied in the Learning context.

"Learning for anyone, at any time, at any place" is the motto. With the shift towards the knowledge society, the change of working conditions and the high-speed evolution of information and communication technologies, peoples' knowledge and skills need continuous updating. Learning based on collaborative working, creativity, multidisciplinary, adaptiveness, intercultural communication and problem solving has taken on an important role in everyday life. The learning process is becoming pervasive, both for individuals and organizations, in formal education, in the professional context, and as part of leisure activities. Learning should be accessible to every citizen, independent of age, education, and social status and tailored to individual needs.

Meeting these social challenges is a leading issue of research on the use of technology to support learning (e.g., the 6th and 7th EU Framework Programme for Research and Technological Development, 2002-2013).

In the context of Knowledge Society, the focus of research in this area has been on applications of technologies for user-centered learning, building on the concept of human learning and on sound pedagogical principles with the key objectives to be:

- To increase the efficiency of learning for individuals and groups
- To facilitate transfer and sharing of knowledge in organizations
- To contribute to a deeper understanding of the learning process by exploring links between human learning, cognition, and technologies

In this book, we applied a clear editing strategy. We wanted and, thanks to the excellent contributors, we made it:

- Go beyond the traditional discussion on Technology Enhanced Learning
- Provide a reference book for the area with main emphasis to be paid on practical aspects.
- Make learning oriented edition; in other words, the proposed book can be seen as a textbook for everybody interested in TEL.

The whole book is organized around the following pillars of the Technology Enhanced Learning Agenda:

Technology Enhanced Learning: An Emerging Episteme

- **The technology enhanced learning domain:** Philosophical routes, demonstration of various communities, success stories, lessons learned
- **Technology enhanced learning key issues:** Effective strategies, learning models and theories, deploymenent of ict's in education, policy issues of TEL, integration issues, extensibility, interoperability

Technology Enhanced Learning: The Theories

- Pedagogical theories and models of TEL
- Constructivist approaches to TEL
- Collaborative/Context Aware/Personalized TEL approaches
- Communities of learners and TEL

Technology Enhanced Learning: The Practices

- TEL practices in primary and secondary educations
- Surveys of ICT's adoption in K-12 education
- Future of TEL

Technology Enhanced Learning: The Applications in Domains

- TEL tools / Emerging technologies and New generation TEL
- Challenges for the future/Specification of Government Policies for the Promotion of TEL in education.
- Roadmaps for the future

We are very happy since during the preparation of this edited book we also launched the *International Journal of Technology Enhanced Learning* (IJTEL), which can be found at http://www.inderscience.com/ijtel

IJTEL fosters multidisciplinary discussion and research on technology enhanced learning (TEL) approaches at the individual, organisational, national, and global levels. Its key objective is to be the leading scholarly scientific journal for all those interested in researching and contributing to the technology enhanced learning episteme. For this reason, IJTEL delivers research articles, position papers, surveys, and case studies aiming to:

- Provide a holistic and multidisciplinary discussion on technology enhanced learning research issues
- Promote the international collaboration and exchange of ideas and know how on technology enhanced learning
- Investigate strategies on how technology enhanced learning can promote sustainable development

Our wonderful journey in the research and vision for the knowledge society has one more stop. In September 2008 (and in each forthcoming September), we organize the Athens World Summit on the Knowledge Society (for more information, e-mail Lytras@ceid.upatras.gr).

The Athens World Summit on the Knowledge Society aims at becoming the leading forum for the dissemination of the latest research on the intersection of Information and Communications technology (ICT) and any area of human activity including production, economy, interaction, and culture.

The Athens World Summit on the Knowledge Society brings together:

- Academics
- Business people and industry
- Politicians and policy makers
- Think tanks
- Government officers

The underlying idea is to define, discuss, and contribute to the overall agenda on how emerging technologies reshape the basic pillars of our societies towards a better world for all. This is why five general pillars provide the constitutional elements of the Summit:

- Government in the knowledge society
- Research and sustainable development in the knowledge society
- Social and humanistic computing for the knowledge society
- Information technologies for the knowledge society

- Education, culture, business, tourism, entertainment in the knowledge society.

The **Athens World Summit on Knowledge Society** event series provide a distinct, unique forum for cross-disciplinary fertilization of research, favouring the dissemination of research that is relevant to international research agendas as the EU FP7.

We do believe that this edition contributes to the literature. We invite you to be part of the exciting Technology Enhanced Learning Community and we are really looking forward to your comments, ideas, and suggestions for future editions.

Structure/Edititng Strategy/Synopsis of the Book

When dealing with technology enhanced learning (TEL), it is really of no sense to try to be exhaustive, not only because of the fast pace in technologies that support technology enhanced learning but mostly due to the many different aspects of the domains. Moreover, when you are trying to investigate the new insights of TEL, like social networks, Wemantic Web, assessment, and knowledge and learning management, the mission becomes even more complex.

This is why from the beginning we knew that our book should be selective and focused. In simple words, we decided to develop a book with characteristics that would help the reader to follow several different journeys through the contents. We also decided to open the book to big audiences. While we could pursue through our excellent contacts and great network of collaborators a publication aiming to promote the discipline, we decided that it would be most significant (from a value adding perspective) to develop a reference book. And this is what we made with the support of great contributors: a state of the art reference book for technology enhanced learning providing an excellent overview of the emerging research agenda. Having the experience of the edition of four edited books and feedback from hundreds of researchers from all over the world, we decided to keep the same presentation strategy. We tried, and succeeded, we think, in developing a book that has three characteristics:

- It discusses the key issues of the relevant research agenda
- It provides practical guidelines and presents several technologies and
- It has a teaching orientation.

The last characteristic is a novelty of our book. Several times editions seem like a compilation of chapters without an orientation to the reader. This is why every edited chapter is accompanied by a number of additional resources that increase the impact for the reader.

In each chapter, we follow a common didactic-learning approach:

- At the beginning of each chapter, authors provide a section entitled Inside Chapter, which is an abstract-like short synopsis of the chapter.

At the end of each chapter there are some very interesting sections where reader can spend many creative hours. More specifically the relevant sections are entitled:

- **Internet session:** In this section authors present one or more Web sites, relevant to the discussed theme in each chapter. The short presentation of each Internet session is followed by the description of an *Interaction* where the reader (student) is motivated to have a guided tour in the Web site and to complete an assignment.

- **Case study:** For each chapter, contributors provide "realistic" descriptions for one case study that readers must consider in order to provide strategic advice.

- **Useful links:** These refer to Web sites with content capable of exploiting the knowledge communicated in each chapter. We decided to provide these links in every chapter, even though we know that several of them will be broken in the future, since their synergy with the contents of the chapter can support the final learning outcome.

- **Further readings:** These refer to high quality articles available both in Web and electronic libraries. We have evaluated these resources as of significant value.

Acknowledgment

"To the happiness..." That we are all looking for, With the wish to inspire our minds, to stay in our souls and rock our hearts forever.

We finalized this book "Technology Enhanced Learning: Best Practices" in early August 2007, Miltiadis in Athens, Greece, of 42C, Dragan in Canada, and Patricia in Gijon, Spain.

So the time has come for us to express our deepest appreciation and respect to the 30 contributors of this edition. Their knowledge, expertise, and experience are evident in every line of this edition. It sounds typical, but it is the ultimate truth. Every edition is just an outlet where the world of ideas is seeking a fertile ground. And this ground is not self-admiring. It requires the interest and insights of people. Hence our second deepest thank you goes to our readers in academia, industry, government, and in society in general.

It is also typical to acknowledge the publishers and all the supporting staff in all the stages of the book production. But in IGI Global, we have found more than just publishers and excellent professionals. We have found great supporters of a shared vision to develop books/editions and knowledge for a highly demanding society. So dear Mehdi, Jan, Kristin, Jessica, Anthony, Meg, please accept our warmest compliments for your encouragement and inspiration. You prove to us every day that IGI-Global is not only a high quality publishing organization but also a community that cares for its people.

Our deepest appreciation and respect to Professor Kinshuk, for his excellent foreword.

If you judge the type of our "job," then you have to admit from the beginning that editing books is not an income-generating case. We must laugh when we go to DHL with a bulk package of all the required materials for the book and they ask us to pay about 250-300 euros for sending them to the United States. We are joking and saying that with this money one of us could fly in person to the States. But when we have posted the package, the Ithaca is there and we really enjoyed the trip, so our only real anxiety is to open our book to our audiences. So, once again, the journey was full of exciting experiences and we are really grateful to all the people who stand by us.

We are looking forward to the next one.

A personal note from Miltiadis: I want to thank from the bottom of my heart Patricia for the new journey we started together concerning our magazine about China, ORLY, and D++, a lifetime project, and also my aderfos Dragan for the mutual Agapi and respect. Sve najbolje za brata Dragan. Hola y buenas noches Espanola.☺

Chapter I

Technology Enhanced Learning Tools

Goran Shimic, University of Belgrade, Serbia

Inside Chapter

This chapter emphasizes the variety of today's e-learning systems. They have both positive and negative characteristics. Several useful tools are common for these systems. The main part of this chapter contains a detailed description of e-learning systems and their tools. If a system is appropriate for the needs of the learner then it has more intelligent behavior and its tools are more specialized. Some systems have separate tools that act as standalone applications. Others contain built in tools. In this chapter, the e-learning tools are grouped by their functions. Owing to standardization efforts, the differences between the e-learning tools become their advantages, and the e-learning systems become interoperable. The intelligent learning management systems (ILMS) become a new way to integrate the benefits of the different e-learning systems. At the end of the chapter there is a short description of an ILMS named Multitutor. This represents a possible way of future e-learning systems development.

Introduction

Using current Internet technology to support learning in the classroom is recently becoming much easier and much more feasible than it used to be. If a network of computers or workstations is available in a classroom (the same is on the global network), it is easy to install and use Apache, Tomcat, or another Web server. It can distribute HTML pages generated statically or dynamically by an educational application. Client computers/workstations should only have an Internet browser. Hardware and software requirements for the client machines are minimal. TEL tools are strongly related to e-learning (as the other technology enhanced tools are related to e-commerce, e-banking, e-government).

There are three groups of the e-learning systems which are the most frequently used on the Web: adaptive systems: adaptive hypermedia (AH), intelligent tutoring systems (ITS), and nonadaptive systems (learning management systems, or LMS). The AH systems are focused on adaptable structure of the educational materials (Brusilovsky, 2003). They provide different adaptation techniques: conditional or stretch text, variations of pages and fragments, and frames linked to the concepts. There are many good examples of the AH systems. ISIS-tutor (Brusilovsky & Pesin, 1994) has adaptability based on the directed graph of concepts. The concepts are *based-on* and *is-basis-for* relations. KN-AHS (http://wwwis.win.tue.nl/ah94/Kobsa.html) has implemented the presentational adaptation. The learning materials are composed by-fly. In the Hyperflex (http://www.cs.mdx.ac.uk/staffpages/serengul/HYPERFLEX. htm), the navigational adaptation is implemented in the system. The student has a full list of topics, but the order of items is changeable.

While the AH systems have a compact system design with high coupled components, the ITS have high-level modularity. ITS provide user (student) oriented design and much more pedagogical knowledge implemented in the system. These systems are focused on problem-based learning (PBL). The Cognitive Tutor (Ritter, 1997) is designed for learning math; the LISP TUTOR [naci referencu] is focused on the using of LISP programming language, while the SQL Tutor helps students master the structured query language (SQL). PBL requires a precisely defined student profile and a high level of interaction between the system and the student. Therefore, the behaviour of ITS is more intelligent than in the other e-learning systems. Both of them (AHS and ITS) are focused on the specific area of one domain.

LMS represent the domain independent systems. They enable the teachers the possibility of composing their courses of newly created and existed learning units or so called learning objects (LO). These objects are modelled and described by standard structure and metadata. This means that LO would be reused in many courses and for different purposes. Teachers can use a LMS to develop Web-based course materials and tests, to communicate with students, and to monitor their students' progress. Students can use it for learning and collaboration The LMS are much more successful in Web-enhanced education (related to a number of users) because they have better administration capabilities than adaptive systems mentioned above. WebCT and Blackboard represent two typical LMS systems.

There are several TEL tools in the e-learning systems. They can be categorized in three main groups depending on their functions: teacher tools, learner tools, and administration tools (Figure 1). Implicitly there are three basic actors in the e-learning system (named as their functionalities). Most of them are shared between these actors.

The collaborating tools (e-mail, forum, whiteboard, news, discussion groups) are shared by all actors. Teacher functions imply both the teacher and the domain expert functions. The authoring tools enable the teacher/expert to design, to describe, to organize, and to publish learning resources (e.g., learning content, tests). These resources are used by the learner through learning tools and assessment tools. The learners can annotate (personalize) the learning contents (by annotation tools). The annotation tools allow the teacher to point out the important parts of the learning contents. The teachers can see and analyze the progress of the learners by using the assessment tools and the User&group management tools. The managing of the user and group data includes the add/edit/remove actions. These tools also enable the teachers and administrators to track and analyze learner actions at an individual and group level. The administrator manages the overall e-learning system by System management tools (user accounts, setup, and configuration data, database administration). Also he manages different kinds of contents (learning resources, collaboration data) as well as the teachers (Content management tools).

Figure 1. Basic tools in the e-learning systems (Copyright 2008, Goran Shimic. Used with permission)

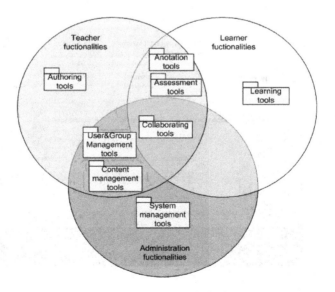

TEL tools mentioned above provide the basic functions of the e-learning systems. They are implemented by different ways on the system. For example, the authoring tools for some ITS act as stand alone applications (REEDEM, LEAP, Authorware, Course Builder). In most cases, the TEL tools are integrated into the system. One e-learning system represents the aggregation of different TEL tools.

Learning Management Systems

The learning management systems (LMS) are integrated systems that support teachers' and students' needs. The LMS provide a complete platform in the areas of logging, assessing, planning, delivering contents, managing records, and reporting. They improve both self-paced and instructor-led learning processes (Beck, Stern, & Haugsjaa, 1996). The LMS architecture is more complex than the one of ITS (Figure 2). As mentioned, these systems have three basic kinds of functions:

- Teacher functions (creating, describing, and publishing the learning resources, organizing resources in the courses/lessons/tests/exams, collaborating with the other teachers and learners, monitoring learners' progressions, etc.).

Figure 2. LMS architecture (Copyright 2008, Goran Shimic. Used with permission)

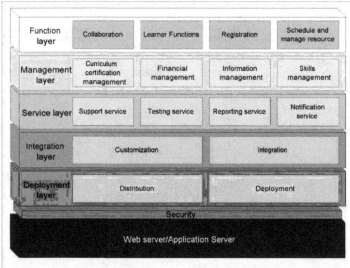

- Learner functions (using of a learning/test materials, collaborating with the other learners and teachers, etc.).
- Administration functions (managing of overall system data).

The system complexity is layered to distribute responsibility through the system (for different users: administrators, Web designers, software designers, and implementers, domain experts, teachers, etc.). This way LMS have greater efficiency in course productions than other e-learning systems.

LMS are domain-independent systems that provide the design and publishing of reusable learning resources (learning resources that can be used for different courses and for different learner groups). These resources are structured and described on different ways in the different LMS (e.g., e-packs in WebCT or building blocks in Blackboard). The commercial nature of most of LMS and difference of content packaging and user profiling standards decrease the interoperability between different LMS. The producers of today's LMS try to incorporate learning standards in to the their products (e.g., WebCT Vista, Blackboard, Atlas Pro).

The Examples of LMS

The WebCT (http://www.webct.com) and the Blackboard (http://www.blackboard.com) are two similar LMS that store a great amount of learning contents. The teachers can combine the existing contents or they can create new ones. WebCT and Blackboard are not open source systems and whole learning resources are hosted on their URLs.

The WebCT is a commercial product implemented as pure Web application—collection of Perl scripts. Content and configuration data are stored in text files without XML support but resource management is well designed. The WebCT has strong communication features. The courses are built by LO so called e-packs. The user interface is difficult to use (Piendl, 1999). Therefore WebCT provides different types of wizards that simplify the course production. The newest version of this LMS (WebCT Vista) represents the integration effort of WebCT and Blackboard.

The Blackboard is designed as a toolset that provides different functions. My Faculty Tools are designed for the course design. The course is represented as a package named Course Cartridge. This package is composed by building blocks (see previous section). The course designers can reuse the existing LO by the BuildingBlock Catalog tool. The learners can search the learning topics by the Search Content tool. The user management is provided by the Seneca Toolkit tool. There is a plug-in tool named LinkMaker designed for linking the learning resources and course items. The FAQTool represents the tool for managing FAQ lists. The FAQ lists are grouped according to contents that are accessible to the learners (FAQTool). The colaboration between users is possible by e-mailing and forums.

The Moodle (Modular Object–Oriented Dynamic Learnign Environment) (Brayan, 2006) is a high interactive LMS. The courses can be created in three different formats (aspects): topic (conceptual), social, and weekly (chronological) (Figure 3). The Moodle is the open source modular LMS (exactly Course Management System) based on ideas of social constructivism. This means that e-learning systems have to provide the learners the number of tools for the customization of the learning environments according to their individual needs and experiences. Activities (the concept of the SCORM content packaging standard represent the heart of Moodle architecture.

The Moodle is implemented as a collection of PHP modules with MySQL or Posgres7 DBMS on the backend side. These modules represent Moodle tools (Figure 3). The Choices module is designed for survey purposes. There is a separate Survey module. These modules help teachers evaluate and adapt created learning environments, regarding preferred learning methods and perceptions of specific learners' groups. The Quiz module enables the teachers to create online quizzes. The Forums module provides users endless group discussions on teacher managed topics. The Resource module is a tool that provides the direct resource creating (plain text only), uploading, or linking external resource. The ChatRoom is a synchronous collaboration tool that is also controlled by the teacher. The Journals is designed for teachers and students for writing and revising ideas. The Dialog module enables users to have a one-on-one written conversation. The Assignment enables teachers to give students tasks to complete online or off-line.

Figure 3. Moodle LMS (Copyright 2008, Goran Shimic. Used with permission)

a. Activities

b. User interface

The main disadvantage of the existing LMS is a low interoperability with similar outdoor systems. The learning process includes different user activities and different ways of organizing it. The LMS producers try to offer as much more functions as possible to the users. Therefore LMS are difficult to exploit by teachers and learners.

On the other side, the domain independence, the integrated authoring tools, the great collaboration support, the management of the overall learning process, and the content reusability are the great advantages of LMS.

Adaptive E-Learning Systems (AEH&ITS)

The two most frequently used groups of the adaptive education systems on the Web are the Adaptive Education Hypermedia (AEH) and the Intelligent Tutoring Systems (ITS).

AEH

The AH systems are focused on non-linear and adaptable structure of the educational contents (Brusilovsky, 2003). The AEH architecture consists of the adaptation module (adaptation engine), the domain model (relationships between concepts), and the learner model (the row data source of adaptation) (Figure 4). The difference between the general purpose AH systems and the AEH is in the additional pedagogical module that is designed to emphasize the educational functionality of the system.

The AEH systems provide the user easy navigation, referencing, and global view of the contents. The adaptability of AEH is provided by the learner model. The AEH can be adaptable on the content level (adaptive presentation) and on the link level (adaptive navigation) (Brusilovsky, 1998).

Figure 4. Architecture of adaptive e-learning systems Copyright 2008, Goran Shimic. Used with permission)

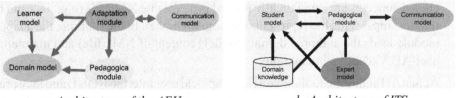

a. Architecture of the AEH   *b. Architecture of ITS*

Figure 5. Adaptive education hypermedia Copyright 2008, Goran Shimic. Used with permission)

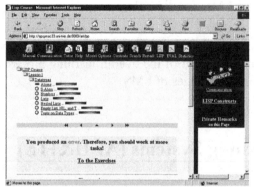

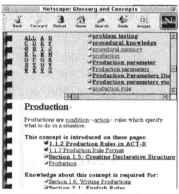

a. ELM ART navigation   b. InterBook AH

The ELM ART (http://www.psihologiue.uni-trier.de:8000/project/ELM/elmart.html) is a LISP programming AEH with the episodic student model (Figure 5). This model consists of different learner stereotypes. Based on a questionnaire and a pretest, the profile of the student is classified in one of the offered stereotypes. The ELM ART content is organized in a concept based hyperspace (one concept, one page). Annotation is used to markup the concept page that is not ready to be learned (e.g., prerequisite concepts are not learned yet).

The InterBook (Figure 5) is another example of AEH. As in the ELM ART, in the InterBook indexing of the concepts is used to create the glossary and to recommend the next best page to the learner.

In the AEH authoring tools enable the authors to translate the domain concept structure (space) to the adaptive hypertext structure (hyperspace) (Brusilovsky, 2006). There are several techniques that provide this function. The first AH authoring tools are mainly based on the hypertext markup. For example, InterBook (Figure 7) uses comment tags (<!—embedded markup tags—>) to relate the specified HTML contents with the prerequisite and outcome concepts.

Another markup approach is a XML based authoring tool. In the AHA! tool (De Bra, Aerts, & Rousseau, 2002), the page content is represented in HTML. The XML extensions in pages are used for indexing authors conditional fragments. The included concepts are semantically related in a separate XML file (e.g., is-a and has-a relationships). This file represents the domain model. In the runtime, the adaptation module loads the authored domain model (content of XML file) and maintains the user-AHA adaptive interaction.

Actual AH authoring tools have a rich graphical user interface (GUI) and they provide easy annotation possibilities. The NetCoach (Figure 6) authoring tool (Weber, Kuhl,

Figure 6. Adaptive hypermedia authoring tools (Copyright 2008, Goran Shimic. Used with permission)

a. NetCoach AH authorinng tool

b. ALE authoring tool

& Weibelzahl, 2001) uses a concept-based hyperspace approach and supports both concept authoring, and page authoring. The contents have a hierarchical organization and the authors can add background and behaviour to every separate page.

Another example of a rich interface AH authoring tool is ALE (Specht, Kravcik, Klemke, Pesin, & Hüttenhain, 2002) (Figure 6.b). The content has a tree structure, and the concepts are indexed such as in the InterBook. The concepts are represented as sets of synonyms. This way, the concept level of user modelling is avoided. Automatic concept indexing produces content searching by simple text analysis.

ITS

The other group of adaptive systems are ITS. As mentioned, they provide the most sophisticated tutoring to the learner. These systems are focused on a specific domain and on the learning process (pedagogy, user modelling, and user evaluation). While the AH systems are focused on the content design, representation, and adaptation, the main task of the ITS is tutoring the learner. The general concepts that support the above mentioned aspects are implemented as components of the ITS architecture. There are five basic ITS modules (Figure 5) the student model, the domain knowledge, the pedagogical module, the expert model, and the communication model (Beck et al., 1996).

Most ITS are focused on problem-based learning. The Cognitive Tutor (Ritter, 1997), http://www.carnegielearning.com, is ITS based on a cognitive student model. The first version of Cognitive Tutor is PAT OnLine (Ritter, 1997), an algebra tutor. The students' knowledge level is estimated regarding capabilities.

Figure 7. Cognitive tutor (Copyright 2008, Goran Shimic. Used with permission)

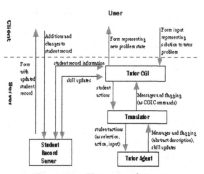 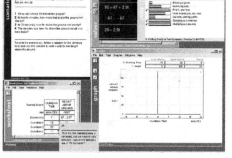

a. Cognitive Tutor architecture   b. Cognitive Tutor GUI

Cognitive Tutor is the rule based system designed for the mathematic tutoring. The core of the Cognitive Tutor is the Tutor Agent (Figure 7), which consists of the expert module (problem generator and inferring engine), the student model (cognitive model), and the pedagogical module (step by step evaluating student skills and adapting future tasks). Student records are stored on a separate server. Students' row data are collected directly form the client, while the processed data are received from Tutor Agent (via Translator and Tutor CGI). The rich user interface provides great support to the learning process (Figure 7).

The SQL Tutor (http://www.cosc.canterbury.ac.nz/~tanja/sql-tut.html) represents a ITS designed for learning SQL queries. The constraint-based reasoning represents a specific property of SQL Tutor. The Student modeller (expert module) profiles the student based on the constraint knowledge base (KB) (Figure 8). There is a separate KB designed for examples of DB entities, problems and solutions.

The SQL Tutor defines a separate model for every learner. While the system is working, this model is filled by session data and conclusions that reflect the learners' level of knowledge (constraint terms). The system infers about the learner by propagating his solutions through the constraint network.

The ITS Authoring Tools

The authoring tools are primary developed for ITS and they are mainly implemented as standalone applications. Therefore, these tools are described in a separate section.

Generally there are two types of authoring tools (Murray & Woolf, 1992). The first one is easy for the teachers and the second one is easy for the programmers. The

Figure 8. SQL tutuor (Copyright 2008, Goran Shimic. Used with permission)

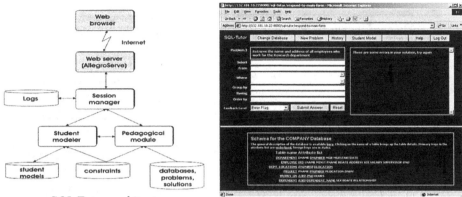

a. SQL Tutor architecture

b. SQL Tutor GUI

first type is focused on the description of the course, the individual student, and the pedagogical strategies and techniques. The examples of the first type are REEDEM (Major, 1995) and RAPIDS II (Towne & Munro, 1992). The second type prefers the domain presentation and the learning strategies. EON (Murray, 1996) and IDE (Russell, 1988) represent the second type of these tools. The ITS tools depend on their functions: the curriculum sequencing and planning, the defining of tutoring strategies, the device simulation and equipment training, and so forth.

The Examples of Authoring Tools

In the REDEEM tool (Major, 1995), a teacher can describe the contents of a course by using the course Meta model. This means that the course can be decomposed into the learning units (chapters and lessons). These units can be semantically linked to the course body. The REDEEM is not designed as a content-producing tool. It is used to describe and relate different contents produced by the ToolBook content authoring tool. The REDEEM enables the teachers to define the system pedagogy (Figure 9) and the learner model (Figure 9).

EON authoring tool (Murray, 1996) is focused on the presentation of the domain concepts (Figure 10), the student modelling, and knowledge structure (Figure 10). The domain concepts are organized in the topic. There are different types of concepts (topics). Every topic is described with attributes such as importance, or difficulty.

The teachers also have to specify the types of relations between topics (e.g., precedes, is part of, etc.). Although the EON is designed for knowledge based ITS, it enables the teacher to define the learner model (Figure 11). This model (Student Model

Figure 9. REEDEM authoring tool (Copyright 2008, Goran Shimic. Used with permission)

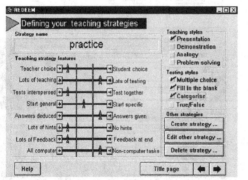
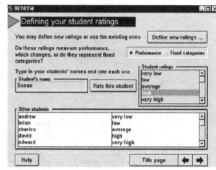

a. Define pedagogic model

b. Define learner model

Editor) is layered depending on the content level. The authors of the course have to define the rules and the values which are used for making conclusions (reasoning) between different levels (event to presentation, presentation to topic, topic to lesson). The transition rules between levels are used for inferring (e.g., presentation level conclusions are based on the facts at event level).

The LEAP authoring tools (Sparks, Dooley, Meiskey, & Blumenthal, 1998) are the special purpose authoring tools. LEAP tools allow experts to easily create courses about interpersonal communications. The LEAP consists of several editing tools: Script editor, Graphical editor (Figure 12), Action editor, Transition editor, Node editor, and so forth.

Figure 10. EON authoring tool (Copyright 2008, Goran Shimic. Used with permission)

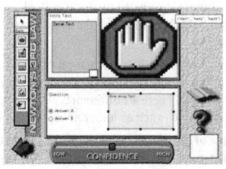
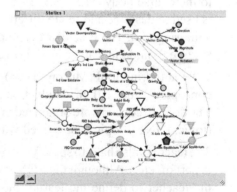

a. Presentation design

b. Knowledge structuring

Figure 11. EON student modeler (Copyright 2008, Goran Shimic. Used with permission)

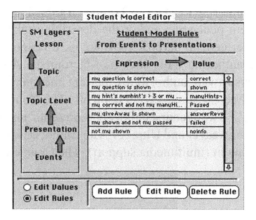

Figure 12. LEAP authoring tool (Copyright 2008, Goran Shimic. Used with permission)

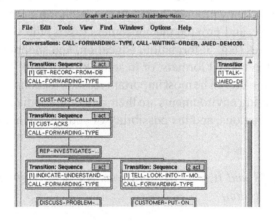

The conversation training is the main goal of these tools; therefore design and pedagogic principles are enforced. The conversation is the set of actions—nodes that contain one or more dialogues. The node can be related to one or more nodes (branches). These connections result in a directed graph. During the runtime, the conversation paths are changeable regarding the learners' communication skills (learner model).

The Role of General Purpose Tools

The represented authoring tools for AEH and ITS are focused on the user modelling, the defining system pedagogy, and/or the describing/relating learning resources. Therefore the other general purpose tools are used for content designing and creating. There are authoring tools such as Macromedia Authorware (http://www. macromedia.com/software/authorware) that are the standalone solutions for the development of Web-based education contents. The Course Builder (http://www. macromedia.com/software/coursebuilder/) represents an additional module for Macromedia Dreamweaver and Ultradev. The Authorware is focused on the design of the learning content (multimedia support). The Course Builder has rich assessment design tools.

CMS, LMS, & ITS

The content management systems (CMS) are Web-based systems designed for two major objectives. They provide the producers (authors) storage for their contents in a Web repository, and provide the consumers (users) the use of these contents for different purposes (e.g., information, education, and shopping). The contents may be represented in textual formats, or in some kind of multimedia formats (photos, video, audio clips, etc.). The most important reasons for considering these systems as potentially learning environments are their rich multimedia support, their advanced management functions, and the possibility of adding extensions.

Figure 13. CMS and typical Web environment (Copyright 2008, Goran Shimic. Used with permission)

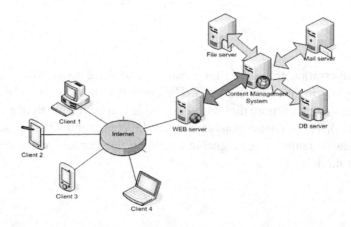

The CMS are multilayered systems that provide by fly composing of delivered content. Usually, they consist of the Web server on the front end and the application and data storage servers at the backend (Figure 13). Usually, the content is composed of different fragments. The statically fragments (hypertext, plaintext, or different kinds of multimedia) can be stored in the file system (file server) or they can be stored as blobs in DB. The dynamic fragments, with the application objects, are stored on the application server. The data from the DB or files are processed by application objects mentioned above. The CMS provide some additional modules/services (e.g., e-mails, forums, searching engines, etc.).

The CMS are based on a variety of technologies. Three technologies are dominant: Java-based systems, Microsoft.NET components, and PHP-based systems. Java-based CMS are usually implemented using JSP (Servlet) technology, with the Apache Web server as the front end server (e.g., Apache Lenya, see http://cocoon.apache. org/lenya; Ariadne LKP, see http://www.ariadne-eu.org/index.html). An alternative is a standalone system with integrated Web and application servers (e.g., OpenCMS, see http://www.opencms.org/opencms/opencms). The DotNET technology integrates well-known Microsoft Web products in the scalable component-based model. There are also many CMS implemented using other technologies: PHP&MySQL (Absolute Engine, see http://absolutengine.com; phpWCMS and PHP Nuke, see http://www. openphpnuke.com; Payton, see http://pyton.org; Plone, see http://plone.org; Joomla, see http://www.joomla.org). The CMS can perform different administration tasks, but all of them are focused on the their contents.

The Integration Prerequisites

The LMS and ITS have different benefits and therefore they are very compatible. On the other side, the CMS are mainly used in institutions. In this case, the learning systems can be developed and installed as standalone systems. There is large amount of contents in CMS that can be used for learning. Separate managing of the user accounts (in CMS and in LMS/ITS) produces many problems in content accessibility and in data consistency. These problems can be solved by incorporation of the TEL tools in the CMS.

Standardization of the Learning Content

For reusability, the learning contents have to be fragmented on so called learning objects (LO). These objects can be used to compose different courses. The authoring tools have to allow teachers the possibility to search the LO. Therefore, LO must be described on a standardized way. The Dublin Core (DC) (http://dublincore.org/documents/dcmes-qualifiers) defines 15 metadata for description of the LO. The IEEE

Figure 14. User models (Copyright 2008, Goran Shimic. Used with permission)

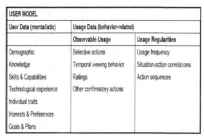

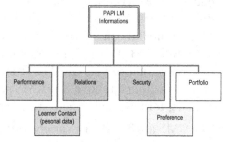

a. UM (Kobsa, Koenemann, Pohl)		b. PAPI LM data types

Learning Object Metamodel (LOM) (http://ltsc.ieee.org/wg12) extends DC standard through nine categories of metadata. The detailed LO description improves searching capabilities, content presentation, better relations between LO and LO classification. The Sharable Content Object Model Metadata (SCORM, http://www.adlnet. org) standard offers all in one packaging to provide better abilities for interchange of the learning contents. The IMS consortium designed many standards: the IMS QMI (http://www.imsglobal.org/question/qtiv1p2) is for test designing, the IMS RCD (http://www.imsproject.org/content/packaging/index.cfm) is for describing LO competence, the IMS CPS is for content packaging, and many others.

The User Modeling Standards

There are many standards of learner modelling. Different models support different user data (Figure 14) (Kobsa, Koenemann, & Pohl, 2001).

The ISO/IEC JTC WG2 recommends PAPI Learner metadata (IEEE P1484.2/D7, 2000). See http://edutool.com/papi/papi_learner_07_main.pdf (Figure 14). This standard is focused on logical division, separate security, and separate administration of several types of learner information.

The IMS consortium designed Learner Information Package (LIP, Figure 15) (ILM LIPv1.0, 2006). This package is designed to provide distributed learner information referencing. This standard is used to easily extend other types of human-related information (i.e., medicine, financial). Ontologging consortium LM is similar to IMS LIP (Figure 15, www.ontologging.com). This ontology is more focused on the learners' activities (type and level of activity and behavior level of knowledge sharing and other social aspects). The EduPerson (EduPerson OCS 200604, 2006) initiative consists of a set of attributes about individuals with higher education. The

Figure 15. User models (2) (Copyright 2008, Goran Shimic. Used with permission)

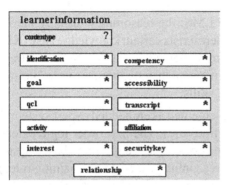
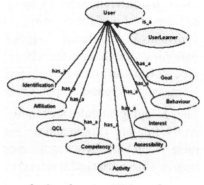

a. IMS LIP LM metadata   b. Ontologging UM ontology

Universal Learning Format (ULF) (http://www.saba.com/standards/ulf/) draws the learners' information like as Dublin Core Metadata Element Set and vCard.

Technology Support

This section represents a brief review of actual technologies that are used in e-learning systems. There are a number of technologies used for content presentations. In the Web-based systems, the contents can be dynamically composed. There are several leader technologies. The Java server pages (JSP, http://jakarta.apache.org/tomcat) represent pure object oriented approach based on the Java platform. The JSP embeds the Java classes and the Java code in a well designed html document. The PHP (http://www.php.net) is focused on the fast and easy designing of Web portals and CMS. In the PHP, HTML tags are embedded in the PHP script. The object-oriented programming is supported from PHP v5. The ASP (Active server pages) (http://www.microsoft.com) are similar to JSP. This is the Microsoft technology based on the IIS (Internet information server) and .NET framework. The Flash (http://www.macromedia.com/) represents the Macromedia product that allows designers to create the interface with a number of rich interface controls and multimedia effects. The main disadvantage of the Flash technology is the hard connection to the data sources (therefore it is mainly used for static contents).

As mentioned, the learning contents can be stored in different ways: as data records in a DBMS (Database Management System), or as files in a file system (Section 5.1). To protect database performances, a number of TEL systems hold short data in the DB and memory expansive learning content is stored in a file system. There can be some difficulties regarding the managing of the file system on different operating system platforms. Therefore, several systems maintain the virtual file system (files stored in the DB, Active directory, Content repository).

There are different kinds of reasoning in TEL systems. The inference engines are implemented in different ways. In the LMS, the reasoning is usually hard coded with many if/then clauses. In the ITS, there exists certain knowledge base (KB). The reasoning module uses the KB (often implemented as a rule base or constraints) to process row and historical data and to infer conclusions about the users' knowledge, interests, preferences, capabilities, and skills.

The reasoning modules are mainly implemented as embedded expert systems based on the first order logic and the production rules. The first order logic extends the proposition logic by using different kinds of entities (e.g., frame based systems or regular object oriented systems) in the reasoning process (e.g., chaining rules). The implementations are based on expert system shells such as CLIPS (http://www.ghg.net/clips/CLIPS.HTML) or Jess (Friendman, 2003) (http://herzberg.ca.sandia.gov/jess/).

Fuzzy logic provides the reasoning engine with the ability to draw reasonable conclusions based on ambiguous data (Zadeh, 1984). Usually, the fuzzy logic is implemented in the industry controllers. Actual e-learning systems collect many implicit data about the learners (e.g., navigation tracks, spending times, visiting frequencies, etc.). The implicit data are often ambiguous and they can not be processed in a conventional way. Therefore, fuzzy logic seems as a more suitable solution for the implementation of reasoning services. There are fuzzy reasoning tools (Ochard, 2006) that can be used in the TEL systems.

Advanced Technologies

The Web services and mobile applications represent advanced technologies that can be used for learning purposes. The main goal of the Web services is to improve interoperability between different systems. The systems offer their services to the external users (other systems). The communication is through interfaces which are defined by Simple Object Access Protocol (SOAP), see http://www.w3.org/TR/soap/, and described by (Web Services Description Language (WSDL). See http://www.w3.org/TR/wsdl. According to the portability of the user (learner) model and the distribution of learning resources, Web service is a possible way to resolve the collaboration between TEL systems.

The use of mobile technologies to support, enhance, and improve access to learning resources is a relatively new idea (Attewell, 2005). As described in the text and Figure 4, the specifics of the mobile platforms (PDA, iPod, hybrid phones) intrude the specific design of the content. The J2ME (http://www.innaworks.com/) and the Midlet (http://java.sun.com/) technology provide development mobile applications for different platforms.

Intelligent LMS (ILMS)

The ILMS represent an effort to associate benefits of adaptive and nonadaptive systems. The LMS collect more learner data than ITS or AH (user results, event logs, collaboration logs). On the other side, the ITS have greater inferring capabilities than LMS. Today, there are many different ITS and LMS. But the educational needs are not yet satisfied. There is no interoperability between these systems. The main problem is that every kind of data on the Web is poorly structured. The existing structures do not have a standardized format, or they implement different standards.

The ILMS structure is based on the structure of both ITS and LMS. As with ITS, in the ILMS there are modelling and representation of relevant aspects of knowledge. This means that it contains the knowledge about the student, the domain, the pedagogy and the communication that are involved.

The lack of learning personalization and the runtime content adaptation (Piendl, 1999) represent the main disadvantage of LMS. An ILMS has the aggregated structure of the LMS framework enriched by embedded core of ITS. The ILMS general architecture is similar to the LMS architecture and also consists of three basic parts: administration tools, teacher tools, and student tools (see Figure 26). The difference between LMS and ILMS is the incorporated intelligence in different parts of the system. The heterogenic functions and the domain independence need the use of different kinds of reasoning.

Figure 16. ILMS architecture (Copyright 2008, Goran Shimic. Used with permission)

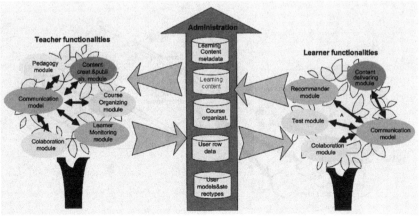

Integration Example: UNIS-MTutor

The MTutor (http://tool.singidunum.ac.yu) represents a domain independent TEL. It consists of three components: administrators' tools, teachers' (authoring) tools, and students' tools. All of them are Web-based applications. MTutor can be deployed as stand alone application, as well as embedded software module in different kinds of Web portals.

MTutor is able to serve intranet and extranet clients at the same time (Figure 17). The system behaves as a standalone application called Multitutor that serves the intranet users (Figure 18). The external users communicate with the MTutor through the university Web portal (University Network Information System) (Figure 18). The portal is designed in the PHP technology, and it is connected with the MTutor by the PHP-Java bridge. The MTutor is able to serve the clients in a conventional way (standard Internet protocols) just like wireless mobile clients through the 3G mobile telephony (e.g., by using the mobile client-server MIDP protocol and the MIDlet Java technology).

The presentation is fully separated from application logic. The system supports different kinds of users. The MTutor contains the IMS LIP LM as a generic model. This model is extended by many additional portable models. They are used on demand. The content packaging is based on the SCORM standard combined with DoublinCore extensions (to describe the content relations) and LOM meta model (to describe the technical formats, classification taxons and language localization). The standardization provides accessibility and reusability of the MTutor learning resources for different kinds of users. Also it provides the system management performances, and uses environmental CMS resources for learning purposes.

Figure 17. General system topology (Copyright 2008, Goran Shimic. Used with permission)

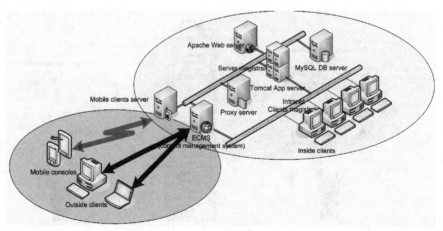

Figure 18. Multitutor as standalone application (Copyright 2008, Goran Shimic. Used with permission)

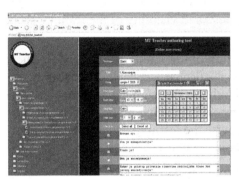

a. Multitutor as standalone application

b. Embedded – MTutor

Different reasoning techniques are used for reasoning about the individual learner in MTutor. The state of the user is explicitly represented by his personal data (collected by the questionnaire, rarely inferred from the sessions). The frequency and sequences of the users' actions (selections, ratings and navigation) are the source of the implicit user data.

The users' results (that clearly reflects the users' state) are processed by the rule-based reasoning engine (rules are designed as Clips rule base and they are processed by JESS shell). Often, the system cannot recognize the users' intentions based on his actions. The information noise complicates reasoning based on the predicate logic. The navigation statistic and the time measuring can produce ambiguous results. Imprecise input data are processed by the Fuzzy inferring engine (implemented as fuzzy sets, terms and rules, that are processed by JESS extension for fuzzy logic— FuzzyJToolkit).

Conclusion

Basically there are two groups of e-learning systems—adaptive and nonadaptive systems. Adaptive systems contain a rich learner model. The adaptation is based on this model. Nonadaptive systems contain an implicit learner model, but this model is not used for adaptation purposes. The adaptation ability also depends on the knowledge design. The system adaptability is proportional to the specialization of the domain. Therefore, it is hard to implement the adaptation in domain independent systems (such LMS or ILMS). The inferring engine represents the third factor of adaptation ability. This module (the expert module in ITS, the adaptation module in AH) uses the system knowledge (usually coded as rules or constraints), row data and defined pedagogy to make conclusions about the learner. These conclusions are used for adapting the learning content. It means that the system can adapt the presentation, navigation support, and visibility of the learning space for the individual learner.

Adaptability represents one manifestation of the intelligent behaviour. There are many others like recommendations, sophisticated feedback, and so forth. The intelligence behaviour is not designated only for the learners. The teachers (experts) need the intelligent feedback regarding their learning materials (exams, lessons, etc.). These messages can help them revise the learning contents according to real students' needs (knowledge level, interests, and preferences).

The adaptive systems are special purpose systems (e.g., specialized for SQL/LISP/ Mathematic learning). Therefore they have compact architecture and they provide a small set of functions. Their producers usually extend the basic set of functions by designing separate specialized tools (e.g., describing and relating the content, defining the user or pedagogy model, etc.). These tools act as standalone applications that can be used only for a specified adaptive system. The nonadaptive systems are designed for a great number of functions. All of these systems have the same feature in that they consist of many different tools. These tools can be implemented as standalone software modules, but usually they act as embedded system modules.

The e-learning tools are designed for three groups of functions: teacher, learner, and administration. There are many subclassifications of e-learning tools. Some tools are designed for the description of the content, others for user modelling or defining the pedagogy.

One of the main goals of the TEL development is to enforce interoperability between different systems. The knowledge about the learners and learning contents has to be reusable and accessible for eveyone. Therefore the mentioned knowledge is described by different metadata formats. If data are well structured, difference can be surmounted by making data transformations (between different formats).

The metadata about the learners, courses, and learning resources acts as the ontology of these domains. The well-formed ontology provides the possibility of semantically interconnecting between learning resources. The ontology improves the searching for learning objects and easy navigation through learning space. This way, the learners can adapt the learning space to their learning styles and preferences (according to theory of constructivism).

The other important objective is to make a greater separation between application logic and data on one side and presentation on the other. This objective can be released by using Web services instead of conventional Web applications and by using XML technologies (XML schemas, XSL transformations). These technologies can be used for marshaling and the representing data. It is easy to say but it is hard to do. Today Web services are limited to simple data interchange, although the SOAP is designed to support the interactions by the objects (whatever this means).

The problem based learning is applicable only to basic mathematical or programming exams. It is difficult to represent expert knowledge of problem solving. The solution is to integrate different reasoning technologies to the same reasoning process.

References

Attewell, J. (2005), *Mobile technologies and learning: A technology update and m-learning project summary*. Learning and Skills Development Agency, London. Retrieved from http://www.m-learning.org/archive/docs/

Beck, J., Stern, M., & Haugsjaa, E. (1996). Applications of AI in Education. *ACM Crossroads*, 3(1), 11-15.

Brayan, C.W. (2006). *Introduction to Moodle*. Retrieved January 2, 2008, from http://www.moodle.org

Brusilovsky, P. (1998). *Methods and techniques of adaptive hypermedia*. School of Computer Science, Carnegie Mellon University. Pittsburgh. Retrieved from http://www2.sis.pitt.edu/~peterb/papers/UMUAI96.pdf

Brusilovsky, P. (2003). A distributed architecture for adaptive and intelligent learning management systems. In *Proceedings of the AIED 2003 Workshop Towards Intelligent Learning Management Systems* (pp. 5-13). Sydney, Australia.

Brusilovsky, P. (2006). *Developing adaptive educational hypermedia systems: From design models to authoring tools*. Retrieved from http://www.sis.pitt.edu/~peterb/papers/KluwerAuthBook.pdf

Brusilovsky, P., & Pesin, L. (1994). ISIS-Tutor: An adaptive hypertext learning environment. In *Proceedings JCKBSE'94, Japanese-CIS Symposium on knowledge-based software engineering* (pp. 83-87). Tokyo, Japan.

De Bra, P., Aerts, A., & Rousseau, B. (2002, October 15-19). Concept relationship Types for AHA! 2.0. In M. Driscoll & T.C. Reeves (Eds.), *Proceedings of World Conference on E-Learning, E-Learn 2002* (pp. 1386-1389). Montreal, Canada.

EduPerson OCS 200604 (2006). EduPerson Object Class Specification (200604), Internet2 Middleware Architecture Committee for Education, Directory Working Group (MACE-Dir).

Friendman, E. (2003). *Jess in action—Rule-based systems in Java*. Livermore, CA: Sandia National Laboratories.

IEEE P1484.2/D7. (2000). IEEE P1484.2/D7, 2000-11-28. Draft Standard for Learning Technology. Public and Private Information (PAPI) for Learners (PAPI Learner). Retrieved January 2, 2008, from http://edutool.com/papi/papi_learner_07_main.pdf

ILM LIPv1.0. (2006). IMS Learner Information Packaging Information. Model Specification v1.0, IMS Global Learning Consortium, Inc.

Kobsa, A., Koenemann, J., & Pohl, W. (2001). Personalized hypermedia presentation techniques for improving online customer relationships. *The Knowledge Engineering Review, 16*(2), 111-155.

Major, N. (1995). REDEEM: Creating reusable intelligent courseware. In J. Greer (Ed.), *Proceedings of The International Conference on Artificial Intelligence in Education* (pp. 75-82). Charlottesville, VA.

Murray, T. (1996). Having it all, maybe: Design tradeoffs in ITS authoring tools. In *Proceedings of the Third International Conference on Intelligent Tutoring Systems*, Montreal.

Murray, T., & Woolf, B. (1992). Results of encoding knowledge with tutor construction tools. In *Proceedings of the Tenth National Conference on Artificial Intelligence* (pp.17-23). San Jose, CA.

Ochard, R. (2006). *NRC FuzzyJ toolkit for the Java(tm) platform user's guide (version 1.9)*. Institute of Information Technology National Research Council of Canada.

Piendl, T. (1999). *Web course authoring tools: An overview.* Workshop 2: The TopClass and WebCT environments. Swiss Virtual Campus.

Ritter, S. (1997). PAT online: A model-tracing tutor on the World Wide Web. In *Proceedings from Workshop about Intelligent Educational Systems on the World Wide Web* (pp. 11-17). Kobe, Japan.

Russell, D. (1988). IDE: The interpreter. In J. Psotka, L. Massey & S. Mutter (Eds.), *Intelligent tutoring systems: Lessons learned* (pp. 323-349). Hillsdale, NJ: Lawrence Erlbaum Associates.

Sparks, R., Dooley, S., Meiskey, L., & Blumenthal, R. (1998). The LEAP authoring tool: Supporting complex courseware authoring through reuse, rapid prototyping, and interactive visualizatioLEAPns. *International Journal of Artificial Intelligence in Education, 10,* 75-97.

Specht, M., Kravcik, M., Klemke, R., Pesin, L., & Hüttenhain, R. (2002). Adaptive LearningEnvironment (ALE) for teaching and learning in WINDS. In *Second International Conference on Adaptive Hypermedia and Adaptive Web-Based Systems (AH'2002) (*Vol. 2347, pp. 572-581). Berlin, Germany: Springer-Verlag.

Towne, D., & Munro, A. (1992). Supporting diverse instructional strategies in a simulation-oriented training environment. In J. Regian & V. Shute (Eds.), *Cognitive approaches to automated instruction* (pp. 107-134). Hillsdale, NY: Lawrence Erlbaum.

Weber, G., Kuhl, H.-C., & Weibelzahl, S. (2001). Developing adaptive Internet-based courses with the authoring system NetCoach. In P.D. Bra, P. Brusilovsky & A. Kobsa (Eds.), *Proceedings of third workshop on adaptive hypertext and hypermedia.*

Zadeh, L. (1984). *Making computers think like people.* IEEE Spectrum.

Further Readings

Zinn, C. (2006). Supporting tutorial feedback to student help requests and errors in symbolic differentiation. In *Proceedings of Intelligent Tutoring Systems 8th. International Conference ITS-2006.*

Feng, D., Kim, J., Shaw, E., & Hovy, E. (2006). Learning to model threaded discussions using induced ontology knowledge. In *Proceedings of the 21st National Conference on Artificial Intelligence (AAAI).*

Mayer, R.E., Johnson, W.L., Shaw, E., & Sandhu, S. (2006). Constructing computer-based tutors that are socially-sensitive: Politeness in educational software. *International Journal of Human-Computer Studies, 64*(1), 36-42.

Lee, H., Beal, C., & Erin Shaw, E. (2006, April 7). *Assessing student motivation with online self-report instruments in Web-based intelligent tutoring system.* Paper presented at the American Educational Research Association Annual Meeting, San Francisco (AERA).

Beal, C., Shaw, E., Vilhjalmsson, H., Chiu, J., Lee, H., & Qu, L. (2005). Enhancing ITS instruction with integrated assessments of learner mood, motivation and gender. In *Proceedings of the 12th International Conference on Artificial Intelligence in Education (AIED).* Amsterdam: IOS Press.

Useful URLs

Artificial intelligence: http://www.aaai.org/AITopics/

PROLEARN project: http://www.prolearn-project.org

ARIADNE: http://www.ariadne-eu.org/index.html

GOOD-OLD-AI: http://goodoldai.org.yu

Learning Management System (LMS) Architecture: http://www.icmgworld.com/corp/ces/ces.lms.asp

S. Smith, HYPERFLEX: http://www.cs.mdx.ac.uk/staffpages/serengul/HYPER-FLEX.htm

Universal Learning Format: http://www.saba.com/standards/ulf/Overview/Frames/overview.htm

Cognitive Tutor: http://www.carnegielearning.com

ELM-ART: http://www.psihologiue.uni-trier.de:8000/project/ELM/elmart.html

SQL Tutor: http://www.cosc.canterbury.ac.nz/~tanja/sql-tut.html

Authorware tool: http://www.macromedia.com/software/authorware

CourseBuilder tool: http://www.macromedia.com/software/coursebuilder

Learning Theories of Instructional Design: http://www.usask.ca/education/course-work/ 802papers/mergel/brenda.htm

Appendix

Figure A1.

Internet Session: International Forum on Education Technology and Society, Educational Technology and Society Journal

http://ifets.ieee.org/

The International Forum on Education Technology and Society is the representative place for the learning technology researchers. The whole year activities give a high status for this forum. Educational Technology and Society Journal is one of the most popular issues about the technology implementation in education.

Interaction:

Visit the home page of the ETS journal at http://ifets.ieee.org/periodical.

Figure A2.

Case Study

A. Development of a software for Basic Studies that provides the teachers and the students distance learning tools.

We have to develop the distance learning system embedded in the university information system. The students' basic data are stored in DB of the university. The learning contents are very distributed and can be stored inside an e-learning DB, university IS DB, or can be found in an external resource (on the Web). The system has to provide basic teacher, student, and administration functions (regarding the described tools in this chapter).

Questions:

1. How to make the project solution (material, human, and time resources).

2. How to design and decompose the software solution regarding the environmental conditions and requested functions.

3. How to find the difficulties and milestones in different project phases.

4. Implementation of DB support for the collaborative learning tool.

Chapter II

TEL Practices in Preschool and Kindergarten Education:
Integrating Computer Use and Computer Programming in Off-Computer Activities

Leonel Morgado, University of Trás-os-Montes e Alto Douro, Quinta de Prados, Portugal

Inside Chapter

The explosion in the use of computing in learning holds great potential for preschool education, and yet information on common educational practices with computers at the level of preschool education is scarce. This chapter shares two distinct goals: first, to provide context for the practitioner by providing a panorama of the information available on actual field practices and recommendations by official bodies from several countries regarding the inclusion of computing technology in the educational practice at the preschool and kindergarten levels; and second, to present a hands-on technical perspective on the matter of immersion of the computer in the daily practice of preschools in the form of a four-way guide, including the use of computer programming in this manner. At the end, a list of readings and activity suggestions is provided to help the reader put these ideas into practice.

Introduction

Young children are immersed in human society and that immersion is reflected upon the daily activities, themes, and events taking place inside their classrooms, or—in the case of preschools and kindergartens—activity rooms. Technology in general, and computers specifically, being nowadays so prevalent in society, has similarly entered these educational spaces, even with all expected constraints of budget allocation, time allocation, and lack of methodological information.

One might therefore expect a deluge of information stemming from field know-how and research on the use of computer technology, and easy-to-find sets of common educational practices. However, such is not the case, and scarcity is the norm, with field surveys tending to focus on formal levels of education for children aged 6 or older (UNESCO, 2003).

This chapter provides the practitioner with the background details that inform and support the practice, and thus the first part of it contains a perspective on the sources of actual information and their content. That information falls short of providing adequate guidance for planning and managing practices, so this chapter also presents a summary of recommendations provided by those sources regarding the inclusion of information and communications technologies (ICT) in the educational practice at the preschool and kindergarten levels. Useful as those recommendations and its sources are, they are either too specific or too generic as guidance for the practitioner that wishes to plan and conduct computer-rich activities. The final section of this chapter thus provides a model to guide the practitioner using a four-way approach to the development of activities.

By means of this four-way approach, this chapter aims to prove itself helpful as a resource for designing and conducting TEL practice at the preliterate levels of education (preschool and kindergarten).

Background

What we as early childhood educators are presently doing most often with computers is what research and NAEYC guidelines say we should be doing least often (Cle-

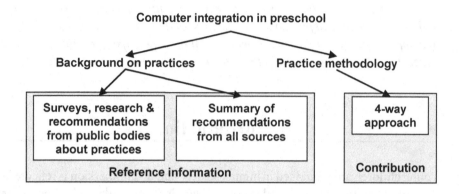

ments, 1994, p. 33). In this quote, Douglas Clements is referring to "most often" uses of computer in early childhood education, but actual field surveys on common practices tend to focus on the formal[1] levels of education for children aged 6 or older: *In most of the countries researched, the studies have been limited to ICT indicators used in the primary and secondary level* (UNESCO, 2003).

At the level of preschool education, field surveys documenting common uses of computers are rare. For instance, a literature review of the field, conducted in 2002, reported, regarding the UK, concluded:

Although observations in preschool playrooms suggest that a computer is commonly available for use during free play (...) a search for survey evidence about the provision of computers or programmable toys in pre-school settings in Scotland (or elsewhere in the UK) revealed no statistical evidence about current usage or playroom availability. (Plowman & Stephen, 2003).

Similar remarks could have been made, and have been made, about other countries. Two years ago, the researchers involved in a project to establish the educational impact of teacher training on preschoolers' learning mentioned how that project provided "hitherto unavailable data and inferences about preschoolers' cognitive, social, and technological capabilities within a technology-enhanced environment" (Swaminathan, Trawick-Smith, & Barbuto, 2005).

However, some survey efforts on the use of ICT in preschools have been taking place in recent years, albeit mostly focusing on the availability of hardware and software, rather than on educational practices (Kinderet,[2] 2002b; Leung, 2003; Lynch & Warner, 2004; Specht, Wood, & Willoughby, 2002). In November 2004, a review study reported "a current surge in research and writing on the use of ICT in early childhood education" (Bolstad, 2004), the results of this surge being grouped in the following categories: (1) *effects* research; (2) investigations of children's behaviour and interactions around computers; (3) research into children's experiences of ICT in early childhood education settings and at home; (4) research about practitioners' professional learning in, or through, ICT; and (5) case studies or exemplars of in-novative use of ICT in early childhood education settings. (Bolstad, 2004)

It is telling that these categories do not include surveys on common uses of ICT or even just computers in preschool education settings. Assorted case studies, obviously, do not provide a picture on how common or representative is each case. Fortunately, two welcome contributions to the field have taken place: a nationwide survey on actual use of computers, conducted by the New Zealand Council for Educational Research, with the cooperation of "242 early childhood managers or co-ordinators, and 402 early childhood teachers" (Bolstad, 2004, p. 62), and a pre-intervention survey on 117 preschool settings in six countries,[3] as part of the research program KidSmart on the improvement of ICT use at this educational level (Siraj-Blatchford & Siraj-Blatchford, 2004).

Thus, one is left with a patchy picture of the use of ICT in the practice, summarized by the following statements (originally made to describe the state of the practice in Sweden, in 2004/2005):

it is more common for the children to have learned how to handle the functions of a computer at home than in pre-school. In pre-school, the children use computers in other activities, that is, to do things, to play and to let time pass. It is extremely unusual for teachers to use ICT as a pedagogical challenge. (...) The ICT are not integrated in other pre-school activities unless the teacher has participated in spe-cial projects (...). (...) teachers who have participated in competence development program[s] (...) are the ones that (...) use the computers in a pedagogical sense. More common is for these teachers to use ICT for documentation of various themes and/or to document children's learning process as well as for the children's own enjoyment. In those cases, a digital camera is used to take photos to be printed out through the computer or stored (...). Teachers who have not participated in com-petence development programs use ICT mostly to relieve the pressure and for the children to have something to do – to devote the children's time. These teachers are more or less just circling around helping the children with various functions and technical support – if they can! (Kinderet, 2002a, p. 40)

In other words, the typical computer use in practice, in preschool contexts, is far from achieving the recommendations published by various public bodies, such as those mentioned, which were based on case studies and specific research on the potential benefits and challenges of computer use in early childhood education.

I therefore base my understanding of current nonprogramming uses of computers in preschool settings on these main reference sources, presented in the diagram below: recommendations from public bodies; analyses of the lectured contents of ICT courses in early childhood education curricula; research articles and reviews; localized surveys on actual practices in the field, conducted at regional, national, or

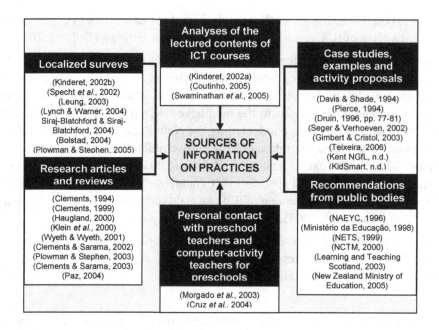

international levels; case studies, personal accounts and examples, sample activities and generic ideas found on the Web or in traditional media; and my own contact with preschool teachers and computer-activity teachers for preschools.

A central research-based concept common in these sources is that "simply providing ICT equipment to schools or teachers will not necessarily make a difference; what makes the difference is the way in which this equipment and other resources are used" (Bolstad, 2004, p. 4). That is, technology should be "integrated into the regular learning environment and used as one of many options to support children's learning" (NAEYC, 1996, p. 2). Table 1, extracted from Bolstad (2004, p. 41), summarizes the evolution and development of the field and provides a framework for situating the various educational practices on the use of ICT.

Even though this table does mention the use of ICT, not just computer, the examples it provides are focused on the use of computers within the preschool classroom. But children are immersed in human society, not just the classroom, and modern preschool education models put considerable importance into children's relationship with the overall society. Under this perspective, the recent explosion in the use of the computer as a communication medium holds great potential for preschool education. It can improve children's and teachers' contact with places, organizations, and people located far from the preschool room, and even allow for better coordination of activities between various teachers and various preschools.

Table 1. Levels of quality of ICT use in an early childhood education setting (Bolstad, 2004, p. 41)

	Physical and technical arrangements	Role of children and adults	Scaffolding of children's learning
A low level of quality ("isolation")	Only one computer is available for children to use, at the teacher's discretion. Only a few software programs are available and the software is unconnected with the current classroom themes and topics. The child operating the computer has his or her back to the other children and is not involved in their activities.	Children seldom use the computer, nor do teachers encourage its use. Teachers often take a controlling and instructing role, partly to ensure that all children have equal opportunities to use the computer.	Teachers stop engaging themselves once children are self-sufficient and have learned basic ICT skills.
A good level of quality ("integration")	The computer is relocated into a more central position among other classroom activities. Computers and other ICT equipment (such as digital cameras) are available for children to use. A range of software programs is available, including pedagogical programs, creativity/multimedia programs, and games.	Sitting together in front of a computer, children help each other, negotiate turn-taking, collaborate, and tutor each other. Children communicate, discuss strategies, solve problems, and have fun together while they use games and educational programs. Children develop different strategies while learning to handle the computer and/or different programs. They ask friends, experiment, guess, move the mouse aimlessly, use help functions, and explore by themselves or with friends. Teachers encourage children to send e-mail, use the Internet for information, and write or illustrate, or lay down soundtracks and narration for their own stories on the computer.	The computer is still not an integrated part of other activities in the preschool. Its uses can be described as learning by doing various activities on the computer, compared to learning through the computer.
A high level of quality ("immersion")	Children use computers and ICT equipment throughout the day as a multifunctional tool that is integrated with other activities and themes. Children learn through the computer and from each other while using a variety of programs or creating their own.	Children explore new topics, are creative in their search for information, ask questions, and express their reflections and feeling. Practitioners and children use computers to document children's activities, make labels and signs as needed, and send messages. Parents can access information while in the setting.	Teachers interact with and guide the children. They create possibilities in which ICT can be used to support children in developing new experiences and to expand their world.

The next section of this chapter provides a hands-on technical perspective on the matter of immersion of the computer in the daily practice of preschools, in the form of a four-step guide, including the use of computer programming in this manner.

The Four-Way Approach to Computer Use in Preschool and Kindergarten

General Guidelines

It would perhaps be expectable to provide this approach divided in two categories: children and teachers. So why haven't I done that? Why did I combine the guidelines into a single integrated section?

Basically, my decision came as a direct consequence of reasoning over hurdles documented in research on children's use of computers in general—and computer programming, specifically. I have no qualms about letting children explore a computer environment by themselves. And indeed for some children this would likely turn out just fine: in various cases, children involved in research learned by themselves and from each other, and in the process developed a strong personal relationship with the products of their exploration (e.g., Morgado, 2006). But for many children, this is not the case: some cannot manage to control the system, others may embrace it, but just repeat over and over similar patterns. It is documented, for instance, that children can easily get weary from unforeseen system behaviour or difficulties (Morgado, 2006), and that "integrating adult mediation in preschool computer learning environments facilitates informed use of computer technologies and has positive effects on children's performance" (Klein, Nir-Gal, & Darom, 2000). Even those children that broadly explore computers on their own can have huge gaps in their understanding, gaps preventing them from reaching more complex patterns of use.

It is therefore the first precept of these guidelines that preschool teachers must be deeply involved in the activities conducted by children. This is not to say that they should be assisting children every step of the way: their involvement can be varied, from direct assistance on computer use, to mere concern with the actual events taking place at the computer or the results of those events, as is clarified further away in the description of the four ways (see also the final row of Table 1).

But teachers can be of little help beyond simple manipulative assistance, if they are themselves groping to achieve some understanding of the whole process. As was mentioned in 2004, in recommendations from the U.S. Department of Education for states, districts and individual schools, on the effective use of technology to enhance learning:

Ensure that every teacher knows how to use data to personalize instruction. This is marked by the ability to interpret data to understand student progress and challenges, drive daily decisions and design instructional interventions to customize instruction for every student's unique needs. (USDE, 2004, p. 41)

The present chapter thus presents this lacking contribution to the use of computers in preschool settings: it focuses on providing teachers with a design and development structure. In other words, it provides a framework to help teachers plan activities, customizing them to suit the context of a particular child, preschool room, activity, or educational theme/project.

In this framework, the key idea is integration or, using the terminology employed in Table 1, "immersion." It relies on the assumption that teachers have a latent professionalism that can be tapped, if it is adequately supported and strengthened.

This key idea is supported by existing research, which recommends that the computer is integrated in other activities with broader scope, rather than simply used to duplicate current educational methods or, worse, be used just as a reward or an electronic babysitter (e.g., Clements & Sarama, 2002; Davis & Shade, 1994; Tsantis, Bewick, & Thouvenelle, 2003).

...computer activities yield the best results when coupled with suitable off-computer activities. For example, children who were exposed to developmental software alone showed gains in intelligence, nonverbal skills, long-term memory, and manual dexterity. Those who also worked with off-computer activities gained in all these areas and improved their scores in verbal, problem-solving, and conceptual skills. (Clements & Sarama, 2002, p. 342)

To integrate computer-programming, my overall guideline is to *use the computational environment, tools, and constructs, making them crucial to non-computer activities, rather than being simple add-ons.* This idea is clarified by the following presentation of the "four ways" (see diagram below).

The Four Ways

As mentioned before, here I present a four-step evolution, progressing in the amount of integration of computer use in educational activities. These steps are presented resorting to small examples that illustrate them, and, with each example, comments specify the actual integration and contextualization idea it aims to cover. However, these steps are not intended as successive steps for the development of activities. Rather, they are simply steps in this presentation of ideas to the reader:

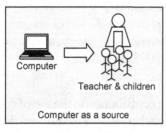

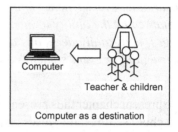

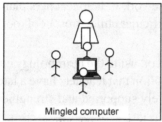

1. **Computer as a destination:** The computer is the final setting of the activity, which originated and develops mostly off the computer.

2. **Computer as a source:** The computer is a source of inspiration or pieces to be used in an activity that takes place mostly off the computer.

3. **Mingled computer:** The computer is both a starting point and an end, but neither the sole starting point nor the sole end, its presence and use varying.

4. **Automated computer:** The computer is a place where programming is employed to automate or accomplish a task designed and under development with one of the three previous steps in mind.

To present these steps, I will use examples from an important set of typical preschool activities: that of world-knowledge activities (Ministério da Educação, 1998). Their aim is to draw the child's attention to particular features of the world, such as the names employed to identify colours, the distinction between geometrical shapes, the composing parts of an animal, the features of each season, the origin of each kind of food, and so forth.

Besides the particular knowledge content of each activity, these activities' strong ties with real-world phenomena render them particularly rich in opportunities for learning. For instance, knowing where milk comes from obviously involves finding out what a cow is, how it is milked, and so on; but it can also involve notions such as the size of a cow and comparing it to the preschool room, and estimating how many cows would fit there; it can involve the exploration of how the milk goes from the cow to the supermarket shelves, and involve social elements such as transactions, buying, selling, advertising; it can involve playing a child-theatre piece or a playground game about herding cows, which will include significant physical activity; and it can include making cow puppets or drawings, with associated skills of representation and fine control.

The use of preschool educational activities in this manner is often within the scope of design projects. In such projects, students design and create artefacts (either alone or in a group), which can then be shared and discussed with others, or enjoyed as a final piece. Such artefacts can be physical items such as a flower garden, or a doll-house (or even a doll-igloo). But they can also be immaterial items, such as a story, a theatre play, or a virtual computer game or environment. The educational value of such design projects has been achieving growing recognition (e.g., Harel, 1991; Kafai, 1995; Papert, 1993), and is fundamentally connected to various pedagogical approaches, such as constructionism (Papert & Harel, 1991) and project learning (Beyer, 1997; Kilpatrick, 1951), and to pedagogical models for preschool, such as High/Scope (Epstein, 2003), Reggio Emilia, Montessori, Waldorf (Edwards, 2002), and Modern School (Vasconcelos, 2001).

Computer as a Destination

To convey the idea covered by this approach, consider the sample computer image-matching game presented in Figure 1: the four circled images on the left are animal parts (top to bottom: hoof, beak, horn, pigtail). One of them belongs to the bird on the right. Typically, this activity might be developed in preschool when the overall context of activities is one of "animals are made of parts." Hopefully, in this way, the child player would be more prone to focus on the concept.

But rather than being mere players, children can be involved in the complete design and development of such an activity.

In Figure 1, its composing drawings are amateurish, and this aims to represent an important feature: the bird and the animal parts are meant to be drawn by children. These images could then be used by the preschool teacher to build the image-match-ing activity, using any program usable for building interactive activities, such as PowerPoint (Microsoft, n.d.) or ToonTalk (Kahn, 1995). The teacher can also cut pieces from each animal picture using any common image-editing program and use those pieces and the original pictures to develop the matching game. With this simple feature, the children when drawing are not just ending their activity there; they are contributing to a game to be developed by the teacher, which they will then play afterwards.

But besides the images themselves, other features of such a game cannot be presented in an image such as Figure 1. There is no need to confine children's participation

Figure 1. Matching animal's parts to an animal

to the drawing of pictures. They could (and I personally believe they should) be involved in the entire design process.

In this example, children's involvement in design could be achieved through some or by all of these actions:

- **Defining the game's rules:** What is right, what is wrong;
- **Define the game structure:** What size is the animal, how many pictures to match, what sizes, what shapes, locations of pictures, and so forth;
- **Define the content organization:** Any animal goes? Or only birds? Can extinct animals be included? What about plants?
- **Define responses:** What should happen when the player fails? What about when the player gets it right?
- **Produce content and assign tasks:** What are the actual images to be used? Where are they coming from (drawn, live photograph, scanned image, objects made & photographed, ...)? Who takes part in producing these images?
- **Produce auxiliary items:** Where do "right" and "wrong" sounds or messages come from (recorded, written, etc.)? What should these messages say? Are they appropriate?

This potential can be explored further if the teacher develops this activity within a computer programming environment that is age-suitable, for then children can be involved in the production of behaviour and responses themselves, as described further ahead in the approach named "Automated computer."

The idea being presented here is: *if the computer is the final setting of the activity, then that activity can originate outside the computer beforehand* (animal parts identification with pets, toy animals, etc.), and in the computer itself it can involve pre-activities (drawing, in this case) aimed at bridging those original off-computer activities with the final intended computer activity.

A more traditional use of this approach is to use the computer as a medium for recording of activities. Figure shows two different examples: on the left side, children selected their preferred photographs from an activity (in this case a Christmas party at their preschool), and then discussed and decided which sentences would better illustrate each one. The preschool teacher then placed those photographs in a presentation, typed the sentences, and in some cases recorded children saying them. The result is a computer-based record of both the party and children's views about it, in text and audio formats. On the right side of Figure 2, a user-controlled figurine is standing inside a virtual house in the ToonTalk program. Given that these houses are quite plain, with just one door and bare walls and floors, they can be used as multidimensional storage places for children's activities. In this case, the wall was used as a place to record pictures of flowers. While the flowers visible in this figure are all from different digital sources, they could just as well be scanned versions of children's hand-made drawings, hand-made objects, photos of real-world flowers, photos found on the Internet, and so forth.

Computer as Source

The converse of the example in the previous section occurs when the final activity takes place off the computer, rather than at the computer. Such is the case when the result of a computer activity determines something in the physical world. Perhaps the simplest example is when the preschool teacher or a preschool child acts as referee or judge to confirm the eligibility of the computer activity.

Figure 2. Recording activities

For instance, suppose that Figure 1, instead of a bird and animal parts, there was the dark silhouette of a fruit and several fruit pictures as matching options.

Getting a proper match could also mean that the child was entitled to receive a real fruit (or a toy one, or a fruit card, Figure 3), and stock it in a "larder" in the preschool room. That, in turn, could be an activity involved in a broader context, such as the benefits of keeping a larder stocked during winter, when one lives far from drugstores or supermarkets, or depending on roads that may become temporarily blocked by snow or landslides.

The idea being presented here is: *in the context of an activity that was planned to take place off the computer, the computer may be integrated, by turning it as a source of pieces to be used off the computer.*

Another example of computer use in this fashion is a multimedia-based activity, from which other activities (off-computer) are derived. Figure 4 shows a computer environment, which children can use to record weather conditions (Teixeira, 2006). In order to fill in the table, children must assemble outside or at the window to check out the current weather. But invariably weather conditions change during the day, and a single icon ("sun," "cloudy," etc.) may not suffice. This is another source of off-computer activities: dealing with conflict mediation and group rules. Further, the elements in this environment speak out aloud information about the weather: for instance, picking up a "snowman" icon, results in the following speech being heard: "When rain drops cool down and freeze, we get snow or haze." Such pieces of information can in themselves cause children to wonder about their meaning or arise the interest to know more about a subject—and from this interest, more off-computer (an on-computer) activities can emerge (Teixeira, 2006).

Mingled Computer

The combination of the two previous ideas is that the computer can be both the destination of off-computer activities and a source of materials for off-computer

Figure 3. Fruit cards and toy fruits, usable in preschool activities

Figure 4. Computer activity: Record the weather conditions

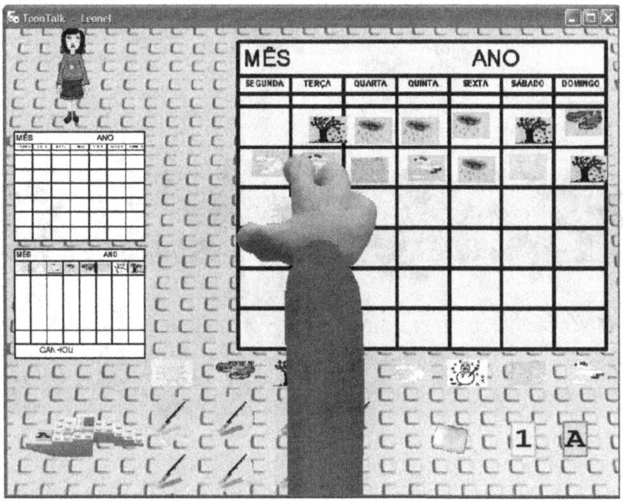

activities. This means that the computer is entirely involved in an activity, rather than being an "extra" part of it.

Figure 5 and the other figures in this section are from an activity developed around the ToonTalk environment, based on the concept of interchanging services among professionals. It was designed and developed in a preschool room where the overall theme/project "professions" was already being developed (Morgado, 2006). The mailman needs bread from the baker, who needs cleaning services from the janitor, who needs letters and bread and so forth (the fourth professional, on the bottom right corner, is a gardener, who provides plants for the decoration of each house).

Children can develop many activities under the context of that general theme/project, and in that process assemble several pictures associated with professions. In this case, with the professions being janitor, mailman, baker, and gardener, those pictures can be uniforms and items such as stamps, garbage cans, pastry, bread, flowers, and so forth. Some of those assembled pictures (originating in Web sites, books, children's own drawings or crafted items and toys, etc.) are then taken into this environment, available for the children to use. Each child, having been acquainted with a specific professional's "tools of the trade," uses the pictures to decorate a house for that professional, with the cooperation of the teacher (in this case, a teacher decided that each house should have a wardrobe, a table, and some shelves, to provide an underlying organization).

So far, nothing renders this activity different from the examples in approach "Computer as destination." But this decoration is just the activity preparation; the actual activity kernel takes place afterwards.

Figure 5. City with houses for four professionals (plus a "pictures" house)

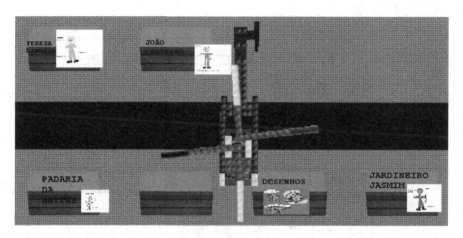

In the course of the preschool day, in another (off-computer) activity, the need may arise (or be created by the teacher) for a specific product—say, a cake from a baker. The child that needs that cake can go to the computer, enter the ToonTalk environment and enter the baker's house. There, that child can leave a request for a cake. This can take several forms: the number "1," the text "cake" and the name of the requesting child; or a picture of a cake and the photograph of the requesting child; or the picture of a cake and an object representing the profession role-played by the requesting child!

For instance, Figure 7 displays several requests found in the janitor's house, on a table laid out for that purpose: left to right, the top row has a parcel (probably delivered by the mailman), and two written-out requests from the mailman (identified as such by pictures of his bag); the middle row has a written-out request from the baker and a cake delivered by her (both identified by a baker's cap), another request

Figure 6. Gardener's house, with wardrobe, products, and tools

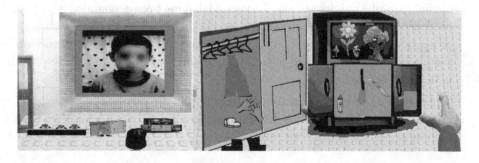

from the mailman, and a flower delivered by with a written note from the gardener; the bottom row has another delivery by the gardener, another request by the baker, and a large delivery by the mailman, with several mail bags and two envelopes.

Clearly, there is a lot for the janitor to do, since both incoming and outgoing requests are found on the table, and there are repeated requests from the same professional. Perhaps the janitor has been neglecting the due tasks, or was absent from preschool for several days. This apparent lack of organization and seemingly "excessive" requests pose a nice learning opportunity. This can be used to start a preschool-wide debate on the organization of requests within a house. Should one's own requests be kept alongside requests from other people? Should one keep a "record" (i.e., a copy) of the sent requests, and if so, should that copy by stored alongside external requests? Why are there so many requests in the janitor's house? Has the janitor been neglecting due tasks? Absent due to sickness? Or simply forgotten to vacuum up completed tasks? Should we help the janitor?

What if some of the requests did not match the janitor's skills (a request for flowers, for instance)? The janitor-playing child could call the child that placed an inadequate request there, and together decide how to solve the problem. However, the teacher could also take part, by prompting the child to decide how a wrong request should be handled. Should it be ignored? Should it be returned to the sender? Should the sender (the real child, a preschool colleague) be called so that he/she could learn about the mistake? Should the request be helpfully forwarded to the proper professional? And if so, should a note about the mistake be sent to the child who made it?

Getting back to the requests in this example, the leftmost in the middle is a request for a cardboard recycling container. A child composed such a request, and placed it in the janitor's house. Probably that child produced a lot of cardboard garbage during the school day, and the teacher leveraged that to introduce the need for a container for that garbage—and introducing recycling as a theme in that process. Sometime during the school day, the janitor-playing child will go to the ToonTalk

Figure 7. Requests in a professional's house, on a table

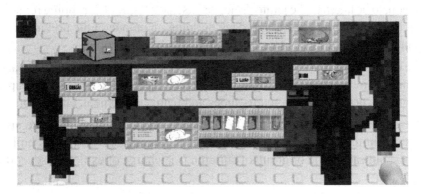

environment and find that there is a request for such a container. That container can be delivered (within the computer) to the house of the child requesting it, who later will find it has been delivered.

Having fulfilled the request for a cardboard recycling container, the teacher or requesting child can be notified, and this can lead to another off-computer activity: for instance, creating the actual container required by the requesting child, or handing the requesting child a toy container, a card representing a container, a container token or something to that effect, for continuing with the activity that originated the request for that container.

But in other cases (requests for cleaning up, for instance) there may not be the necessity for a physical token at all! The consequence of delivering a request in the ToonTalk environment may be that a check mark is painted on the classroom's "today's To Do list" or that beans of toy money needs to be exchanged to "pay" the janitor for that service, which can be an actual clean-up or the virtual cleaning of a virtual house!

The overall idea is: *a computer environment can be used not as a starting point or ending point of a specific activity, but simply as yet another educational play setting in a preschool activity room, completely integrated in the context of other, off-computer activities taking place there.* Actions off the computer can require a computer action to be complete, and a computer-based result can lead to off-computer consequences.

Automated Computer (Programming in Context)

Environments like the ones presented in the previous examples provide a nice context for using programming skills and constructs or even full programs.

In fact, the activity described in the previous example, when developed in a preschool, included the use of a computer construct known as "communication channels." ToonTalk's carrier pigeons were used by children to render easier the sending of requests and the delivery of items: children would give requests to a janitor's carrier pigeon, to be taken to the janitor's house, instead of actually dropping requests there. But rather than present this approach building up on one of the previous examples, I opted to present these ideas in yet another different setting.

The example for this section is centred on sports activities and the necessary equipment. For instance, to swim one needs a bathing suit or shorts and a cap, to play tennis one needs a racket, tennis shoes and tennis equipment, and so forth.

Overall, there are many similarities between this setting and the one about professions in the previous example: instead of houses, one now finds buildings for sports; but each child or group of children is in charge of exploring several notions revolving around the kinds of sports taking place in that building, what equipment is necessary, and so forth.

There is, however, a crucial difference regarding the previous example: no children reside in the sports facilities. Rather, there can also be more houses in the city, where the children "live." And in those houses, pictures for the equipment used in several sports can be made available.

Now one can suppose that for some reason induced by an off-computer activity, a child needs to use a sports facility, such as the tennis court, for instance. That child goes to the child's house and must assemble all the necessary equipment for playing tennis. Taking that equipment into the tennis court, the child in charge of the court must be summoned to check if all the required equipment is being brought in.

But since checking for the equipment is but a matter of comparing pictures, those could be standardized (i.e., same racket picture for all children) and easily compared. So rather than having the child-court-caretaker to be there whenever another child wants to "play tennis," that child-caretaker can be suggested (or come up with the idea) of making a ToonTalk program (or several) to do the necessary comparisons!

This setting places children in a situation where there is a nice motivation for the development of the interactive, animated cartoon-stories of ToonTalk programs. The programs can be as simple as asking, using a prerecorded sound, "Did you bring your racket?" The child wanting to play tennis presents the racket and if the comparison succeeds, then a prerecorded sound can state "you can play."

After playing tennis, the child can proceed with whatever was required by the activity that originated the tennis session (for instance, recording on paper that one tennis session was performed during a specific weekday).

Another way to conduct these activities is for the robot-caretakers to provide an "entry ticket" or some other token when a child presents the suitable equipment, and such tokens can then be presented to the preschool teacher or child acting as referee, or even printed, and used to access some other off-computer activity.

Figure 8. City with buildings for sports and inside the tennis court

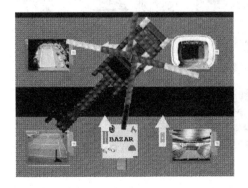 

The overall idea is that *within an integrated activity there are often opportunities for including programming embedded in a larger context. Not just for a purpose, but for a purpose within a context.* Programming in such conditions becomes a tool for automation of the environment – an empowering concept.

ToonTalk is an adequate medium for such activities, since complex programming techniques can be employed by simply acting upon virtual objects, without the necessity to resort to textual or iconic cues. But other media exist that allow programming activities to be developed with preschoolers, even if within a limited pool of programming techniques. Figure 9 presents but five such media: Stagecast Creator (Smith, Cypher, & Tesler, 2001), the physical turtle robot Valiant Roamer (Valiant Technology, n.d.), Electronic Blocks (Wyeth & Wyeth, 2001), My Make Believe Castle (Bearden & Martin, 1998), and Physical Programming (Montemayor, Druin, Farber, Simms, Churaman, & D'Amour, 2002). But other preschool-usable systems are available (Morgado, 2006).

Figure 9. Four programming systems usable in preschool

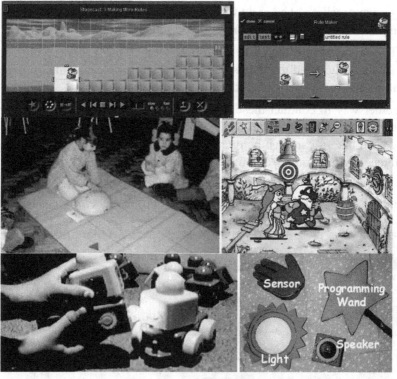

Future Trends and Conclusion

Too often research has sought impacts or effects of computer-use as if it were an environment chemical, rather than an instrument. And an instrument can have its specific features, but a central issue is its use.

Furthermore, there has been ample debate on obstacles poised by current educational and organizational practices in formal schooling levels, but these settings bear little resemblance to the educative environment and practice at the preschool level. Even the experience and know-how developing at the Constructionist Learning Environment (Stager, 2005) is on older, literate students.

How can computers be adequately used in preschool learning environments? There is the need for research to build at the very least a half-baked, half-acceptable answer. Both researchers and practitioners must strive to come to this answer, each in his or her particular way.

The question itself has been amply debated and answered, but mostly at two extremes of its scope. At one end, there has been an adequate provision of "big ideas," such as the political and philosophic analyses of learning potential and objectives; at the other end, there are various examples of projects developed with or by young children (and here I have also provided a few), albeit usually lacking adequate integration with other on-going activities in preschools. It is across this mid-ground of everyday integration within preschool practice that there is simply too little information, something this chapter tried to gather, develop, and convey.

Still much applied research is required. And not just that which can be done within the confines of an educational laboratory or independent research sessions. It is also necessary for research based on the trial and development of detailed models of practice, of detailed accounts over a long time period, so that teachers can build a personal relationship between the large ideas, the accounts of others, and their own practice. Such contributions call for research on the teacher's practice in the field, both from the teachers' own perspective as teachers-researchers, and from researchers not simultaneously acting as teachers.

As an example of a specific issue to which teachers' own research contribution would be central, one can consider the attention-span of teachers to each children. Teachers need to deal with more than a few children at a time, so the level of autonomy that children can have in the use of computers is an essential issue to tackle. In view of the cognitive development, effort, and variety of skills involved, this is not something likely to be immediate or entirely intuitive at these ages, so preschool teachers need to know how to build it up without resorting to long sessions entirely devoted to a single child or pair of children. This is something that shouldn't be addressed just at the level of software or hardware design—even though much more can certainly be done at this level.

In conclusion, one idea should be kept: the computer is now "old" technology, in the sense that its use was widespread before preschool-attending children were born. It should be integrated—immersed—in the practice, just as paper, pens, singing, and dancing are, not turned into a mystical shrine of adults or an isolated activity detached from society and from preschool life.

References

Bearden, D., & Martin, K. (1998). My make believe castl—An epic adventure in problem solving. *Learning and Leading with Technology, 25*(5), 21-25.

Beyer, L.E. (1997). William Heard Kilpatrick (1871-1965). *PROSPECTS: Quarterly Review of Comparative Education, 27*(3), 470-485. ISSN 0033-1538.

Bolstad, R. (2004). *The role and potential of ICT in early childhood education: A review of New Zealand and international literature.* Wellington, New Zealand: Ministry of Education.

Clements, D.H. (1994). The uniqueness of the computer as a learning tool: Insights from research and practice. In J.L. Wright & D.D. Shade (Eds.), *Young children: Active learners in a technological age* (pp. 31-50). Washington, DC: NAEYC.

Clements, D.H. (1999). Concrete manipulatives, concrete ideas. *Contemporary Issues in Early Childhood, 1*(1), 45-60.

Clements, D.H., & Sarama, J. (2002). The role of technology in early childhood learning. *Teaching Children Mathematics, 8,* 340-343. ISSN 1073-5836.

Clements, D.H., & Sarama, J. (2003). Strip mining for gold: Research and policy in educational technology—A response to "Fool's Gold." *Educational Technology Review, 11*(1), 7-69.

Coutinho, C.P. (2005). Os "Conteúdos" da Tecnologia Educativa nos Cursos de Formação de Professores em Portugal: Estudo Analítico em Instituições de Ensino Superior Público. In P. Dias & C.V. de Freitas (Eds.), *Challenges 2005* (conference proceedings on CD-ROM), Centro de Competências Nónio Séc. XXI, Universidade do Minho, Braga, Portugal (pp. 561-573).

Cruz, M.G.M.B., Cristóvão, R., Ferreira, P., Lopes, F., Costa, G., & Claro, A.R. et al. (2004). *Informática em Contextos de Educação de Infância—ICEI. Funcionamento e práticas ao nível da introdução das TIC em Jardins de Infância da Região de Trás-os-Montes e Alto Douro.* Paper presented at the 3rd International Education Congress, O Mundo da Criança, at UTAD, Vila Real, Portugal.

Davis, B.C., & Shade, D.D. (1994). *Integrate, don't isolate!—Computers in the early childhood curriculum.* Washington, DC: U.S. Department of Education. (ERIC Document Reproduction Service No. EDO-PS-94-17)

Druin, A. (1996). CD-ROM Edutainment. In A. Druin & C. Solomon (Eds.), *Designing multimedia environments for children* (pp. 62-93). New York: John Wiley & Sons, Inc.

Edwards, C.P. (2002). Three approaches from Europe: Waldorf, Montessori, and Reggio Emilia. *Early Childhood Research & Practice, 4*(1). ISSN 1524-5039.

Epstein, A.S. (2003, Spring). All about high/scope. *High/Scope ReSource, A Magazine for Educators,* 5-7.

Gimbert, B.G., & Cristol, D.S. (2003). *Technological tools: Enhancing all young children's cognitive and social-emotional learning.* 3er Encuentro Internacional de Educación Inicial y Preescolar, Centros de Desarrollo Infantil del Frente Popular "Tierra y Libertad", Monterrey, Nuevo León, Mexico. Retrieved January 3, 2008, from www.cendi.org/interiores/encuentro2003/talleres/t_07.htm

Harel, I. (1991). *Children designers: Interdisciplinary constructions for learning and knowing mathematics in a computer-rich school.* Norwood, NJ: Ablex Publishing.

Haugland, S.W. (2000). *Computers and young children.* Washington DC: U.S. Department of Education. (ERIC Document Reproduction Service No. ED438926)

Kafai, Y.B. (1995). *Minds in play: Computer game design as a context for children's learning.* Mahwah, NJ: Lawrence Erlbaum.

Kahn, K. (1995, June 17-19). ToonTalk™—An animated programming environment for children. In D. Harris & R. Bailey (Eds.), *NECC '95 proceedings,* Baltimore, MD. Towson, MD: Towson University.

Kent NGfL, National Grid for Learning (n.d.). *Early ICT—A collection of themed ICT activities and resources to support learning in the foundation stage.* Retrieved January 3, 2008, from http://www.naturegrid.org.uk/infant/earlyict/

KidSmart (n.d.). *KidSmart guide to early learning & technology—For home and school.* Retrieved January 3, 2008, from http://www.kidsmartearlylearning.org/

Kilpatrick, W.H. (1951). *Philosophy of education.* New York: The Macmillan Company.

Kinderet. (2002a). *Continuing training of early childhood nurseries: Practices and models—The Portuguese, Spanish, English, Swedish and Bulgarian Contexts* (report). Beja, Portugal: Escola Superior de Educação de Beja.

Kinderet. (2002b). *Diagnóstico Inicial de necessidades de formação contínua de educadores em Tecnologia Educativa* (report). Beja, Portugal: Escola Superior de Educação de Beja.

Klein, P.S., Nir-Gal, O., & Darom, E. (2000). The use of computers in kindergarten, with or without adult mediation; effects on children's cognitive performance and behavior. *Computers in Human Behavior, 16*(6), 591-608.

Learning and Teaching Scotland. (2003). *Early learning, forward thinking: The policy framework for ICT in early years.* Glasgow, Scotland, UK: Learning and Teaching Scotland.

Leung, W.M. (2003). The shift from a traditional to a digital classroom: Hong Kong kindergartens. *Childhood Education: Infancy Through Early Adolescence, 80*(1), 12-17.

Lynch, S.A., & Warner, L. (2004). Computer use in preschools: Directors' reports of the state of the practice. *Early Childhood Research & Practice, 6*(2).

Microsoft. (n.d.). *Microsoft Office PowerPoint.* Retrieved January 3, 2008, from http://www.microsoft.com/powerpoint/

Ministério da Educação. (1998). *Early childhood education in Portugal.* Lisbon, Portugal: Ministério da Educação, Departamento da Educação Básica.

Montemayor, J., Druin, A., Farber, A., Simms, S., Churaman, W., & D'Amour, A. (2002). Physical programming: Designing tools for children to create physical interactive environments. In *Proceedings of the SIGCHI conference on Human factors in Computing Systems: Changing our World, Changing Ourselves* (pp. 299-306). New York: ACM Press.

Morgado, L. (2006). *Framework for computer programming in preschool and kindergarten.* Doctoral thesis, Universidade de Trás-os-Montes e Alto Douro, Vila Real, Portugal.

Morgado, L., Cruz, M.G., & Kahn, K. (2003). ToonTalk in kindergartens: Field motes. In A. Mendez-Vilas, J.A. Mesa González & I. Solo de Zaldívar Maldonado (Eds.), *Information society and education, Proceedings of the International Conference on Information and Communication Technologies in Education (ICTE2002). Journal of Digital Contents, 1*(1), 140-145. Formatex, Badajoz, Spain.

NAEYC. (1996). *Technology and young children—Ages 3 through 8: A position statement of the National Association for the Education of Young Children.* Washington, DC: National Association for the Education of Young Children.

NCTM. (2000). *Principles and standards for school mathematics.* Reston, VA: National Council of Teachers of Mathematics. ISBN 0-87353-480-8.

NETS. (1999). Performance indicators for technology-literate students: Grades preK–2. In *National Educational Technology Standards for Students—Connecting Curriculum & Technology* (pp. 18-19). Washington, DC: International Society for Technology in Education.

New Zealand Ministry of Education. (2005). *Supporting learning in early childhood education through information and communication technologies: A framework for development.* Wellington, New Zealand: Ministry of Education.

Papert, S. (1993). *The children's machine: Rethinking school in the age of the computer.* New York: Basic Books.

Papert, S., & Harel, I. (1991). *Situating constructionism.* In Constructionism (pp. 1-11). Norwood, NJ: Ablex Publishing Corporation.

Paz, Alexandra Maria Serpa Melo da (2004). *Software Educativo Multimédia no Jardim de Infância—Actividades Preferidas pelas Crianças dos 3 aos 5 Anos*, Master's dissertation, Instituto de Educação e Psicologia, Universidade do Minho, Braga, Portugal.

Plowman, L., & Stephen, C. (2003). A benign addition? Research on ICT and preschool children. *Journal of Computer Assisted Learning, 19*(2), 149-164.

Plowman, L., & Stephen, C. (2005). Children, play, and computers in pre-school education. *British Journal of Educational Technology, 36*(2), 145-157.

Seger, E., & Verhoeven, L. (2002). Multimedia support of early literacy learning. *Computers & Education, 39*(3), 207-211.

Siraj-Blatchford, J., & Siraj-Blatchford, I. (2004). *IBM KidSmart early learning programme European Evaluation: France, Germany, Italy, Portugal, Spain and UK – Final Report June 2004.* White Plains, NY: IBM Corporation.

Smith, D.C., Cypher, A., & Tesler, L. (2001). Novice programming comes of age. In H. Lieberman (Ed.), *Your wish is my command: Programming by example* (pp. 7-19). San Francisco, CA: Morgan Kaufmann Publishers.

Specht, J., Wood, E., & Willoughby, T. (2002). What early childhood educators need to know about computers in order to enhance the learning environment. *Canadian Journal of Learning and Technology, 28*(1).

Stager, G.S. (2005, June 27-30). *Constructive technology as the key to entering the community of learners.* Paper presented at the National Educational Computing Conference, Philadelphia, PA, Organized by ISTE—International Society for Technology in Education, Washington, DC.

Swaminathan, S., Trawick-Smith, J., & Barbuto, L.M. (2005, June 27-30). *Technology training at the preschools: Impact on pedagogy and children.* Paper presented at the National Educational Computing Conference, Philadelphia, PA. Organized by ISTE – International Society for Technology in Education, Washington, DC. Retrieved January 3, 2008, from http://www.iste.org/Content/NavigationMenu/Research/NECC_Research_Paper_Archives/NECC_2005/Swaminathan-Sudha-NECC05.pdf

Teixeira, M. (2006). *Informática em Contextos de Educação de Infância: Desenvolvimento de Projectos e Produção de Materiais*, Master dissertation, Universidade de Trás-os-Montes e Alto Douro, Vila Real, Portugal.

Tsantis, L.A., Bewick, C.J., & Thouvenelle, S. (2003, November). Examining some common myths about computer use in the early years. In *Beyond the journal young children*. Washington, DC: National Association for the Education of Young Children. Retrieved January 3, 2008, from http://www.journal.naeyc.org/btj/200311/CommonTechnoMyths.pdf

UNESCO. (2003). *Using indicators to assess impact of ICT in education*. Retrieved January 3, 2008, from http://www2.unescobkk.org/education/ict/v2_2/info.asp?id=13253

USDE, U.S. Department of Education. (2004). *Toward a new golden age in American education—How the Internet, the law and today's students are revolutionizing expectations*. Jessup, MD: Editorial Publications Center, U.S. Department of Education.

Valiant Technology. (n.d.). Valiant roamer user guide. Retrieved January 3, 2008, from http://www.valiant-technology.com/freebies/userguide/user1.htm

Vasconcelos, T. (2001). Conversations around the large table: Building community in a Portuguese public kindergarten. *Early Education and Development, 12*(4), 499-522.

Wyeth, P., & Wyeth, G. (2001). Electronic blocks: Tangible programming elements for preschoolers. In M. Hirose (Ed.), *Human-computer interaction - INTER-ACT'01*. Amsterdam, The Netherlands: IOS Press.

Further Readings

Papert, S. (1980). *Mindstorms: Children, computers, and powerful ideas*. New York: Basic Books. ISBN 0-465-04629-0.

Kay, A. (1991). Computers, networks, and education. *Scientific American, 265*(3), 100-107.

Kafai, Y.B. (1995). *Minds in play: Computer game design as a context for children's learning*. Mahwah, NJ: Lawrence Erlbaum. ISBN 0-805-81513-9.

Jonassen, D.H. (2000). *Computers as Mindtools for schools*. Pearson Education, NJ.

Papert, S. (2000). What's the big idea: Towards a pedagogy of idea power. *IBM Systems Journal, 39*(3-4). Retrieved January 3, 2008, from http://www.research.ibm.com/journal/sj/393/part2/papert.html

Benford, S., Bederson, B.B., Åkesson, K.P., Bayon, V., Druin, A., Hansson, P. et al. (2000). Designing storytelling technologies to encouraging collaboration between young children. In *Proceedings of the SIGCHI Conference on Human Factors in Computing Systems.* New York: ACM Press. ISBN 1-58113-216-6. Retrieved January 3, 2008, from http://doi.acm.org/10.1145/332040.332502

Hourcade, J.P, Bederson, B.B., & Druin, A. (2004). Preschool children's use of mouse buttons. In *CHI '04 Extended Abstracts on Human Factors in Computing Systems.* New York: ACM Press. ISBN 1-58113-703-6. Retrieved January 3, 2008, from http://doi.acm.org/10.1145/985921.986077

Shaffer, D.W., Squire, K.R., Halverson, R., & Gee, J.P. (2005). *Video games and the future of learning. Phi Delta Kappan, 87*(2), 104-111. Retrieved January 3, 2008, from http://coweb.wcer.wisc.edu/cv/papers/videogamesfuturelearning_pdk_2005.pdf

Useful URLs

ToonTalk: Making programming child's play: http://www.toontalk.com/

Playground, Building computer environments for 4-8 year olds: http://www.ioe.ac.uk/playground/

KidSmart. Guide to Early Learning & Technology: http://www.kidsmartearlylearning.org/

Early ICT: http://www.naturegrid.org.uk/infant/earlyict/

MaMaMedia.com, "The Place for Kids on the Net," http://www.mamamedia.com/

Apples4theteacher.com, educational resources for teachers and kids: http://www.apples4theteacher.com/

Pre-Kindergarten Resources: http://www.internet4classrooms.com/prek.htm

Resources: Preschoolers and Interactive Media: http://home.utad.pt/~leonelm/children/resources.html

Computers Boost Preschool Kids' Intelligence: http://webcenter.health.webmd.netscape.com/content/Article/88/99862.htm

Strip Mining for Gold: Research and Policy in Educational Technology-A Response to "*Fool's Gold,*" http://www.editlib.org/index.cfm/files/paper_17793.pdf?fuseaction=Reader.DownloadFullText&paper_id=17793

The role and potential of ICT in early childhood education: A review of New Zealand and international literature: http://www.minedu.govt.nz/web/downloadable/dl10074_v1/ictinecefinal.pdf

A Robot in Kindergarten: http://home.utad.pt/~leonelm/papers/RobotinKinder-garten/RobotinKindergarten.html

Taking Programming into Kindergartens: Exploratory Research Activities Using ToonTalk: http://home.utad.pt/~leonelm/papers/eurologo2003/EuroLogo2003.htm

MicroWorlds JR: http://www.microworlds.com/solutions/mwjunior.html

Stagecast Creator: http://www.stagecast.com/

Endnotes

[1]   That is, "elementary," "primary," "basic," the actual nomenclature varying across national educational systems.

[2]   This survey study encompasses settings in Bulgaria, Portugal, Spain, Sweden, and the UK.

[3]   France, Germany, Italy, Portugal, Spain, and UK.

Appendix

Figure A1.

Internet Session: KidSmart. Guide to Early Learning & Technology

http://www.kidsmartearlylearning.org/

This Web site provides two distinct sections: for Parents, and for Teachers. In each, a deluge of information and ideas is presented, often in comic-book or presentation style, on "Learning & Playing Together," "Integrating Technology," and "Access for All."

Interaction:

From the Teachers section, select the subsection "Integrating Technology," and then, from the left-side menu, "Curriculum Extension" and see the example of a "Promising Practice." Does it involve computers? If not, could you use the ideas in this chapter to integrate computers in that promising practice? If it does involve computers, could you use the ideas in this chapter in order to change the kind of computer use involved?

Figure A2.

Case Study

A. Creating a Computer-Immersed Educational Activity for Preschool

Simon and Pauline (fictional names) wanted to develop an activity for their preschool classrooms about the importance of recycling. They realize that throughout the day the children produce significant amounts of litter: milk cartons, fruit peelings, bits of paper, plastic wrappings, and so forth. T hey decide to create a set of recycling containers for the children to use for the litter being produced throughout the day: a paper/cardboard container, a plastics container, a glass container, and a container for organic litter.

Now children can learn to deposit their litter in separate containers and this can be used as a leverage for discussing recycling, the possibility of producing less litter, or even about ecology and the environment.

Simon and Pauline developed similar activities at their classrooms and are quite happy with the results. However, one issue bugs them: sometimes a child places litter in the wrong container, and if no-one notices it, that mistaken action is not worked upon. However, going through litter inside the containers is neither convenient nor hygienic.

They reckon that they could use the computer to overcome part of the problem. Children could use it to make a record of the litter deposited in the containers, as long as making that record is quick and convenient. Then that record could be used to evaluate adequate use of the containers—and even to help them realize the amount of litter they produce.

Using ToonTalk and its virtual city, they decorate four houses as if they were containers, simply by applying adequate images to the façades and roofs (the picture below, on the left, shows a house before and after applying a picture).

continued on following page

Figure A2. continued

Now children can easily enter containers to place virtual litter there or analyze their contents. But where can that litter come from? Simon and Pauline realize that they could use a fourth house as a storage place for litter "icons" or samples. That way, when a child want to record, for instance, that he/she placed a milk carton in the paper container, all that child has to do is enter ToonTalk, go to the storage place, pick up a virtual milk carton, and lay it in the paper container.

They proceed to implement this approach. However, soon they find a problem with it: when something wrong happens (for instance, a glass bottle is found inside the paper container), who placed it there? It would be nice to have children "in charge" of specific containers, and responsible for explaining to other children that their litter was in the wrong place. But if litter is untraceable, then that much is not possible.

Fortunately, they realize there is a simple solution to this problem: the storage place can have not only litter icons, but also photographs or nametags for each children. This way, children can place pieces of litter inside ToonTalk boxes, along with their photographs, and take these boxes to the recycling containers. This way, the source of each litter piece is traceable (see picture above, on the right). Note: in order to drop a picture on the floor and make it usable as an infinite source of icons – an "infinite stack," in ToonTalk terms—one simply presses Ctrl+S before dropping it.

To complete this activity, children "in charge" of specific containers could do daily or weekly checks of its contents, and help other children correct their distribution of litter, or even combine all deposited litter and make a weekly or daily total, which in turn could be employed to render visible the amount of litter we as humans produce daily.

Questions:

1. Visit http://www.toontalk.com/ and download a trial version of ToonTalk. Try to implement this example.

2. Try to implement this activity in another software tool. For instance, use presentation software such as Microsoft PowerPoint, employing a slide for each container (instead of a ToonTalk house), to implement this activity.

3. Could you devise different ways to integrate the computer in educational activities about recycling? This case employs the third approach, "Mingled computer." Try to devise different recycling activities using the computer under "Computer as source" and "Computer as destination" approaches, and then try to devise a different "Mingled computer" activity.

4. Try to program a ToonTalk robot to play the sound "thank you" if given a milk carton.

Chapter III

The Blended Learning Classroom:
An Online Teacher Training Program

Karen García, University of Massachusetts, USA

Renata Suzuki, Sophia University, Japan

Inside Chapter

This blended learning classroom (BLC) case study identifies and describes successful procedures and methodologies that widen the use of online tools in virtual environments. It provides a systematic and organized access to the plethora of free social software available online for the development of collaborative learning activities. The goal of this particular BLC professional development activity was to offer a face-to-face group of English teachers in Venezuela the opportunity to meet members of an international community of practice (CoP) and together review a packaged learning course material online. Blended technology, the mix and match of available tools, served to display the wide use of resources and each person's skills. By exploring online tools, participants gained an opportunity for learning about both educational theory and the use of technology. The experience described here shows a prototype of future pathways towards educational content use and development.

Inside Chapter

This chapter describes a spontaneous collaborative learning activity initiated by members of a virtual community of learners involved in the exploration of online tools for English language instruction. The procedures followed to carry this teacher training experience were instrumental to the thorough review of pedagogical theory that took place in terms of their applicability and suitability as technology enhanced learning approaches. This chapter addresses the following achievements:

- The blended course creates and facilitates expansive discussion of content adaptation for online delivery, aiding learners to become producers of knowledge while gaining functional computer skills.

- A North American educational curriculum served to highlight constructivist learning among English language teachers within a virtual environment, showing that a culture bound pedagogical content holds relevance in international online settings.

- This project showed a great potential, moving from the predictive review of established curriculum to offering educators an invigorating international instructional approach to professional development.

- The blended learning experience offers a glimpse at future educational trends in which learning materials are easily available from unlimited knowledge repositories and spontaneously used in virtual settings.

A review of educational theory and socio ecological models of teaching in virtual environments leads our description of a blended learning experience. Procedures are offered, used by members of a virtual community of English teachers and a group of teachers in a computer laboratory in Venezuela to meet online weekly for 13 weeks for the review of an educational curriculum. The learner-based approach to teaching and learning described here served to expand the limits of online tools and the application of existing educational materials beyond traditional methods as they held relevance in a virtual classroom.

This chapter describes a blended learning activity in which volunteers from distant countries and time zones gathered weekly for an hour in a virtual classroom to examine an educational unit from a pre-packaged K-12 teacher-training course. The group's weekly meetings are examined, illustrating how "The Learning Classroom: Theory and Practice" course materials gave structure and content to the teacher training, facilitating both substantial review of materials, and examination of its relevance to language teaching for adults. In this 13-week peer mentoring learning experience members of an international online community of practice (CoP) located at various places around the world joined a face-to-face group of English language teachers in Venezuela in a virtual classroom for the examination of the curriculum and exposure to online tools. This blended synchronous approach to joining online and face-to-face participants also served to build delivery skills and teaching styles in a virtual classroom environment.

A socio-ecological model examines the context in which a homogeneous language is instrumental to representation and interaction in virtual learning experiences. The socioconstructive application of technical skills was a source of support for teachers and a major asset. Modeling from experienced peers was also crucial for success in the virtual environment. Online interaction strengthened the virtual CoP and showed how multivalent representations of this international aggregate of educators achieved diversity in an era of supposed digital homogenization.

The applied nature of the blended experience is evidence of the depth of applicability and relevance of technology enhanced learning applications available to educators online. In addition to the technological challenges of gaining distinct skill sets for online interaction, the added face-to-face group served to validate the boundaries of meaning and the suitability of the curriculum explored in the virtual classroom. Hence, the blended learning experience offers a unique experience facilitated by a constructivistic approach to teaching and learning beyond geographical confines.

A Socio-Ecological Approach to Education

This online "blended" learning experience follows along the lines of the "socio-ecological field theory" attributed to Brofenbrenner (1979), "constructivism" to Vygotsky (1978), and called "Situated Learning" by Herrington and Oliver (1995). These approaches share three common elements: the agent, the interaction, and the context in which action takes place. Our approach also integrates a critical pedagogy (Fassett & Warren, 2007) by promoting the exploring of how the educational content was relevant to each participant. A central element in this socio-ecological model is the ability of a virtual learning environment to host and integrate synchronous interaction between participants from the entire world. Examination of the function of language to achieve online interaction and the contextual formulation of CoPs as hosts to that emergent pedagogy are fundamental to our work.

In addition to exploring the limits of technology on pedagogical methods, the blended classroom served to address the subjective nature of teaching and learning within its expansive global context.

Teaching in Virtual Environments

Issues of language, technological literacy, and how to best use online tools for teaching are central to understanding the challenges posed by the blended learning experience. A critical review of social presence and interaction dynamics between expert-learners and moderators-presenters in the blended format allows for recommending ways to advance teacher-training activities online. How the literature explains virtual representations of diversity is a primary concern of this work. The literature on learning technology and language use in the formulation of virtual CoPs offers that understanding.

Lacking physicality, virtual representations more strongly rely on social presence, achieved by interaction. Social presence is recognized in the literature as a central concept in building online communities (Aragon, 2003), directly related to learning outcomes (Richardson & Swan, 2003), and crucial in the improvement of instructional effectiveness (Tu, 2002). This literature acknowledges the affective function of social presence, or as Rourke, Anderson, Garrison, and Archer (2001) call it, "the ability of learners to project themselves socially and affectively into a community of inquiry" (p.3). Interest in the measurement of social presence is also growing (Rourke et al., 2001; Tu, 2002).

Some definitions of social presence entail the perception of online participants as being real (Richardson & Swan, in Garber, 2004); others (Short, Williams & Christie, in Aragon, 2003) emphasize its salience as the interpersonal nature of interaction. Short et al. (Rourke et al., 2001, p. 4) define social presence as interaction, that is, "the salience of the other in a mediated communication and the consequent salience of their interpersonal interactions." Cutler (Rovai, 2002, p. 6) also notices the interactive quality of social presence since "in cyberspace (it) takes more of a complexion of reciprocal awareness of others… to create a mutual sense of interaction that is essential to the feeling that others are there." For Gunawardena (1995) "(i)nteractivity is a quality (potential) that may be realized by some, or remain an unfulfilled option. When it is realized, and when participants notice it, there is *social presence*" (p.152).

Although interaction in asynchronous and synchronous environments pose rather different challenges, it seems safe to assert that in general, social presence is a function of interaction rather than the converse. Nevertheless, the construct of a teaching presence is more appropriate to address the ability to steer online interaction beyond just transmitting information. Rourke et al.'s (2001) definition is applicable to our experience: "We define (text based) *teaching presence* as the design, facilitation, and direction of cognitive and social processes for the purpose of realizing personally meaningful and educationally worthwhile learning outcomes" (p. 5).

For our purposes, gaining and refining a teaching presence became most important for the success of the blended learning experience.

In order to fully use technology for self-representation, participants must use online tools expansively (Aragon, 2003), build an identity (Macfadyen, 2004) or an interactional self (Vieta, 2003). Devoid of physical cues, reliance on text is critical for social presence (Miller & Miller, 1999). The required ability to mediate language (in speech and/or text) and technology results in a distinct self-portrayal. For instance, in text-only environments icons become gestures, eye contact, and tone of voice. On synchronous experiences involving speech, the content allows communication to more closely resemble face-to-face transactions in which the greater the interaction the greater the learning. Yet reaching an accurate virtual representation of society is arguable since a filtering process takes place where those with at least basic language competence and social skills for disclosure and/or technological competence are the ones rendered as present and representative of the population.

The nature of interaction is of interest to educators and a wide range of variations is discussed in the literature. Hawkes (2001) looks at the ability of asynchronous computer networks to host critically reflective dialogue; McAlister, Ravenscroft, and Scanlon (2004) look at the use of text in synchronous environments; Burnham and Walden (1997) audio and text. McKenna and Green (2002) and Kern, Ware, and Warschauer (2004) address differences between face-to-face and virtual interaction and how language is used to negotiate meaning. Graham (2005) also looks at blended settings. What seems certain is that interaction in computer supported learning environments is essential for "effective knowledge acquisition and increased understanding" (Orvis & Lassiter, 2006, p. 1). Both the social and instrumental function of interaction in distance education are acknowledged by Collins and Berge (1996) and Thurmond and Wambach (2004) and aids in reaching a teaching presence (Anderson, Rourke, Garrison, & Archer, 2001). We now turn to considering how teaching presence is the medium for knowledge management in the virtual classroom.

Critical Pedagogy in Virtual Classrooms

Using online tools for teaching and learning generates participation in learning environments (Brook & Oliver, 2003; Hill, Wiley, Nelson, & Han, 2003), leads to competency in utilizing their components (Mabrito, 2004; Miller & Miller, 1999), serves for delineating strategies to achieve best results (Preece, & Maloney-Krichmar, 2003; Ryba, Selby, & Mentis, 2002), and leads to professional development activities for teachers (Eib & Miller, 2006; Hinson & LaPrairie, 2005). In these environments, online tools allow interaction, transmit information, and serve for the construction of knowledge (Dalgarno, 2001; Khan, 2000; Pahl, 2003). As communication instruments, online tools serve to interact privately, to broadcast publicly, to announce, and/or to archive.

Online educational experiences are bound to limits of the technology and the us-ers' ability to transcend those limits while also gaining personal competency in the transfer of knowledge content in teaching. According to Miller and Miller (1999) "(c)omputer technologies used to develop and deliver Web-based instruction vary depending on factors such as learning goals, pedagogical approach, and instructor expertise or access to expertise in using these technologies" (p. 1). While the literature on learning styles (Schrum & Berge, 1998) addresses important considerations ap-plicable to online education, we concur with Muirhead (2004) in that there is a need to ascertain which is the best instrumental teaching stance in online environments: "researchers have neglected to study individual differences in teachers' facilitator skills that can influence the quality of interactivity" (p. 5). In the BLC we focused on the development of interactive pedagogical approached to transmitting educational content while gaining expertise in the use of the virtual classroom. Approaches ranged from expert presentations, to moderation and facilitation of classroom participation, to the delivery of participatory and highly interactive activities.

An emergent critical pedagogy worth noting leads to Walker (2004), who examined strategies to encourage participation in synchronous text utilizing Socratic ques-tioning, and to Elder and Paul (1998), who examined how it may lead to critical thinking. The literature on constructivism in online education is worth highlight-ing. Honebein (1996) establishes pedagogical goals, Lefoe (1998) and Adriaen (2002) offer guidelines for designing constructivistic learning environments. This literature is also sensitive to the online social context in which learning takes place (Verneil & Berge, (2000). In addition, Schrum and Berge (1998) describe how teachers' functional roles are turning into that of brokers, questioners, providers of structure, encouragers of self direction, team membership, collegiality, leading towards sensitivity to all learning styles and breaking vertical hierarchies between teachers and learners.

The Blended Learning Experience

The professional development experience featured here took place in a virtual classroom housed at Learning Times (http://www.learningtimes.org), a learning environment supporting an open community of educators. The goal of the learning experience was twofold: first, to offer a local face-to-face group of educators the opportunity to meet members of an international CoP and study learning material together online; and second, to explore this novel use of the available tools towards displaying the most expansive use of resources and the individual's skills. In doing so, participants gained an opportunity to learn about both content and the use of technology. The blended learning classroom became a study group, the packaged curriculum the object of observation, and the delivery of the materials online a means to achieving a blended experience. The overall design of the activity evolved in practice as described below.

Set Up Procedure

A higher education institution in Venezuela, South America, endorsed the course as a formal teacher training activity. Participants met face-to-face in a computer laboratory with Internet uplink to study the "Learning Classroom: Theory into Practice," a self-contained course developed in North America by the Annenberg Foundation (2004). This rich collection of educational resources is freely available online for use formally within the Foundation's leadership, or independently as in the virtual experience described here. First, The Learning Classroom Course Web portal is reviewed. The "packaged" video-based course explores learning theory and application to grades K-12. It includes 13 half-hour video programs, a print guide and a Web site with background readings, questions for discussion, and assignments. All materials and full description of the course are available at the Foundation's Web site: http://www.learner.org/resources/series172.html. Graduate credit is available after completion.

The educational materials were relevant to teachers in Venezuela and to a virtual CoP of educators, a nexus of English language instructors whose main purpose is to use the Web as a means for teaching. Members of the CoP use free communication tools and readily available technologies to explore applications in the teaching of english to speakers of other languages (TESOL) context (Stevens, 2005). Planning discussions led to their sponsorship of the professional development activity. Participation was encouraged by means of announcements through an asynchronous Yahoo-group based mailing system and solicited at a weekly gathering at Tapped In (a synchronous text based virtual environment hosting a community of educators). Participants in the blended experience registered in the course's own Yahoo-group to receive messages describing our Blended Learning Classroom (BLC) course and explaining its requirements: weekly video and readings, keeping journals on reflections, a final project, and weekly 1-hour synchronous meetings in a virtual classroom.

Online tools used for communication and interaction emulated features generally available in "contained" asynchronous learning environments. Text messages served as forums for asynchronous communication and Web pages built to publish participants' profiles. The actual weekly performance varied among participants and their access to technology; it centered on readings, videos, blended classroom participation, and revolving leadership moderating study of one unit. Once the synchronous blended format was established, the focus shifted from the curriculum per se to encompass online presentation and moderating skills for each unit. The BLC approach is similar to McCarty's (2005) "hybrid" approach regarding online education in which a face-to-face group in Japan used voice technologies and a learning management system to communicate with mentors in different points of the world. In our case, an already established curriculum served for discussion about its appropriate use in a virtual classroom.

Who are the Participants?

All of the participants in the virtual classroom were teachers. While most were language instructors, their teaching of English varied according to fluency, geography and access to materials. The use of a common language is central to carrying out the teacher development project showcased in this chapter. During sessions, participants connected unit topics to their teaching around the globe. Core group teachers recounted experiences from Brazil, Portugal, Denmark, the USA, Japan, and Venezuela. Sporadic participants from Columbia, Abu Dhabi, Taiwan, Russia, Poland, Greece, and Kuwait filled the palette of descriptions about schools and local English teaching circumstances. Twenty-eight individuals representing 13 countries of the world participated. Although the regular meeting time (Fridays at 16 GMT) presented a challenge to participants residing in scattered locations around the globe, on average, 12 participants attended each session. The open-door style classroom in which guests would present a topic of their choice created a flexible atmosphere of group attendance, giving it a sense of being a seminar. The next section describes innovative uses of asynchronous and synchronous tools in the blended classroom.

Online Tools

Members from the CoP highlighted their mastery of the electronic medium by documenting their experiences with asynchronous tools ranging from profile-sharing Web pages, e-mail posts reporting hurdles and/or achievements, to blogs and blokis (electronic journals). Recordings of lessons were archived for absent members. The integration of asynchronous features within the "live" Blended Classroom experience may have served a significant unifying function by shortening the participants' "threshold(,) from feeling like outsiders to feeling like insiders" (Wegerirf, 1998, p. 34). These tools not only served to archive the general content, they also allowed continuity of expression throughout the 13-week period, keeping the virtual context alive beyond the one hour synchronous meeting.

Synchronous tools for communication within the virtual classroom and beyond included an interactive whiteboard for slides and shared Web page viewing, voice chat, text chat, and instant messaging. A world map helped pinpoint the geographical location of participants present each week, building a strong sense of the global network. Other visual tools such as pictures, images and doodles on the white board built spontaneity and familiarity among course participants. A significant feature of the course over and above the benefits of each particular session involved a learning curve, or rather, the challenge of how to mix and match tools for personal expression. Beginning sessions entailed not only gaining mastery of the virtual classroom platform and the hardware each participant had available, but also finding the best means to convey curriculum material. Beyond the "show and tell" nature of online presentations, the virtual classroom's most outstanding feature was its "multiliteracy" dimension: audio capacity, text messaging, and coordinated projection of visual information by means of an interactive whiteboard. Navigating or leading a session involved addressing the communication taking place in the text, audio, manipulating visual slides, and coordinating the use of the white board. Managing all of the virtual classroom features is complex and requires skills and practice. As a participant stated: "This is not so easy, the scrolling and the text chat, and the copy and pasting."

Gaining a voice became an ongoing goal much like Honebein's (Cox, Carr, & Hall, 2004, p. 183) constructivistic approach to reaching "… sensitivity toward learners' previous knowledge and the encouragement of *ownership* and *voice* in the learning process." Close to the end of the course, innovative use of tools achieved highly generative activities. For example, during the Motivation session, participants working in pairs researched pictures, Googled quotes, scripted role-plays, or shared personal stories. The interactive whiteboard and audio served to gather and present the results to the whole group. The final session also pooled useful learning strategies and practices integrated into the classroom.

Language

The key function of English as an international global language in Internet environments is acknowledged in the literature (Chew, 1999; Wallace, 2002; Yang, 2002) to the extent of computers being considered as "extremely resistant to any language using nonRoman alphabets (Holderness in Selwyn, 1999, p. 71). Indeed, Warshchauer (2002) speaks of the "de facto *lingua franca* of online communication" (p. 64). However, the homogenous and dominant use of English for communication in the Internet may pose a challenge to those whose language is different. Moreover, Crystal (2001) clearly analyses how "Netspeak" has distinct linguistic parameters different from the written or spoken word, raising the bar for speakers of other language Internet users. For instance, the ability to use words as nonverbal communication <grin>, and to convey the depth of face-to-face encounters is a challenge shared in virtual environments relying on text and/or audio. Again, repartee in text or audio utterances must be expressed almost simultaneously with mental processing.

For the local group in Venezuela, using the audio feature was indeed a hurdle involving technical configuration of equipment and linguistic stage presence. Nevertheless, once accustomed, as English instructors they welcomed the access to an international English speaking community, and the opportunity to learn from the experience. Access to online tools allowed them contact with other language teachers, and the virtual classroom offered all participants a destination in which to meet and learn together, solidify bonds, and strengthen skills in using online tools. In the voice of a participant: "Learning a language is not only words, it is also contact with viewing different ways of viewing life."

The following statement from the coordinator in Venezuela illustrates the group's positive attitude to the instrumental function of the English language in reaching the virtual global community: "We are citizens of the world ... Teaching a second language allows us to teach a new culture. ... When we are English speakers we belong to a larger community from what we are now."

As these statements and experiences clearly indicate, for the BLC participants, the collaborative, supportive environment of the course lowered barriers in its approach to communication per se, be it via technological or linguistic tools. In this way, the classroom was able to embrace benefits of a global English language as an acceptable expression of community identity.

In the blended experience, the participant's use of text to represent their immediate local surroundings increased the appeal of text communication. Synchronous media offers teachers immediacy, an important component of social presence, with more explicit visual and/or audio content. In turn, the quality of interaction serves to achieve teaching presence.

The Virtual Learning Sessions

Each session started with greetings among participants, checking their audio and introducing themselves. Those without audio capacity participated by greetings in the text-messaging window, establishing a smooth integration and interweaving of social presence in text and audio conversation. Not only would technical adjustments take place at this point, but this practice also allowed the development of comfort with the classroom's audio broadcast feature. During the course, all participants had the opportunity to project their personal and unique voice, irrespective of volubility. Indeed, it was exciting and motivating to hear the mix of voices from far-flung places and make the auditory connection to the Web of learning across the planet.

The interactive whiteboard served as an important visual tool to establish social presence. Members posted up pictures of themselves or their country's beauty spots on the "ice-breaker" world map, or grabbed a seat next to a friend in a doodled classroom diagram. Preferences for particular font colors and sizes in whiteboard brainstorming also served to establish personality and presence. The virtual classroom software offered tools such as visual checkmarks and polling function, mini surveys, hand-clapping and smiley icons which popped up next to participants names when clicked. These icons served to convey presence, personal appreciation and interested involvement in proceedings.

Interaction

Even if we accept the expressive power of visual tools, as stated before, the role of language literacy in social presence is unquestionable, and in online environments requires competence with text and oral speech. At the beginning of the blended experience, preference for text exchange prevailed and silence was noticeable. Later in the 13-week period, audio and text interaction appeared complementary, as all members developed these basic competencies. It seemed possible that participants came to know each other, felt more confident to state their views verbally, and were more skilled in following the text thread. Oren, Mioduser, and Nachmias (2002) support our observation that the quality of interaction changing over time was possibly due to the participants' comfort with each other and with the technology.

The virtual classroom became the principal locale for group interaction and where social and didactic activity was managed in each session. A linear text chat accompanied a turn taking access to the audio in which people could be required to raise their hands to ask for a turn to speak. While the platform could nurture strong regulatory norms similar to a well-controlled face-to-face environment, in practice, teachers shared spontaneously. Moderators and participants invited others to speak either by voice or by text, and took turns in a fluid reciprocal exchange. There was consensus that text chat as a tool was beneficial, interactive, and unobtrusive. Its capacity to serve as a "vehicle for the development of social cohesion" was also evident as concluded by Cox et al. (2004, p. 192) and Wang (2005).

The synchronous nature of the text chat while others speak was a distinct asset of the virtual classroom, offering opportunities for reflection and expansion of ideas without disruption. As stated in the text window by a participant, "Text complements voice and it gives us a chance to comment while someone speaks." In addition to the communication devices within the virtual classroom, the use of instant messaging also offered important complementary functions such as rehearsals prior to public statements within the classroom. Although we were virtually blind to witnessing the interaction that took place in the local group, their rich face-to-face and online encounter possibly lead to richer interaction and reflection.

Becoming a facilitator in the virtual classroom entailed both the construction and broadcasting of knowledge, and participants faced the challenge of making the Learning Classroom course material interactive. The topics presented allowed for a review of teaching approaches, and the experience offered an opportunity to practice those skills online. In this way, the Blended Classroom became a showcase for different teaching styles ranging from reliance on the original curriculum, to a shower of ideas visually represented by means of text and/or pictures, and even to teamwork. Further examination of variations in the facilitation of the teaching process found in the BLC seems warranted.

Gaining Teaching Presence at the Blended Learning Classroom

Like Hawkes (2001), who wonders if the quality of asynchronous interaction approximates face-to-face interaction, looking at styles of online instruction also seems crucial to reaching all learning styles. The ability to convey educational content diversely might address the expected gaps in learning, established in the literature by Cox et al. (2004) and Wang (2005). These learning gaps attributed to limits in online tools might instead be a function of the participant's preference and the leader's style.

The roles of facilitator as presenter and as moderator parallel Miller and Miller's (1999) view of the cognitive process and cognitive constructivist approaches. The former transmits expert knowledge and the latter leads to individuals gaining knowledge through social interaction. Following the packaged curriculum with a presentation style corresponds to a cognitive processing approach to transmit knowledge. In turn, a constructivist approach would lead to a moderating facilitator style, since "(t)he constructivist paradigm reflects a position that knowledge is not independent of the learner but is internally constructed by the learner as a way of making meaning of experiences" (Cronin & Jonassen, et al., in Miller & Miller, 1999, p. 6).

Further examination of the facilitator's roles according to Moshman's (Dalgarno, 2001) distinction of endogenous, exogenous, and dialectical constructivism is beyond our consideration. However, it is important to highlight that the dialectical constructivistic approach permeated, since the "role of social interaction in the learner's knowledge construction process, leading to an emphasis on cooperative and collaborative learning strategies" (p. 190) was evident. Likewise, varied use of open, comparing, proving, and synthesizing questions among moderators could have lead to different pedagogical benefits as noted by Wang (2005). The virtual nature of the experience allows for another parallel, this time between Riley's (2002) focus on modeling and the distinction between presenting, moderating, and facilitating a learning experience in a virtual classroom. He posits "(v)irtual culture affords the wider educational sweep (of communicative interactions) and highlights the activity of modeling to represent and to communicate, rather than the activity of communicating in order to model" (p. 50).

A dialogical process promoted reflection on the roles of language used by teachers as educators, the function of learning styles as they relate to students' persistence and success in school, group work as a means to reduce the fear in learning a second language, and teaching being more than sharing thoughts. The participants used and witnessed a comprehensively designed curriculum on education using divergent methods for transmission of the material within and beyond the boundaries of the technology. The virtual classroom as the place for interaction allowed for a construction of knowledge shared by the whole group. Such an experience approximates the concept of multiculturalism offered by Shaffer (2004) as a "diversity of means rather than ends" (p. 25). Nevertheless, the work of Holliday (2001) offers insights in examining the challenges faced by facilitators in reaching this diversity in the delivery of the curriculum:

We must come to terms with the fact that the bridges we build to reach other cultures might only be meaningful to our culture. The concept of learner-centredness and stakeholder-centredness are products of our own discourse, and may not belong to the differently constructed worlds of those we wish to reach. We thus need to look deeply and critically at our own discourses before judging those of others. (p. 176)

In other words, expecting dialog or a particular approach to facilitating is in itself already colored by our own bias. Observing the whole repertoire of facilitator styles allows each educator to begin to consider when a particular style and use of tool is most appropriate.

A cross-fertilization among teachers around the world allowed for a wide support loop as theory was put into practice. Thus, as the material was covered, participants were gaining access to patterns of coping with a new style of teaching delivery. By witnessing the shared modeling, they developed their teaching skills. This knowledge and modeling on how teachers adapt new theory and approaches and implement them in their environment was a major asset in the blended learning experience.

Conclusion

Our experience followed that of Rovai and Jordan's (2004), which identified the trend of education as "moving away from a faculty-centered and lecture based paradigm to a model where learners are the focus, where faculty members become learning environment designers, and where students are taught critical thinking skills" (p. 2). This new blended system of professional development offered the benefits of collaborative dialog, linking up educators with others in diverse international locations to share common educational concerns. It also offered congruence in purpose in a teacher development activity by the transferring or construction of knowledge resulting in social interaction, which in turn ultimately facilitates and is required for that process of knowledge creation. The BLC experience also heightened the groups' competence as language teachers in a manner similar to Duemer et al.'s (2002) description of the formation of online professional communities. Furthermore, this transfer of information and communication through contact in the virtual classroom also strengthened and bonded the blended global community.

We have described a dynamic approach to professional development, a learning experience in which face-to-face educators met weekly with an international community of practice to study about teaching and learning synchronously online. This new approach takes basic and generally available technology and extends its capacity into a vibrant and expansive application of human interaction. The multivalent representations of this international aggregate of educators suggest how online diversity is achieved in an era of supposed digital homogenization.

A major asset of the blended learning experience was the support offered teachers by the socioconstructive modeling loop of practical application conducive to affective gains in approaching technolinguistic issues. Examination of methodological approaches leading to such supports is crucial for success in blended environments. Moreover, the facilitating function of text as a speech rehearsal/unobtrusive discussion tool in synchronous environments deserves further investigation. The teaching competence of participants and the volunteer nature of the project served to overcome the concerns expressed by McDonald (2002) for suitability of educational materials and feasibility of technological access. Her identification of benchmarks for success in Internet based Distance Education is worth addressing in the future.

This project showed much potential, moving from the established curriculum and offering educators an invigorating international instructional approach to professional development. It exemplifies innovative uses of technology in its application of reusable procedures for learning packages (Finnis, 2004). Further use of socio-ecological field theory could explain how various virtual environments serve as efficient contexts to support experiential education. The interactive approach described here offers an applicable structure leading to the successful integration of learning objects, pre-packaged curriculum and open content digitalized materials for educational purposes. While this chapter described procedures used to implement a successful professional development activity, next steps must certify and protect the quality, value, and equitable access of online resources through out the world.

Our blended classroom experience became spontaneously available to a global community of practice whose cooperative experimentation and exploration of online tools served as the basis for a teacher development activity. The virtual setting allowed for intercultural interaction in a collaborative global environment. Access to the unlimited plethora of educational materials and tools that ease social interaction online increased the potential to develop the technical, theoretical and social skills required for ongoing teacher training. The procedure that emerged from harvesting resources from a community of practice is the foundation for the development of extended activities like the blended classroom. The face-to-face complement also deepened the interaction and created a unique group composition. In addition to these blended group compositions, an explorative and innovative climate built by experienced virtual participants furthered the student centered learning. The potential use of online tools and educational materials within multicultural contexts seems promising and worth pursuing.

Acknowledgment

The authors would like to thank all Blended Course participants, the Webheads Online Community of Practice and the Venezuela coordinator Doris de Martins for their invaluable support in the project. The generous support from Learningtimes. org is also acknowledged in providing access to the virtual classroom in which the learning experience took place.

References

Adriaen, M. (2002). Instruction design principles for language teaching. *Distances,* 5, 143-153.

Anderson, T., Rourke, L., Garrison, D. R., & Archer, W. (2001). Assessing teaching presence in a computer conferencing context. *Journal of Asynchronous Learning Networks*, 5(2). Retrieved January 4, 2008, from http://www.aln. org/publications/jaln/v5n2/v5n2_anderson.asp

The Annenberg Foundation. (2004). The Annenberg Foundation's mission statement. Retrieved January 4, 2008, from http://www.annenbergfoundation. org/about/about_show.htm?doc_id=209617

Aragon, S. R. (2003). Creating social presence in online environments. *New Directions for Adult & Continuing Education, 100,* 57-68.

Bronfenbrenner, U. (1979). *The ecology of human development: Experiments by nature and design.* Cambridge, MA: Harvard University Press.

Brook, C., & Oliver, R. (2003). Online learning communities: Investigating a design framework. *Australian Journal of Educational Technology, 19*(2), 139-160. Retrieved January 4, 2008, from http://www.ascilite.org.au/ajet/ajet19/brook. html

Burnham, B. R., & Walden, B. (1997). *Interactions in distance education: A report from the other side.* In *Proceedings of the Adult Education Research Conference (AERC).* Stillwater, OK: Oklahoma State University.

Chew, P. G. (1999). Linguistic imperialism, globalism and the English language. In D. Graddol & U.M. Meinboff (Eds.), *English in a changing world. AILA Review, 13,* 37-47.

Collins, M., & Berge, Z. (1996). *Facilitating interaction in computer mediated online courses.* Retrieved January 4, 2008, from http://www.emoderators.com/moderators/flcc.html

Cox, G., Carr, T., & Hall, M. (2004). Evaluating the use of synchronous communication in two blended courses. *Journal of Computer Assisted Learning, 20,* 183-193.

Crystal, D. (2001). *Language and the Internet.* Cambridge: Cambridge University Press.

Dalgarno, B. (2001). Interpretations of constructivism and consequences for computer assisted learning. *British Journal of Educational Technology, 32*(2), 183-194.

Duemer, L., Fontenot, D., Gumfory, K., Kallus, M., Larsen, J., Schafer, S. et al. (2002). The use of online synchronous discussion groups to enhance community formation and professional identity development. *The Journal of Interactive Online Learning, 1*(2). Retrieved January 4, 2008, from http://www.ncolr.org/jiol/issues/PDF/1.2.4.pdf

Eib, B., & Miller, P. (2006). Faculty development as community building. *International Review of Research in Open and Distance Learning, 3*(2), 1-15.

Elder, L., & Paul, R. (1998). The role of Socratic questioning in thinking, teaching, and learning. *The Clearing House, 71,* 297-301.

Fassett, D., & Warren, J. (2007). *Critical communication pedagogy.* Thousand Oaks, CA: Sage Publications.

Finnis, J.A. (2004). Learning technology: The myths and facts. *International Journal of Instructional Technology and Distance Learning, 1*(5). Retrieved January 4, 2008, from http://www.itdl.org/Journal/May_04/article07.htm

Garber, D. (2004). *Growing virtual communities.* The International Review of Research in Open and Distance Report # 34.

Graham, C. R. (2005). Blended learning systems. Definition, current trends, and future directions. In C. J. Bonk & C. R. Graham (Eds.), *Handbook of blended learning: Global perspectives, local designs.* San Francisco: Pfeiffer.

Gunawardena, C. (1995). Social presence theory and implications for interaction and collaborative learning in computer conferences. *International Journal of Educational Telecommunications, 1*(2/3), 147-166.

Hawkes, M. (2001). An analysis of critically reflective teacher dialogue in asynchronous computer-mediated communication. *International Conference on Advanced Learning Technologies*, 0247.

Herrington, J., & Oliver, R. (1995). Critical characteristics of situated learning: Implications for the instructional design of multimedia. In *Proceedings ASCILITE '95*, University of Melbourne. Retrieved January 4, 2008, from http://www.ascilite.org.au/conferences/melbourne95/smtu/papers/herrington.pdf

Hill, J. R., Wiley, D., Nelson, L. M., & Han, S. (2003). Exploring research on Internet-based learning: From infrastructure to interactions. In D. Jonassen (Ed.), *Handbook of research on educational communications and technology* (2nd ed.) (pp. 433-460). Columbia, MO: University of Missouri.

Hinson, J., & LaPrairie, K. (2005). Learning to teach online: Promoting success through professional development. *Community College Journal of Research and Practice, 29*(6), 483-493.

Holliday, A. (2001). Achieving cultural continuity in curriculum innovation. In D. Hall & A. Hewings (Eds.), *Innovation in English language teaching*. London: Routledge.

Honebein, P. (1996). Seven goals for the design of constructivist learning environments. In B. Wilson (Ed.), *Constructivist learning environments*. New York: Educational Technology Publications.

Kern, R., Ware, P., & Warschauer, M. (2004). Crossing frontiers: New directions in online pedagogy and research. *Annual Review of Applied Linguistics, 24*(1), 243.

Khan, B. H. (2000). Discussion of resources and attributes of the Web for the creation of meaningful learning environments. *CyberPsychology and Behavior, 3*(1), 17-23.

Lefoe, G. (1998). Creating constructivist learning environments on the Web: The challenge in higher education. In *ASCILITE '98 Conference*, Wollongong, New South Wales, Australia. Retrieved January 4, 2008, from http://www.ascilite.org.au/conferences/wollongong98/asc98-pdf/lefoe00162.pdf

Mabrito, M. (2004). Guidelines for establishing interactivity in online courses. *Innovate: Journal of On-Line Education, 1*(2). Retrieved January 4, 2008, from http://innovateonline.info/index.php?view=article&id=12

McAlister, S., Ravenscroft, A., & Scanlon, E. (2004). Combining interaction and context design to support collaborative argumentation using a tool for synchronous CMC. *Journal of Computer Assisted Learning: Special Issue: Developing Dialogue for Learning, 20*(3), 194-204.

McCarty, S. (2005). Global communications in a graduate course on online education at the University of Tsukuba. In *GLOCOM Platform, Colloquium #60*.

Tokyo: Japanese Institute of Global Communications, International University of Japan.

Macfadyen, L. (2004). *The prospects for identity and community in cyberspace: A survey of current literature.* The University of British Columbia: Centre for Intercultural Communication.

McDonald, J. (2002). Is as good as face-to-face as good as it gets? *JALN, 6*(2), 10-23.

McKenna, K., & Green, A. (2002). Virtual group dynamics. *Group Dynamics: Theory, Research, and Practice, 6*(1), 116-127.

Miller, S., & Miller, K. (1999). Using instructional theory to facilitate communication in Web-based courses. *Educational Technology & Society, 2*(3). Retrieved January 4, 2008, from hhttp://ifets.ieee.org/periodical/vol_3_99/miller.html

Muirhead, B. (2004). Encouraging interaction in online classes. Learning technology: The myths and facts. *International Journal of Instructional Technology and Distance Learning, 1*(6). Retrieved January 4, 2008, from http://www.itdl.org/Journal/Jun_04/article07.htm

Oren, A., Mioduser, D., & Nachmias, R. (2002). The development of social climate in virtual learning discussion group. *The International Review of Research in Open and Distance Learning, 3*(1), 1-19.

Orvis, K., & Lassiter, A. (2006). Computer-supported collaborative learning: The role of the instructor. In S. Ferris & S. Godar (Eds.), *Teaching and learning with virtual teams* (pp. 158-179). Hershey, PA: Idea Group.

Pahl, C. (2003). Managing evolution and change in Web-based teaching and learning environments. *Computers and Education, 40*(2), 99-114.

Preece, J., & Maloney-Krichmar, D. (2003). Online communities: Focusing on sociability and usability. In J. A. Jacko & A. Sears (Eds.), *The human-computer interaction handbook* (pp. 596-620). Mahwah, NJ: Lawrence Erlbaum.

Richardson, J. C., & Swan, K. (2003). Examining social presence in online courses in relation to students' perceived learning and satisfaction. *Journal of Asynchronous LearningNetworks, 7*(1), 68-88. Retrieved January 4, 2008, from http://www.sloan-c.org/publications/jaln/v7n1/pdf/v7n1_richardson.pdf

Riley, D. (2002). Educational innovation, learning technologies and virtual culture potential. *Association for Learning Technology Journal, 10*(1), 45-51.

Rourke, L., Anderson, T., Garrison, D., & Archer, W. (2001). Assessing social presence in asynchronous text-based computer conferencing. *Journal of Distance Education.* Retrieved January 4, 2008, from http://cade.icaap.org/vol14.2/rourke_et_al.html

Rovai, A. (2002, April). Building sense of community at a distance. *International Review of Research in Open and Distance Learning (IRRODL), 3,* 1. Retrieved

January 4, 2008, from http://www.irrodl.org/index.php/irrodl/article/download/79/153

Rovai, A. P., & Jordan, H. M. (2004). Blended learning and sense of community: A comparative analysis with traditional and fully online graduate courses. *International Review of Research in Open and Distance Learning*, 13. Retrieved January 4, 2008, from http://www.irrodl.org/index.php/irrodl/article/view/192/274

Ryba, K., Selby, L., & Mentis, M. (2002). Analysing the effectiveness of on-line learning communities. In *Proceedings of the 2002 Annual International Conference of the Higher Education Research and Development Society of Australasia (HERDSA)*, Perth, Australia. Retrieved January 4, 2008, from http://www.ecu.edu.au/conferences/herdsa/main/papers/nonref/pdf/KenRyba.pdf

Schrum, L., & Berge, Z. L. (1998). Creating student interaction within the educational experience: A challenge for online teachers. *Canadian Journal of Educational Communication, 26*(3), 133-144.

Selwyn, N. (1999). Virtual concerns: Restrictions of the Internet as a learning environment. *British Journal of Educational Technology, 30*(1), 69-71.

Shaffer, D. W. (2004). Multisubculturalism: Computers and the end of progressive education. *In Submission to Educational Researcher.* Retrieved January 4, 2008, from http://www.education.wisc.edu/edpsych/facstaff/dws/papers/multisubculturalism-draft1.pdf

Stevens, V. (2005). Computer-mediated communications tools used with teachers and students in virtual communities of practice. In S. M. Stewart & J. E. Olearski (Eds.), *Proceedings of the First Annual Conference for Middle East Teachers of Science, Mathematics and Computing* (pp. 204-218). Abu Dhabi: Middle East Teachers of Science, Mathematics and Computing.

Thurmond, V., & Wambach, K. (2004). Understanding interactions in distance education: A review of the literature. *International Journal of Instructional Technology and Distance Learning, 1*(1), Retrieved January 4, 2008, from http://www.itdl.org/journal/Jan_04/article02.htm

Tu, C. (2002, April-June). The measurement of social presence in an online learning environment. *International Journal of E-Learning,* 34-45. Retrieved January 4, 2008, from http://www.aace.org/dl/files/IJEL/IJEL1234.pdf

Verneil, M., & Berge, Z. L. (2000, Spring/Summer). Going online: Guidelines for the faculty in higher education. *Educational Technology Review: International Forum on Educational Technology Issues and Applications, 13*, 13-18.

Vieta, M. (2003, October 16-19). *The interactional self and the experiences of Internet mediated communication as seen through Heidegger, Mead, and Schutz.* Paper presented at the Peer Reviewed Conference at the Association of Internet Researcher's "Broadening the Band" Conference in Toronto, Canada.

Retrieved January 4, 2008, from http://aoir.org/members/papers42/Vieta_Interactional_Self_v3.pdf

Vygotsky, L. S. (1978). *Mind in society: The development of higher psychological process*. Cambridge, MA: Harvard University Press.

Walker, S. A. (2004). Socratic strategies and devil's advocacy in synchronous CMC debate. *Journal of Computer Assisted Learning, 20*(3), 172-182.

Wallace, C. (2002). Local literacies and global literacies. In D. Block & D. Cameron (Eds.), *Globalization and language teaching* (pp. 101-14). London: Routledge.

Wang, C. (2005). Questioning skills facilitate online synchronous discussions. *Journal of Computer Assisted Learning, 21*, 303-313.

Warschauer, M. (2002). The Internet and linguistic pluralism. In I. Snyder (Ed.), *Silicon literacies: Communication, innovation and education in the electronic age* (pp. 62-74). London: Routledge.

Wegerirf, R. (1998). The social dimension of asynchronous learning networks. *JALN, 2*(1), 34-49.

Yang, S. (2002, September 11-14). *Educational research for the dialectic process of globalization and localization*. Paper presented at the European Conference on Educational Research, University of Lisbon. Retrieved January 4, 2008, from http://www.leeds.ac.uk/educol/documents/00002276.htm

Further Reading

Allen, S., Ure, D., & Evans, S. (2003). *Virtual communities of practice as learning networks*. Retrieved January 4, 2008, from http://www.masie.com/research-grants/2003/BY_Final_Report.pdf

Brookfield, S. (1995). *Becoming a critically reflective teacher*. San Francisco, CA: Jossey Bass.

Conrad, R., & Donaldson, J. A. (2004). *Engaging the online learner activities and resources for creative instruction*. Guides to online teaching and learning, vol. 1. San Francisco: Jossey Bass.

Hewitt, T. W. (2006). *Understanding and shaping curriculum: What we teach and why*. Thousand Oaks, CA; London.

Hofmann, J. (2004). *Live and online: Tips, techniques, and ready-to-use activities for the virtual classroom*. San Francisco: Pfeiffer.

Hofmann, J. (2004). *The synchronous trainer's survival guide: Facilitating successful live and online courses, meetings, and events*. San Francisco: Pfeiffer.

Moore, G. S, Winograd, K., & Lange, D. (2001). You can teach online! Building creative learning environments. New York: McGraw Hill.

Pallof, R., & Pratt, K. (2003). *The virtual student a profile and guide to working with online learners.* San Francisco: Jossey Bass.

Pallof, R., & Pratt, K. (1999). *Building learning communities in cyberspace: Effective strategies for the online classroom.* San Francisco: Jossey Bass.

Piskurich, G. M. (Ed.) (2004). *Getting the most from online learning: A learner's guide.* San Francisco: Pfeiffer.

Roblyer, M. D., Edwards, J., & Havriluk, M. A. (1997). *Integrating educational technology into teaching.* New Jersey: Prentice Hall.

Useful Links

Communities of Practice

http://www.webheads.info/: Webheads in action communities of practice online

http://www.zope.org/: Zope is an open source application server for building content management systems, intranets, portals, and custom applications. The Zope community consists of hundreds of companies and thousands of developers all over the world, working on building the platform and Zope applications.

http://www.ocwconsortium.org/: Universities working together to advance education and empower people worldwide through opencourseware.

http://p2p.internet2.edu/: The Peer-to-Peer WG (P2Pwg) has its beginnings from a grassroots effort to investigate and explore the many aspects of peer-to-peer, beyond the resource management issues that bring the most notoriety.

http://www.internet2.edu/projects/: Developing advanced networking technology is at the heart of Internet2. Members have access to a unique nationwide high-performance network infrastructure that removes boundaries of today's Internet. Internet2 actively supports our community as it pioneers developments in areas such as middleware, security, network research and performance measurement capabilities.

http://www.education-world.com/a_curr/curr062.shtml: Getting started in the internet—a resource guide to listserves

http://www.gse.harvard.edu/news/features/dede03012003.html: Interview with Professor Chris Dede who believes that emerging technologies expand our capability to create, share, and master knowledge. His current project is the development of Multi-User Virtual Environment Experiential Simulators (MUVEES).

http://kngforge.uwc.ac.za/santec/: SANTEC is an enabling network of educational technology practitioners with an interest in educational technology in developing environments. The aim of SANTEC is to be a community of practice that facilitates and supports collaborative ventures and effects synergies amongst members.

Educational Content

http://courses.durhamtech.edu/tlc/www/html/Special_Feature/hybridclasses. htm: The Teaching-Learning Center (TLC) is dedicated to enhancing teaching and learning excellence for faculty, students, and staff at Durham Technical Community College and for educational colleagues in public schools and universities across the community.

http://www.georgetown.edu/crossroads/webcourses.html: Dynamic syllabi serve as online platforms upon which to stage, manage, and enhance a course and can include electronic resources, instructors' notes, exercises and assignments, course projects, virtual exhibitions, links between course readings and Web resources, rich multimedia resources and students' projects.

http://careo.ucalgary.ca/cgi-bin/WebObjects/CAREO.woa: Learning Commons Educational Object Repository

http://www.ibritt.com/resources/dc_objects.htm: Designing Courses: Learning Objects, SCOs, IMS Standards, XML, SGML, and so forth.

http://www.lolaexchange.org/cgi-perl/lolaexchange/lola.cgi?function=f54&us ername=: Learning Objects Repositories

http://ocw.mit.edu/OcwWeb/: MIT's OpenCourseWare: a free and open educational resource (OER) for educators, students, and self-learners around the world. It is true to MIT's values of excellence, innovation, and leadership.

http://www.cloudnet.com/~edrbsass/affectiveeducation.html: Lesson Plans for the affective domain

Affective Education Lesson Plans and Resources

http://www.eduref.org/: The Educator's Reference Desk builds on over a quarter century of experience providing high-quality resources and services to the education community.

http://www.free.ed.gov/?sid=2: Federal Resources for Educational Excellence

Teaching and Learning Resources from Federal Agencies

http://www.merlot.org/merlot/index.htm: Multimedia Educational Resource for Learning and Online Teaching

http://thenode.org/: Resources to support an international community of educators and trainers interested in understanding online learning technologies and harnessing their potential.

http://blogs.law.harvard.edu/cyberone/: The course Web site for Law in the Court of Public Opinion.

http://www.nln.ac.uk/Materials/default.asp: National Learning Network

http://www.mcli.dist.maricopa.edu/mlx/: The Maricopa Learning eXchange (MLX) is an electronic warehouse of ideas, examples, and resources (represented as "packages") that support student learning at the Maricopa Community Colleges.

http://www.intime.uni.edu/terms.html: The mission of INTIME is to help educators improve student learning at all levels (PK thru University work) and in all content areas.

http://oerwiki.iiep-unesco.org/index.php?title=OER_useful_resources: OER useful resources

http://creativecommons.org/: Enabling the legal sharing and reuse of cultural, educational, and scientific works.

http://nsdl.org/: The National Science Digital Library

http://opencontent.org/ocwfinder/: The Open Content Finder

http://www-jime.open.ac.uk/98/5/: A Model for Distributed Curriculum on the World Wide Web

Online Tools

http://www.edutools.com/: WCET's EduTools provides independent reviews, side-by-side comparisons, and consulting services to assist decision-making in the e-learning community

http://www.google.com/literacy: A resource for teachers, literacy organisations and anyone interested in reading and education, created in collaboration with LitCam, Google, and UNESCO's Institute for Lifelong Learning.

http://www.google.com/educators/: Google recognizes the central role that teachers play in breaking down the barriers between people and information, and we support educators who work each day to empower their students and expand the frontiers of human knowledge. This Web site is one of the ways we're working to bolster that support and explore how Google and educators can work together.

http://www.lamsfoundation.org/: LAMS is a revolutionary new tool for designing, managing and delivering online collaborative learning activities. It provides teachers with a highly intuitive visual authoring environment for creating sequences of learning activities. These activities can include a range of individual tasks, small group work and whole class activities based on both content and collaboration.

http://scout.wisc.edu/: The Internet Scout Project. Since 1994, the Scout Project has focused on developing better tools and services for finding, filtering, and presenting online information and metadata.

http://plone.org/: Opensource content management system

http://cosl.usu.edu/projects/educommons/: What is eduCommons? eduCommons is an OpenCourseWare management system designed specifically to support OpenCourseWare projects like USU OCW. eduCommons will help you develop and manage an open access collection of course materials.

Chapter IV

Collaborative Online Learning and Accessibility

Martin D. Beer, Sheffield Hallam University, UK

Paul Crowther, Sheffield Hallam University, UK

Elizabeth Uruchurtu, Sheffield Hallam University, UK

Inside Chapter

This chapter looks at how the issues of accessibility have developed over a number of collaborative learning projects that have investigated the use of various technologies to provide effective communication mechanisms between students in various virtual learning scenarios:

1. *Occupational Therapy Internet School (OTIS) investigated the use of a graphical virtual college environment to allow occupational therapy students to discover how practice differed in various European Union countries.*

2. *MOBIlearn investigated the new opportunities offered by mobile devices to develop a new paradigm of mobile learning.*

3. *The Health Informatics module allows Foundation Degree students working in Health Informatics to discover the different aspects of their various roles and to*

reflect on the way in which they interface with clinical and other professionals and their role within the wider National Health Service (NHS) agenda.

The use of different technologies has raised various accessibility issues that need to be addressed if this type of learning is to be adopted more widely and accepted best practices are to be followed. These are discussed and indicators are given as to how they may be addressed systematically to provide an effective learning experience for all.

Introduction

This chapter discusses a number of projects all with similar aims: that is, to engage students spread geographically over often a considerable distance in a collaborative learning activity in which they share their experiences and learn from them. They have led to a better understanding of the need to follow best practice guidelines for accessibility so that technical and pedagogic developments are used inclusively and do not unnecessarily exclude individuals because of their inability to engage with the technology.

The first example is the Occupational Therapy Internet School (OTIS) (Armitt, Green, & Beer, 2001), in which occupational therapy students from across Europe came together to discuss the practice of their subject in each country. The objective was for them to identify similarities and differences based on a series of case studies which were presented within a virtual college environment in which the students could navigate to find the various course materials and meet other students who were studying the same thing. This provided an environment which was much more like that experienced in the typical simulation type computer game, at least to the extent that the technology and network capabilities at the time would allow.

The second example is the MOBIlearn prototype (MOBILearn, 2002), which exploited mobile technology to allow students to move round the real environment (for example, a museum, a university campus, or a first aid training area) and to access both the learning materials they required and discuss their findings with their peers as they explored. The aim was to provide a learning experience similar to that of OTIS but for the students to explore a real space, or series of spaces, rather than sitting at a computer and exploring the virtual world.

These examples used prototype environments which concentrated on the communication needs of the staff and students and operated in synchronous communication mode. The third example considers the attempt to integrate a collaborative learning environment into a learning portal by making innovative use of the standard facilities provided. The module is part of a Foundation Degree in Health Informatics and aims to introduce students to the range of working environments that they can experience. Any student is unlikely to have direct experience of more than a small fraction of these environments. The situation is also changing rapidly as the National Health Service National Program for IT (Brennan, 2005) is rolled out, an operation with which the students are actively engaged through their work experience. The students engage in online discussion groups based on the learning materials provided and their own work and medical experiences to share the richness of the domain which they demonstrate by preparing a reflective log of their learning.

The chapter will introduce the pedagogic principles on which each of the learning projects was based and then will discuss some of the lessons learned. A major issue as these projects move from pilots to full scale deployment is accessibility. Some of the issues are discussed and the adaptations required to meet these requirements are highlighted. These projects give some indications of the requirements for online collaborative learning and show how such a teaching environment can be achieved in practice.

Background

Virtual Communities of Practice

A key feature in meeting the educational requirements of all these examples has been the development of communities of practice through collaborative interaction online. A community of practice has been defined as "a flexible group of professionals, internally bound by common interests, who interact through interdependent tasks guided by a common purpose thereby embodying a store of common knowledge" (Jubert, 1999, p. 166).

In the health care environment, paramedics or professions allied to medicine, such as occupational therapists, clearly fall under this definition. However, when you consider Ellis, Oldridge, and Vasconcelos (2003), not all the criteria suggested are strictly met for all health care workers. For example, the concept of a voluntary and emergent group of individuals and self regulation are not effectively supported. By the nature of the profession, the community cannot be self regulating and it is arguable whether membership is voluntary, even for the first aiders covered by the MOBIlearn example. Other criteria are less controversial, for example, mutual sources of gain, shared practices, mutual trust and tacit understanding of common interests and issues of concern.

All of the examples are primarily about learning. However, core to the methodology is an assumption that users will work in a collaborative way, no matter which scenario is being considered. For an e-learning system to encourage the formation of a community of practice, it is useful to consider the guidelines of Desanctis, Fayard, Roach, and Jiang (2003) who suggest collaborative learning should:

- Aim for frequent interactions
- Foster the technology as a platform for group discourse
- Aim for deep discussion (over time)
- Recognize the importance of facilitators
- Recognize the importance of routines
- Encourage groups to experiment

All of these points relate to features found in each of the examples in different ways with the intention of encouraging the formation of a community of practice. The first point is particularly important as Koh and Kim (2004) reported that the amount of interaction, specifically knowledge sharing, is an indication of the state of health of a community.

Learning

Engagement, learning, and transfer are, according to Waight and Stewart (2005), the major outcomes which can be achieved via e-learning. MOBIlearn provided a tool to facilitate collaboration and teamwork. It expanded on systems such as OTIS (Beer, Slack, & Armitt, 2005) to provide a framework which could be used in a variety of learning situations. It also allowed a variety of learning styles. The Health Informatics module attempted to provide a similar experience through a standard learning portal.

Learners today want to learn when and where they want, in formal, nonformal, and informal ways (Brand, Petrak, & Zitterbart, 2002; Cook & Smith, 2004). The types of learning, shown in Figure 1, are characterized by the following attributes:

- **Formal**
  - Mandatory participation
  - Objectives and means controlled by a facilitator
- **Nonformal**
  - Voluntary participation
  - Objectives controlled by learners
  - Means controlled by a facilitator

- **Informal**
  - ◦ Grows out of spontaneous situations
  - ◦ Objectives and means controlled by learners
  - ◦ There may be a facilitator who may provide some content and moderation

Figure 1 shows the relationships of the various MOBIlearn scenarios to the different types of learning. OTIS attempted to exploit the formal and informal aspects by encouraging learning developing out of the informal interaction over the learning materials whereas the health informatics module exploited the formal and informal aspects by the learners developing groups that allowed them to gain sets of experiences that no single learner could possibly experience on their own.

The Projects

OTIS

The OTIS system was developed specially to facilitate the collaborative educational philosophy, while being sympathetic to a non-technical user base. Above all, it had to facilitate a high degree of synchronous (real time) communication. This permitted groups of students to meet both formally and in an ad hoc manner to discuss different matters separately from other groups who might be meeting within the virtual environment at the same time.

Figure 1. Learning and the position of the MOBIlearn scenarios

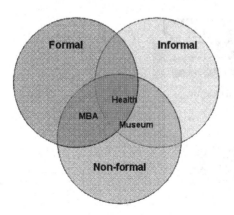

Site navigation had to be intuitive so that students did not spend much time learning a new system and could locate meetings, case studies, library materials, and course details quickly and easily. The online library of resources was organized to support the problem-based learning approach. The system also exploited the opportunities offered by new technology to deliver educational materials in innovative ways, including multimedia, such as video footage of patients and audio clips of interviews. Completed assignments were subject to peer review by other students and had to be made available electronically to tutors and external markers for assessment. This was innovative at the time and was essential because the tutors were also dispersed across Europe and did not meet except within the virtual environment.

The OTIS system design identified the need for a core system which would be common to all future courses and a course-specific element comprising the course materials. The core included the user and document management facilities and communications and was based on CoMentor, a collaborative learning environment from the University of Huddersfield (Gibbs, Skinner, & Teal, 1999). The course materials were developed in HTML using standard Internet tools such as Microsoft FrontPage, which provided a rapid development medium in which materials could readily be adapted in collaboration with the occupational therapists. Multimedia was "plugged in" to the HTML using well established technologies. Users accessed the OTIS system using a standard Java-enabled Web browser.

The OTIS user screen was divided into two halves. The course materials occupied the left hand side of the screen and the right hand side comprised the communications suite (Figure 2). The communications capabilities provided are shown in Table 1.

Figure 2. A typical student view of OTIS

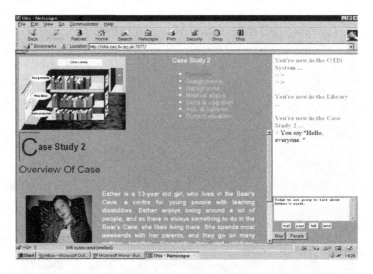

Table 1. Communications types supported

Method		Description
Talk	Synchronous	A broadcast chat message to all users present in the same virtual room as the sender
Page	Synchronous	A private chat message to one or more users logged on anywhere in the OTIS system
E-mail	Asynchronous	An e-mail message to one or more users

Figure 3. OTIS circulation areas

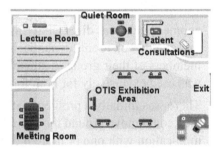

OTIS main map   OTIS courtyard map

The course materials interface was developed using a Virtual Campus metaphor (Ginsberg, Hodge, Lindstrom, Sampieri, & Shiau, 1998). The Virtual Campus comprised a number of virtual rooms such as the library, student work area, and so forth. This facilitated navigation around the OTIS site, as students readily identified the purpose of each room and knew intuitively what activities would take place in that room. Figure 3 shows the main maps giving the layout of the OTIS virtual campus.

Students clicked on the relevant part of the map in order to enter a room, and once in the room, they clicked on the door in the room map (Figure 4) to return to the entrance hall or courtyard. They were never more than one click away from one of these two central areas. This was important as it was easy for students to lose each other in the virtual world and they would return to the entrance hall to regroup before returning to discuss the learning materials.

The virtual rooms also provided the means by which groups of users congregated to discuss specific issues. When Talk was used, the message was displayed in the communication area of every occupant of that room. This provided an effective way in which a group could discuss for example Case Study 1, at the same time as

Figure 4. Typical room maps

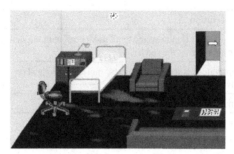 

OTIS patient consultation area   OTIS meeting room

another group was discussing Case Study 2 in another room. Both students and tutors could book rooms dynamically in the Room Booking area, and invite the other members of their group to attend. Once understood, this proved very popular and was used extensively for both formal and informal meetings.

There was initially a problem with participants finding the rest of the group, since they could move around the virtual campus. The Page facility allowed direct communication with one or more individuals, wherever they were on the system, and could be used to locate and shepherd wayward members of the group, or to conduct personal conversations.

The OTIS project showed that problem-based learning techniques could be used effectively in a distance-learning environment to bring members of a highly practical profession together across different countries. This allowed experiences to be shared across a wide range of problems and best practices to be disseminated rapidly across many national boundaries. An important feature of the OTIS course structure was the use of multinational tutorial groups and tutorials. The relatively high level of synchronous communication encouraged by the system meant that mock consultations were practical, and the use of role playing characters were easy to arrange as different tutors (or indeed students) could act the patient whenever necessary. This led to an extremely dynamic and flexible learning environment in which students, staff, and others interacted much more closely than with electronic mail based tutorial systems.

The regular liaison and negotiation between all parties closely mirrored the advanced communication necessary in a team of health professionals aiming to deliver the best possible integrated health care package to a consumer. In the case of OTIS, the student as the consumer needed to both experience the results of such integration and be trained in the methods to achieve such ends. The student consumer therefore played a valid role in all the stages of early pilot rounds, evaluating both the system and the materials.

MOBIlearn

This example is based on experiences from the MOBIlearn project funded by the European Framework V IST programme. MOBIIlearn met learners' requirements utilizing mobile communications and personal computing devices such as PDAs, smart phones, or portable computers; in other words, mobile or ubiquitous computing. A key part of the MOBIlearn project was the integration of new technologies in education. It aimed to improve access to knowledge for selected target users giving them ubiquitous access to appropriate learning objects (Taylor, 2003). Initially the MOBIlearn requirements were provided by four scenarios:

- A visit to an art gallery
- Access to training and basic medical knowledge in a hospital
- A master's course in business administration
- University orientation for new students

The aim of MOBIlearn was therefore "the creation of a virtual network for the diffusion of knowledge and learning via a mobile environment...to...demonstrate the convergence and merging of learning supported by new technology, knowledge management, and new forms of mobile communication" (MOBILearn, 2002, p. 7).

The pedagogic basis of the system was the learner who interacted with a mobile learning portal to access learning objects and participates in online activities. Each of the test scenarios had its own learning objects. However, all these learning objects had to be delivered in a flexible way to a variety of devices (Kinshuk & Goh, 2003). One challenge was therefore to deliver the correct interface to a learning object to the mobile device. There are a variety of ways of delivering learning materials to devices with differing characteristics including re-authoring, transcoding, and the functional-based object model (Stone, 2003). Ideally, an open standard should be used to allow different content providers to make their material available on mobile devices. The approach taken in MOBIlearn was to use re-authoring where page descriptions were held as XML which were compatible with the standard suggested by (Loidl, 2005).

This example concentrates on the knowledge management aspects of the system as illustrated by the health care scenario explained in the next section. Here users were encouraged to share practices and discuss possible solutions to problems encountered in the health domain.

The Health Care Scenario

There is a constant need to rapidly train employees and update their skills in all types of working environments, and especially in the health care environment. It is further stated that e-learning and knowledge management are core to achieving this. Young (2003) provides the example of e-learning to improve leadership skills among nurses. The majority of nurses preferred engaging with material at home and over the Internet in their own time and own pace. A survey of the nurses suggested a high percentage had applied the knowledge they had gained.

The health care scenario was a nonformal learning environment where a community of practice was encouraged. The system was designed to deliver training case studies which could then be discussed and developed. Learning had no start or end point and new members could join (and leave) at any time. It might well however be a condition of employment that staffs engage with this as continuing professional development. As already stated, this contradicted some of Ellis et al.'s (2003) criteria for a community of practice, specifically a voluntary and emergent group. However, if staff engaged with the learning environment, a virtual community of practice could develop, meeting other criteria including a mutual source of gain. Users were motivated by their own interests as well as the organization's interests (MOBILearn, 2002), making this an example of a sponsored community.

Within the health care scenario, quiz game, visualization, enactment, and self-evaluation were all required as well as the more generic requirements of the MOBIlearn system as a whole. Figure 5 shows a use case diagram, a Unified Modelling Language (UML) (Rumbaugh, Jacobson, & Booch, 1999) model which documents user requirements.

Although primarily a nonformal learning environment, the health care scenario had elements of both formal and informal learning associated with it, as shown in Figure 5. There were basic proficiencies, skills, and responses to situations which had to be learned. These could be delivered by the quiz and the evaluation of a case study. Using criteria-based assessment, a health care worker could improve their certification. This was formal learning and would need to be validated by appropriate professional bodies if it is to be used as such.

There was also an informal component where health care workers with particular interests could develop their knowledge in a more spontaneous and unstructured way. Again, individuals and groups could develop a knowledge base in a specific type of case study rather than a broad range.

The system also allowed reference material to be created and managed. For example, a user could call up instructions on how to deal with minor wounds. The template that was used for detailing the procedure is illustrated in Table 2.

Figure 5. Use case diagram of the health care scenario

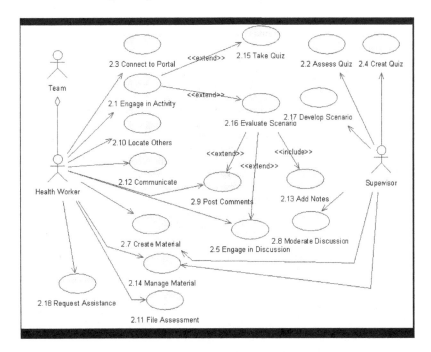

An Example of a Case Study

One of the activities in the scenario was "visualization," or as labeled in the use case diagram, "Evaluate Scenario." This was designed to test a variety of skills of individuals and teams of individuals. Specifically it aimed to:

- Improve observation and appraisal skills
- Improve decision making under pressure
- Encourage learners to examine their response
- Facilitate collaboration with other learners

An example of how a case study would be presented to a learner is shown in Figure 6, where an incident has been staged. Learners were stepped through the incident and were required to give an assessment at each stage. This assessment could then be discussed by other members of the community.

Figure 6 shows the first of three images in the case study "Collapse 2" which showed an incident of a collapsed unconscious IT worker. It was discovered that a series of still images was more effective than a video clip for a user to add observations and

Table 2. Template for instructions illustrated by minor wounds

Condition	**Minor wounds**
Aim:	Prevent **infection**
Treatment:	<ul><li>wash and dry your **own hands**</li><li>cover any **wounds** on your own hands</li><li>put on **disposable gloves**</li><li>clean wound, if dirty, under **running water**</li><li>**pat dry** with **sterile dressing**</li><li>cover wound temporarily with sterile dressing while you clean surrounding skin with soap and water</li><li>always swab **away** from the wound, using a fresh dressing for each stroke pat surrounding skin dry</li><li>cover **wound** completely with **sterile dressing**</li><li>advise **casualty** to see doctor if there is a special risk of **infection** because, for example, the **wound** was caused by :<ul><li>an **animal bite**</li><li>a dirty object (puncture wound)</li></ul></li></ul>
	Remember – there is a risk of infection by tetanus for ALL open wounds

Figure 6. PDA-based version of the learning object 'Collapse 2'

assessments. Each subsequent image showed a section of the case study in close up and allowed assessments to be made and refined.

The Health Informatics Module

One of the difficulties in designing work-based learning into e-learning courses is that, particularly in technical areas, it is very rare for students to obtain the necessary range of experience to meet the full range of learning outcomes necessary to achieve the academic objectives of the module. For example, students taking the FdSc in Health Informatics are likely to have experience of the use of informatics in either primary or secondary care, but not both. They are also likely to be involved in a limited range of specialisms within those categories. The traditional way of dealing with this issue is to establish a system of circuits, which provide the necessary range of experiences for each student. This is a major management overhead that requires absolute cooperation between employers and the University. In an e-learning environment where the students are spread geographically across the country, and potentially across the world, such cooperation is unlikely to occur in a timely and effective manner.

In this approach, groups of students with a range of experiences reported on and discussed their experiences within tutor moderated discussion groups. Students therefore gained the range of competences across a wide range of positive experiences to meet the learning outcomes timely and effectively. By sharing their practice they reinforced their understanding of the issues that they personally experience and would be better able to apply their knowledge to new situations in their professional lives.

This example discusses the experience of developing and delivering the first year module that introduced the basic concepts of working in the Health Informatics domain. It will be followed in subsequent years by further modules which will introduce more specialist topics as the students' experience grows.

One of the issues in establishing this module was how to stimulate the students and promote the deep learning essential to operate effectively with today's health professionals. Educators suggest that students who are personally involved in learning from real life situations are the ones who are most likely to experience deep learning; McAllister, Lincoln, McLeod, and Maloney (1997, p. 8), for example, argue that:

deep approaches to learning are found in students who are affectively involved in searching for personal meaning and understanding (their own personal practical knowledge), seeing the whole picture or person—not just the isolated features or disembodied problems—drawing on their personal experience to make sense of new ideas and experiences and relating evidence to conclusion. These deep learning ap-

proaches are in marked contrast to surface approaches exhibited by students who seek only to memorize and reproduce information or skills, see only the discrete "bits," expect the educator to be in control of their learning, and are largely motivated by the external imperative to pass an assignment or gain their qualification.

The requirement that UK Foundation degrees include an element of work-based learning provides an ideal opportunity to encourage deep learning based on their real-life experiences. This not only ensures quality learning but it is also a safeguard for the future in that they are most likely to display a holistic approach to their clients in a rapidly changing environment, with a clear emphasis on quality of care. Clinical education has been shown to be effective in facilitating deep learning (Boud, 1988; Hagadorn, 1992) and for students in the academic environment realistic case studies explored via a stimulating problem-solving approach can form a close approximation to learning from real life. This synergy is further strengthened by the use of discussion forums to provide input from students with current relevant experience.

This problem-based approach provides the scaffolding on which students can bring their collective work experiences to bear on a range of problems so that they learn together, and allows us to tap into the accepted benefits which are normally described as:

- Integration of knowledge is encouraged, so that the complete environment is studied, rather than just the technical context.
- Essential core skills are fostered, such as problem solving, communication, and team working.
- A deeper approach to learning is encouraged; not merely the learning of taught facts, memorized in order to pass an examination.

It has been found that medical courses which use a formal problem-based learning (PBL) approach are systematic in the way the cases are presented; study is conducted via small groups, each facilitated by a tutor, and face to face feedback sessions are held regularly. While the use of a PBL approach would be beneficial in relating the students' work-based activities to their learning, it was clear from the beginning that an Internet-based delivery mechanism could not meet the formal structure of problem-based learning groups. Instead, the course design team aimed to develop essential professional skills by designing materials which could be addressed via the use of a problem solving model (Hagadorn, 1992).

The class was divided into groups to assist management of the discussion boards and each group was provided with a set of discussion forums specifically for their use. Each group had a nominated tutor who monitored the discussions and guided the students through the various tasks involved. The module started with 71 students divided into four groups, ranging in size from 13 to 21.

The pedagogic basis of the module was the learner who interacts with the learning portal to access learning objects and participates in a wide range of individual and collaborative online activities. As such, it expanded on systems such as OTIS (Armitt et al., 2001) and MOBIlearn to provide a framework which can be used in variety of learning situations. It also allows a variety of learning styles.

Organization of the Module

The module materials were presented as a series of online activities within the University's Blackboard online learning portal. These consisted of five major units, each of which was expected to take about 2 weeks, although tutors had discretion over exactly how long each group took, depending on individual circumstances. The units were:

1. Introduction to the Module
2. Security and Confidentiality
3. Primary Care
4. Secondary Care
5. Finishing Off

Units 2-4 were semi-independent and could be delivered in any order. Communications facilities were provided in a number of ways, each providing access to a different audience:

- **Discussion board:** For general discussions across everyone taking the course, for example to share useful information with all members of the cohort.
- **Group pages:** For formal and nonformal learning activities within groups, as were required by the activities throughout the module. Separate Discussion groups were provided for each unit and threads for each collaborative exercise.
- **E-mail:** Available to send e-mail to one or more members of the group. In practice, this was used mainly by tutors issuing formal notices such as instructions to move on to the next unit or to submit work for feedback.

Informal learning was supported by the students' ability to create their own discussion threads when they considered that there was a need to do so. In practice this has not happened yet.

There were two discussion forums set up for general use by all members of the module. These were:

- **General topics**—for general topics of interest to the whole cohort.
- **Technical issues**—specifically to report technical issues, such as broken links and download problems, to the technical developers so that they can locate and fix them.

There was no general student discussion area available (although any student could initiate one at any time) as it was felt that there were already too many communication channels available and that adding another without a clear purpose would only cause confusion. Certainly in the early weeks of the module there was enough confusion, with students introducing themselves on the "General Topics" forum, rather than to their group board. Tutors had to guide them to the proper place and encourage them to repost so that everyone could find their contribution. This has not always proved easy in an online situation where tutors and students never actually meet. Towards the end of the module, a wider forum for all modules on the course was established to give students the opportunity to comment on their experiences more generally.

Assessment

The principle item of assessment was the module log that each student produced as they processed through the module. It had spaces for them to record each activity that they undertook. These were simply text boxes and could be expanded and contracted as required. This was because each student would have more or less to say about individual activities, depending on their own and their group experiences. The log was not meant to be simply a précis of the messages that had appeared in the relevant discussions, but to provide an opportunity for the students to reflect on their learning on each topic. Students were therefore expected to compare their experiences with those of other members of the group and to show how their understanding of the subject had changed throughout the module.

The log was split into sections, one for each unit, and students were asked to submit completed sections to tutors at regular intervals. This allowed tutors to advise on the students' work, and to encourage them to take appropriate action if necessary, to ensure a successful final outcome to the module. The log was finally completed, taking note of the tutor's feedback, and submitted for marking at the end of the module. With the first cohort, the students were given no opportunity to indicate what action they had taken on the feedback given by tutors, which they found rather dispiriting, so it is proposed to add an additional component to each section of the student log to indicate what action they had taken on the feedback to encourage them to make more effective use of the feedback.

Results

Initial results have been very positive, despite a number of organizational issues at the start of the module.

* Initial engagement was significantly higher than in earlier modules on this course (approximately 75% compared with just over 50% with the earlier modules).

* The students have been willing to participate in quite wide ranging discussions and share their experiences effectively with the rest of the tutorial group.

* The intermediate moderation of the student learning log was a major factor in encouraging early engagement and students welcomed the possibility of obtaining early feedback which would hopefully ensure that they correct any issues and develop their learning style effectively throughout the module.

* Unfortunately the tutorial groups broke up later in the module with tutors having difficulties maintaining any meaningful relationship with their groups. A major contributor to this was the variation in speed in which students moved from unit to unit. The communications facilities within Blackboard did not provide an effective location mechanism for current activity and both students and tutors found themselves hunting for each other around the various groups. There is an urgent requirement at least for some indication of the latest activity for each participant. Blackboard provides comprehensive logging facilities but for our purposes they proved difficult to interpret and were very expensive in terms of resources to collect.

* At the end of the module, 32 students submitted learning logs out of the 48 who remained on the course. This as a proportion was a considerable improvement on other, similar modules. Whilst engagement remained unsatisfactory, student feedback indicated that this was because of a conception of the workload of the module (it carried 50% more credit than the other modules) and the learning through discussion groups was considered to be very effective. This was evidenced by the proportion of high marks achieved by the students.

There was considerable initial resistance from some students to share their experiences, but so far this has been shown to be because of unfamiliarity with the learning paradigm rather than uncooperativeness as such. This resistance is diminishing rapidly with familiarity and with the better understanding of what is necessary to successfully complete the module.

Comparing the Experiences

The three examples discussed attempt to develop the students' learning by involving them directly in the collaborative learning process. OTIS did this by developing a geographic virtual space around the learning materials in which both students and staff could move both to locate the materials of interest and to find others with similar current interests. The metaphor used was often that of a virtual college environment with tutorial rooms, the library, a help desk, exhibition rooms, and so forth. This had the effect of turning the learning experience into something much more like an immersive game with the synchronous communications adding much to the immediacy of the experience. This was despite the service level of the international networks at the time often causing noticeable delays. Informal groupings around particular learning materials did happen, but not as much as had been intended. This was attributed to the very sparsely populated nature of the test world where apart from at set tutorial times there would only be one or two students present.

The MOBIlearn prototypes acted in a different way in that the objective was to provide effective communication to the learner as they moved around a real scenario. In many ways this could be compared with turning the real world into a virtual reality type of experience. The use of mobile phones and PDAs to communicate meant that students were fully aware of and familiar with the use of the communications facilities from the start and communicated freely both to share experiences and to leave comments as they moved around the real environment. So, for example, in the museums scenario this led to what was effectively the sticking of post-it notes with comments on some very well known paintings. These shared views became a major part of the learning experience. The health care scenario described in rather more detail in this chapter was very much an attempt to guide students through particular scenarios required by competency programmes aimed at providing confidence in dealing with certain types of situation that a first aider is likely to find in the real world. The object was therefore to deliver the training as it was required, without the student having to wait for the next available face-to-face course but without losing the learning associated with the conventional group interactions and peer support.

The Health Informatics module has been a rather different experience. The need to use the standard university portal put severe constraints on the facilities that could be utilised. In particular, only having asynchronous group discussion facilities caused many more problems with both staff and students loosing any real concept of presence about mid-way through the module. While there had been issues with staff and students losing track of each other in OTIS, they had always managed to find each other again quite quickly using the hailing mechanism. Asynchronous communication does not provide this facility.

Accessibility Issues

Accessibility refers to the extent to which individual users can easily access a Web site and its related electronic services, regardless of the devices they use to interface (JISC Legal, 2005).

In the examples analyzed through this chapter, collaborative learning was sought by means of different platforms and approaches as discussed in the previous sections. While the firs two examples (OTIS and MOBIlearn) refer to custom made platforms specifically designed to test certain hypotheses in live trials, with carefully selected participants, the Health Informatics module has been delivered through the University's Virtual Leaning Environment (VLE). Therefore, another important issue that these approaches highlight is that of accessibility.

As a matter of law, accessibility places an obligation on HE institutions to ensure equal access to Web sites and e-learning services. Educational institutions must take such steps as it is reasonable for it to have to take to ensure that …in relation to students services provided for, or offered to, students by it, disabled students are not placed at a substantial disadvantage in comparison with students who are not disabled. (JISC Legal, 2005, p. 2)

In order to avoid placing students at a substantial disadvantage, institutions are expected to make reasonable adjustment to the service if such a substantial disadvantage arises, or if the institution anticipated that it could do so at some time in the future.

Some accessibility issues that arise from the OTIS project relate to its graphical features and the cognitive load that places on students with visual impairments or cognitive disabilities. For this approach to be more accessible to a wide range of learners, and especially those with disabilities, support would be required for features such as "live" text-to-speech for screen reading and document reading, speech recognition for text transcription and "actioning" commands, and simple graphical navigational aids (TechDis, 2005).

In the case of MOBIlearn, it has to be noted that accessibility of mobile devices can be viewed from two perspectives: (1) the accessibility and usability of the mobile device for a particular purpose (learning, in this case), and (2) the use of a mobile device as an assistive technology. While many features of mobile devices have potential benefits for disabled learners, see, for example, the extensive analysis available at TechDis (2005), there are significant accessibility issues that impact the inclusion of some groups of learners into collaborative learning, such as:

- Learners with visual impairment will experience difficulties with the small screen size and the limited options for altering sizes, colours and backgrounds.

- Another disadvantaged group includes those students with motor control problems. Learners with poor fine motor coordination may find it difficult or impossible to operate the device.

- Many learners, but especially those with cognitive difficulties, can struggle with the nonintuitive, minimalist interfaces of many mobile devices.

Some technologies are available that make accessibility possible, such as text-to-speech for screen and document reading, speech recognition for text transcription and activation of commands, screen magnifier, keyboard commands with navigational prompts, keyboards, or other hardware data input devices. Some other features that may help relate to the design of the devices themselves, such as cases designed with materials that increase friction and grip and larger more ergonomic styli that are more easily gripped (TechDis, 2005).

In the case of using VLE for collaborative learning, accessibility relates mainly to the design of the learning materials and student activities. Most VLE are now being developed to meet accessibility legislation. Many of them (e.g., WebCT and Blackboard) are customizable to suit the corporate look and feel of the institution and offer a degree of flexibility for the teacher in terms of choosing the content, tools and the way they are displayed (Runa, 2004). Nevertheless, VLE allow for the creation of learning content in a variety of formats that are not verified by the application to comply with accessibility standards (Elaine, Stockton, & Green, 2004).

Some good practice advice for flexibility and simplicity in the design of learning content, general accessibility design principles include (Elaine et al., 2004; W3C, 2005):

- Support availability of information in visual, auditory, tactile modalities

- Choose language level to support ease of understanding

- Emphasise structure by using proper HTML (or otherwise) markup—for example, using <H1> for the highest level of content, <H2> for the next level, and so on

- Establish a clear and consistent navigation pattern

- Allow user to choose display options

- Ensure accessibility of the user interface
- Ensure interoperability between mainstream applications and assistive technologies

While recommendations and advice exist as to what represents good practice, the issue is that there is no official guidance on the standards required for designing learning content. Students with disabilities are likely to have particular requirements which go beyond the current available levels of configurability, which also includes access to alternative means of communication and interaction that may enable them to effectively work independently and collaboratively (Elaine et al., 2004). The question then remains as to whether institutions and practitioners are making "reasonable adjustments" in order to make learning fully accessible for all students, including those using assistive technologies. What would happen if a learner within a group of students has a disability?

Future Trends

With increasing diversification of student backgrounds and modes of study, traditional classroom teaching methods are becoming considerably more difficult to organize and deliver. Students are unwilling to wait for the next run of a particular course, and want increasingly to study at or close to home. All these drivers are leading universities to investigate online learning environments as an effective way of supporting these students. If the traditional advantages of a university education are not to be lost, there is a need to ensure that facilities for both peer and tutor communication are provided equally to all students. This is proving challenging both technically and educationally. It is unlikely that the iPOD generation will be willing to sit down in front of a computer screen to study when they conduct the rest of their lives on the move. MOBIlearn attempted to map out how this sort of mobile learning could be designed and delivered. OTIS would have been greatly enhanced if students could have provided video and audio mterials to enhance their discussions if the technology had been adequately robust at the time. It is, however, essential that accessibility issues are properly addressed in these new forms of delivery.

Students who require assistance are also developing capabilities that have previously been thought impossible. They make use of technology to access a wide range of material that is not naturally accessibly to them, but appropriate technology can make provide these capabilities. Speech-to-text and text-to-speech converters are just examples of what can be used, but students rapidly develop a toolbox of facilities that are suitable for their own use. These will often not meet preconceptions on the systems required to deliver the learning materials. It is therefore essential to use appropriate standards whenever possible so that the student (or indeed teacher) can use whatever facilities they are familiar with to access the learning materials whenever they require them.

Conclusion

Our experiences over these three examples show how effective matching of the technology and changing student expectations of how it should be used can improve the learning experience and encourage collaborative activity in the virtual world. At the time of OTIS, students were still generally very technologically unaware and needed a lot of encouragement to engage with the online world. By the time of MOBIlearn, they were all very familiar with mobile phones and texting and took to the synchronous communication immediately and made considerable use of it. The Health Informatics module was frustrating as it started well and looked as if the virtual tutorial groups would work well, but they then just faded away because of the "lost in hyperspace" syndrome. This needs more work to ensure that the community is maintained in an effective manner.

One of the arguments for online collaborative learning has been that anyone can participate fully and equally no matter what their accessibility issues, as all that is required is that they are provided with an appropriate means of joining the discussions. In practice this has been found much more difficult to achieve because of the need to provide positive and exciting interfaces. These are not easy to fit into an accessibility framework and much more work is required if attempting to meet these requirements is not to lead to bland and uninteresting interfaces for the majority of learners.

References

Armitt, G. M., Green, S., & Beer, M. D. (2001, March 22-24). Building a European Internet school: Developing the OTIS learning environment. In *Proceedings of the European Conference on Computer-Supported Collaborative Learning*, Euro-CSCL 2001, Maastricht, Netherlands (pp. 67-74).

Beer, M., Slack, F., & Armitt, G. (2005). Collaboration and teamwork: Immersion and presence in an online learning environment. *Information Systems Frontiers, 7*(1), 27- 35.

Boud, D. (1988). *Developing student autonomy in learning* (2nd ed.). London: Kogan Page.

Brand, O., Petrak, L., & Zitterbart, M. (2002). Support for mobile learners in distributed space. In *Learning Lab Lower Saxony Proceedings of E-Learn 2002,* Montreal, Canada.

Brennan, S. (2005). *The NHS IT project: The biggest computer project in the world ever.* Oxford: Radcliffe Publishing.

Cook, J., & Smith, M. (2004). Beyond formal learning: Informal community e-learning. *Computers and Education, 43,* 35-37.

Desanctis, G., Fayard, A-L., Roach, M., & Jiang, L. (2003). Learning in oline forums. *European Management Journal, 21*(5), 565-577.

Elaine, P., Stockton, C., & Green, S. (2004). Individual students, individual difficulties, individual solutions: A virtual learning environment for learners with severe disabilities. In P. Kommers & G. Richards (Eds.), *Proceedings of World Conference on Educational Multimedia, Hypermedia and Telecommunications,* Chesapeake, VA, AACE (pp. 5375-5381).

Ellis, D., Oldridge, R., & Vasconcelos, A. (2003). Community and virtual community. In B. Cronin (Ed.), *Annual review of information science and technology, 37,* 145-146.

Gibbs, G., Skinner, C., & Teal, A. (1999). *CoMentor: A collaborative learning environment on the WWW for philosophy and social theory students.* Retrieved January 5, 2008, from http://comentor.hud.ac.uk

Ginsberg, A., Hodge, P., Lindstrom, T., Sampieri, B., & Shiau, D. (1998, September 13-16). The little Web schoolhouse: Using virtual rooms to create a multimedia distance learning environment. *ACM Multimedia 98,* Bristol, UK (pp. 89-98).

Hagedorn, R. (1992). *Occupational therapy: Foundations for practice.* Edinburgh: Churchill Livingstone.

JISC Legal. (2005). *Accessibility law for e-learning authors.* Retrieved January 5, 2008, from http://www.jisclegal.ac.uk/publications/elearningseries.htm

Jubert, A. (1999). Developing an infrastructure for communities of practice: The Siemens experience. In *Proceedings of the 3rd International Online Information Meeting, Online Information 99,* London (pp. 165-158).

Kinshuk, & Goh, T. (2003) Mobile adaptation with multiple representation approach as educational pedagogy. In *Proceedings of Wirtschaftsinformatik 2003 - Medien - Markte – Mobilitat,* Heidelberg, Germany (pp. 747–763).

Koh, J., & Kim, Y. G. (2004). Knowledge sharing in virtual communities: An e-business perspective. *Expert Systems with Applications, 26,* 155-166.

Loidl, S. (2005). Towards pervasive learning: WeLearn.Mobile, a CPS package viewer for handhelds. *Journal of Network and Computer Applications, 29*(4), 277-293.

McAllister, L., Lincoln, M., McLeod, S., & Maloney, D. (Eds.). (1997). *Facilitating learning in clinical settings*. Cheltenham: Stanley Thornes.

MOBIlearn. (2002). Next generation paradigms and interfaces for technology supported learning in a mobile environment exploring the potential of ambient intelligence, Annex 1'. Information Society Technologies Program EU Proposal/Contract: IST-2001-37187.

Rumbaugh, J., Jacobson, I., & Booch, G. (1999). *The unified modelling language reference manual*. Addison Wesley.

Runa, J. (2004). Accessibility and usability in e-learning systems. In G. Richards (Ed.), *Proceedings of World Conference on E-Llearning in Corporate, Government, Healthcare and Higher Education*, Chesapeake, VA, AACE (pp. 2894-2899)

Stone, A. (2003, May 19-20). Designing scalable, effective m-learning for multiple technologies. In *Proceedings of MLEARN 2003*, London, UK (pp. 145-153).

Taylor, J. (2003, May 19-20). A task-centred approach to evaluating a mobile learning environment for pedagogical soundness. In *Proceedings of MLEARN 2003*, London, UK (pp. 167-171).

TechDis. (2005). *Accessibility perspectives on e-learning*. Retrieved January 5, 2008, from http://www.techdis.ac.uk

W3C. (2005). *How people with disabilities use the Web*. Retrieved January 5, 2008, from http://www.w3.org/WAI/EO/Drafsts/PWD-Use-Web/

Waight, C. L., & Stewart, B. L. (2005). Valuing the adult learner in e-learning: Part one - a conceptual model for corporate settings. *The Journal of Workplace Learning, 17*, 337-345.

Young, K. (2003). Using e-learning to liberate the talents of nurses. *Industrial and Commercial Training, 35*(4), 137-141.

Further Reading

Chan, T-W., Roschelle, J., Hsi, S., Kinshuk, Sharples, M., Brown, T., et al. (2006). One-to-one technology enhanced learning: An opportunity for global research collaboration. *Research and Practice in Technology Enhanced Learning, 1*(1), 3-29.

Corlett, D., Sharples, M., Chan, T., & Bull, S. (2005) A mobile learning organiser for university students. *Journal of Computer Assisted Learning, 21*, 162-170.

Sharples, M., & Beale, R. (2003). A technical review of mobile computational devices. *Journal of Computer Assisted Learning, 19*(3), 392-395.

Sharples, M. (2003). Disruptive devices: Mobile technology for conversational learning. *International Journal of Continuing Engineering Education and Lifelong Learning, 12*(5/6), 504-520.

Sharples, M., Corlett, D., & Westmancott, O. (2002). The design and implementation of a mobile learning resource. *Personal and Ubiquitous Computing, 6,* 220-234.

Schenker, K. (2002). Accessible distance education based on collaborative learning. In *Proceedings of World Conference on Educational Multimedia, Hypermedia and Telecommunications (*pp. 1752-1753).

Pearson, E., & Koppi, T. (2002). Inclusion and online learning opportunities: Designing for accessibility. *Association for Learning Technology Journal, 10*(2), 17-28.

Willder, B. (2002). Disability legislation: Implications for learning technologists in the UK. In L. Phipps, A. Sutherland & J. Seale (Eds.), *Access all areas: Disability, technology and learning* (pp. 6-9). ALT/JISC/TechDis.

Useful URLs

Chris Argyris. Theories of action, double-loop learning and organizational learning: http://www.infed.org/thinkers/argyris.htm

TechDis Service. Provides helps and advice to staff in further and higher education on all aspects of technology and disabilities: http://www.techdis.ac.uk

JISC Legal Information Service. Publications related to legal aspects of online learning, including accessibility issues: http://www.jisclegal.ac.uk/publications/elearningseries.htm

World Wide Web Consortium (W3C), Web Accessibility Initiative (WAI). Develops strategies, guidelines, and resources to help make the Web accessible to people with disabilities: http://www.w3.org/WAI/

Disability Discrimination Act 1995: http://www.opsi.gov.uk/acts/acts1995/1995050.htm

Special Educational Needs and Disability Act 2001: http://www.opsi.gov.uk/acts/acts2001/20010010.htm

U.S. Section 508 Guidelines: http://www.section508.gov/

Appendix

Figure A1.

Internet Session: The MOBIlearn Project Web Site
http://www.MOBIlearn.org

interaction:
The public deliverable

http://www.MOBIlearn.org/download/results/public_deliverables/MOBIlearn_D4.1_
Final.pdf

Gives the guidelines used by the project in developing the scenarios used. To what extent
were accessibility issues considered in designing these scenarios and, if not, what more
could have been done to embed accessibility into the underlying design

Figure A2.

Case Study

A. Campus Discovery Quiz

Novel methods of technology enhanced learning inevitably lead to accessibility issues. Care needs
to be taken in designing activities to ensure that all students can have a full and profitable learning
experience whatever their physical capabilities. This case study is intended to allow you to look at
possibilities within your own teaching environment and assess how novel learning methods can be
used effectively without disadvantaging specific students because of their accessibility needs.

You are asked to organize a campus discovery quiz for new students to your university or college.
Students are divided into small groups and each is given a hand held computing device that can deliver
multimedia material based on its location on the campus and surrounding area and collect answers to
questions. Groups can also communicate with each other either by messaging or verbally.

As part of the exercise, you want each student to register with the library, the computing services,
and so forth, and to meet with various members of staff. Instructions are provided as multimedia
messages when the group has found the appropriate locations.

Questions:

1.   Look at your own induction process and develop a set of activities that you would think
      appropriate for your students to learn about your campus and the facilities offered.

2.   Identify how you would like to present the activities to the students in a novel and effective
      way so that they become familiar with the layout and facilities offered as quickly as pos-
      sible.

3. Consider whether each student should have a mobile device or one for each group. Consider the
      differences in the way the groups will work in each case and what effects this will have on
      students with accessibility issues.

3.   What accessibility issues do you foresee and how would you expect to overcome them?

Chapter V

The Importance of Training Needs Analysis in Authoring Technology Enhanced Learning for Companies

Emma O'Brien, University of Limerick, Ireland

Timothy Hall, University of Limerick, Ireland

Kevin Johnson, University of Limerick, Ireland

Inside Chapter

This chapter looks at the potential to exploit existing technology enhanced learning (TEL) authoring tools to provide customised learning solutions that address both businesses' needs and employees learning requirements. It examines the feasibility of integrating training needs analysis into existing authoring tools to automate customisation. The chapter outlines a framework for such using best practices in the technology enhanced learning field such as sound instructional design theo-

ries, standard compliant metadata sets, and LO granularity while exploiting well established TEL authoring models. The chapter also highlights how this framework was implemented in practice in the form of an electronic tool that ties closely with existing learning content management systems.

Introduction

This chapter examines the potential of existing technology to enable the effortless tailoring of technology enhanced learning (TEL) courses. A framework for such by combing training needs analysis (TNA) and instructional design theories with existing TEL authoring models is outlined. Figure 1 illustrates how these areas contribute to the outcome.

The outcome is an integrated authoring solution that overcomes the limitations associated with existing TEL authoring models.

Traditional Authoring Models and Existing Problems examines existing TEL authoring models and their limitations.

The Requirement for Training Needs Analysis explores why training needs analysis is necessary to ensure training in organisations meets their real needs.

Integrating TNA into TEL Authoring outlines a model of incorporating training needs analysis into existing e-learning authoring models.

Figure 1. Chapter overview

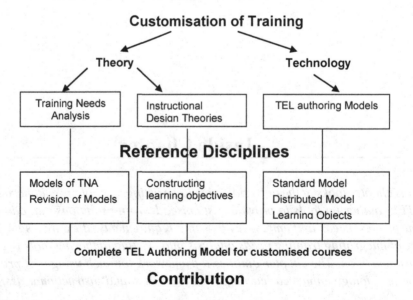

Linking TNA to TEL Authoring Models investigates different instructional design theories in terms of their ability to integration of TNA into TEL authoring using a pedagogically sound framework.

Tailoring Training outlines how to customise training in the context of an integrated framework combining all theories outlined in previous chapters together.

Future Developments explores potential research that may emerge from the outlined framework.

Figure 2 outlines the key theorists in these areas.

The framework outlined in this chapter creates a best practice solution for authoring TEL solutions by exploiting existing best practices in the TEL field. It ensures that the framework builds upon existing TEL authoring models and technologies such as learning content management and reusable learning objects. The model takes care to ensure that it remains compliant at all times with TEL standards such as learning object granularity, metadata standards, and interoperability. In addition it uses well established and proven instructional design theories to ensure the model is pedagogically sound. In all, the framework offers a best practice solution to authoring customised TEL solutions by extending existing work and overcoming the

Figure 2. Key theorists

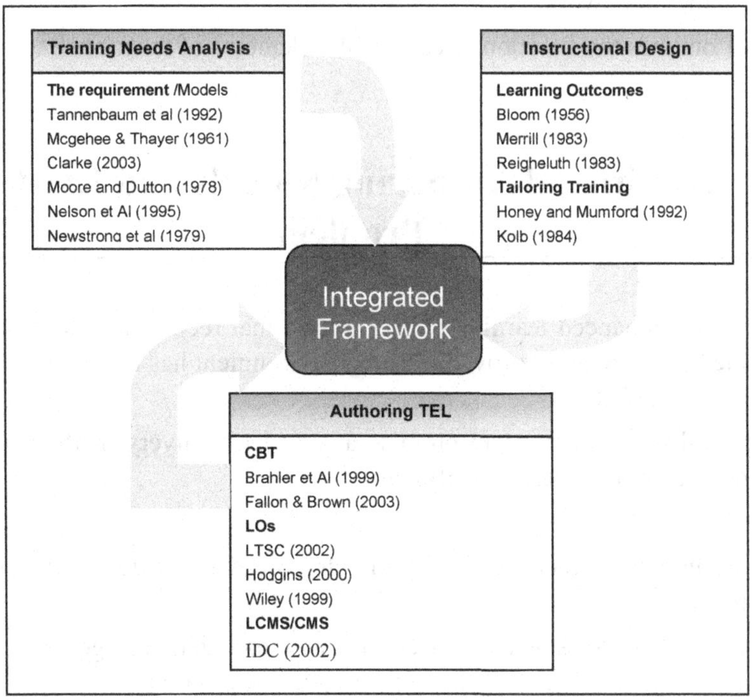

Figure 3. Summary of best practice TEL Authoring model outlined in this chapter

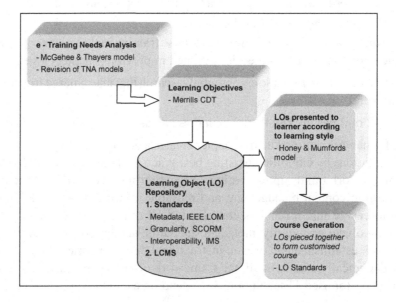

limitations associated with traditional TEL authoring models. Figure 3 summarises the best practice model outlined in this changer and the TEL areas exploited to develop the framework.

Table 1 outlines the function of each of the elements of the model.

Traditional Authoring Models and Existing Problems

Technology enhanced learning (TEL), a term that recognises the contribution to be made by ICT to an improved learning environment has its origins in computer-based training (CBT).

Computer-based training had promise as an ideal delivery medium to meet the training need of companies. It offered:

- Media rich interactivity; it offered a far more effective training tool that printed manuals.

- Integrated assessment and user tracking meant that management could be assured that their personnel met the required standards.

Table 1. Summary of the elements of the TEL authoring model

Element	Function
E-Training Needs Analysis	To identify granular training topics for each individual in the organisation in accordance with the organisational goals. This element is currently manual in the existing TEL authoring model. This chapter looks at automating TNA and integrating it into authoring tools.
Learning objectives	Once training topics are identified, these are translated into learning objectives by the framework using Merrill's CDT. Currently in the TEL authoring model, learning objectives are generated by pedagogical experts. To allow non experts to automate customisation of courses the generation of learning objectives has been made electronic in the new best practice framework.
Search for Learning Objects (LOs)	Once the learning objectives have been identified segments of learning or course material that can satisfy these objectives are searched for in a learning object repository. The LOs have metadata attached which have fields identified by standard bodies. In addition because these pieces of learning can be of different sizes, SCORM have identified a granularity model, in the framework outlined in this chapter only LOs of a similar granularity are searched for. Many of these are created and hosted on a learning content management system (LCMS).
Segments are presented	Once LOs associated with the individuals' training needs are identified, a suggested presentation sequence is displayed to the user in a form that corresponds with their learning style. For example, if an individual is a pragmatist, the learner might be presented with tests and questions first. The learner can alter the sequence of the LOs if they wish.
Course generation	Once the individual approves the sequence of the Los, a course manifest is developed which details how the course is to be run and how LOs are to be presented according to specific standards.

- CBT was available 24 hours per day, 7 days per week (24/7).
- Employees could access the training material on a just-in-time basis, so that they could carry out a particular task immediately after reviewing the latest information (Fallon & Brown, 2003).

CBT was delivered standalone on a terminal or across a local area network from CD-ROM. However the huge authoring resource needed was less than ideal; some 100 hours of development being required for each hour of course content. Also each course was designed for a specific end user and reuse of the content was not an important factor (Brahler et al., 1999).

TEL has evolved to keep the good aspects of CBT but to overcome the challenges associated with content development and reusability. TEL encompasses any type of learning content that is delivered electronically. For the scope of this chapter, TEL will be defined as "any learning, training or education that is facilitated by the use of well-known and proven computer technologies, specifically networks based on Internet technology" (Fallon & Brown, 2003, p. 4). TEL offers two authoring paradigms: standard and distributed solutions. The standard solution is a one-size fits all option offered by vendors for general public sale or created with a specific audience in mind. This paradigm emerged from the traditional CBT model discussed above.

Distributed TEL is a possible authoring paradigm at the heart of best practices in TEL authoring that is gaining popularity and credibility as it provides a flexible and more cost-effective solution as opposed to standard TEL solution. Instead of creating a single course containing material that cannot be reused easily, a number of segments are created. These are then pieced together to form a course, which is then hosted and presented to the learner.

In this process:

1.   A general needs analysis is conducted to ensure there is a need for training in a specific area. This can be done in a number of ways, by speculating, asking managers, responding to changes in the company such as the introduction of new technology or in a structured form.

2.   From the needs analysis, generic learning objectives are generated.

3.   Once this has been completed, a manual search for relevant learning segments is done.

4.   If the relevant learning segments do not exist in the database, they are authored and then saved into the database.

5.   These are then pieced together to form a course that is deliverable to the users.

The result from the distributed method is a number of reusable learning segments, saved in a repository that can be searched to provide small snippets of learning to individuals as required or can be pieced together to form a tailored course.

Advantages include creating learning material can be easily reused by searching for the required segments and editing where applicable, it is cost-effective solution as material can be continuously reused, which permits the user to take fragments of courses if required rather than undertaking a whole course and sifting through irrelevant material, and finally it offers the potential to provide tailored courses de-

Figure 4. Distributed e-learning solution

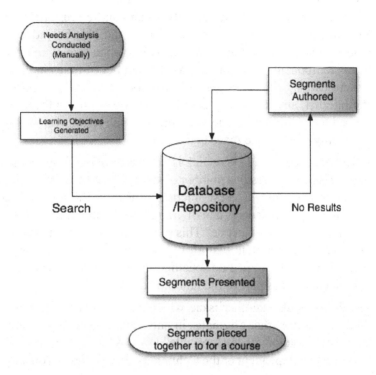

pending on the individual's training needs. Disadvantages are that without formalised standards, searching databases may be difficult. And in order to allow individual segments to be pieced together standards may be required.

This method provides an ideal solution for organisations that regularly create TEL solutions, especially those courses requiring similar material. Moreover, it is suitable for organisations wishing to offer individualised training courses based on their business needs. However, the dynamic potential of this has not been explored in depth until now.

The distributed TEL solution provides a more flexible, cost-effective, and adaptive training method to assist organisations to achieve increased productivity and improved quality. Thus many companies are opting for this method over standard TEL.

The segments of learning outlined in Figure 4 in the distributed TEL model are known as learning objects (LOs), according to LTSC (2002). These are at the core of best practices in TEL today including aspects of instructional design, development, and delivery, due to their potential for reusability, generativity, adaptability, and scalability (Gibbons, Nelson, & Richards, 2000; Hodgins, 2000; Urdan & Weggen, 2000). It is these learning objects and their sequencing that are key to this authoring paradigm.

Learning objects are elements of computer-based instruction grounded in the object-oriented paradigm of computer science. Object-orientation highly values the creation of components (called "objects") that can be reused (Dahl & Nygaard, 1966) in multiple contexts. This is the fundamental idea behind learning objects: instructional designers can build small (relative to the size of an entire course) instructional components that can be reused a number of times in different learning contexts. As learning objects are generally understood to be digital entities deliverable over the Internet, any number of people can access and use them simultaneously (as opposed to traditional instructional media, such as an overhead or video tape, which can only exist in one place at a time).

The subject of sequencing LOs, which is at the core of our framework, leads to several issues arising. As a result a number of standards have been developed to ensure LOs remain in line with TEL best practices. The most difficult problem facing the designers of learning objects is that of granularity (Wiley et al., 1999). How big (or small) should a learning object be? This chapter is not concerned with constructing LOs, however it is important that all LOs are of the same size (or granularity) to ensure consistency. This must be specified in the search criteria when identifying LOs to be sequenced as part of the tailored course.

Interoperability is also another issue which causes concern. It can be defined as "enabling information that originates in one context to be used in another in ways that are as highly automated as possible" (Rust & Bide, p. 6). It is important that LOs can operate independent of the technology they are hosted on and best practice standards such as SCORM's runtime model and the IMS overcome this problem (Sciore, Siegel, & Rosenthal, 1994). Thus it is important that only standard compliant LOs are selected to ensure interoperability

Reusability falls into several categories when associated with TEL and content management systems. Within the scope of this chapter, the main focus of reusability is that of content reusability, that is, the material that is delivered to the learner to achieve a learning goal and the ability to reuse such content without any significant changes (Duval & Hodgins, 2003). In the framework outlined in this chapter it is important that all LOs selected are reusable to ensure maximum efficiency.

Although it is easy enough to provide access to a piece of learning content directly from a Web page, many organisations want to control access to the courseware and track data such as who is using the content, the level of usage of the content, and the outcome of that usage. A learning management system (LMS)/learning content management system (LCMS) is the technology widely used to implement the best practice TEL authoring model outlined earlier. It is a Web server based software application that provides the administrative and data-tracking functions necessary to achieve this. The specific features and functions of an LMS vary considerably from one system to another, but generally they include administrative functions, learning interfaces, and sequencing options.

An LMS will enable organisations to collect data about the level of usage and effectiveness of the courses that are running online. Usage data includes the number of learners taking a course, the average amount of time spent on a course, and the number of learners completing a course.

The international research consultants at IDC (2002) in their paper "Learning Content Management Systems: A New E-Learning Market Segment Emerges," identify the components of an LCMS as consisting of an authoring application, a data repository, a delivery interface and administration tools. LCMS are the technology that implements the distributed TEL authoring model in practice. It is this technology which will be exploited to enable tailoring of courses, particularly the functionality of the data repository of LOs.

These systems, whether a LMS or LCMS, are a viable solution for the delivery of learning objectives based on the structuring of course content by a teacher or course creator. However they do not offer the facility for nonexperts to structure such courses. In addition TNA, currently an analysis needs to be done off-line. None of the systems permit for an online training needs analysis. Therefore a solution to enable a nonexpert to structure courses is to define, specify and build a LCMS with a TNA feature already integrated. The best method of doing this is through open source technologies and programming languages. The outcome was a system that was flexible, adaptive, customisable allowing access any time, anywhere, catering for diverse and changing needs of the users, and allowing custom content to be added. At its core is the reuse and sequencing of standard compliant LOs into individualised seamless courses which would provide a more complete best practice TEL authoring model.

The Requirement for Training Needs Analysis

The current changing business needs requirements for a more personalised approach to learning and the advent of new technology are placing new demands on the development of online courses. Organisations, particularly SMEs, are looking for courses that can be customised based on their business needs at an affordable price (The European Observatory for SMEs, 2003). The current distributed authoring model affords the possibility to tailor training with ease by piecing together only relevant segments of learning or learning objects. Currently, such models enable the manual development of generic courses, however they do not provide the tools to facilitate the tailoring of such courses based on individual and company learning and training needs. The extension of the current model to facilitate this functionality would provide huge advancement for the authoring of customised courses without the need for expertise. This section examines the feasibility of using training needs analysis (TNA) to enable this to take place.

Returning to current authoring frameworks (Figure 3), the first step in the process consisted of conducting a TNA. In the present model, TNA is often carried out manually and is a lengthy process requiring experts. If electronic tools are used to conduct the TNA, they are not integrated into the authoring environment and thus do not facilitate the ability to customise material. However integrating the TNA concept into existing authoring tools will provide the functionality to allow companies to plan training and customise relevant training material based on their business and learner needs.

What is Training Needs Analysis

To determine the definition of Training Needs Analysis, first let us identify what is a training need. Dalziel (1992) provides the simplest and most specific explanation of a training need. "At its simplest a training need exists when there is a gap between the present skills and knowledge of its employees and the skills and knowledge they will require for effective performance" (Dalziel, 1992, p. 184). A training need may apply to any individual in a company; however, what training that individual needs may vary according to the individual's job function in the organisation. A training need may arise as a result of the introduction of new technologies, procedures or policies in the organisation if an employee changes job roles or when an employee first joins a company.

To discover who requires training and what areas training is required a Training Needs Analysis (or training needs assessment) is conducted. A Training Needs Analysis can be carried out using a number of different frameworks and methods, for example using questionnaires and interviews focus groups, amongst other methods. These methods and frameworks will be discussed in more detail later.

Benefits of Conducting a Training Needs Analysis

Training can be an expensive activity and as a result many researchers have empha-sised the importance of Training Needs Analysis as a first step in the training process (Clarke, 2003; Moore & Dutton, 1978; Tannenbaum & Yuki, 1992). Training Needs Analysis is "a determination of the [organisational] goals which can be served by training, the people who require training, for what purposes they require training and the content of the training" (McGehee & Thayer, 1961, p. 9).

From the definition outlined by McGehee and Thayer (1961), it can be concluded that Training Needs Analysis provides the potential to identify content in which employees require training in accordance with organisational goals. Moreover, it reduces the probability of companies spending large amounts of money on training efforts which are not required, allowing them to focus their training budgets on areas which will help the company improve its competitive advantage. Thus it assists the organisation to plan its training process so it is the most effective it can possibly be providing a means to address SMEs training issues or lack of planning. Furthermore, it provides information which is helpful in developing learning objectives.

The next section will examine this process in detail to determine how it may be useful in identifying relevant content to enable the development of tailored courses.

Integrating TNA into TEL Authoring

Models of TNA

Despite the emphasis on the importance of the TNA step in the training process, there is an absence of a comprehensive model to assist those wishing to conduct a Training Needs Analysis (Newstrom & Lilyquist, 1979; Smith, Delahaye, & Gates, 1986). The most well established and highly commended method for identifying training needs is that of McGehee and Thayer (1961), according to Leat and Lovell (1997), Moore and Dutton (2001), Nelson et al. (1995), and Tannenbaum and Yuki (1992).

McGehee and Thayer's (1961) framework outlines a three stage integrated approach to identifying training needs which ensures that training is tied to the organisations missions, goals, and objectives. The framework can be summarised in the following steps:

1. **Organisational analysis:** This allows companies to determine where training can be implemented to achieve the organisational goals.

2. **Operations analysis:** This identifies what training should consist of. It involves a task analysis, which identifies the activities required to achieve a goal or carry out a job function.

3. **Man analysis**: This focuses on the employee's performance at the tasks identified in the operations analysis to identify potential skills gaps/weaknesses at such tasks.

Hence it can be stated that a Training Needs Analysis assists the identification of areas where training is needed in the organisation and in which individual employees need training relevant to their organisational and job needs. The analysis allows the identification of the learning materials employees need to satisfy their training needs.

Revision of TNA Models

McGehee and Thayer's (1961) model has been around some time and its validity in current day business practices must be questioned due to the difference when comparing today's business world with that of 45 years ago; thus, some additional research was conducted to examine the applicability of McGehee and Thayer's (1961) model today.

Focus Groups, surveys, and case study analysis were used to identify whether this model was still valid in the current business environment.

Based on the combined analysis it has resulted in a revision of McGehee and Thayer's (1961) model of Training Needs Analysis. From the research, it has emerged that McGehee and Thayer (1961) is still an applicable model for identifying training needs in organisations. However it has been highlighted that training can take place at a number of different levels and training needs to be tailored to mirror this. Thus McGhee and Thayer's (1961) model has been updated to reflect the following:

- **Step 1. Organisational analysis:** Identifies the missions and goals of the company and specify skills and the level of skill required by all persons in the organisation to achieve these (overall training).

- **Step 2. Level analysis:** Identifies the skills and the level of skill required by persons at each level in the organisation to achieve the organisational missions and goals (level training).

- **Step 3. Functional analysis:** Identifies the departmental goals to achieve the organisational missions and goals and specifies the skills and the level of skill required by each department to achieve this (functional training).

- **Step 4. Job role analysis:** Identifies the skills and the level of skill required by each individual to conduct their daily tasks and achieve the functional goals (job role training).

- **Step 5. Individual analysis:** The individual specifies their competency (experience) at skills specified in each of the above steps and a skills gap analysis is done to identify the individuals training needs and thus training plan.

Figure 5 shows a diagram of these steps.

This provides a comprehensive and practical framework that ties training closely with a company's business requirements assisting them to effectively plan this activity. It is linked closely with McGehee and Thayer's (1961) model. However it goes further in identifying different levels of training to ensure a user only has to undertake the training relevant to them. Moreover it takes account of the individual's experiences, providing a first step to enable the personalisation of training solutions.

Figure 5. An updated TNA framework

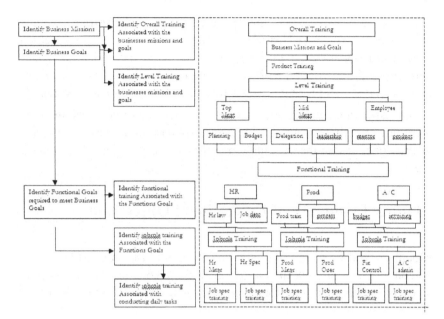

The framework will provide the basis for integration into TEL authoring. Once the individuals training needs have been specified relative to their experiences and relevant requirements, it is possible to construct a personalised training solution.

Linking TNA to TEL Authoring Models

Looking at the distributed authoring model, the connection between TNA and the authoring environment was the construction of learning objectives. This is the means for integrating TNA into the authoring environment.

Now that a means of specifying relevant content to present to the user has been identified, a method of how to identify personalised learning objectives for the learner is required. As identified previously in the TEL distributed model learning, objectives are created manually and are used to search for relevant learning material in the authoring system (see Figure 3).

Learning objectives identify the performance level you wish the learner to attain at a specific task and are used as an indication that learning has been accomplished (Gagne, Briggs, & Wager, 1992). For example, if an employee requires training in market research techniques at the end of taking a course you may wish them to list the types of market research, identify the steps involved in conducting a market research and demonstrate how to conduct a market research.

Once tasks are identified as training needs, these then must be translated into learning objectives, that is, desired learning outcomes to allow the user to search for relevant LOs. Instructional Design theories can assist this by specifying ideal outcomes depending on the content type of the training need. This will assist in the creation of tailored courses by piecing together relevant LOs, to achieve learning outcomes.

Most instructional design theories identify methods of how best to help people to learn however they do not specify how to determine learner's performance. Two instructional design theories that do assist the construction of learning objectives are:

Blooms Taxonomy of Educational Objectives

Bloom created taxonomy that allowed the classification of different educational outcomes. There are six major classes in the taxonomy. These can represent six levels of learning ranging from least to most complex (Bloom, 1956):

1. **Knowledge:** The learner is required to recall what they have learned.
2. **Comprehension:** The learner is required to explain what they have learned..
3. **Application:** The learner is required to apply what they have learned to a situation.
4. **Analysis:** The learner is required to breakdown material and detect the relationships between the materials.
5. **Synthesis:** The learner is required to piece together elements and parts to form a whole.
6. **Evaluation:** The learner is required to make judgements about the value, for some purpose of ideas, works, solutions, methods, or material.

Bloom (1956) provides an ideal generic framework to assist educators to identify levels of performance educator's wish their students to obtain. However, he does not prescribe situations in which to use each level of the taxonomy thus a noneducationalist (or a system) is not capable of constructing such. A theory is required that will allow the selection of the most appropriate educational objectives associated with the learners' requirements.

Merrill's Component Display theory

Merrill's component display theory (CDT) is an instructional design theory that indicates what set of components is most likely to achieve the desired learning outcomes under certain conditions (Reigheluth, 1983). The CDT classifies learning objectives on two dimensions:

1. **The type of content:** Content is classified as a fact, concept, principle, or procedure.
2. **Performance level:** This step specifies the level of learning a student is required to achieve based on the content to be learned.

Merrill outlined a performance-content matrix based on content and performance level based on the type of content different levels of performances are expected from the learner.

Firstly a piece of content is defined as: (*Examples are identified in the next phase*)

- **Fact:** "Facts are arbitrarily associated pieces of information" (Merrill, 1983, p. 287).
- **Concepts:** "Concepts are groups of objects, events or symbols that all share common characteristics and are identified by the same name" (Merrill, 1983, p. 287).
- **Procedure:** "Procedures are an ordered sequence of steps necessary to accomplish some goal, solve a particular class of problem or produce some product" (Merrill, 1983, p. 287).
- **Principle:** "Principles are explanations or predictions of why things happen in the world" (Merrill, 1983, p. 288).

When the performance level is identified, a student may be required to remember what they have learned, use it, or find a new use for the information they have learned (note the only performance level that is required for a fact is remember):

Remember—Simply ask the user to remember a fact, concept, procedure, or principle:

- Remember Fact. Example: Define (performance level) the capital of Ireland (fact).

Use—Requires the learner to use the piece of information learned.

- Use Concept – Example: From the above description is this animal a mammal.

Find—Requires the learner to use the information in a different scenario:

- **Find Procedure:** Example: Write a program that checks if a temperature is in Celsius and if not changes it to this format.
- **Find Principle:** Example: What would happen to the ice if you increased the temperature to 100 degrees.

Once the content type is specified learning objectives can be generated by attaching a desired performance outcome to the content. The content then can be developed to teach this learning objective.

Once these are created, the CDT identifies a presentation form for teaching the content associated with the learning objective to the student. Merrill states that all subject matter can be represented on two dimensions (Merrill, 1983):

1. **Generalities:** These are general statements of definition. For example a generality for a fact may be define.
2. **Instances:** These are specific cases of concepts, procedures, and principles, for example, give an example of a mammal.

Moreover, material is presented in an expository and inquisitory manner, that is, the material is explained to the student or the student question. A combination of these presentation types ensures optimum learning for the student.

The CDT provides an ideal instructional design theory for creating learning objectives from the content to be taught and an optimum presentation format for these objectives. Furthermore to this it describes an instructional design method to teach these objectives in an optimum format. In addition, it provides a prescriptive model which could be easily programmed and automated. The next section examines how the CDT is applied in association with the TNA model and a learning styles theory to tailor training in an online system.

Tailoring Training

Once the learning objectives are identified ways of sequencing LOs are mapped the individuals learning styles.

To determine the sequencing content relevant to an individual's personal learning preferences, it was first necessary to determine their learning style. Honey and Mumford's learning styles model (Honey & Mumford, 1992) has been adopted to assist the system to determine this.

This model focuses on adults' preferences of specific types of activities and instructional material and provides useful guidance for associating the sequencing of type specific instructional material with learners' preferences and studying attitudes in order to achieve certain learning outcomes. (Papanikolaou & Grigoriadou, 2003)

Furthermore this has been used with Merrill's CDT in a previously in a project known as INSPIRE in an adaptive hypermedia context and has proven to be successful in personalising the presentation of content at an individual level (Papanikolaou & Grigoriadou, 2003).

Honey and Mumford's model (1992) classifies learners as Activists, Pragmatists, Reflectors, and Theorists.

- **Activists:** These are individuals who learn through new experiences. In terms of the CDT this means that such individuals may be presented with a LO that satisfies the learning outcome to conduct a market research.

- **Pragmatists:** These are individuals who learn best by applying new ideas immediately. They like to see the real world value in learning.

- **Reflectors:** These are individuals who learn best by collecting all data regarding a subject first and then taking time to consider all possible angles.

- **Theorists:** These are individuals who learn best by understanding the basic assumptions first and then determining logical models.

It builds on a previous model developed by Kolb known as the Learning Styles Inventory, which was based on experiential learning (Kolb, 1983) and which was extended to a more practical based format to assist individuals to determine their learning style.

This questionnaire is used in the framework to determine individuals' learning styles and present content in an appropriate format to that learner.

The diagram in Figure 6 illustrates how the TNA is integrated into the authoring tool to tailor training using instructional design and learning styles models. The next section will explain how this framework has been applied to extending the TEL distributed model.

Figure 6. Framework for final prototype

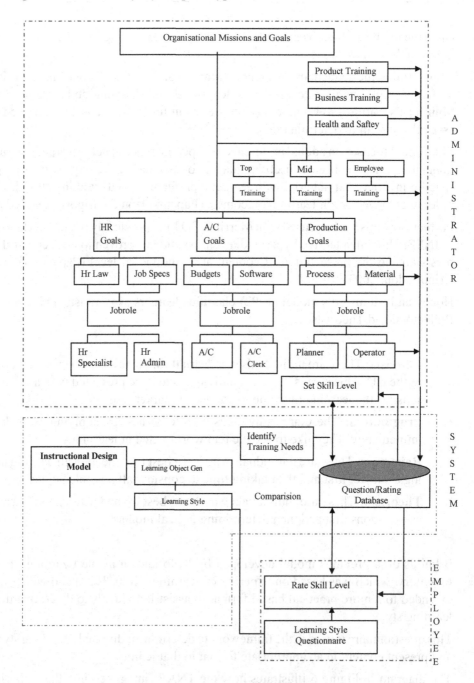

System Outline

There are two types of user of the system:

1. **An administrator:** Who is responsible for maintaining the information and populating the database with company information for the TNA
2. **An employee:** Who is responsible for identifying their learning style, individual training needs, and tailoring their training

Administrator

When an administrator enters the system for the first time, the administration is required to enter the companies organisational missions and goals and overall training associated with this (training for all staff). For example, if the organisational goal is to cut costs, all staff might receive training in cost cutting measures. The administrator will be asked to enter the competencies associated with the training course and identify whether it is a fact, procedure, principle, or concept (or a combination of these) based on Merrill's CDT. For example a competency associated with cost cutting measures might be evaluating your work area, this may be a procedure. Figure 7 illustrates how this work.

Once these are set up, an administrator for each department (most likely the manager of that department) is required to enter their department name and functional goals required to achieve the organisational goals. For example, if an organisational goal is to cut costs,the production department's functional goal might be to reduce waste or defects thus resulting in quality training. In addition the administrator will be required to identify competencies associated with the training and classify the competency according to Merrill's CDT.

The same procedure will also occur for job role training and level training. Once these are identified, the administrator will specify skills levels they wish their staff to achieve for these competencies.

Staff/Employee

When an employee enters the site for the first time, the employee is required to identify a learning style by answering 80 questions from Honey and Mumford's (1992) questionnaire. They system then identifies their learning style.

They are then required to identify their skills gap at the competencies outlined by the administrator. Once they complete this at each level, the system identifies where

Figure 7. A screen grab if the "enter the competenices to achieve goals" screen

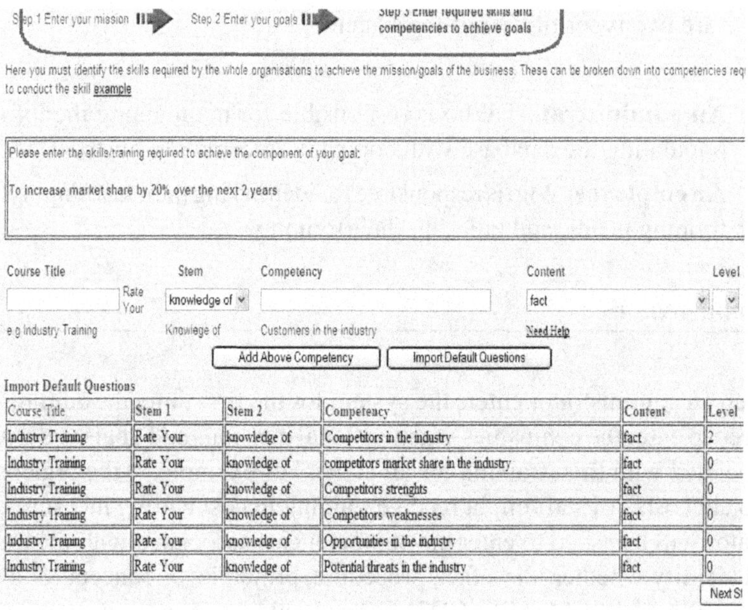

shortfalls exists and generates a training plan for the employee based on the skills gaps for each competency and the classification according to Merrill's CDT.

For example, in the case above where there is a skills gap in "evaluating your work area," Mr Jones' plan will state that you will need training in this competency and generate learning objectives based on Merrills CDT. See Figure 8 for an example.

The individual can then generate tailored courses based on their training plan and learning style. The system will use the learning objectives to search the learning object repository/database in the distributed TEL model for relevant LOs. The system will use the learning objective to search description field of the metadata for each LO until an LO that matches that description is found. This is then put into a sequence depending on the individuals learning style. For example, if someone is an Activist they might be asked to evaluate their workspace first rather than taking LOs that explain the steps in evaluating their workspace. Thus generating a tailored course based on the individuals learning needs and the organisations business needs is then presented to the learner via the LCMS. These steps continue for each competency with a skills gap.

The framework uses a combination of TNA and Instructional Design theories with existing technologies to generate a model that enables the development of tailored courses to both individual and business needs without the need for expertise. The next section explores how the framework can be exploited further to offer a more personalised solution in terms of the individuals learning requirements.

Figure 8. Sample training plan with learning outcomes

Training Plan for Mr Jones

Overall Training

Cost Cutting Measures

- Evaluating your Work Space:
- List the steps in evaluating your work space
- Outline the steps for evaluating your work space
- Give an Example of Evaluating your work space
- Ask the student to list the steps in evaluating your work space
- Ask the student to outline the steps in evaluating your work space
- Ask the student to evaluate their work space

Organisational Goals:
To cut costs by 10%

Functional Goals – Production
To reduce defect goods by improving quality

Overall training for Organisational Goal

Training title	Competency	Classification	Skill Level
Waste reduction	How to eliminate waste in your working area	procedure	3

Level training for Organisational Goal

Training title	Competency	Classification	Skill Level
Budgeting	Forecasting expenditure	procedure	2

Functional training for Functional goal - Production

Training title	Competency	Classification	Skill Level
Identifying defects	the causes of common defects	principle	3

Jobrole training for Functional Goal – Production operator

Training title	Competency	Classification	Skill Level
Quality training	checking your machine settings	procedure	3

Joe Bloggs meets the skills level for each of the above competencies however he has a shortfall for the competency *How to eliminate waste in your working area*. The required skill level is 3 and he rated his skills level as only 1, thus this has been identified as a training need by the system. As a result this has written to his training plan and the system will generate learning objectives for this.

continued on following page

Figure 8. continued

> The competency How to eliminate waste in your working area has been defined as a procedure so according to Merrills CDT the optimum method for teaching a procedure is at three levels remember, use and find. Thus the learning objectives for this may be:
> - List the steps in eliminating waste in your working area
> - Demonstrate the steps in eliminating waste in the production area
> - Conduct a procedure for eliminating the waste in your working area and report on it
>
> These learning objectives are then used to search for learning objects with a metadata description similar to the learning objective. If these are found then they are presented to the learner in a sequence that corresponds to the individuals learning style which has been identified prior to the TNA. For example a pragmatist (person who likes to apply their learning in the real world) might prefer to undertake the learning objective *Demonstrate the steps in eliminating* waste first
>
> Once the individual finalises the presentation format the course manifest is generated and stored for that learner. Once the learner has completed the topic they can record this in their training plan and the topic disappears from their course outline

Future Developments

The future of TNA associated with TEL is tied in with the developing of its sophistication as educators and pedagogues build more successful models and techniques which are able to exploit the promise offered by the relentless advance of ICT. A key associated shift for SME employees is the move to Life Long Learning (LLL) away from employer driven training. This leads to two seemingly opposing developments. On the one hand there is the increased personalisation of TEL that focuses on the needs of the individual worker within a company, whilst on the other there is a societal shift to a more open Learning-Community model that emphasises the role of the learner's peer group.

Focussing initially on techniques of personalisation, we can accept that in the near future the commonest form of best practices in TEL authoring will deliver learning material online with content dynamically generated by aggregating learning objects drawn from some form of repository, delivered through a LCMS,[2] resulting in three nonexclusive developments that must be considered:

1. Content dictated by reference to a personal learning passport
2. Content determined and structured by a personal learning environment PLE
3. Content that self adapts to a person's preferred learning style.

In all three cases, the technological implementation route is probably more easily mapped out than the pedagogical one!

Learning passport: A Learning Passport (Barker, 1999) ultimately contains a detailed record of an individual's past learning in terms of direction (learning, aptitude, and career aspirations), structure (the order in which topics were studied), content (breadth and depth down to learning object level), and time frame (when, and for how long). As this passport is built up, TNA is absorbed into the routine functioning of the passport. The passport and an LCMS together will be able to select and present material based on the individuals profile (employment or career related, for academic credit or personal interest): at the right level, be built on previous knowledge, and not leave information gaps.

Personal learning environment (PLE): The functions and functionality currently carried out centrally by a VLE or LCMS are designed to accommodate many different learning situations and to support a wide learner/teacher base, they cannot be ideal in all cases.[5] If these software tools were distributed to a client application, thus becoming a Personal Learning Environment, a learner would be able to configure and adapt them so as to addresses her/his individual learning preferences and process. Such a PLE, being a personal tool, will seek for material based on the known past study of the learner, and presented in a preferred learning style. Such tools should incorporate self adaptive techniques so a PLE will continuously adapt to the learners maturing learning. A less appealing possibility is that more intelligent PLEs could monitor a person as they work and offer training or learning episodes to help improve their performance and becoming an integration of work and training. The further development of PLEs as a viable learning environment will arise in the need for the framework outlined in this chapter to be extended to incorporate the functionality of PLEs.

Self adapting content: The optimum way of presenting learning material to a learner depends upon their personal learning style and techniques and the context of their learning, current e-learning and learning objects cannot accommodate all of these factors; however, it is technically possible for LOs to self-adapt to an individuals preferred (or observed) learning style. So the way in which an LO runs will be different for, say, a pragmatist or a theorist, using Honey and Mumford's (1992) learner styles.[6] The implication is that LOs themselves will be dynamically constructed from constituent parts at a much finer granularity by an internal engine based on a knowledge (discovered from a learning passport?) of the learner's preferred learning style. This concept poses technological as well as conceptual difficulties that are yet to be adequately solved.[7]

Turning now to our other theme: that of the learner as a member of a group. Many educators are merging the techniques of Problem and Enquiry Based Learning (PEBL), and Collaborative Learning with TEL environments. An enriched environment is created for the learner through involvement and collaboration with a peer group, whilst the TEL provides communication, structuring and archiving tools. Also, since ICT offers easy communication with other wherever they may be, less structured collaboration for learning is evolving through the creation of online *learning com-*

munities. Such communities introduce another conceptual shift through a blurring of the boundary between teacher and learner. They more nearly model the natural processes of learning on the job and ubiquitous learning, where a work colleague becomes a teacher and a learner, by showing someone else how to do something, confirming heir own skills and knowledge. The structure and behaviour of online learning communities is again a combination of the development of enabling technology, ICT, and TEL, and the evolution of techniques and ability to benefit from them. The use of learning communities to support the learners using the framework outlined in this chapter would provide an enriched learning environment. An extension of the framework to direct individuals to suitable learning communities associated with their individual learning objectives would offer a more blended and less isolated learning solution.

However these two themes develop and blend, they enhance the future capabilities of TEL by the integration a wider range of possible actions and activities, but they make effective tools for needs analysis more necessary as the responsibility for learning planning is thrown back on the individual.

Conclusion

This chapter explored the integration of TNA with existing TEL authoring techniques to facilitate the tailoring of training. The chapter highlighted that:

1.   Existing authoring tools offer enormous potential to tailor training

2.   It is possible to tailor courses using existing theories and technologies

3.   TNA is a feasible method of assisting the tailoring of training

4.   It is possible to automate the generation of learning outcomes based on Merrills CDT

5.   With the emergence of new technologies further personalisation is possible with the integration of learning passports, PLEs rather than LCMS, and adaptive LOs

For those wishing to integrate TNA into existing TEL authoring, it is recommended that, if possible, it should be done so electronically as manual TNA is a time consuming process and training can be difficult to customise based on several learners' requirements. The integration should be conducted in line with the existing functionality of the LCMS/LMS tools. It is recommended that the TNA follow a number of key steps to ensure successful integration:

1.   Identify organisational goals

2.   Identify functional goals to achieve the organisational goals

3.   Identify training required to achieve both functional and organisational goals. Training should be specified to a high level of granularity and can be defined within a number of contexts to ensure successful customisation:

   •   Overall training required to achieve organisational goals. This is training which is required by everyone in the company.

   •   Level training required to achieve organisational goals. This is training which is given to certain levels in the organisation. For example managerial level training may be how to successfully lead an interdisciplinary team whereas employee level training may be how to be a successful mentor.

   •   Functional training required to achieve functional goals. This is training which is given to all individuals in a department. For example the HR department might receive training on how to operate the new HR computer system

   •   Job role training required to achieve functional goals. This is training which is required by an individual depending on the job role they are in. For example a HR specialist might need training on new HR Laws.

By following these steps one can ensure that the training offers meet the overall needs of the organization. This is because the needs analysis ensures that learning objectives generated are very specific to allow the search of relevant learning material. The granularity also allows training courses to be customised to individuals training needs, as often some LOs may offer the potential to be reused in a number of contexts.

It is hoped that this chapter will provide a "hands on" guide for practitioners wishing to adopt TNA into their course development and inspire individuals to examine existing best practices in TEL technologies and exploit their potential through their integration with other tools and theories. This will enable the development of a holistic and integrated approach to TEL which together offer more benefit to the learner than individual standalone models.

References

Barker, K. (1999). *The electronic learning record: Assessment and management of skills and knowledge: A literature survey.* BC Literacy. 1999 FuturEd.

Retrieved January 5, 2008, from www.futured.com/pdf/FuturEd%20ELR%
20lit%20review.pdf

Bloom, B. S. (1956). *Taxonomy of educational objectives.* New York.

Brahler, C. J., Peterson, N. S., & Johnson, E. C. (1999). Developing on-line learning materials for higher education: An overview of current issues. *Educational Technology and Society, 2*(2).

Clarke, N. (2003). The politics of training needs analysis. *Journal of Workplace Learning, 15*(4), 141-153.

Dahl, O. J., & Nygaard, K. (1966). SIMULA - an algol based simulation language. *Communications of the ACM, 9*(9), 671-678.

Dalziel, S. (1992). Organisational training needs. In J. Prior (Ed.), *Gower handbook of training and development* (pp. 183-192). Worcester, Great Britain: B Billing Sons Ltd.

Duval, E., & Hodgins, W. (2003). *A LOM research agenda.* Paper presented at the WWW2003, Budapest, Hungary.

Fallon, C., & Brown, S. (2003). *E-learning standards: A guide to purchasing, developing and deploying standards-conformant e-learning.* St. Lucie Press.

Gagne, R., Briggs, L., & Wager, W. (1992). *Principles of instructional design.* Fort Worth, TX: Harcourt Brace Jovanovich College Publishers.

Gibbons, A. S., Nelson, J., & Richards, R. (2000). The nature and origin of instructional objects. In D. A. Wiley (Ed.), *The instructional use of learning objects: Online version.* Agency for Instructional Technology.

Hodgins, W. (2000). *Into the future.* Retrieved January 5, 2008, from http://www.learnativity.com/download/MP7.PDF

Honey, P., & Mumford, A., (1992) *The manual of learning styles* (3rd ed.). Berkshire UK: P Honey.

IMS. (2003). *IMS digital repositories spedification.* Retrieved January 5, 2008, from www.imsglobal.org/digitalrepositories/

Irlbeck, S., & Mowat, J. (2007). Learning content management system (LCMS). In K. Harman & A. Koohang (Eds.), *Learning objects: Standards, metadata, repositories, and LCMS* (pp. 157-184). Santa Rosa, CA: Informing Science Press.

Johnson, K., & Hall, T. (2007). Granularity, reusability and learning objects. In A. Koohang & K. Harman (Eds.), *Learning objects: Theory, praxis, issues, and trends* (pp. 181-208). Santa Rosa, CA: Informing Science Press.

Kolb, D. A. (1984). *Experiential learning: Experience as the source of learning and development.* London: Englewood Cliffs, Prentice-Hall

Leat, M.J., & Lovell, J. (1997). Training needs analysis: Weaknesses in the conventional approach. *Journal of European Industrial Training, 21*(4), 143-153.

LTSC. (2002). *IEEE learning technology standards committee mission.* Retrieved January 5, 2008, from http://grouper.ieee.org/groups/ltsc/index.html

McGehee, W., & Thayer, P. (1961). *Training in business and industry.* Wiley.

Merrill, D. (1983). Component display theory. In C. Reigeluth (Ed.), *Instructional-design theories and models: An overview of their current status.* Hillsdale, NJ, London: Lawrence Erlbaum Associates.

Merrill, M. D. (1999). Using knowledge objects to design instructional learning environments. In T. Murray, S. Blessing & S. Ainsworth (Eds.), *Authoring tools for advanced technology learning environments.* Springer.

Moore, M. L., & Dutton, P. (1978, July). Training needs analysis: Review and critique. *Academy of Management Review,* 532-545.

Nelson, R. R., Whitener, E. M., & Philcox, H. H. (1995). The assessment of end-user training needs. *Communications of the ACM, 38*(7), 27-39. Retrieved January 5, 2008, from http://portal.acm.org/citation.cfm?id=214793&coll=portal&dl=ACM&CFID=20974446&CFTOKEN=85476952

Newstrom, J. W., & Lilyquist, J. M. (1979, October). Selecting needs analysis methods. *Training and Development Journal,* 52-56.

Observatory of European SMEs (2003). *SMEs in Europe 2003.* Retrieved from http://ec.europa.eu/enterprise/enterprise_policy/analysis/doc/smes_observatory_2003_report7_en.pdf

Papanikolaou, K.A., & Grigoriadou, M. (2003). An instructional framework supporting personalized learning on the Web. In *3rd International Conference on Advanced Learning Technologies,* Athens, Greece.

Pea, R. D. (1993-1994). Seeing what we build together: Distributed multimedia learning environments for transformative communications. *Journal of the Learning Sciences, 3*(3), 285-299.

Reigeluth, C., & Stein, F. S. (1983). The elaboration theory of instruction. In C. Reigeluth (Ed.), *Instructional-design theories and models: An overview of their current status* (pp. 339-381). Hillsdale, NJ, London: Lawrence Erlbaum Associates.

Rust, G., & Bide, M. (2000). *The indecs metadata framework:Principles, model and data dictionary.* Retrieved January 5, 2008, from http://www.indecs.org/pdf/framework.pdf

Saljo, R. (1999). Learning as the use of tools: A socio-cultural perspective on the human-technology link. In K. Littleton & P. Light (Eds.), *Learning with computers: Analysing productive interactions* (pp. 144-161). New York: Routledge.

Sciore, E., Siegel, M., & Rosenthal, A. (1994). Using semantic values to facilitate interoperability among heterogeneous information systems. *ACM Transactions on Database Systems (TODS), 19*(2), 254-290.

Smith, B., Delahaye, B., & Gates, P. (1986, August). Some observations on TNA. *Training and Development Journal,* 63-68.

Tannenbaum, S., & Yuki, G. (1992). Training and development in work organisations. *Annual Review of Psychology, 43*(1), 399-441.

Urdan, T. A., & Weggen, C. C. (2000). *Corporate e-learning: Exploring a new frontier.* Retrieved January 5, 2008, from http://wrhambrecht.com/research/coverage/elearning/ir/ir_explore.pdf

Wiley, D. A., South, J. B., Bassett, J., Nelson, L. M., Seawright, L. L., Peterson, T., et al. (1999). Three common properties of efficient online instructional support systems. *The ALN Magazine, 3*(2).

Further Readings

Barker, K. (1999). *The electronic learning record: Assessment and management of skills and knowledge: A literature survey.* BC Literacy. 1999 FuturEd. Retrieved January 5, 2008, from www.futured.com/pdf/FuturEd%20ELR%20lit%20review.pdf

Brennan, M., Funke, S., Anderson, C. (2001). *The learning content management system.* IDC White Paper.

Moore, M. L., & Dutton, P. (1978, July). Training needs analysis: Review and critique. *Academy of Management Review,* 532-545.

Smith, B., Delahaye, B., & Gates, P. (1986, August). Some observations on TNA. *Training and Development Journal,* 63-68.

Chapter VI

Metacognition for Enhancing Online Learning

Giuseppe Chiazzese, Italian National Research Council, Italy

Antonella Chifari, Italian National Research Council, Italy

Gianluca Merlo, Italian National Research Council, Italy

Simona Ottaviano, Italian National Research Council, Italy

Luciano Seta, Italian National Research Council, Italy

Inside Chapter

The existing research in the field of traditional didactics shows that students who have good metacognitive skills often achieve better scholastic results. Therefore, it seems that students who are aware of their cognitive processes and are able to self-monitor their learning activities tackle didactic tasks with greater success. The chapter presents an analysis of studies regarding applications of metacognition within technological learning environments which have been implemented in the last few years, and this is followed by a description of the features of the Gym2learn system. This system aims to reveal self-regulating processes and guide the student in acquiring all the steps of the executive control of some important comprehension strategies for understanding hypertexts.

Introduction

The concept of metacognition has its origin in the field of cognitive science and is an open and multifaceted concept within which many different types of research problems are investigated, giving rise to the definition of a "fuzzy concept" (Flavell, 1981; Wellman, 1985).

Originally, metacognition represented an important regulatory strategy regarding awareness of the organization and functioning of our thought processes.

Early studies of metacognition were of historical importance since they emphasized the active involvement of the student in the learning process; this involvement was achieved by informing the student about the advantages of using self-regulating cognitive strategies and allowing the student to apply them to different tasks (Brown & Palincsar, 1982).

The cognitive sciences have identified two main aspects of metacognition, namely *metacognitive knowledge,* possessed or to learn, and *metacognitive skills* related to the control and the monitoring of mental activity.

For a more detailed analysis, it may be useful to mention the principal theoretical models which have contributed to clarifying the more controversial aspects of this field of studies.

Following the theories of Flavell (1976), who was the first person to use the term metacognition in his "model of cognitive monitoring" (Flavell, 1981), it is possible to recognize four classes of phenomena which interact among themselves:

1. Metacognitive knowledge is a stable set of knowledge about cognitive processes and consists of two main features:
    *   The sensitivity which a subject shows in applying an appropriate strategy to resolve a particular cognitive problem;
    *   The variables, declarative knowledge (what I know) and procedural knowledge (I know how to do it) which the subject has about himself, a task to solve and the strategies to use.

2. Goals (or tasks) or, rather, the aims the subject intends to achieve which are of many kinds.

3. Metacognitive experiences allow the subject to organize his actions according to his aims, increasing the probability of success.

4. Actions (or strategies) refer to the cognitions or other behaviours employed to achieve the set goals and vary according to the desired outcome.

Following this model metacognitive knowledge is therefore capable of influencing goals, actions, and experiences.

For a further explanation of the metacognition concept, we consider Brown, Brandsford, Ferrara, and Campione's model (1983) where it is possible to identify four kinds of metacognitive processes:

- Predicting, which consists of the ability to hypothesise cognitive acts which may be used later;
- Planning, which consists of the ability to identify and plan a sequence of actions to reach a goal;
- Monitoring, which consists of the ability to control and progressively supervise ongoing cognitive operations;
- Evaluating, which consists of the ability to finally control the overall strategy and, if necessary, to modify it.

According to the author, metacognition is involved in all the phases of the study activities, and, in particular:

- Recognizing the need for a strategic behaviour;
- Evaluating the features of the task and searching for the most appropriate strategies from one's repertoire;
- Applying the strategy and checking its effectiveness (Campione & Brown, 1978).

Consequently, Brown states that metacognition does not consist only in an awareness of how cognitive processes function (that is the comprehension of information processing involved in complex skills), but also in the ability to plan, control, ask oneself questions and regulate oneself in the cognitive processes.

In synthesis, monitoring of the cognitive components and executive control are the two main metacognitive constructs that emerge from the cited models.

The former, which is identified in Flavell's model, implies a knowledge of one's own learning modalities, of the kinds of task to carry out and of the strategies to apply during the different study activities. The latter results from the set of actions to carry out during the learning process and which Brown identifies in predicting, planning, monitoring, and evaluating.

Jacobs and Paris (1987) in their "multicomponential model" regarding metacognition emphasize how, on their own, declarative and procedural knowledge do not guarantee the correct performance of learning tasks, where the student is required to be aware not only of *what* and *how*, but also of *when* and *why* to adopt particular strategies.

The authors therefore introduce a third kind of knowledge, defined as "conditional knowledge"; in particular, this can indicate the conditions in which learning is facilitated, when to use a certain strategy, and the cases in which it is most effective.

In this sense, the most useful and innovative implication in the metacognitive didactic approach consists of leading the student towards self-regulation, that is, to recognizing the skills needed for carrying out learning tasks and choosing with more awareness the most productive strategies to reach goals which bring scholastic success.

More in detail, among the range of explicit actions to be implemented in didactic activity we can mention: showing how a strategy is applied, introducing the practice of self-regulation,promoting the anticipated planning of procedures, reflecting on predictable obstacles, sustaining individual monitoring during the execution of tasks, discussing the relationship between actions and purpose, generalizing to other contexts, and maintaining the acquisitions over time.

These theoretical assumptions had and continue to have meaningful spin-off on didactics, so that today working on metacognitive learning aspects satisfies the most pressing needs within the school of transmitting not only concepts but also tools that allow students to learn to learn.

This means, in particular, developing in the student an awareness of what he is doing, why he is doing it, when and in which conditions it is appropriate to do it, as well as stimulating the skills for managing his own cognitive processes, which he can actively direct with practical evaluations and indications.

As described above, the possession of metacognitive skills draws on cognition, and to achieve this aim for some time we have seen an abundance of training programs to teach students both learning strategies, appropriate to different didactic settings, and the ability to apply techniques for their self-regulation.

Schneider and Pressley (1989) have referred to a list of items to take into consideration for teaching a strategy. This list is reproduced here:

1. Provide a detailed strategy
2. Teach it using a model to copy (modeling)
3. Repeat the first two phases well
4. Obtain observations and comments from the students
5. Emphasize how having a strategy makes it possible to control the learning processes
6. Reinforce the subject when he has shown he can use the strategy appropriately

7. Invite the subject to monitor himself, that is, to observe himself while he is learning to use the strategies and when he meets contexts in which it is appropriate to use them

8. Compare the results obtained using the strategy with those achieved in a traditional way

9. Encourage the student to generalize the strategy to different contexts

10. Teach the use of the strategy in different subjects and contexts and with different materials

These programs, although based on different theories, often have a series of implicit rules in common which are essential requirements for effective training:

•   Explicit instruction for using strategies with feedback during training has proved more efficient than asking the students to infer or abstract characteristics of the strategies without further help (Eliot-Faust, Pressley, & Dalecki, 1986; Gelzheiser, Sheperd, & Wozniak, 1986);

•   The interactive activities permit learners to carry on a constructive dialog on thought and learning processes (Duffy & Roehler, 1989);

•   The effect of self-monitoring can be observed only if students are free to use this information to regulate their studies (Thiede & Anderson, 2003);

•   The students who are aware of the importance of a strategic approach to studying learn more and become able to generalize better compared to those who simply use the strategy (Ianes, 1991).

Figure 1. Metacognition for enhancing online learning map

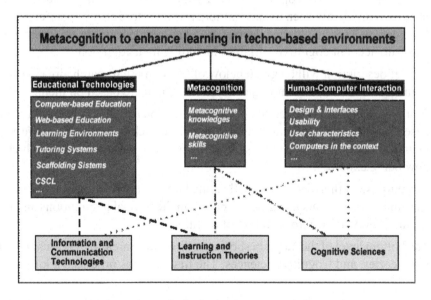

The training methods described are a valid tool with meaningful spin-off in scholastic settings, but they are rarely used in traditional didactic contexts. There are various reasons for this, such as the large number of hours required to carry out metacognitive training programs and the difficulty for teachers to effectively monitor the training path of each student. Moreover, as Duffy (1990) reveals, teachers tend to confuse content and processes and they often find it difficult to present the strategies to the students as sets of mental operations which can be modified to suit different situations.

The next section presents an analysis of studies regarding applications of metacognition within technological learning environments which have been implemented in the last few years, and this is followed by a description of the features of the Gym2learn system. This system aims to reveal self-regulating processes and guide the student in acquiring all the steps of the executive control of some important comprehension strategies for understanding hypertexts.

Metacognition and Technology Based Learning

A feature of the last few years has been the increased integration of the different learning theories and practices and ICT. This has resulted in innovative educational technologies which, however, require teachers and researchers to reflect on the way in which students study and learn with the new media. These reflections must take account not only of traditional aspects of learning models and instructional design, but also of the results of the cognitive sciences.

One of the concepts of cognitive science which has had the most influence on learning has undoubtedly been metacognition. It is therefore easy to predict that the next few years will see heightened interest in technological learning environments which take into account cognitive variables including metacognition.

A brief description will be given below of some of the research already carried out in this sector and the technological systems which are based on them.

It proves difficult, however, to compare the various studies because they are often based on different theoretical assumptions. To tackle this problem we present a map (see Figure 1) which allows us to find our way through territory which is only now being explored.

The purpose of this diagram is to illustrate how the application of metacognition in learning environments using ICT is based on theoretical assumptions and practical results from very different sectors of research.

The bottom level of the diagram shows the three main areas of research: ICT, Learning theories, and Cognitive sciences. The first area has produced a lot of tools and technological systems; the second has given rise to a large number of models and practices; and the last sector has suggested mechanisms to describe the working of the human brain. These fields of research are largely autonomous but, recently, new results have been obtained by combining them in various ways.

This has typically come about in the sector of educational technologies, where ICT and learning theories have both contributed to producing different educational tools, some of which are indicated in the diagram. A similar trend can be observed in studies of metacognition, where cognitive sciences and learning theories have highlighted different aspects of metacognition, also indicated in the diagram. Finally, human-computer interaction studies have been influenced by both ICT and cognitive sciences.

All these studies have contributed to the definition of the topic under consideration, that is, the use of metacognition to enhance learning in educational environments based on technology.

This topic can be studied from many different points of view and the results of the research are often difficult to compare.

To give an example of this, we can consider metacognition either as a framework to improve the comprehension of a topic when the student uses the computer for studying, or as an aid to improve the use of technological tools for learning.

Our diagram makes it easier to understand some of the interesting links between research studies of very different types which apparently have little in common, but it can also be used to plan interesting new research in fields which have not yet been thoroughly explored. If we restrict our analysis to the current situation of the studies on this topic, we can identify the following lines of research:

- Studies which aim to integrate cognitive strategies into educational environments based on technology (Romero, 2004; Zachary & Le Mentec, 2000). The studies consider that these environments are especially appropriate for supporting the metacognitive approach. The research is oriented towards the development of specific tools which permit metacognitive monitoring and control.

- Studies of new cognitive strategies adapted to the new media used during the learning activities, such as hypertexts, multimedia, and the Web (Azevedo, 2001; Després & Leroux, 2003; Marais & Bharat, 1997; Moore, Hobbs, Mullier, & Bell, 1997; Protopsaltis & Bouki, 2004; Puntambekar & Stylianou, 2003). In this respect, metacognition is considered as a specific framework which can improve the performance of the students working with these technological systems.

- Studies which aim to use the new technologies as a support for teachers and students while they are engaged in learning activities based on metacognition (Kramarski & Ritkof, 2002; Moreno & Saldana, 2004; Teong, 2003). Experiences have shown that the employment of metacognition in educational settings requires a considerable effort to plan and carry out. Technologies can provide new tools to help teachers and to involve students during these activities.

In the following section, we will indicate some specific examples for each of the study types described above and we will illustrate the strengths and weaknesses of these different approaches considering the following four variables:

- *Theoretical background*, that is the explicit ideas underlying the systems designed. The theoretical background can include general theories about cognitive processes, learning and instruction, interaction between people, and technological systems;
- *Metacognitive aspects*, that is, the way in which metacognition is considered in the systems and the specific tools developed to sustain metacognitive processes;
- *The student's role*, which may be active, for example, when the student decides how and when to use the functionalities, or passive if the student is subject to the organization of the system;
- *The field of application*, that is, the type of learning activities where the system can be employed successfully. For example, some tools may be designed exclusively for using on the Web, while the student is interacting with a CD-ROM or while engaged in other technology based educational settings.

Integrating Cognitive Strategies into Technology Based Educational Environments

Cognitive Tutor Geometry

Cognitive Tutor Geometry is a computer-based learning environment that supports students through guided and active learning. The assumption is that by using the strategy of self-explanation, metacognition, in its theoretical framework, can improve a student's ability to learn and solve a geometrical problem. In particular, the study of geometry is supported by tools that promote learning by doing and explaining. The student is faced with a problem and, by interacting with a menu, has to explain every step of his process of problem-solving. Moreover, Cognitive Tutor Geometry

Table 1. Some systems using metacognition

System	Variables	Data	References
Cognitive tutor	Theoretical background	Self-explanation	Aleven, Koedinger, 2002
	Metacognitive Aspects	Metacognitive Knowledge	
	Student's role	Active	
	Application Field	Computer-based learning environment	
Gstudy	Theoretical background	Self regulated learning	MacAllister, Winne, Nesbit, Jamieson-Noel, Zhou, Bennet, 2005; Winne, Nesbit, Kumar, Hadwin, Lajoie, Azevedo, Perry, 2006
	Metacognitive Aspects	Executive Control	
	Student's role	Active	
	Application Field	Learning Kit	
RiverWeb	Theoretical background	Self regulated learning	Azevedo, Ragan, Cromley, Pritchett, 2002
	Metacognitive Aspects	Executive Control	
	Student's role	Active	
	Application Field	Hypertextual environment for research purposes	
I-Search	Theoretical background	Metacognition as a higher order skill	Lloyd, 2001a; 2001b
	Metacognitive Aspects	Metacognitive Knowledge	
	Student's role	Active	
	Application Field	Web application	
Metacognitive Maps	Theoretical background	The four main skills of metacognition (planning, monitoring, evaluating, revising)	Lee, Baylor, 2006
	Metacognitive Aspects	Metacognitive Knowledge	
	Student's role	Active	
	Application Field	Web application	
Nestor	Theoretical background	Constructivism	Zeileger, 1999
	Metacognitive Aspects	Executive Control	
	Student's role	Active	
	Application Field	Web application	
Did@browser	Theoretical background	Metacognitive questions	Chiazzese et al. 2004a; 2004b
	Metacognitive Aspects	Executive Control	
	Student's role	Active during the surfing management; passive during stimulus prompting	
	Application Field	Web application	
iSTART	Theoretical background	Self-explanation reading training	McNamara, Levinstein, Boonthum, 2004
	Metacognitive Aspects	Metacognitive Knowledge and Executive Control	
	Student's role	Passive during the teaching of the strategies; active in the practical activities	
	Application Field	Web-based application	

also includes advice and feedback to the student about the work he has done in order to avoid interruptions in the study activity and to promote self-explanation.

gStudy

gStudy is a Web browser that allows students to use numerous tools (e.g., annotation tools, a highlighter, etc.) to manipulate hypertextual contents called *Learning Kit*. When the student is working on hypertextual content, the system provides cognitive scaffolding procedures to promote knowledge and management of study strategies that are usually applied in traditional settings. Metacognition is involved when the student uses the functionalities and has to control and monitor his cognitive processes.

The RiverWeb Water Quality Simulator

The RiverWeb Water Quality Simulator is a hypertextual enviroment designed to evaluate experimentally the influence of different goal settings on a student's ability to comprehend and control his learning process. The system is based on self-regulated learning theory: the best performing students are the ones who are able to manage their learning autonomously. In particular, The RiverWeb Water Quality Simulator enables students to evaluate the impact of certain variables on water quality through the observation and modification of a series of indicators. The student receives information by interpreting graphs that he can generate, answers some general questions and constructs a conceptual map.

Adapting Cognitive Strategies to the New Media

I-Search

I-Search is a meta-tool that supports a novice Web user during the process of online research. The system encourages awareness both of the variables involved during the search activity and useful strategies for tackling each step. It presents the student with a graphical overview of the various search phases, accompanied by textual prompts for the correct execution of every phase. I-Search thus uses metacognition as a tool to stimulate higher order skills and improve the results of Web searching. The system was one of the first to alert the scientific community to the need to support Web users with media specific procedures.

Metacognitive Maps

Metacognitive Maps is a tool for drawing conceptual maps in a Web-based environment. In this system, the metacognition is activated when students control and regulate the cognitive processes involved in Web surfing in order to improve learning and decrease the risk of getting lost in hyperspace. Students can use a *global map* to understand the structure of the whole hypertext; a *local tracking map* to monitor what they have done and decide what they have to do; a *planning space*, where they have to define their learning aims. The student himself establishes his learning aims, strategies to use, and the time necessary to carry out a task.

Nestor

Nestor is a software that implements "constructivist surfing" of the Web and considers online study as a process that can be active, self-organized, and collaborative if the student can use tools to comprehend his navigation and the structure of the contents he studies. While the student is surfing, the system draws a map which represents the Web space visited, allows the construction of personal Web pages, and enables the personalization (through notes, keywords, etc.) of the pages studied. A student using Nestor plays an active role and manages his cognitive processes metacognitively when he uses the system's functionalities.

Did@browser

Did@browser is an educational tool for secondary schools which poses metacognitive questions to students, enabling them to monitor their learning processes during Web surfing. According to the theoretical framework, the use of metacognitive questions is a support for activating and engaging learners' awareness and it facilitates their learning and improves the outcomes of a task. Students receive prompts to reflect on during their Web surfing, answer questions and then manage their surfing freely.

Supporting Metacognition with New Technologies

iSTART

iSTART is a Web-based application that provides high-level reading strategies to young adolescents. The theoretical background is the Self-Explanation Reading Training (SERT), that is, a model in which self-explanation improves students' comprehension and learning. In iSTART, students read/listen to the explanations of a virtual trainer and then use the strategies they have learned in a guided context. The system implements traditional metacognitive training in a tech-based environment: the student learns both cognitive strategies and how to control them metacognitively.

Methodological Consideration on Gym2Learn System

The above analysis of the metacognitive environments reveals differences between the systems which, despite involving all the metacognitive skills, vary with respect to their theoretical, methodological, and technological aspects. However, the categories identified for comparison are to be considered only for speculative purposes and in some cases may be reductive if used to describe functions which are common to more than one category. The review of this set of metacognitive environments has led to a series of reflections regarding margins for their improvement, on the basis of the theoretical aspects described in the introduction.

They have also been fundamental in the design of Gym2Learn, a metacognitive environment for the comprehension of online texts which will be presented below.

First of all, it appears to us that the majority of existing systems assume that the student is already familiar with the cognitive strategies activated by the functionalities as well as with the metacognitive skills of executive control.

The most immediate effect of this observation is that less able students are impeded, rather than supported, by the use of functionalities which are not self-explanatory.

Moreover, in our opinion, without explicit teaching of the strategies, the executive control, and the effects of their application, there is a risk of the user becoming an executor who is unaware of the cognitive strategies he is using.

These considerations have led us to propose integrating specific training into the systems; this training would include both the learning strategies and how to control them autonomously and with awareness.

Secondly, the metacognitive systems sometimes do not provide support for the supervision of a task *during* its execution. In our opinion, it is instead important to allow the students to observe their learning processes constantly so it is easy for them to monitor their work and, consequently, modify/improve it before they finish. It would therefore be useful to integrate monitoring areas into the systems where the students can observe the work in progress while using the functionalities.

Finally, no attention is paid to the possibility of generalizing the metacognitive experience which the tools stimulate in the student to other contexts. For this to take place, the student needs to recognize the importance of a strategic approach which can be applied to different types of contents. One possible solution to the problem is to make the student aware that the procedures he has learned can be applied to the contents of everyday life as well as to traditional topics of study.

These considerations lead us to conclude that good practices for designing metacognitive environments would be to:

- Support teachers in structuring metacognitive didactic activities simply and quickly;

- Teach (explicitly) students how it is possible to use new study strategies and how to control them effectively and autonomously;

- Exploit the autonomy and interactivity of media implementing functionalities to make students active participants in their own learning processes;

- Enable students to self-monitor their activities;

- Help students to generalize, that is, to become aware of how strategies they have learned can be applied in different contexts from those in which they studied.

Technological Consideration on Gym2Learn System

The methodological aspects described so far have encouraged us to develop the GymToLearn system to support online text comprehension. In particular, the system provides specific tools for training and controlling some of the mental strategies employed during Web study at a metacognitive level.

The student is engaged within the system in two distinct phases: a training phase in which he learns some strategies for text comprehension and an executive phase in which he can use functionalities to support the application of learned strategies. These functionalities are available as an add-on of the Firefox browser.

Training Phase

The training phase consists of a series of practical exercises to perform on hypertext pages, whereby students begin to familiarize with the use and control of some cognitive strategies for understanding hypertexts (recalling previous knowledge; constructing hypotheses and verifying them in the text; asking and answering questions to check their comprehension; identifying the most important parts of texts; understanding and interpreting figures, graphics, and pictures in the texts).

The training phase, based on the vademecum proposed by Schneider, is articulated around some strategies (Brown, Armbuster, & Baker, 1986) which can improve text comprehension. In particular:

Scrolling down the text to recall previous knowledge

If we accept the supposition that comprehension improves when the reader already knows something about the topic considered in the text, it is a useful strategy to glance rapidly through the text in order to recall previous knowledge and thus associate it more easily with the new information.

Formulating hypotheses and verify them during surfing

As in a problem solving process, this strategy requires the reader to formulate hypotheses based on the information given at the beginning of the text and to verify them as they read on.

Answering and asking oneself questions to verify comprehension

Different studies (Pressley, Tannenbaum, McDaniel, & Wood, 1990) have shown that during the reading of a text, answering questions has positive effects on learning. Besides, by asking himself questions, the student plays an active role in checking and self-evaluating his comprehension of the text.

Identifying important parts of the text

During the reading of the text, a valid strategy for reducing the cognitive overload is to separate the main concept from the secondary ones, bearing in mind the purpose of the reading activity.

The training for each of the above mentioned strategies is structured in the following way:

- A description of the cognitive strategy;
- A series of exercises for training in the use of the strategy;
- An exercise in the generalization of the learned strategy;
- A self evaluation page where the student assesses his application of the learned strategy.

Each exercise aims to promote the activation of metacognitive processes proposed by Brown's model and consists of the following items:

- A task that describes the learning activity to be carried out;
- A plan of action that represents the sequence of steps to perform in order to use the cognitive strategy correctly;

- A training text;
- An assessment area that proposes a set of questions for stimulating the monitoring of the operation performed;
- A monitoring area that allows the student to self-evaluate his use of the learned strategy.

Executive Phase

The executive phase allows students to put into practice on the Web all the knowledge acquired during the training phase. The student can surf freely through Web sites proposed by teachers or selected independently and use the system support to apply the cognitive strategies and thus facilitate the learning of the Web content. The Web surfing in G2L is free while in the other solutions described above the student surfs only learning content developed by the teacher. Moreover, in G2L the student has an active role because he can decide when and which functionality he wants to use to support his learning activities.

Each functionality stimulates the cognitive strategy associated with it through a semantic annotation mechanism on the Web page. This mechanism saves the following information loaded by the user in a note: the time and the text selected by the user. The note is saved on the annotation server and an icon appears next to the selected text. In this way, during surfing, the student can review the comprehension strategy he used before. By clicking on an icon it is possible to view and edit a note. For example, if the student intends to use the strategy "formulate hypothesis," he will select the relevant portion of the text and will activate the corresponding functionality for formulating a hypothesis and saving it.

The advantage of using an annotation mechanism like this is that it is possible to track all the student's notes related to each strategy and thus to monitor how he has employed them during surfing. It is possible to argue that the student's annotations created during surfing could provide us with information about his content comprehension process.

The information is saved by an RDF file that tracks the student's use of the four strategies of text comprehension.

In conclusion, our semantic annotation mechanism enables the system to:

- Classify the student's annotations in relation to the strategies he has used;
- Monitor the student's activities both at diachronic level by a temporal reconstruction of the strategy employed and at synchronic level by analyzing the set of strategies employed during the comprehension of the individual content;

- Display the annotations to the student through specific icons placed in the hypertext.

Conclusion

In this chapter, we have considered two parallel phenomena: the introduction of the Web as a didactic resource and the interest in metacognition as a valid support during online learning processes.

However, with respect to the latter phenomenon, we have to underline that the theoretical framework does not appear sufficiently clear and the experimental studies are limited and not exhaustive.

Our rationale is that metacognition can be useful in improving the student's performance in learning online only if it is introduced by adapting practices and technological tools to the media used.

Besides, this work aims to promote the idea that the active involvement of students in learning activities is an essential step towards acquiring autonomy during study, and it provides tools and strategies which can be used in all fields of education and can be generalized to other situations in everyday life.

It is therefore important that research in this area continues to investigate effective ways of including metacognitive support in the design of user friendly, computer-based learning environments.

References

Aleven, V. A. W. M. M., & Koedinger, K. R. (2002). An effective metacognitive strategy: Learning by doing and explaining with a computer-based cognitive tutor. *Cognitive Science, 26*(2), 147-179.

Azevedo, R. (2001). Using hypermedia to learn about complex systems: A self-regulation model. In *Proceedings of the 10th International Conference on Artificial Intelligence in Education* (pp. 65-71), Amsterdam.

Azevedo, R., Ragan, S., Cromley, J. G., & Pritchett, S. (2002). *Do different goal-setting conditions facilitate students' ability to regulate their learning of complex science topics with RiverWeb?* Paper presented at the Annual Conference of the American Educational Research Association, USA. (ERIC Document Reproduction Service No. ED 482509)

Brown, A. L., Brandsford, J. D., Ferrara, R. A., & Campione, J. C. (1983). Learning, remembering and understanding. In P. Mussen (Ed.), *Handbook of child psychology: Cognitive development* (Vol. 3, pp. 77-166). NY: John Wiley.

Brown, A. L., & Palincsar, A. S. (1982). Inducing strategic learning from text by means of informed, self-controlled training. *Topics in Learning and Learning Disabilities, 2,* 1-17.

Campione, J. C., & Brown, A. L. (1978). Towards a theory of intelligence: Contributions from research with retarded children. *Intelligence, 2,* 279-304.

Chiazzese, G., Todaro, G., Chifari, A., Ottaviano, S., Seta, L., & Allegra, M. (2004a). Surfing to learn. *IADAT Journal of Advanced Technology.* ISSN 1698-1073.

Chiazzese, G., Todaro, G., Chifari, A., Ottaviano, S., Seta, L., & Allegra, M. (2004b). Did@browser: A tool to support the surfing activities of students. In *Proceedings of IADAT – e2004 The IADAT International Conference on Education Bilbao* (pp. 6-9), Spain.

Desprès, C., & Leroux, P. (2003). Le tutorat synchrone en formation à distance: un modèle pour le suivi pédagogique synchrone d'activités d'apprentissage à distance. In C. Desmoulins, P. Marquet & D. Bouhineau (Dir.), *Environnements Informatiques pour l'Apprentissage Humain* (pp. 139-150). Strasbourg: ATIEF; INRP.

Duffy, G. G. (1990). *Reading in the middle school* (2nd ed.). Newark, DE: International Reading Association.

Duffy, G. G., & Roehler, L. (1989). *Improving classroom reading instruction: A decision-making approach.* NY: Random House.

Eliott-Faust, D. J., Pressley, M., & Dalecki, L. B. (1986). Process training to improve children's referential communication: Asher and Wigfield (1981) revisited. *Journal of Educational Psychology, 78,* 22-26.

Flavell, J. H. (1976). Metacognitive aspects of problem solving. In L. B. Resnick (Ed.), *The nature of intelligence* (pp. 231-323). Hillsdale, NJ: Erlbaum.

Flavell, J. H. (1981). Cognitive monitoring. In W. P. Dickson (Ed.), *Children's oral communication skills.* NY: Academic Press.

Ianes, D. (1991). *Metacognizione e insegnamento.* Trento: Edizioni Erickson.

Jacobs, J., & Paris, S. (1987). Children metacognition about reading: Issues in definition, easurement and instruction. *Educational Psychologist, 22,* 255-278.

Kramarski, B., & Ritkof, R. (2002). The effects of metacognition and e-mail conversation on learning graphing. *Journal of Computer Assisted Learning, 18,* 33-43.

Lee, M., & Baylor, A. L. (2006). Designing metacognitive maps for Web-based learning. *Educational Technology & Society, 9*(1), 344-348.

Lloyd, A. (2001a). A software tool for supporting the acquisition of metacognitive skills for WebSearching. In *Proceedings of the International Conference on Artificial Intelligence in Education* (pp. 19-23).

Lloyd, A. (2001b). *I-Search: A meta-tool for novice Web searchers.* Retrieved January 6, 2008, from http://citeseer.ist.psu.edu/560801.html

MacAllister, K., Winne, P. H., Nesbit, J., Jamieson-Noel, D., Zhou, M., & Bennet, N. (2005). Tools for investigating self-regulated learning: An overview. In D. Jamieson-Noel (Organizer), *New tools, approaches and issues in researching self-regulated learning in authentic settings.* Washington, DC: American Psychological Association.

Marais, H., & Bharat, K. (1997). Supporting cooperative and personal surfing with a desktop assistant. In *Proceedings of ACM UIST'97*, Canada (pp. 129-138).

McNamara, D. S., Levinstein, I. B., & Boonthum, C. (2004). Istart: Interactive strategy training for active reading and thinking. *Behavior Research Methods, Instruments, & Computers, 36*(2), 222-233.

Moore, D., Hobbs, D., Mullier, D., & Bell, C. (1997). Interaction paradigms with educational hypermedia. In *Euromicro 97* (pp. 65-71), Budapest.

Protopsaltis, A., & Bouki, V. (2004). Cognitive model for Web based hypertext comprehension. In *Web-Based Education* (pp. 604-606), Austria.

Puntambekar, S., & Stylianou, A. (2003). Designing metacognitive support for learning from hypertext: What factors come into play? In U. Hoppe, F. Verdejo & J. Kay (Eds.), *Artificial intelligence in education: Shaping the future of learning through intelligent technologies.* Amsterdam: IOS Press.

Romero, M. (2004). *Metacognition dans les EIAH.* Retrieved January 6, 2008, from http://margarida-romero.com/cursus/dea_chm_ie/content/romero_transversal.pdf

Schneider, W., & Pressley, M. (1989). *Memory development between 2 and 20.* NY: Springer-Verlag.

Teong, S. K. (2003). The effect of metacognitive training on mathematical word-problem solving. *J. Comp. Assisted Learning, 19*(1), 46-55.

Thiede, K. W., & Anderson, M. C. M. (2003). Summarizing can improve metacomprehension accuracy. *Contemporary Educational Psychology, 28,* 129-160.

Wellman, H. M. (1985). The origins of metacognition. In D. L. Forrest-Pressley, G. E. MacKinnon & T. G. Waller (Eds.), *Metacognition, cognition, and human performance.* NY: Academic Press.

Winne, P. H., Nesbit, J. C., Kumar, V., & Hadwin, A. F. (2006). Supporting self-regulated learning with gStudy software: The learning kit project. *Technology, Instruction, Cognition and Learning, 3,* 105-113.

Zachary, W., & Le Mentec, J. C. (2000). Incorporating metacognitive capabilities in synthetic cognition. In *Proceedings of The Ninth Conference on Computer Generated Forces* (pp. 513-521), Orlando.

Zeiliger, R., Belisle, C., & Cerratto, T. (1999). Implementing a constructivist approach to Web navigation support. In *Proceedings of the ED-MEDIA'99 Conference* (pp. 403-408).

Chapter VII

A Research-Led Approach to Technology Enhanced Learning:
Strategies, Programmes, Projects, & Pedagogies in UK Higher Education

Jacqueline A. Dempster, University of Warwick, UK

Introduction

This chapter focuses on national and institutional initiatives in UK higher education (HE) to support and embed technology enhanced learning, and in particular with regard to the development in undergraduate students of research-oriented capabilities. The term "research-led" is widely used in the HE sector to describe universities that demonstrate a high capacity for good quality research whilst claiming that their research informs and enhances their teaching. The approaches described are based on the premise that developments should be led by clear pedagogical objectives coupled with the opportunities afforded to the curriculum by the technologies.

The chapter begins with an overview of technology enhanced learning (TEL) initiatives in UK higher education, though it should be noted that the term "TEL" is not used ubiquitously; other terms have been in fashion, such as C&IT (following the Dearing report, 1998) and e-learning (following international trends). The first part outlines national policies and programmes that have had a significant impact on TEL practice, development of accreditation schemes to standardise and recognise teaching and learning practice, and, recently, a national benchmark exercise to review institutional progress in TEL and find new paths for future policy and practice.

The second part of the chapter focuses on the importance of good pedagogical models for TEL as a means to foster, support, and assess specifically students' development of research-based learning. Finally, based around a study in eight research-led or research-informed UK universities and the aforementioned national e-learning benchmarking exercise, the approaches to working with faculty to embed these ideas into their everyday use of technology are explored.

Keywords: Teaching and Learning Technology Program, Research-Led Learning, Benchmarking E-Learning, Strategies and Pedagogies, Pedagogical Models for TEL

Technology Enhanced Learning Initiatives in UK HE

The Rise of National Policy and Programmes

Over the last 50 years, the impact that technology has made on our lives and work is remarkable. More remarkable still is the relatively low impact that it has had on teaching and learning practices. While technology has been used in universities and colleges since the dawn of computers in the late 1940s and early 1950s, for the first 30 years or more it was mostly used to support research analysis and improve the efficiency of administration.

In the United Kingdom, several national schemes were established in the 1980s and 1990s that put TEL into vogue. At this time, the terms used were computer assisted learning (CAL) and computer based training (CBT) and some interesting educational software developments began to emerge. Of these, the Computers in Teaching Initiative (CTI), set up in 1989 as one of the first publicly funded HE teaching support networks, was most significant. It comprised 24 discipline based support centres around the country that assisted in sharing expertise and TEL materials across the community.

A few years on and a Teaching and Learning Technology Programme (TLTP) was established, which prompted large-scale development across the UK HE sector. It supported a high number of projects in producing discipline specific TEL packages as well as projects to aid implementation of TEL. A joint initiative of all the UK Higher Education Funding Councils with a remit to "make teaching and learning more productive and efficient by harnessing modern technology," TLTP was unique. The first two phases spanned 1992-96, with over £11 million from all the Funding Councils, plus institutional investments, creating a high volume of TEL materials in a wide range of HE subjects. These projects were in the main consortium-based endeavours in an attempt to overcome the "not-invented-here syndrome" of previous developments by ensuring that at least the institutional partners would own, and therefore use, the TEL packages produced. A third phase followed in 1998 focused specifically on implementation and embedding of the TEL materials and practices developed.

Evaluations of TLTP (Sommerlad, Pettigew, Ramsden, & Stern, 1999; University of Edinburgh, 1998) indicated that the programme was successful in many of its various aims. It is clear that with such substantial breadth of involvement of universities and their staff, there are likely to be outcomes beyond the materials that were created and the uses to which these were put. The collaborative nature of the programme raised awareness of the opportunities offered by TEL. Assessment, student and staff support, curriculum design, and infrastructure issues all came into sharper focus. Communities of practice were formed both within and between academic departments and central support units, many of who continue to work together to varying degrees. These networks brought a substantial expertise to higher education—in teaching, project management, and technology enhanced learning and teaching.

Uptake, however, was limited by the localised nature of the medium, predominantly single machine courseware (e.g., floppy disk, CD-ROM, videodisc) delivered. Further externally funded development, such as that initiated by the Joint Information Systems Committee (JISC), European Union, Fund for the Development of Teaching and Learning (FDTL) and the Teaching and Learning Research Programme (TLRP) funded by the Economic and Social Research Council (ESRC), has built upon the expertise that resides in individuals and networks resulting in an impressive track record in the UK from these early initiatives.

Concurrently, institutional learning and teaching strategies were being emphasised with grants from the HE funding councils to support universities for their development and implementation of strategic objectives, many of which including TEL. Out of such funding, many institutions set up 'teaching innovation funds' and recruited academic support staff (if these did not exist already) to assist with sustaining developments and support further innovations at a local level.

Emerging Technologies and Opportunities for Curriculum Change

The widespread changes affecting HE internationally are nothing new (Taylor, 1998). There appears to be a greater homogeneity within the UK HE sector with respect to use of TEL than in other countries, largely due to the impact of these centrally funded initiatives (University of Edinburgh, 1999). Nevertheless, across this era, uptake was patchy and sustainable practice was challenged by poor infrastructure capacities and the limitations of personal computing. It is only with the birth of the Internet, connecting millions of computers, coupled with improvements in personal computers and high-speed networks that significant impact is evident (Fallows & Bhanot, 2002). The Web shifted the balance from the sending of information to publishing of information, and later the restriction of materials based on membership of a particular organisation or group. More than any other tool, the Web changed the way we think about the possibilities of technology enhanced learning. The access to materials and modes of interaction to support learning and teaching is limited only by the imagination.

And therein lies a further challenge. The Internet with its wealth of information and communication raises the issue of how local teachers make best use of the technological options to provide for the needs of their students. How can courses be designed to develop in the students' the capacity to engage with technology as a tool for learning at university and in their on-going work and lives? There is no consensus of best practice for technology enhanced learning; it depends crucially on the nature of the learning desired and the skill of the teacher in the deployment of appropriate methods. Despite the prevalence of CTI and TLTP, pedagogical support for teaching staff at the local level was still lacking in most HE institutions, which restricted their capacity to integrate TEL materials into courses and assist students to learn with the new technologies. As the technical barriers came down, many HE institutions started to address this issue by appointing "TLTP" officers, and later "e-learning" specialists, and by acquiring a greater understanding of the factors influencing the embedding of technology into teaching and learning practices (Dempster & Deepwell, 2003; Oliver & Dempster, 2003).

Professionalising HE Teaching and Learning

Around the same time, in the late 1990s, emphasis on the professionalism of teaching gained support. A number of forward-looking universities established accredited programmes to assist in enhancing the quality of teaching and learning. Institutional teaching certificate programmes for new lecturers were quickly followed by professional standards that recognised these qualifications at a national level. However, few such programmes truly embraced the newer techniques afforded by technology, and focused very much on enhancing traditional lecture/seminar and assessment formats.

In 1997, the Institute for Learning and Teaching in Higher Education (ILTHE, now subsumed within the Higher Education Academy) established itself as the professional body for academic staff (and to a lesser extent academic related support staff) in UK HE. It was an important element in raising the status of teaching as a core part of the professional role of the university academic. However, the ILTHE found mixed favour amongst the community; not everyone desired to be a "member." Many academics resented (as they perceived it) being "told how to teach," increasingly so as institutional programmes recognised by ILTHE became mandatory for probationary lecturers. Those in supporting roles for technology enhanced learning and teaching, were restricted to "associate" membership only, perpetuating the divide (and apparent inferior status) of educational support roles from that of lecturers.

Many institutions started to develop specific accreditation programmes for staff interested or involved in the application of technology in learning and teaching (review by Smith & Oliver, 2000). Such programmes attracted both lecturers and educational support staff. One TLTP phase 3 project, *Effective Framework for Embedding C&IT Using Targeted Support* (EFFECTS: www.elt.ac.uk/), was particularly important in initiating developments of this kind. The EFFECTS project began in 1998 to support both new and experienced academic lecturers and learning and teaching support staff in applying information and communications technologies. As a result of excellent dissemination and networking of the team, this well-known, nationally funded project led to the implementation of several professional development courses in a growing number of UK HE institutions. Some were accredited locally, such as the M-level programme we run at Warwick (www.go.warwick.ac.uk/cap/wela/), and/or through recognition under the Embedding Learning Technologies Professional Development Framework (ELT PDF) of the UK's Staff and Educational Development Association (SEDA). These courses follow a variety of formats, from a series of short, intensive face-to-face workshops and online activities to year long development programmes with tailored support for staff to undertake a small-scale TEL project.

In 2004, the Association for Learning Technology (ALT), a long standing professional body for learning technology professionals across HE, FE, and industry, developed a specialised accreditation scheme for its growing community in order to provide the much-needed recognition of their specialised role and expertise in learning technology (Oliver, 2000). The "CMALT" scheme (CMALT: www.alt.ac.uk/cmalt/) was launched formally in July 2005 and is growing steadily in its certified membership.

Benchmarking E-Learning

In 2006, the University of Warwick, along with 11 other HE institutions, took part in the pilot of a national benchmarking exercise (see www.heacademy.ac.uk/bench-marking.htm), funded jointly by the Higher Education Academy (formerly ILTHE) and the JISC. The purpose is to identify, review and share institutional strategies and activities to promote and support technology enhanced learning and teaching.

A push for efficient and more effective education has been a constant feature in many technology enhanced learning initiatives. Foster proposes five essential ingredients of "good" TEL (Foster, 2002). Interestingly, most early developments stemmed from an adaptation of traditional practice rather than the introduction of innovation per se. Institutions that looked to increase the productivity of the teaching and learning function while maintaining quality and minimising risk, experienced a kind of educational inertia that preserves and perpetuates the direct face-to-face style of teaching. Those with a nonstatus quo orientation saw educational development (read: quality enhancement) as constantly changing, adapting and refreshing within the context of the values held by the institution.

The benchmarking exercise facilitated an in-depth review of an institution's e-learning activities and experiences over recent years alongside access to the approaches and lessons learned in other institutions. The work has identified both strategic and operational strengths and weaknesses, making us better informed and equipped to further develop and embed TEL across the University. The focus of our continuing work is on providing examples of the large-scale activities necessary to embed TEL within an institution. Warwick's view of "embedding" means staff ideally choose from a range of teaching methodologies and ways of providing learning opportunities. These may include electronic resources and online activities alongside nontechnological ones.

To do so, lecturers need to be equipped with the pedagogical and technical skills to make informed decisions about how best to integrate e-learning into their teaching. Such decisions are best based on properly evaluated, evidence-based approaches to developing students' learning, whilst assuming an absence of the often significant obstacles to choosing an e-learning method over any other method. Without a viable model for the kinds of pedagogy one wishes to support, these choices are a stab in the dark. What follows is an attempt to provide some possible frameworks for research-led learning supported by technology as a blueprint for future design and evaluation of our strategic educational objectives for TEL.

Strategies and Pedagogies for Research-Led Technology Enhanced Learning

Linking Research and Teaching

There is already a wealth of literature debating the existence of linkages between research and teaching. See Hattie and Marsh (1996) and Jenkins (2005) for reviews. This was brought into sharp focus by the Boyer (1998) report, which proposed a reinvention of undergraduate education in the United States. Boyer's (1998) model promotes a strategy for involving students with real social problems outside of the academy, referred to as the "scholarship of engagement." Such ideas have been taken on board in the UK and elsewhere. Studies suggest that undergraduate research opportunities have a significant impact on the quality of student learning, as well as giving students a sense of the potential of their subjects (Blackmore & Cousin, 2003; Jenkins, 2006).

As previously discussed, evaluation of TLTP suggested that while there were many benefits of a national programme of this kind, uptake of TEL products was not as widespread as the funding investment might have hoped. It was notable that, in general, staff in research-led universities were more reluctant to take up TLTP-like packages. This stems from a clash with existing teaching paradigms, which are strongly informed by research interests and in which learners are encouraged to act as apprentice researchers in their undergraduate as well as postgraduate studies rather than consumers of disciplinary "content."

Identifying Pedagogical Models for Research-Led Learning

Warwick has always taken the view that good research can inform and strengthen the quality of education that it is able to offer its students and its learning and teaching strategy has reflected this for a number of years. While strategies and the policies for linking research and teaching are important, an understanding of the pedagogy underpinning such a link is crucial. In the light of the tension between research and teaching, the question that all research-intensive universities need to ask themselves is whether the research activity can add value to curricula in terms of learning. The pedagogic level of this question has always been a fruitful area to explore. Various projects over the last 8 years spring from this emphasis, culminating in development of a Centre for Excellence in Teaching and Learning

Table 1. From Roach et al. (2001)

ADOPTIVE LEARNING	ADAPTIVE LEARNING
Knowledge and Practice of....	**Formation and Generation of....**
Facts, Assertions, Rules and Laws	Personal Interpretation, Meaning and Expression
Language and Protocols	Evaluation, Decisions and Justification
Techniques and Procedures	Arguments, Reasoning and Explanations
Organisation, Structure and Strategy	Synthesis, Conceptualisation and Understanding
Established Relationships and Principles	Originality, Creativity and Innovation

(CETL), the Reinvention Centre for Undergraduate Research (www.go.warwick. ac.uk/reinvention/), in partnership with Oxford Brookes University. This model of education places students at the centre of the learning experience and their learning is enhanced through active engagement in their own research. These activities provide significant impetus to this important pedagogical aspiration, drawing in an increasing number of departments and other institutions.

Much of the shift in our thinking in this area arose originally from work on a TLTP phase 3 project, Technology Enhanced Learning in Research-Led Institutions (TELRI) project, based at Warwick, with Warwick and Oxford working in partnership, followed at a later stage by Durham, Birmingham, and Southampton Universities. The project sought to tackle two interrelated challenges. The first is a particular feature of research-intensive universities, which is that the two main activities of research and teaching were not as closely linked as they might be, and the former has a higher status in terms of career progression for academic staff. The second was that the potential to make effective use of the growing range of technological tools available is hampered by the lack of a suitable pedagogical framework for using technology to support higher cognitive aspects of learning required for research practice.

The TELRI work sought to identify and define some of the research-related graduate attributes such as the skills of enquiry, analysis, synthesis, creativity, and evaluation and to map the ways in which different types of technology supported their development in students. We first focused on the cognitive processes of researchers and used this as a model for defining research-led learning outcomes in a language that academic staff could recognise and relate to, taking on board the need for (re)interpretations across subject disciplines. Two complementary types of capability were established, *adoptive* and *adaptive,* to signify the difference between the use of established knowledge and techniques of the discipline and the creation of new knowledge and its application in novel situations (Roach, Blackmore, & Dempster, 2001; see Table 1). These terms were felt to offer a distinction in strategies and processes beyond that previously described as "deep" and "surface" learning (Marton

Table 2. Mapping technology to curriculum activities (Updated from Roach et al., 2001)

	Learning resources	Learning support	Assessment	Integration medium
ADOPTIVE learning	Provision of course materials, exercises	Guidance and feedback on knowledge, practice of ... (see Table 1)		
Traditional	Lectures Guidance notes Books Journals	Seminars Group classes Lab work Study guides	Essays Work/lab books Multiple choice tests Oral presentations	
				Virtual Learning Environments
TEL-based	Web-based resources CAL/CBT Simulations Bibliographic databases Internet sites Podcasts	Interactive TEL Simulations Applications software *(e.g., spreadsheets, statistical or textual analysis packages, CAD/CAM, 3-D modelling, multimedia)*	Electronic marking Computerised tests CAL, simulations (that include feedback)	
ADAPTIVE learning	Student led content	Guidance and feedback on the formation and generation of... (see Table 1)		
Traditional	Discussion of work in progress Distribution of marked work	Seminars Group classes		*Virtual Learning Environments*
TEL-based	Web publishing Discussion archives Students' research journal	Web publishing and critical analysis Discussion lists/boards and student blogs Text/audio or video conferencing	e-submissions Students' published work Discussion contributions	

& Saljo, 1986; Ramsden, 1992), arguing that there are both deep and surface forms of adoptive and adaptive learning.

Having now a set of explicitly defined, if generic, set of learning outcomes, we then set out to identify and test those technologies that encouraged and supported enhancement of adaptive learning, equating these to the higher order capabilities required for research and thus, research-led learning (see Table 2). There is a natural tendency to use previously formed concepts before creating new ones. Thus, the two forms of learning must be fostered through different teaching and learning activities and must be assessed differently (see Table 1). The choice and combination of methods will dictate the balance of the learning towards adoptive or adaptive outcomes.

Research-led activities aim to foster development of creative and collaborative capabilities of students through the technologies that support the sharing and discussion of work. Practice from across the disciplines (Dempster, 2003) show ways in which technology can support critical thinking and debate that is focussed on the students' own work (or work in progress). Learning activities may draw on primary resources, including disciplinary research, for which Web-based (virtual) learning environments can provide highly flexible access integrated with other learning support and assessment.

If the form of assignment is familiar, then students will fall on adoptive learning, that is "adopting" the strategies and procedures of established processes in the discipline. If, on the other hand, students are to be encouraged towards adaptive learning, assignments will need to offer novel and open scenarios that foster the formation of new ideas and concepts by the student. Put another way, the requirement in research-led learning is to undertake activities that allow the demonstration of adaptive learning capabilities and qualities in the students' work and to assess accordingly. Thus, the emphasis in the curriculum design needs to be placed firmly on the activities of the students rather than on the subject content. The only exception would be where the students themselves are creating "content," in the sense that they contribute to the course by researching and bringing in resources that support the expression and justification of their ideas.

Embedding Technology Enhanced Learning into Institutional Practice

A Strategy for Diversity of Innovation

Such pedagogic frameworks for research-led learning can provide a means for institutions and individual course leaders to make explicit statements about otherwise implicit and subjective learning outcomes. In so doing, they can act as a guide to learning and assessment criteria for the research-based "skills of transfer" that are of immense value to employers and in later lifelong learning. Equally, they act as a guide for the application of technology to enhance specific types of learning and assessment strategies, in line with the real, desirable curriculum aims (see TELRI course design guidelines available online at www.telri.ac.uk/guidelines.pdf).

There is also an impending need to raise awareness and develop techniques not only for pedagogical good practice of using TEL, but also the social dimension. This implies a need to support staff as well as students in developing the skills of a modern information society. The strategy for TEL adopted at Warwick is, however, certainly not intended to impose models of practice or procedure on the University's faculty. Instead, we take the approach of both fostering bottom-up diversity and establishing the necessary degree of common service standards, whilst recognising the inevitable and ongoing tension between the two.

Overall, we believe this "managed diversity" is responsive to individual and departmental need; it encourages innovation and distinctiveness; it establishes a sense of ownership by faculty; and its development is highly dialogic. We believe this gives us a degree of flexibility and breathing space that is not always available with commercial virtual learning environments (VLEs), and allows the university to respond effectively when new needs and requirements emerge.

It is true to say our e-learning strategy has been more aspirational than target-driven. The model is to evolve tools and services in response to demand. Naturally, this is often led by innovators. The challenge then becomes how to disseminate and encourage use by "late adopters."

Disseminating and Promoting TEL

There are many different approaches that HE institutions have taken to embedding technology enhanced learning into their "everyday" educational practice (Oliver & Dempster, 2003), from introduction of virtual learning environments to broad teaching enhancement initiatives as a focus. Many rely on innovations of a small number of individuals or departments to inspire and drive uptake, whilst others have developed large-scale, institution-wide implementation projects. Some institutions have sophisticated strategies and specialised development units to support use of technology by academics, some have a more dispersed structure. There is clearly no one model of "best practice" for the introduction of TEL that ensures it will be embedded into academic practice.

What is clear is that in developing their own practice, staff cannot simply reproduce the "innovative" approaches of others. On the whole, institutions have looked to promote change through encouragement, identification of "effective" practice and dissemination of approaches, and lessons learned. A significant informal driver for the spread of TEL, or particular features of TEL, is pressure from students. Changing practice is not simply a matter of information flow, in which staff, once aware of a TEL technique, will automatically embrace it—instead, these practices must be reinterpreted through the specific context of the academic. Our approach is based on incremental and cooperative activity. The emphasis is on pedagogy as the driver and departments and teachers in the lead. This is backed up with high quality support and resources along with evaluation and the sharing of good practice. Any development needs to start from the premise that change is appropriate for the department in terms of enhancing teaching and the student learning experience and in enabling staff and students to do new things or to do the same things better or more efficiently.

Generally, staff and educational development focuses not on the e-learning product but on the process, "going with the grain" of academics' own interest, in the case of research-intensive universities this being research, and working with specific educational processes or technologies that lecturers are known to be enthusiastic about (Dempster & Blackmore, 2002).

Conclusion

Understanding the impact of technology enhanced learning is wholly dependent on having clear strategic and educational goals for its development and deployment. We need to work out in advance, as far as possible, what we want to achieve before we consider what is working to most effect and what we mean by "best practice" of our TEL activities on academic thinking, practices and legacies.

For lecturers to engage in TEL, they need time for pedagogic analysis, development and evaluation—and, as identified in the Dearing report (Dearing, 1997), very little academic time is spent explicitly on such professional development activities. Development of expertise in TEL has been an increasingly offered to staff as a component of the accredited courses (some mandatory for new lecturers) now prevalent in UK universities. At Warwick, a specific postgraduate award was introduced in 2004 as a means for academic and related staff to gain recognition in this specialist area (www.go.warwick.ac.uk/wela/).

Practices change constantly, but without "joined-up" technical and pedagogic support alongside an appropriate reward scheme for TEL, this change will be undirected or even misdirected (Oliver & Dempster, 2003). Furthermore, to succeed in any attempt to identify and encourage "best practice," recognition for innovative or excellent teaching practice is critical. The visibility of promotional routes for staff who contribute to specific institutional objectives (in our case, this is towards research-led learning) offers a means of demonstrating the value that the institution places on achieving that goal.

References

Blackmore, P., & Cousin, G. (2003). Linking teaching and research through research-based learning. *Educational Developments, 4*(4), 24-27.

Boyer, E. (1998). *Reinventing undergraduate education: A blueprint for America's research universities.* US Boyer Commission. Retrieved January 6, 2008, from http://naples.cc.sunysb.edu/Pres/boyer.nsf/

Dearing, R. (1997). *Higher education in the learning society.* National Committee of Inquiry into Higher Education. London: HMSO. Retrieved January 6, 2008, from http://www.leeds.ac.uk/educol/ncihe/

Dempster, J.A. (2003). Developing and supporting research-based learning and teaching through technology. In C. Ghaoui (Ed.), *Usability evaluation of online learning programs* (pp. 128-158). Idea Group Publishing.

Dempster, J. A., & Blackmore, P. (2002). Developing research-based learning using ICT in HE cirricula: The role of research and evaluation. In R. MacDonald & J. Wisdom (Eds.), *Academic and educational development: Research, evaluation, and changing practice in HE* (pp. 129-139).

Dempster, J.A., & Deepwell, F. (2003). Experiences of national projects in embedding learning technology into institutional practices in UK higher education. In J. Seale (Ed.), *Learning technology in transition: From individual enthusiasm to institutional implementation* (pp. 45-62). Lisse: Zwets & Zeitlinger.

Fallows, S., & Bhanot, R. (2002). Educational development and ICT: An introduction. In S. Fallows & R. Bhanot (Eds.), *Educational development through information and communications technology* (pp. 1-7).

Foster, S. (2002). Implementing an institution-wide ICT strategy for university education. In S. Fallows & R. Bhanot (Eds.), *Educational development through information and communications technology* (pp. 9-16).

Hattie, J., & Marsh, H.W. (1996). The relationship between research and teaching: A meta-analysis. *Review of Educational Research, 66*(4), 507-542.

Jenkins, A. (2005). *Implementing change on your campus: Institutional strategies for integrating research and teaching.* Retrieved January 6, 2008, from http://www.uofaweb.ualberta.ca/researchandstudents//pdfs/AlanJenkins-ImplementingChangeonYourCampus.pdf

Jenkins, A. (2006). *Reshaping teaching in higher education: Linking teaching and research.* London: Routledge/Falmar.

Marton, F., & Säljö, R. (1986). A cognitive approach in learning. In F. Marton, D. Hounsell, & N. Entwistle (Eds.), *The experience of learning.*

Oliver, M. (2000). What learning technologists do. *Innovations in Education and Training International, 39*(4), 1-8.

Oliver, M., & Dempster, J.A. (2003). Embedding e-learning practices. In R. Blackwell & P. Blackmore (Eds.), *Towards strategic staff development* (pp. 142-153). Buckingham: SRHE/Open University Press.

Ramsden, P. (1992). *Learning to teach in higher education.* Routledge, London.

Roach, M., Blackmore, P., & Dempster, J.A. (2001). Supporting high level learning through research-based methods: A framework for course development. *Innovation in Education and Training International, 38*(4), 160-169.

Smith, J., & Oliver, M. (2000). Academic development: A framework for embedding learning technology. *International Journal of Academic Development,* 5(2), 129-137.

Sommerlad, E., Pettigew, M., Ramsden, C., & Stern, E. (1999). *Synthesis of TLTP annual reports.* Unpublished report, Tavistock Institute, London.

Taylor, P.G. (1998). Institutional change in uncertain times: Lone ranging is not enough. *Studies in Higher Education, 23*(3), 269-279.

TELRI Project transferability work (2002). Retrieved January 6, 2008, from www. telri.ac.uk/Transfer/

University of Edinburgh. (1999). *Use of TLTP Materials in UK Higher Education: A HEFCE Commissioned Study.* University of Edinburgh. Retrieved January 6, 2008, from http://www.hefce.ac.uk/pubs/hefce/1999/99_39.htm

Chapter VIII

A Framework for Building Emotional-Motivational Agents as Intelligent Tutoring Entities

Bogdan-Florin Marin, University Of Duisburg-Essen, Germany

Axel Hunger, University Of Duisburg-Essen, Germany

Inside Chapter

This chapter presents our efforts to integrate role theory and agent technology in order to support collaborative work/learning processes between users spatially distributed within a synchronous collaborative virtual environment. Our work aims to overcome a major inconvenience in distance education systems: tutors' difficulties when following up a distance collaborative learning process and in particular those students who cannot keep up progress with their team-mates. Our approach embraces the learning paradigms mentioned above and the work on pedagogical and intelligent agents as a mechanism for modelling and analyzing student-tutor interactions.

Introduction

Several studies (Glaser, Chi, & Farr, 1988) have established that knowledge needs to be connected and organized in important concepts and this structure should allow transfer to other contexts. It was also shown that the learning process improves when the students are in charge with their own learning, develop meta-cognitive strategies to assess what they know, and acquire more knowledge if necessary. In other words, the learning process must help students build knowledge from existing knowledge (constructivist learning), guide students to discover learning opportunities while problem solving (explorative learning), and help students to define learning goals and monitor their progress in achieving them (metacognitive strategies).

Applying these theories to distance education systems can lead us to a constructivist learning environment which encourages students to be more proactive in determining learning paths and synthesizing information from multiple sources. Hence, learners should not be constrained to a predefined learning path (Kinshuk & Ashok, 1997). This requires not only adequate tools but also the environment to allow meaningful interaction between the student and the learning system. According to Sims, meaningful interaction is not merely pacing back and forth in a linear manner along prescribed paths but involves engaging the student with the learning content in a proactive manner.

Current distance and open learning devices attempt to mitigate the difficulties encountered by learners when they follow a distance course. Then it is necessary to take account of these difficulties when distance learning is set up, avoiding insulation and a loss of motivation by learners that are the cause of many giving up (Rene-Boullier, 2003). Keeping this in mind, an interesting question arises from a system design and implementation viewpoint: "How do we design a truly interactive environment based on the learning paradigms presented above?" By truly interactive environments, one can understand an environment which keeps the learner(s) motivated and interacts with them.

This chapter presents our efforts to integrate role theory and agent technology in order to support collaborative work/learning processes between users spatially distributed within a synchronous collaborative virtual environment. Our work aims to overcome a major inconvenience in distance education systems: tutors' difficulties when following up a distance collaborative learning process and in particular those students who cannot keep up progress with their team-mates. Our approach embraces the learning paradigms mentioned and the work on pedagogical and intelligent agents as a mechanism for modelling and analyzing student-tutor interactions. Our motivation comes from the fact that German students are required to spend at least one semester abroad. With the usage of the new media and communication technologies, it should be easier for foreign students to follow the studies in Germany. Further, it can provide to German students the opportunity to take part in a Software-Engineering Course, which is held at their home location during their abroad period of study, but also have the chance of getting knowledge in systems known as CSCW environments.

Why Agents as Tutoring Knowledge Entities?

The application of intelligent agents in the educational sector comes about mainly in the form of personal assistants, user guides, alternative help systems, dynamic distributed system architectures, human-system mediators, and others.

The choice of intelligent pedagogical agents is based on online students' need for good support in distributed collaborative learning environments. The role these agents have to play is new, and they have to deal with three simultaneous dimensions:

1.   The technical (how to work with- and use the environment's available tools)

2.   The pedagogical (how to construct their own representation about a given domain and use a graphic environment to represent it)

3.   The strategic (how to use and develop their own social competences to achieve their goals in the collaborative learning scenario)

Educators responsible for following up details from all three dimensions would not be able to pay sufficient attention to the aim of the learning process. Intelligent agents can monitor students' steps and, according to the knowledge models they have, inform students about procedures the students are not yet used to.

As a result of all of the changes that have taken place in the educational system, one now sees the increasing emergence of complex and dynamic educational infrastructure that needs to be efficiently managed. Corroborating this, new (types of) educational mechanisms and services need to be developed and supplied. In particular, these services need to satisfy a series of requirements such as personalization, adaptation, support for user mobility, and support for users while they are dealing with new technologies, among others. Agents emerge to provide solutions for these require-ments in a way that is more efficient when compared to other existing technologies (Aroyo & Kommers, 1999).

According to Aroyo and Kommers (1999), agents can influence different aspects in educational systems. They supply new educational paradigms, support theories, and can be very helpful both for learners and for teachers in the task of computer-aided learning.

Lees and Ye (2001) believe that the application of the agent paradigm to CSCW potentially can exchange information more fluid among the participants of groupware systems (as decision-making systems), help in control of the process flows, and also supply groupware interfaces. These ideas also are applicable to other domains, such as is the case of interactive learning.

According to Kay (2001), in the first computer-assisted teaching environments the idea was to build "teachers" who could transmit knowledge to the learners. Currently, these types of environments are more geared up for exploration on the part of the learners, designing, building, and using adaptive systems as tools. These environments also are being built to give greater responsibility to the learners regarding aspects of the learning process, and especially regarding control of its model, which is the central aspect in the adaptability of the tools.

For McCalla, Vassileva, Greer, and Bull (2000), learner models may have a variety of purposes depending upon the type of knowledge that needs to be stored and processed. For them, the computation of all of the learner (sub-) models of an environment can be computationally expensive and not always necessary. In the work cited four purposes are presented for a model: reflection, validation, matchmakers, and negotiation.

For Kay (2001), there are several problems from the learners' point of view. One is the increase in the power of choice and control over the model. This could increase the learners' workloads or even turn into a distraction. In this case, the learners should take advantage of the moments such as the end of a course or a topic to evaluate and reflect upon their participation and the learning process. Another potential problem is incorrect data being supplied by the learners. The solution adopted in this work for that problem was to store the type of information learners are providing and the type the environment extracts.

In their work Lester, Converse, Kahler, Barlow, Stone, and Bhogal (1997) provides the result of his investigation on the impact of animated agents along the dimensions of motivations and helpfulness in an interactive learning environment. They coin the notion of "persona effect" as "the presence of a life-like character in an interactive learning environment—even one that is not expressive—can have a strong positive effect on student's perception of their learning experiences" (Lester et al., 1997, pp. 359-366)

Motivation in Pedagogical Agents

The *Motivational Strategy* models sets of behaviour patterns that may indicate student's lack of motivation, to allow actions to keep motivation according to the expert recommendations. The expression "strategy" refers to a set of rules to orient the tutor in the decision taking process. The Emotional Strategy orients the tutoring system on identifying which primary variables are related to which behaviours in order to assemble the Behavioural Structures. The tutoring system also models the Temperament Structure based on these strategies and on the student's performance information. In our case, we choose three strategies based on the progress of the student.

1. Learning by Doing. In this strategy the tutor is very active. Within the context of the scenario, it coaches the student step-by-step to perform the appropriate activity. At each step, the student can inquire about the purpose of the actions and activities performed. The tutor uses the structure of the activity trees to provide explanations (see Figure 1).

The tutorial goals (activities) in Figure 6 give rise to a contextualized dialogue in the following ways:

1. In turn (1) of the dialogue, it is the tutor's first mention of this problem, so the *situate_problem_context* activity is added to the activity tree, and the tutor describes the type of problem while highlighting its location in the ship display (regions are colored according to the type of crisis, e.g., red for fire, grey for smoke).
2. In turn (2) of the dialogue, the tutor tells the student why it chose to review this sequence so that the student will understand the tutor's subsequent turns. This corresponds to the activity *explain_review_sequence.*

Figure 1. Sample activity tree

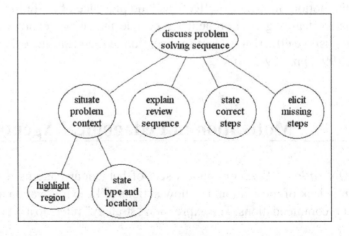

3. In turn (3) of the dialogue, the tutor contextualizes the problem by reminding the student what they did (they sent repair 3 to set fire boundaries). This corresponds to the activity *state_correct_steps.*

4. Also in turn (3), the tutor asks the student what step of the sequence they omitted. Since the student does not provide the information the tutor is looking for (in turn (4)), the tutor provides further information about the context (turn (5)), and re-asks the question (turn (7)). This interaction is specified in the decomposition of the *elicit_missing_steps* activity (not shown in Figure 6).

Modelling Pedagogical Agent's Roles

We integrated animated-agents in Passenger (see Figure1) in order to overcome the lack of tutor like also tutor's inability to follow-up the learning process. We consider agents in a virtual society of learners as entities that occupy a social position and perform several roles.

Roles have been introduced in multi-agent systems(MAS) community as a way to coordinate the behaviour of individual agents by means of a normative system or an organization. According to Cabri, Ferrari, and Leonardi (2004) a role "is a set of capabilities/knowledge and expected behavior which can be assumed, used and released, accordingly to a set of starting-requirements." The above requirements are needed to assume the role and must be matched by current capabilities of the agent. The capabilities/knowledge added by the role improve the agent ones (intended before the assumption), in the case allowing it to assume other roles. Finally the expected behavior represents a set of duties that the agent playing the role has to take into account and that other agents (playing other roles) can rely on during interactions.

We view agents in a virtual society of learners as entities that occupy a social position and perform several roles. Giddens (1997) defines social position within a group as the social identity an individual has in a given group or society. Biddle and Thomas (1979) define roles as those behaviours, characteristic of one or more persons in a context. In our case, a role specifies a characteristics pattern of behaviour for the interactions of the agent so that the agent which plays that role behaves in a specific way under certain situations involving other learner(s) or agents.

Figure 2 shows the Role class written in BNF specification. Role ID is used to distinguish a role from other roles. A skill can be defined as the ability to carry out a task at a predefined level of competence. In our concept Skills of a role describe the properties (or the abilities) that the agent will need to possess in order to perform successfully the role. Skills should be linked together with roles: if an agent

Figure 2. BNF specification of role class

```
<Role >::= "ROLE"
      <Role ID>
      <Skills>
      <Roleset>
   <Prerequisites>
  <Responsibilities>
      "END ROLE"
```

knows what role it has to play then it also knows the skill(s) required to successfully accomplish that role. As far as the procedures (the agent is developed in Borland Delphi, and a class in Delphi has procedures similar with the methods from a Java class) of the Role class, yhere are a group of procedures which associate Role class with skill class:

- *TAddSkill()*: This procedure is used to bind a particular role with a particular skill
- *TRemoveSkill()*: Destroys the link created by TAddSkill
- *TGetSkill()*: Returns all skills relevant to the role under consideration.

Roleset refers to a set of roles that agent interacts with given this role. Prerequisites of the role refer to the credentials an agent needs in order to occupy the social position under that role. Responsibilities of a role refer to the duties of an agent undertaken within the context of the actual role.

To exemplify the concept in an educational environment the tutor-agent should have the following skills (capabilities) within a group of students:

- **Interrogator:** Poses questions and the students of a collaborative group then provide answers. The questions should provide help for the students to reach a common learning goal.
- **Reviewer:** Analyzes the students' answers, including whether it is correct or not.
- **Monitor:** Records the answers from all the students and the communications among students during the collaborative learning process.

- **Instructor:** Gives individualized instructions and helps those students who cannot keep up with the progress of their group-mates.
- **Group manager:** Has the ability to control the coherence of the group.

Let's take for example the *Reviewer* role. The skills required for this role are: agent should be able to understand the student's answer (natural language processing), then it should analyze whether it is correct or not. An important skill of this role can be considered the ability to display emotions and gestures (animations) to students' answers. Our prototype responds to the students' answers (also to questions) by synthetic speech, facial display, and gestures.

The *Roleset* for this role can be considered as the set composed from the roles ={*Interrogator, Instructor*}. Of course the *Prerequisites* for this role can be simply deducted: if the students answer to the question posed by agent (during the *Interrogator* role—here is also the link between these 2 roles: *Interrogator* and *Reviewer*).

Further, we introduce a new modelling paradigm: the Agent-Object-Relationship (AOR) metamodel (Wagner, 2003) for modelling agent-oriented information systems. In AOR modelling, an entity is either an event, an action, a claim, a commitment, an agent, or an object. Only agents can communicate, perceive, act, make commitments, and satisfy claims. Objects do not communicate, cannot perceive anything, are unable to act, and do not have any commitments or claims. Being entities, agents and objects of the same type share a number of attributes representing their properties or characteristics. So, in AOR modelling, there are the same notions as in entry relation (ER) modelling (such as entity types, relationship types, attributes, etc.).

For showing how to model pedagogical agents with AORML, let us model the role of *Instructor*, assuming the following scenario: during a learning session a student needs help on a certain topic. There are two possibilities:

Figure 3. The core elements of AOR modelling

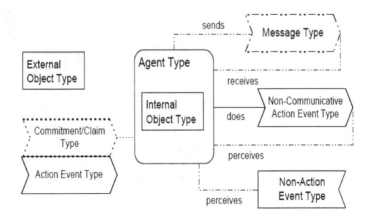

a.   As shown in Figure 4, the pedagogical agent can decide using the tutoring module about the way of providing help or hints to the student

b.   The pedagogical agent does not posses enough knowledge to answer the question, therefore it "claims" an answer to the mobile agent. Mobile agent is responsible for pedagogical-agent's *"knowledge needs[1]"* when it needs to communicate with other tutors (humans or agents) in order to receive help for accomplishing its task. In our case we assume that the mobile agent can find another "Peer" Tutoring Agent which can provide help.

One can easily notice that our Agent based learning systems needs to incorporate two more agent types:

1.   **The *mobile agent* type:** Responsible for providing help for pedagogical agents' "knowledge needs"

2.   **The *coordinator agent* type:** It exists on the server-side, responsible for coordinating all pedagogical (there can be more than two pedagogical agents due to the simultaneous learning sessions) and mobile agents working in reasonable orders in case of chaos. Its work is to receive incoming mobile agents, supply to mobile agents the host list in the network, and send the mobile agents to their destinations. Coordinator agents are always watching the status of the whole network, and they can offer the best path for mobile agents' migrating. Also, it is responsible for starting a new tutor-agent for every new session started.

Figure 4. Scenario solution A

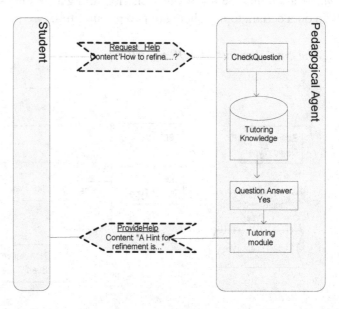

Figure 5. Scenario solution B

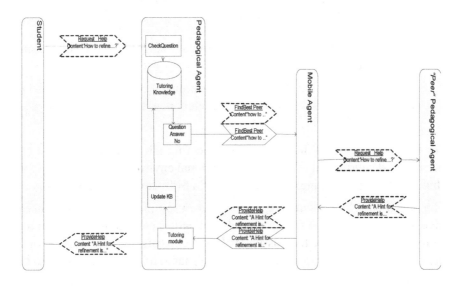

Nevertheless, this work does not focus on modelling these two types of agents. A more detailed description of these two agents can be found in work of Marin, Hunger, Werner, Meila, and Schuetz (2004a, 2005)

The Passenger Learning Environment

Motivation is one of the key terms used in education. The emotional state of the student contributes a lot to whether a student is motivated or challenged, which are key conditions for certain actions. Curiosity and puzzlement may lead to investigate problems. But also frustration may lead to action, although it is a more negative affect. The tutor can choose to consider taking certain actions to bring about a change in the emotional state. Lepper (1993) identified four main goals in motivating learners: challenge, confidence, curiosity, and control.

Modern Software Engineering in any case signifies teamwork. The worldwide extension of the data networks and continuing globalization add another component software engineering: the development of worldwide distributed teams. The use of this forward-looking form in university education could make a special contribution to the way in which students work, and are worked with, in the future (Hunger, Werner, & Schwarz, 1999).

When comparing the professional field of Software Engineering with the Software Engineering education the following aspects have to be taken into consideration:

1. Working in a team, dividing up the given task into subtasks, discussing intermediate results.

2. The usage of the new media and communication technologies also requires that students should work in a completely new scenario.

For the special case of the software engineering lab regarded here, the emphasis lies on the development of a proper educational environment for the support of the students during a meeting in the context of a Software Engineering lab.

The specified requirements for a groupware used in a Software-Engineering lab give a direction how the function- and application-classes of the Passenger-Client were defined. Therefore the Passenger-Client consists of a communication component, a cooperation component, and several shared tools and resources to carry out Software Engineering tasks.

In local laboratory experiments, students usually work together in groups of two or more. This learning paradigm is often called collaborative learning. One solution for this problem is usage of virtual collaborative environments, which bring together users who are geographically distributed but connected via a network. Therefore the students can be trained using the virtual lab concept to work in spatially distributed teams.

Within the past years a synchronous groupware named PASSENGER was developed for this purpose at our university. This groupware (see Figure 6) is composed of modules: the communication component which contains video screens of each participant and a cooperation component which allows students to interact together on a common artifact. The participants can be three students and one tutor. Three essential differences of this groupware compared to publicly available solutions can be specified:

1. **Passenger floor-control (PFC)** (Dommel & Garcia-Luna Aceves, 1994): the main advantage of the developed Floor-Control protocol is to guarantee a defined fairness and to prevent the mutual exclusion and blocking. Thereby, the fairness definition is based on a theoretically equal distribution of the Floor-holding concerning the occurrence. In particular, the Passenger Floor Control does not limit Floor-holding duration.

2. **A user interface designed to support group awareness** (Dourish & Bellotti, 1992): The design is based on common requirements and the special requirements from the analyzed group behavior. For all design decisions, thought has been given to the requirement for measures to increase the group-awareness.

Therefore a concept for the positioning and resizing of the communication windows was developed and implemented. Especially, solutions for the Floor-Control and the group-awareness were developed during the design of the user interface. Group awareness functions were implemented by means of providing all needed information for a late coming participant to discover the actual conference state. This is implemented by highlighting the video screen of the person who has access to the shared resources.

3. The whiteboard concept materialized in tools to carry out software engineering tasks. The implemented PASSENGER-CASE tool for the software design features its concept for realizing the private and public work area and its process specified support for software engineering. The separated realization between the work and the display area enables the Floor-Holder first to simultaneously access the last two design documents. Due to this fact, he is simply able to compare the two schemes by switching between the work and display window. The rest of the participants have the same possibility under the condition that they transfuse the content of the display field of their work area.

Each member has the same view of the public window according to the What You See Is What I See (WYSIWIS) principle, but only one of them—the actual floor holder—can alter the document at a certain time. Each member is also equipped with a private working window to try out own ideas and to work simultaneous on an individual solution. A more detailed description of the Passenger environment can be found in work of Marin, Hunger, Werner, Meila, and Schuetz (2004b).

Figure 6. Passenger agent tutor

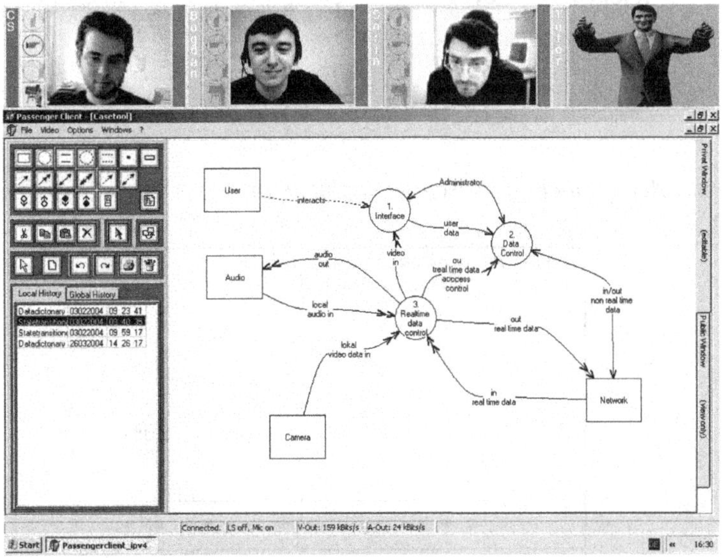

The Software-Engineering lab at the University of Duisburg Essen (UDE) is conducted as a project setup of student teams, each consisting of four participants: 3 students and one tutor, where the same tutor can be in several virtual teams. That can cause problems in terms of availability if the virtual teams meet at the same time but also if the teams meet at times outside the tutor consultation hours. In the context of distributed collaborative learning, it is usually difficult for students to be aware of others' activities and for instructors to overview the process and regulate the collaboration. In order to facilitate collaborative learning, intelligent agents were developed to support the awareness and regulation of the collaboration. The next sections will highlight our prototype's results from practice.

Theory in Practice

Our agent is an animated cartoon with human like gestures. Our agent responds to the students' questions/actions by synthetic speech, facial display, and gestures. We choose to design and implement our own animated agent instead of using Microsoft Agent to ensure Passenger platform independence and extensibility. We choose Borland Delphi environment to realize the Passenger environment and also for our prototype implementation. The evaluation study for this prototype concerns two levels:

- **Usefulness level:** The usefulness of the agent facilities within Passenger groupware needs to be evaluated by human teachers.

- **User friendliness level**: This level highlights how the agent was accepted by students.

Figure 7. Acceptance of passenger-agent-tutor

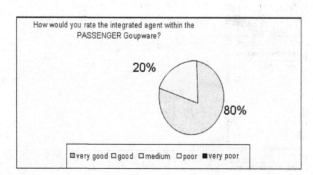

Several experiments took place in the local area network of our institute. Only the second part of the evaluation study was conducted among 25 first year Master students.

Each session consisted of three students and one tutor (human or agent). The student experienced the traditional lab with the human tutor and also with the agent feature of the Passenger system. After these experiments, students had to answer to questionnaires files. A sample of questions concerning the second level that were asked to the students is the following:

1. Do you consider the application attractive? If yes, what did you like about it?

2. Do you think that the "agent" features prevented you from understanding the educational process better?

3. Do you prefer the agent tutor instead of the human tutor? Please justify your answer.

Based on the above mentioned questionnaires, several evaluations could be made. Some results concerning the agent integration and acceptance are shown in the Figure7. Although the number of participants in the evaluation test was rather small for a quantitative evaluation, the trends seem to be unambiguous.

Conclusion

Within this chapter, it was shown how to corroborate role theory with agent technology in a synchronous virtual environment in order to overcome several major inconveniences of distance education systems like: awareness, communication, or tutors' inability to follow-up a learning process. The main contribution of this work in the "Agents in CSCW" research field is conception of a Distance Learning System in which humans and artificial agents can collaborate to achieve a common learning goal.

However, it would be a mistake to conclude that current and forthcoming developments can make intelligent tutor-agents to replace human teachers. Given the fact that learning is a complex cognitive activity, learners cannot rely solely on machines when capturing and mastering knowledge of a certain domain.

References

Aroyo, L., & Kommers, P. (1999). Preface—intelligent agents for educational computer-aided systems. *Journal of Interactive Learning Research, 10*(3/4), 235-242.

Biddle, B.J., & Thomas, E.J. (1979). *Role theory: Concepts and research.* New York: K.E. Kriger Publishing Company

Cabri, G., Ferrari, L., & Leonardi, L. (2004). Rethinking agent roles: Extending the role definition in the BRAIN framework. In *Proceedings of IEEE Int. Conf. on Systems, Man and Cybernetics,* Hague, The Netherlands.

Dommel, H.-P., & Garcia-Luna Aceves, J.J. (1994, March-April). Group coordination support for synchronous Internet collaboration. IEEE Internet Computing, 74-80.

Dourish, P., & Bellotti, V. (1992). Awareness and coordination in shared workspaces. In J. Turnier & R. Kraut (Eds.), *Proceedings of CSCW'92- Sharing Perspectives* (pp. 107-114). Toronto: ACM Press.

Giddens, A. (1997). *Sociology* (3rd ed.). London: Polity Pressedition (pp. 585). ISBN: 0745618030.

Glaser, R., Chi, M.T.H., & Farr, M.J. (1988). *The nature of expertise.* Hillsdale, NJ: Erlbaum.

Hunger, A., Werner, S., & Schwarz, F. (1999). Measures to improve the globalization in higher education. In Proceedings of ICCE 99, Chiba, Japan, II (pp. 803-804).

Kay, J. (2001). *Learner control. User modeling and user adapted interaction.* The Netherlands: Kluwer Academic Publishers (pp. 11, 111-127).

Kinshuk, P., & Ashok, P. (1997). A conceptual framework for Internet-based intelligent tutoring systems. *Knowledge Transfer, 2,* 117-124.

Lepper, M.R. (1993). *Motivational techniques of human-tutors: Lessons for the design of computer-based tutors.* Lawrence Elbaum Associates.

Lees, B., & Ye, Y. (2001). Preface. In *Proceedings of ASCW01—Workshop of Agent-Supported Cooperative Work. 5th International Conference on Autonomous Agents.*

Lester, J.C., Converse, S.A., Kahler, S.E., Barlow, S.T., Stone, B.A., & Bhogal, R.S. (1997). The persona effect: Affective impact of animated pedagogical agents. In *Proceedings of CHI-97* (pp. 359-366).

Marin, B., Hunger, A., Werner, A., Meila, S., & Schuetz, C. (2004a). A synchronous groupware tool to conduct a spatially distributed collaborative learning process. In Proceedings of the 5th IEEE International Conference on Information Technology Based Higher Education and Training (pp. 269-274).

Marin, B., Hunger, A., Werner, A., Meila, S., & Schuetz, C. (2004b). An intelligent tutor-agent to support collaborative learning within a virtual environment. In *Proceedings of IEEE Int. Conf. on Systems, Man and Cybernetics*, Hague, The Netherlands.

Marin, B., Hunger, A., Werner, A., Meila, S., & Schuetz, C. (2005). Roles of an intelligent tutor-agent within a virtual society. In *Proceedings of IEEE International Symposium on Applications and the Internet.*

McCalla, G., Vassileva, J., Greer, J., & Bull, S. (2000). Active learner modeling. In Proceedings of ITS'2000. Springer (LNCS 1839, pp. 53-62).

Rene-Boullier, L. (2003). Pedagogical coordination: A global vision of the personalized accompaniment of DESS DICIT. Revue Sticef, 10.

Sims, R. Interactivity: A forgotten art? Retrieved January 7, 2008, from http://intro.base.org/docs/interact/

Wagner, G. (2003). The agent-object-relationship metamodel: Towards a unified view of state and behavior. *Information Systems, 28*(5).

Further Reading

Borghoff, U.M., & Schlichter, J.H. (2000). *Computer supported cooperative work: Introduction to distributed applications.* Springer-Verlag.

Guizzardi, R.S.S., Wagner, G., & Aroyo, L. (2002). Agent-oriented modeling for collaborative learning environments: A peer-to-peer helpdesk case study. In *XIII-Brazilian Symposium on Computers in Education.*

Marin, B., Hunger, A., & Werner, S. (2006). A framework for designing emotional agents as tutoring entities. In Pivec, M. (Ed.), *Affective and emotional aspects of human-computer interaction: Game-based and innovative learning approaches (vol. 1). The Future of Learning*, 266-285. IOS Press: The Netherlands.

Marin, B., Hunger, A., & Werner, S. (2006). Corroborating emotion theory with role theory and agent technology: A framework for designing emotional agents as tutoring entities. *Journal of Networks, 4.*

Weiss, G. (2000). *Multiagent systems: A modern approach to distributed artificial intelligence.* MIT Press.

Useful URLs

Sims, R. *Interactivity: A forgotten art?:* http://intro.base.org/docs/interact/

Agent-Oriented Relationship Modeling Language: http://www.informatik.tu-cottbus.de/~gwagner/AORML/

Foundation for Physical Intelligent Agents: http://www.fipa.org/

Odell, J. Van Dyke Parunak, H., & Bauer, B. (2001). Representing agent interaction protocols in UML. In P. Ciancarini & M. Wooldridge (Eds.), Agent-oriented software engineering (pp. 121-140). Berlin: Springer. Retrieved January 7, 2008, from http://www.fipa.org/docs/input/f-in-00077/

Intelligent Tutoring Systems: http://www.aaai.org/AITopics/html/tutor.html,

ABITS: An Agent Based Intelligent Tutoring System for Distance Learning: http://www.capuano.biz/Papers/ITS_2000.pdf

An Agent Based Intelligent Tutoring System for Enhancing E-Learning/ E-Teaching: http://www.itdl.org/Journal/Nov_05/article02.htm

International Forum of Educational technology and Society (IFETS): http://ifets.ieee.org/

Endnote

[1]   Here knowledge need denote the fact that pedagogical agent lacks the proper knowledge to fulfill successfully its tutoring goal.

Chapter IX

Pedagogical Uses of Multimedia Annotators and Players

Tetyana Sydorenko, Michigan State University, USA

Tom Myers, CTO, N-topus Software, USA

Alexander Nakhimovsky, Colgate University, USA

Inside Chapter

Multimedia materials form an increasingly important part of technology-enhanced learning (TEL). We present two kinds of related computer programs, multimedia annotators and multimedia players, which provide greatly improved control over how the user navigates, searches, and displays multimedia materials. Our main focus will be on MannX (Multimedia Annotator—XML). The objective of this chapter is to familiarize the reader with multimedia annotators and players, explain why and how they should be used for learning and especially for foreign language learning, present the best practices for their design, and outline the future directions for developing this new technology and its pedagogical applications. We believe that for many fields of study annotated and searchable multimedia materials are the best vehicle for instruction and learning.

Introduction

Multimedia materials form an increasingly important part of technology-enhanced learning (TEL). We present two kinds of related computer programs that provide greatly improved control over how the user navigates, searches and displays multimedia materials. The programs are recent and do not yet have standard names, but at least two groups of developers (Nakhimovsky & Myers, 2003; University of Wisconsin Language Institute, 2003) call them *multimedia annotator* and *multimedia player*. These programs conform to the best practices of TEL:

- They can be accessed online, which assures "Learning for anyone, at any time, at any place."

- These programs are user-centered because they let the user take control of the program (and therefore of acquiring knowledge) and accommodate various learning styles.

- Such programs allow for the inclusion of a variety of authentic materials in various media.

- They motivate the learners by using authentic material and by providing a non-stressful learning environment.

According to the constructivist approach to learning, the above concepts are very important in education. Let's look at some examples of these concepts. We will start

Figure 1. Chapter key issues: Multimedia annotators and players for learning

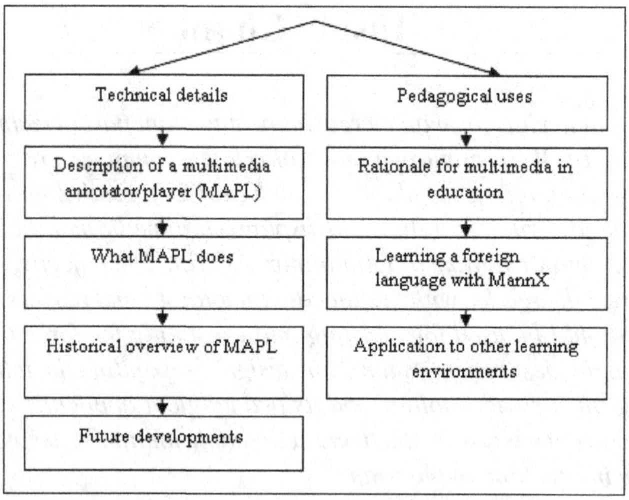

with the user control because the point about online learning probably does not need to be explained. Imagine that you are at a conference presentation. You know the topic of the presentation well and wish you could skip to the main points. However, at a live presentation this is not possible. On the other hand, if this presentation was video recorded and annotated with text, you would be able to search for a keyword, such as *findings* or *results* and skip to the part of the video where this keyword is located. In this case, you would have control over the information that you wished to access. People have different experiences and background knowledge, and that is why it is best to allow the learners to choose what they want or need to learn.

The next example is on the variability in learning styles. This time imagine that you are taking a tennis class, and you have never seen a tennis match before. The first day of class the instructor gives you a sheet with the tennis terms and the rules of the game, and the next class the instructor shows you how to play. However, you are a visual rather than a verbal learner, so you do not get much out of the sheet with the terms and rules; instead, you wish you were shown video clips illustrating each of the rules. For other people, however, a well-organized printed handout worked very well, and they could ignore the video. It is known that people have various learning styles; for this reason, good multimedia programs allow the learners to choose the order and the type of the activities.

Finally, a third example of a concept concerning a multimedia program design is about authentic material. Imagine that you are taking a class on child language development. You are required to read chapters in your textbook on the research that has been done in this area, but you cannot really witness the process of child language development because you do not know anybody who has small children. So the only sources of knowledge for you are the teacher and the textbook. However, you would probably be also interested in observing the children developing their language ability so that you could draw your own conclusions. That is, you would want to gain some knowledge from authentic, real life situations. Good multimedia programs do contain authentic material to which the learner might not have had access otherwise.

It seems that learners would be more motivated if they could control what they are learning, when, and how, and if they were exposed to experiences resembling real life; in fact, the research on multimedia programs and motivation has found exactly this.

We will proceed with our chapter in the following order. First, we will provide the rationale for multimedia in education, particularly in language learning. Next, we will discuss multimedia annotators and players with the main focus on MannX (Multimedia Annotator—XML), the annotator and player developed by N-Topus Software and extensively tested in the classroom, at Colgate, and other places. We will also provide an overview of several other available programs. We then discuss new pedagogical opportunities made possible by multimedia annotators and players, as well as their future technological development. We will primarily apply these pedagogical opportunities to foreign language learning, although other learning contexts can also benefit from multimedia annotators.

Background: Multimedia Annotator/Player

Rationale for Multimedia

Multimedia is widely used today in education: it simultaneously presents audiovisual information and text; it carries more information than other instructional materials; it is perceived as "cool" by students. Of all disciplines, language learning can benefit most obviously from using multimedia, for these reasons:

Table 1. Literature review of pedagogical reasons for multimedia

Issue	Reference	Main contribution
Technology and perception of teachers	Schrodt & Turman (2005)	Students find teachers who use technology to be more reliable and knowledgeable than those teachers who do not.
The role of input in a foreign language	Gass (2003)	Discusses the historical and current views on input.
	Blake (2001)	Technology, as opposed to traditional materials, might speed up learning by providing more input.
Learning styles	Paivio (1986)	According to dual coding theory, visual, and verbal input is processed differently.
	Mayer (2001)	Provides a review of well-designed multimedia materials tailored to different learners.
	Levine (2004), Luke (2006)	Emphasize the importance of learner autonomy and individual differences.
	Pujola (2002)	Investigates different learning styles when people are using a multimedia program.
Motivation	Shawback & Terhune (2002)	Multimedia programs increase learner motivation when compared with traditional materials.
	Luke (2006)	Provides an overview of studies on motivation.
Authentic input	Kramsch & Andersen (1999)	The importance of culture for language learning is emphasized.
	Weyers (1999)	Students who had authentic video input rather than traditional instruction improved significantly in foreign language comprehension and production.

- Language is primarily an oral medium.

- Facial expression, gestures, and body language are important components of oral communication.

- Language is deeply embedded in culture, and visual images, especially moving images, are incomparably more effective than text in presenting cultural detail, providing richer input in the target language.

In addition, present-day students are more used to absorbing information from the screen (TV or computer) than from a printed page, and they find teachers who use technology to be more reliable and knowledgeable than those who do not (Schrodt & Turman, 2005). Table 1 summarizes the advantages of multimedia in education in general and language learning in particular.

Multimedia provides more information than a textbook due to a much greater bandwidth. In language learning, information that is in a foreign language is called *input*. Input plays a vital role in language learning (Gass, 2003), and technology, as opposed to traditional materials, might speed up learning by providing more input (Blake, 2001). Because all resources are included in one program, learners spend more time learning new information rather than searching for it. Since input is provided in various media, multimedia programs accommodate people's different learning styles. For example, some people are visual learners, while others are verbal learners (Mayer, 2001). Learners also differ in proficiency level, prior knowledge and experience, goals, aptitude, and motivation, to name a few. Thus, many have emphasized the importance of individualized learning, as well as of learner autonomy, that is, that learners should take control of their education (Levine, 2004; Luke, 2006). For example, Pujola's (2002) software program allows learners to watch a video or read a text as many times as they want, to turn subtitles on or off, and to use a monolingual or a bilingual dictionary. Tailoring a program to individual learners is what makes a multimedia program an educational success. Such success, in a form of learners' increased motivation, is also caused by better understanding of and engagement with the material (Shawback & Terhune, 2002). The material can be understood and learned better if learners receive instant feedback (Brett, 1995), which is often not possible in a regular classroom. Engagement with the material can be induced by presenting learners with real situations that take place in the foreign culture, and learning the culture is a part of learning a language (Kramsch & Andersen, 1999). Materials that were made in the foreign culture and that have not been modified are called *authentic*. Such materials not only raise learners' interest, but also often improve their comprehension and production of a foreign language (Weyers, 1999).

Rationale for Multimedia Annotators and Players

On the other hand, multimedia presents certain technical challenges: compared to text, it is more difficult to navigate, to search, and to annotate; and it is more difficult to do a close study of a segment of video than of a paragraph of text: replaying a specific segment takes more effort than just going back to the beginning of the paragraph. Considerations of this nature led us to develop the first multimedia annotator. We wanted to replace text, consisting of words separated by spaces on a printed page, with digital video, consisting of sentences that characters exchange in a dialog. However, to be really effective, movies as language instruction texts and other real materials should be introduced early in the curriculum. The difficulty with such an early introduction is that students are not yet ready to deal with "unabridged" material created without an expressed pedagogical purpose in mind. We had to build a support system for students to handle unabridged digital video. Such a support system would include the ability to stop, pause, and rewind video or audio material, to see the transcript, to click on the word in the transcript and see its definition or translation, a corresponding picture, or a grammatical rule.

This chapter presents two computer programs that operate together to address these technological problems: multimedia annotator and multimedia player. Since they operate together and are frequently bundled in a single application, we will talk about a Media Annotator/Player, or MAPL for short. In this section, we provide technical background. The main thrust of the chapter is a specific example of MAPL called MannX (Multimedia Annotator—XML) and its pedagogical uses, primarily for language teaching.

Primary Media Players

A MAPL operates in the software context that includes a *primary media player*. By a primary media player (PMP) we mean a software library that is used by a programmer to control navigation and playback of the media at the most elementary level, in terms of individual frames or milliseconds, depending on the format of the media. (We will use the term "media point" to refer to either a specific frame or a specific millisecond, as appropriate.) In more specialized vocabulary, a PMP makes available to a programmer an "application programming interface" (API) that specifies the commands available to the programmer. A typical set of commands that would make a multimedia annotator possible would consist of:

- Start and stop playing
- Go to a specific media point
- Report the current media point

- Report the total number of media points in the media object
- Report the percentage of media object that has been already loaded
- Report the state of the media object: playing or not playing

Until quite recently, PMPs were few and limited in their capabilities. The last couple of years have seen a proliferation of them, including some open-source initiatives. Table 2 presents the most important ones, providing four important characteristics for each:

- What programming languages can the programmer use with them?
- What media formats can they handle?
- What platforms (Windows, Mac, Linux, Web browser) are they available for?
- Are they easy to install (EtI)?

Table 2. Most important PMPs and their characteristics

Name	Program. Language	EtI	Media Formats	Platform
JMF (Java Media Framework)	Java	No	QT, MPEG1,	Java (all platforms) Browser (via an applet)
QTJava	Java	No	QT, MPEG1,	Java (Win, Mac) Browser (via an applet)
QuickTime	JavaScript	Yes	QT, MPEG, AVI	All platforms Browser (via plug-in)
RealVideo	JavaScript	Yes	RealVideo	All platforms Browser (via plug-in)
SWF	ActionScript¹ JavaScript	Yes	SWF	All platforms Browser (via plug-in)
FLV	ActionScript, JavaScript	Yes	FLV	All platforms Browser (via plug-in)
Windows Media Player	VBScript (IE), JavaScript	Yes	AVI, QT	Windows, Browser
MPlayer	JavaScript	Yes on Linux	AVI, FLV, QT, OGG	All platforms
VLC	JavaScript	Yes on Linux	AVI, FLV, QT, OGG	All platforms

What is and is not easy to install can be a subject of debate in some cases, but the contrasts between the opposites (e.g., QTJava as quite complex vs. Flash as completely trivial and frequently pre-installed) is clear and very important for acceptance.

Since MannX (unlike most other annotators/players) is intended to work within a Web browser, the most important primary players for us are those that support Java and JavaScript. Using Java is less dependent on the browser but more cumbersome: a Java plug-in for the browser needs to be installed and media is displayed in a special container, such as an applet. JavaScript does not require an additional installation, but its behavior is more browser dependant; in particular, Internet Explorer (IE) usually requires a special treatment.

What Does a MAPL Do?

Given a primary media player, a media file, and a text file that needs to be time-aligned with the media, what specifically does the annotator have to do? Let us assume that the user has stopped the media at some media point M, and positioned the cursor at some text time location T, intending to make this a synchronization point: the end of the current segment and the beginning of the next one. The annotator needs to perform two operations:

- Find out the value of M from the primary media player.
- Insert markup at text location T that contains the value of M.

Some multimedia annotators can have an interval-based interface: instead of selecting the text and media points, the user selects a text segment and a time interval. Internally, the annotator will simply go through this sequence of operations twice, once for each end-point of the segment. Note that either the text segment or the time interval can be empty: we can have text corresponding to no playback, or a video segment corresponding to no text.

With markup in place, the player of multimedia annotations, in response to the user action that selects a segment to play, will perform at least these two operations:

- Scroll into view and highlight the selected text segment.
- Instruct the primary media player to play the corresponding media segment.

In addition to segment playback, multimedia players provide a variety of capabilities for navigation, search and dictionary lookup.

History and Overview of Programs

Historically, the first multimedia annotator was COMMAS (COlgate MultiMedia Annotating System), later revised as MANNA (Multimedia ANNotator Application) developed by Myers and Nakhimovsky in the mid-1990s (Nakhimovsky, 1997; Nakhimovsky & Myers, 2003; Nakhimovsky, Nakhimovsky, & Myers, 1996). These programs predate the wide spread of Java and the Web. MANNA's main characteristics are as follows:

- **Media format:** QuickTime video and audio
- **Programming language:** C++
- **Platforms:** Windows and Macintosh
- **Markup:** A proprietary data structure

By 2002, MANNA had been reworked into MannX, where X stands for XML (Nakhimovsky & Myers, 2003). At the same time, work on multimedia annotators and players began in linguistics, especially in two areas in which annotating video recordings is of primary importance: endangered languages (which need to be preserved on digital recordings) and sign languages of the deaf. By now, there are several annotators and players. They are listed in Table 3, classified by these parameters (letters in parentheses indicate abbreviations in the table).

- Does it support both Audio (A) and Video (V) or only Audio?
- What primary media player does it use? (This determines on which platforms it is available, see Table 2).
- Is the annotator a self-standing desktop program (D) or is it a browser-based application (B)?

Table 3. MAPLs in linguistics and their features

Name	FOS	Media	PMP	D/B	XML
MannX	Yes	AV	QTJava, JMF SWF	B	Yes
MmA	No	AV	SWF, FLV	B	Yes
ELAN	Yes	AV	QTJava, JMF	D	Yes
Transcriber	Yes	A	snack	D	Yes
Transana	Yes	AV	snack	D	No
SoundIndex	Yes	A	snack	D	Yes

- Does it use XML for time-alignment markup?

- What is the primary emphasis: language teaching (T) or linguistic research (R)? Within the latter, most programs are for language analysis and interlinear glossing, especially for endangered languages, but Transana addresses the needs of Qualitative Data Analysis.)

- Is it free and open-source? (FOS)

Multimedia Annotators developed for linguistic research (all except MannX and MmA in the table) usually come with sophisticated machinery for linguistic analysis. In that sense, MannX is more of a presentation tool, albeit open-ended in its possibilities. However, instead of adding more features to MannX, it is more effective to develop it further as a player while using one of the existing programs as an annotator. ELAN is a natural choice because it is Java based, open source, and under active development.

Using a Web Server

Annotators/Players that operate within a browser have the additional choice of using or not using a Web server. There is a frequent confusion here that needs to be addressed: using a Web server program does not necessarily require Internet access. The source of confusion is the ambiguity of the term "Web server": it may refer to a piece of software, a computer program that communicates with a Web browser and responds to its requests, or it may mean a piece of hardware, a computer on the Internet that runs one or several Web server programs. What is not well-known is that a Web server program can run on the same computer as the browser. There is, in fact, a reserved URL for such a Web server program: http://localhost. This URL directs the browser request to the same Web-server computer on which the browser is running.

Put differently, there are two well-known ways of opening a Web page in the browser: as a local file or as an Internet location. For instance, there is a page on the Web that shows a table of English irregular verbs, http://www2.gsu.edu/~wwwesl/egw/verbs.htm. If you copy that file to your hard drive, as, for example, (assuming you use Windows) C:\example\verbs.htm, and open it locally in the browser, it will show this URL: file:///C:/example/verbs.htm. (Or, more precisely, this is the URL the browser is supposed to show according to the URL standard, and this is what the standard-conformant Firefox browser will show. Microsoft's Internet Explorer will ignore the standard and display Microsoft's proprietary directory path, C:\example\verbs.htm).

The difference between file:///C:/example/verbs.htm and http://example/verbs.htm is the difference in *the protocol of communication*. In the first URL, the browser communicates with the operating system on your computer, asking it to open a local file. In the second URL, the browser communicates with a Web server program on a different computer, using the HTTP protocol, asking it to send a page over the Internet, also using the HTTP protocol. It is the difference in protocol that is crucial here, not the fact that in the first instance the files are on the same computer and in the second instance on two different computers. If your computer runs a Web server program, you can open the file on your computer using the HTTP protocol. For instance, if you are on Windows, the IIS Web server is running, and the "Web root" is C:\inetpub\wwwroot, then you can put the same verb.htm file into the directory C:\inetpub\wwwroot\example and open it with this URL: http://localhost/example/verbs.htm.

Why would one want to run a Web server locally, on the same computer? There are two good reasons for doing so. First, there is an enormous amount of software that supports every stage of the HTTP protocol, especially the stage between the moment when the server receives a URL request from the browser and the moment when the server sends back the page to be displayed (or some other data, such as a zip archive to be saved on disk). If you use the HTTP protocol locally, all these software tools are available to you, and you can develop and/or use a *Web application* without leaving your computer, and without depending on an Internet connection. Second, a Web application so developed is usually Internet-ready: if you copy your Web application directory to a remote server on the Internet, it should work exactly as it does on your local Web server. (Of course, the bandwidth will be more restricted, so if you use huge image files or stream videos, the application may break.)

Finally, there is one more rather technical reason that applies if your application is mostly written in JavaScript. JavaScript is an excellent language that is available in every browser. However, it has severe security limitations; in particular, it cannot modify files on your computer. In fact, it cannot even open most files on your computer, other than files with JavaScript code. On the other hand, JavaScript within an HTML file communicates easily with the Web server from which that HTML file was sent via the HTTP protocol. So, if you run a Web server locally, you can always make JavaScript requests to it to open, modify and save a local file, thus overcoming the security constraints on JavaScript. This is how the Web server is used in MannX.

MANNX and its Pedagogical Uses

In the fall of 1994, the Russian Department at Colgate taught a course whose "reading matter" consisted of digitized excerpts from a Russian movie and the text of that movie, supplemented by an on-screen dictionary and commentary. Students prepared on their own in the lab. They worked through the segments of the movie, looping through a segment as many times as necessary, inspecting the corresponding text, and working with that text using available help with comprehension. The students came to class knowing the excerpt inside-out and ready to discuss it. The course was both a popular and pedagogical success. We think this success can be attributed to the fact that students were learning from an authentic video, which they could understand because there were enough tools available. These tools can be seen in Figure 1, which shows a MannX lecture on the HTTP protocol (in English) for speakers of Pashto. In the top left frame, there is a video clip, playback controls, and text corresponding to a segment of the video. In the bottom left frame, there is a transcript, the highlighted part of which corresponds to the current segment of the video. In the top right frame, there is a monolingual dictionary, although it can also be bilingual for foreign language learning. In the bottom right frame, some terms or concepts from the video are explained in details. In the Russian course created with MannX, clicking the button *On* enables the grammar manual which appears instead of the two frames on the right. The users can enable or disable each frame by dragging the inside border of the frames.

The advantage of MAPL over other materials is that all support features are available at the same time. However, when students are watching a video on a DVD or a VHS tape, they can at best get either the subtitles in the same language as the audio, which is equivalent to a transcript, or subtitles in the students' first language, which

Figure 2. Screenshot of MannX interface

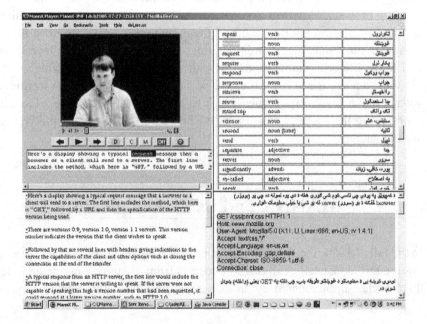

is equivalent to a translation. Of course, the teacher can provide the transcripts or the translations and the explanations for each segment of the video on paper. The paper transcripts and translations can also be matched with the segments of the DVD, but this will not be as convenient because the segments in a commercially made DVD are quite long and cannot be modified by the teacher. In MAPL, the teacher or creator of the lesson can divide the video into different types of segments. One lesson can be created for beginners in which the segments are very short (for example, 5-10 words), while another lesson can be created for more advanced learners with the video divided into longer segments, for example, two to three sentences. The teacher can even annotate separate words rather than fragments of the video. Moreover, students do not have to work with each segment in order: they can skip freely from one segment to another. When working with each segment, the students can try to understand it using all available tools, or they can practice their pronunciation by repeating the phrases over and over. With a DVD or a regular media player, it is not easy to play exactly the same short segment of the video over and over.

Even though in MannX students can access all tools at once, they should not necessarily do so. Students should try to do their best with the least help, first replaying the video several times and trying to understand as much as they can. After that, they can enable the transcript and attempt to understand more of the video. They can also do exercises to help them figure out the gist and the details. Only after these activities, the students should enable translations of words and phrases and their explanations. The harder the students try, the more they will remember later. The reason for this is that students notice more when they try to figure out the meaning rather than look up the words in the dictionary. Noticing has been claimed to be one of the vital components of successful language learning (Schmidt, 1990, 2001). Of course, the teacher can decide in which order these tools should be used. Alternatively, teachers can let the students decide which tools they want to use based on their learning styles. For example, some people learn words better if they see translations, while others do better if they see corresponding pictures or video clips (Chun & Payne, 2004). The main point is that the tools can be enabled or disabled for each learner.

Once the students have worked with the video, they get to check their understanding of it through exercises and feedback. One group of exercises can be used to check the understanding of the plot. For example, the question can be "Why does Воробьянинов visit his dying grandmother?" The students will first need to choose the answer, after which they will receive some feedback. However, the feedback would not contain the correct answer but would rather be a corresponding segment (or several segments) of the video, with or without transcription, that can help with the answer. After that, the students can be provided with the correct answer or the teacher might ask the students to compare their answers in class, and only then give them the correct answer. Another group of exercises can deal with vocabulary. Students will be asked to choose or provide the meaning of a word or a phrase.

Then several segments of the video where this word occurs will be displayed. If the word has more than one meaning in the same video, the students can be given video segments where the word occurs and asked to compare the different meanings. Finally, they can get the correct answer from the program or in class. The third group of questions can be used to review the material from previous lessons. The students can be asked to compare how the word was used in different lessons, or how the behavior of a certain character changed. For feedback, they will be given relevant segments of the video from other lessons. (Searching across lessons rather than within one lesson will soon be possible with MannX). In short, the feedback will consist of the relevant segments of the video and/or transcript. If the students have to figure out if their answer is plausible, they can notice more than they would from just seeing the correct answer.

It is necessary to explain the role that we assigned to the computer in our program. First, the computer does not try to do any "teaching": all the learning takes place between the student and the (video) narrative, not between the student and the computer. The computer's main role is to deliver the narrative and to help the student cope with it. Second, the computer does not try to "understand" the language or the student. In our project, we eschew all applications of artificial intelligence techniques to computer-assisted instruction, which means that the program is not stand-alone and requires teacher involvement. Finally, the computer does not dazzle and distract the student by the interactive and multidimensional capabilities of multimedia, keeping the attention focused on the content of the narrative and the linguistic support systems. We sought to minimize the number of buttons on the screen, providing only the navigational controls for moving around in the one-dimensional movie and for studying its text.

Any multimedia program, in addition to presenting meaningful material to the learners and helping to comprehend it, should also include activities that will help the learners remember new input and use it. This claim is based on Ausubel's concept of meaningful learning (Brown, 2000), which suggests that to achieve high retention of new input, the latter must be related to the knowledge that the learner has already internalized. Otherwise, the new material will be forgotten because it is not incorporated into the person's cognitive system. These activities should include language production for communication, negotiation, and problem solving purposes. Since MannX is not interactive in a sense that it cannot understand learners' open-ended responses, such activities have to be done separately. These activities can be in a form of discussion through e-mails, forums, and chat rooms to prepare students for a classroom discussion. If students are prepared, their anxiety to speak is lower because they are not afraid to talk about something they have already practiced. According to Krashen, lowering the learners' affective filter (i.e., anxiety) will help them acquire the foreign language faster (1985).

In summary, the benefits of multimedia programs are that they contain more information the learners can assess than traditional materials, they are more convenient, they provide many tools to help learners comprehend authentic information, they provide more feedback than the teacher can due to time constraints, and as a result increase learner motivation. However, MAPL presents information and tools that help with comprehension in a different way (video aligned with text), and provides feedback that is a relevant segment or segments of the input, which can induce the learner to notice more information in the feedback.

Future Trends: MannX

Currently MannX manipulates digital media using Java code that runs within an applet. In the earlier version of the program (still used in MIRC) Java support is provided by QTJava from Apple, available only on Macintosh and Windows. The most recent version uses Java Media Framework (JMF) from Sun that is more authentically cross-platform (Linux, Windows, Mac OS, Solaris). JMF is also more stable and reliable than QTJava but it has not been actively developed since its initial introduction and therefore lacks support for the more recent codecs, such as Sorenson. In addition, both QTJava and JMF require a somewhat cumbersome installation, because not all users have Java on their computers, and very few have QTJava or JMF pre-installed.

For these reasons, we have recently developed a version of MannX that uses SWF Flash files, written entirely in JavaScript, bypassing the Java code. With version 9 of Flash, we expect to support Flash FLV files, which provide much better video quality. At that point, we will be able to dispense with Java and cumbersome installations because Flash is pre-installed on almost every browser. We should also be able to start using YouTube or Google Video files with transcripts and commentaries without requiring a download of the video: the text components of the MannX lesson can be on the user's computer while the video remains on YouTube.

The next version of MannX will also extend its search function. Currently, MannX performs both a string-match search and a more sophisticated semantic search within a single lesson or episode. (See Nakhimovsky & Myers, 2003). The next version will search for a given string across all episodes of the movie, making it possible to see the target string in many contexts. For words and fixed phrases, such contexts can be precomputed, together with their video-synchronization markup. This will create a video concordance of the text of the movie and its annotations.

We are also planning to introduce standard markup for the beginning and end points of the media segment corresponding to the marked-up text segment. (The markup will probably be based on the TimedText and SMIL specifications developed by the World Wide Web Consortium, w3c.org. If the markup includes enough metadata about the media format and the API used to access it, we can effectively decouple authoring systems from players and make annotated-media player a separate software category. This may lead to healthy competition among the players, both commercial and open-source: annotators would compete on tools for creating pedagogical materials; players would compete on search capabilities and pedagogical features, such as exercises and testing.

Application to other Disciplines and Conclusion

Even though we mostly discussed the pedagogical application of MannX to language learning, multimedia annotators/players are applicable to any other discipline. Since the annotator can create an extensive support system for studying the media content, the resulting materials are appropriate for self study. Browser-based multimedia players can also be used for distance learning. Any discipline or skill that can benefit from a close study of and interactions with annotated video recordings should use materials prepared with a multimedia annotator and delivered by an interactive player.

To conclude, we would like to remind the readers about the best practice guidelines we mentioned throughout the chapter for the design and evaluation of MAPL.

- MAPL should be online-based so that everybody can access them.
- These programs should include authentic material.
- Their design should be driven by learning theories rather than technological possibilities.
- MAPL should be user-centered to account for the knowledge background and learning styles of the learners.
- MAPL should contain or be supplemented with activities promoting learner interaction with the material and with other learners.
- The readers should remember that these guidelines apply not only to MAPL, but to TEL in general.

References

Blake, R. (2001). What language professionals need to know about technology. *ADFL Bulletin, 32,* 93-99.

Brett, P. (1995). Multimedia for listening comprehension: The design of a multimedia-based resource for developing listening skills. *System, 23*, 77-85.

Brown, H. D. (2000). *Principles of language learning and teaching* (4th ed.). New York: Addison Wesley Longman.

Chun, D., & Payne, S. (2004). What makes students click: Working memory and look-up behavior. *System, 32*, 481-503.

Gass, S. (2003). Input and interaction. In C. J. Doughty & M. H. Long (Eds.), *The handbook of second language acquisition* (pp. 224-255). Malden, MA: Blackwell.

Kramsch, C., & Andersen, R. W. (1999). Teaching text and context through multimedia. *Language Learning & Technology, 2*, 31-42. Retrieved January 7, 2008, from http://llt.msu.edu/vol2num2/article1/index.html

Krashen, S. (1985). *The input hypothesis: Issues and implications*. New York: Longman Press.

Levine, G. S. (2004). Global simulation: A student-centered, task-based format for intermediate foreign language courses. *Foreign Language Annals, 37*, 26-36.

Luke, C. (2006). Situating CALL in the broader methodological context of foreign language teaching and learning: Promises and possibilities. In L. Ducate & N. Arnold (Eds.), *Calling on CALL: From theory and research to new directions in foreign language teaching* (Vol. 5, pp. 21-41). San Marcos, TX: CALICO.

Mayer, R. (2001). *Multimedia learning*. Cambridge: Cambridge University Press.

Nakhimovsky, A. D. (1997). A multimedia authoring tool for language instruction: Interactions of pedagogy and design. *Journal of Educational Computing Research, 17*, 261-274.

Nakhimovsky, A. D., & Myers, T. (2003, July). *Digital video annotations for education*. Paper presented at the International Conference on Engineering Education, Valencia, Spain.

Nakhimovsky, A. D., Nakhimovsky, A. S., & Myers, T. (1996). *Frameworks for developing multimedia authoring systems*. Paper presented at the Annual joint conference of the Association for Computing in the Humanities and the Association of Literary and Linguistic Computing, Bergen, Norway.

Paivio, A. (1986). *Mental representations: A dual coding approach*. Oxford: Oxford University Press.

Pujola, J. (2002). CALLing for help: Researching language learning strategies using help facilities in a Web-based multimedia program. *ReCALL, 14*, 235-262.

Schmidt, R. (1990). The role of consciousness in second language learning. *Applied Linguistics, 11*, 129-158.

Schmidt, R. (2001). Attention. In P. Robinson (Ed.), *Cognition and second language instruction* (pp. 3-32). Cambridge, MA: Cambridge University Press.

Schrodt, P., & Turman, P. (2005). The impact of instructional technology use, course design, and sex differences on students' initial perceptions of instructor credibility. *Communication Quarterly, 53,* 177-196.

Shawback, M. J., & Terhune, N. M. (2002). Online interactive courseware: Using movies to promote cultural understanding in a CALL environment. *ReCALL, 14,* 85-95.

University of Wisconsin Language Institute. (2003). Multimedia Annotator and Multimedia Language Builder. Retrieved January 7, 2008, from http://www.languageinstitute.wisc.edu/content/projects/authoring_tools.htm

Weyers, J. (1999). The effect of authentic video on communicative competence. *Modern Language Journal, 83,* 339-349.

Further Readings

Bai, J. (n.d.). *Making multimedia an integral part of curricular innovation.* Retrieved January 7, 2008, from http://www2.kenyon.edu/People/bai/Research/Multimedia.pdf

Brugman, H., Russel, A., Broeder, D., & Wittenburg, P. (n.d.). *EUDICO, annotation and exploitation of multi media corpora over the Internet.* Retrieved January 7, 2008, from http://www.mpi.nl/ISLE/documents/papers/brugman%20-%20Eudico%20paper.pdf

Chapelle, C. A. (1998). Multimedia CALL: Lessons to be learned from research on instructed SLA. *Language Learning & Technology, 2,* 22-34. Retrieved January 7, 2008, from http://llt.msu.edu/vol2num1/article1/

Harold, W., & Means, S. (2004). *XML in a nutshell* (3rd ed.). Sebastopol, CA: O'Reilly Media, Inc. Retrieved January 7, 2008, from http://proquest.safaribooksonline.com/0596007647

Nakhimovsky, A. D., & Myers, T. (2002). *XML Programming.* Berkeley CA: Apress.

Plass, J. L. (1998). Design and evaluation of the user interface of foreign language multimedia software: A cognitive approach. *Language Learning and Technology, 2,* 40-53. Retrieved January 7, 2008, from http://llt.msu.edu/vol2num1/pdf/article2.pdf

Useful URLs

Randall Bass: Bibliography of multimedia software for general education http://www.georgetown.edu/faculty/bassr/mmbiblio.html

Randall Bass: On the use of multimedia for general education http://www.georgetown.edu/faculty/bassr/multimedia.html

Han Slöetjes: On ELAN—multimedia annotator in linguistic research: http://www.ncess.ac.uk/events/ASW/video/e-ss-agenda-video-sloetjes.pdf

Max Plank Institute for Psycholinguistics: ELAN download: http://www.mpi.nl/tools/elan.html

THDL: On QuillDriver—an authoring tool for creation and editing of audio and video files: http://www.thdl.org/tools/quilldriver/

Transcriber: http://trans.sourceforge.net/en/presentation.php

Transana: http://www.transana.org/

W3C: resources on XML: http://www.w3.org/XML/

Endnote

[1] ActionScript is a language, loosely based on JavaScript, that was developed by Macromedia (acquired by Adobe in 2005) to script the Flash player. The differences between ActionScript and JavaScript have always been minor; with the latest version of ActionScript, they were eliminated and the language was folded into the latest version of JavaScript.

Appendix

Figure A1.

Internet Session: Exploring MANNX

http://www.n-topus.com/mx/KeeneFlood/

Open the above Web site in a browser, preferably in Firefox. It will lead to an annotated version of Jon Udell's screencast on the Keene, NH, flood of October 8-9, 2005, which has been annotated in MannX. Wait for the video to load. Then click on the "?" button to learn how to use the MannX player. Explore the text of the video segment by segment. Also explore any facts/concepts that interest you in the commentary section (bottom left frame). Click on "D" to look up words in the dictionary. Use "T" (stands for topic) to find how certain words are used in the video. For example, click on the word "flood" in the dictionary, then click on "T" to see in which contexts it appears throughout the text.

Interaction: after you have learned how MannX interface works, discuss your experience and come up with other possible uses of any MAPL in class or in a discussion board/forum.

Chapter X

Knowledge Mining for Adaptive Multimedia Web-Based Educational Platform

Leyla Zhuhadar, University of Louisville,USA

Olfa Nasraoui, University of Louisville, USA

Robert Wyatt, Western Kentucky University, USA

Inside Chapter

This chapter introduces an Adaptive Web-Based Educational platform that maximizes the usefulness of the online information that online students retrieve from the Web. It shows in a data driven format that information has to be personalized and adapted to the needs of individual students; therefore, educational materials need to be tailored to fit these needs: learning styles, prior knowledge of individual students, and recommendations. This approach offers several techniques to present the learning material for different types of learners and for different learning styles. User models (user profiles) are created using a combination of clustering techniques and association rules mining. These models represent the learning technique, learning style, and learning sequence, which can help improve the learn-

ing experience on the Web site for new users. Furthermore, the user models can be used to create an intelligent system that provides recommendations for future online students whose profile matches one of the mined profiles that represents the discovered user models.

Introduction

Today, an educational Web site can be a gold-mining repository rather than a static Web site—a voyage in space, time, and technology to discover the hidden student behavior and experience. At the department of Distance Learning at Western Kentucky University, an interactive Web environment was developed whereby teachers, researchers, and knowledge seekers can discover information about their distance learning students. Every single access to our platform, from each individual student to different types of learning material, such as *text*, *audio*, *podcasting*, and *video lectures* were traced and recorded in log files. The audio and video lectures were presented through the latest technology, Podcasting and VODcasting, to enhance the learning *mobility*. By tracking the behavior of each online student and knowing which lectures he/she has selected, the sequence of lectures that were selected, the type of the selection (text, audio, or video), and the method used (online or off-line), we can build a user model (user profile), which is a system representation of how the learner relates to the conceptual structure of the application.

According to De Bra, Aroyo, and Cristea (2004), education has been (and still is) changing dramatically: several changes are occurring simultaneously, which are characterized by the three *A*'s: *anyplace, anytime, anyhow* (p. 387). For the last few years, there has been a noticeable cultural trend among students who prefer to combine study and work. Online courses and the Internet play a major role in helping the students become independent of the physical availability of the teacher. However, online courses do not automatically make the teacher available anyplace and anytime. Some researchers have tried to create automatic teaching systems that simulate the intelligence of the teacher like SQL-Tutor (Mitrovic, 2002) and ELM-ART (Weber, 2001) or Beal's Artificial Intelligence inspired system (Beal, Qu, & Lee, 2006). According to Beal et al. (2006),

Intelligent tutoring systems (ITS) can provide effective instruction, but learners do not always use such systems effectively. Motivated students interested in course material take to ITS readily, but others will improvise ways to get through without putting in much effort.

As we can see, the ITS approach in general does not rely on the intelligence of the learner to select the information that he or she needs. In our approach, we allowed the students to choose the lectures that were needed, the sequence that was desired, and the learning style/format that was preferred. Moreover, data mining algorithms were applied on the system's usage data in order to allow the students to benefit from the learning experience that some previous students have already gone through. The system discovers some patterns in students' behaviors in their process of learning and observing the materials on the Web site over a period of time. Each collection of these patterns can then be transformed into user models (user profiles), which form the foundation of a recommender system. When future students log into the learning system, their initial behaviors would be observed and mapped to the previously discovered user models and recommendations of lectures and their formats would be offered. This approach provides answers to four A's: *automatic synchronization, accessibility, availability,* and *adaptivity. automatic synchronization* distinguishes both Podcasting and VODcasting from the traditional multimedia (audio and video) on the Web: Most likely Pod/VODcasting will not replace traditional multimedia on the Web, but will rather become a more flexible extension of it, offering more diversity to a considerably larger audience. The key element of this intelligent technology is the *automatic feed*, which allows online students to subscribe to this feed only once and then the updated lectures, audio recordings of textbooks, texts, recent audio or video interviews, and so forth, will automatically be transferred to students' MP3 devices. *Accessibility* means offering learners with different needs alternative ways to navigate through the information. For instance, the inclusion of closed caption text was embedded into our system to help different ways of information delivery (hearing impaired students need the caption as an alternative to sound). Using this method, we can provide students with disabilities (hearing impaired) with alternative ways of accessing online course materials. *Availability* means enabling online students to access lectures any way and anyhow, that is, through the Internet via streaming the media online to a browser or an MP3 device, streaming the media off-line which allows students to "read" or "review" texts while walking or driving. *Adaptivity* refers to learner preferences regarding different learning styles. Some learners prefer learning by reading (text), others by listening (audio) and yet others prefer a visual learning style (video). What is innovative about our system is that the four A's can be encapsulated into the personalization aspect, which includes all aspects of the learning situation, such as personal preferences of student learning style and needs. We will call this system, which is illustrated in Figure 1, the *My Way adaptive e-learning platform.*

Background

Personalization

According to (Nasraoui, 2005), the move from *traditional physical* stores of products or information to *virtual* stores of products or information has eliminated physical constraints traditionally limiting the number and variety of products in a typical inventory. Unfortunately, this move has drastically limited the traditional three dimensional layouts of products for which access is further facilitated thanks to the sales representative or librarian, to a dismal *planar* interface *without* the sales representative or librarian. As a result, users of the Web can drown in the huge number of options, most of which they may never get to see. In the late 1990s, Jeff Bezos, CEO of Amazon™ said, "If I have 3 million customers on the Web, I should have 3 million stores on the Web" (Schafer, Konstan, & Reidel, 1999). Hence, in online environments, Web personalization has become more of a necessity than an option. As shown in Table 1, personalization can be used to achieve several goals

Figure 1. Recommendation system for multimedia Web-based educational platform "© 2008, Leyla Zhuhadar. Used with permission."

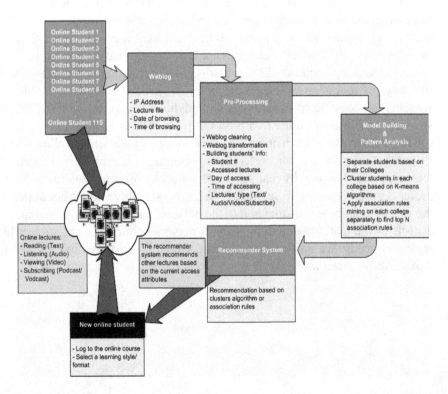

Table 1. Possible goals of Web personalization

• Adapting e-learning systems to their users • Converting browsers into buyers • Improving Web site design and usability • Improving customer retention and loyalty • Increasing cross-sell by recommending items related to the ones being considered • Helping visitors to quickly find relevant information on a Web site • Making results of information retrieval/search more aware of the context and user interests

that range from increasing customer loyalty on e-commerce sites (Schafer et al., 1999) to enabling better search (Joachims, 2002). The information explosion on the World Wide Web has made personalization a necessity (Nasraoui, 2005; Nasraoui, Krishnapuram, & Joshi, 1999).

Personalization can either be done via information agents (e.g., Web search engines) or in an end-to-end manner by making Web sites adaptive (Nasraoui, 1999).

Modes of Personalization

Personalization falls into four basic categories, ordered from the simplest to the most advanced (Nasraoui, 2005):

1. **Memorization:** In this simple and widespread form, user information such as name and browsing history are stored (e.g., using *cookies*), to be later used to greet the returning user. This mode, usually implemented on the Web server, depends more on Web technology than on adaptive or intelligent learning and may raise some problems of user privacy.

2. **Customization:** In this form of server-implemented personalization, the user's preferences are taken from registration forms and then used to customize the content and structure of a Web page. This mode is typically not adaptive to change and is performed manually or at best semi-automatically. A typical example of this form is My Yahoo!™'s personalized Web portal.

3. **Guidance or recommender systems:** This mode of server-based personalization system *automatically* recommends hyperlinks that are relevant to the user's interests. Access to the needed information on a large Web site is facilitated (Mobasher, Cooley, and Srivastava, 2000; Nasraoui, Krishnapuram, Joshi, & Kamdar, 2002; Schafer et al., 1999). It relies on data reflecting the user's *implicit* interest (e.g., browsing history that is recorded in Web server

logs) or *explicit* interest (*user profile* that is entered through a Web registration form). This approach forms the focus of our effort in Web personalization in e-learning environments.

4.   **Task performance support:** This is a client-side personalization system where a personal assistant executes actions on behalf of the user so that access to relevant information is facilitated. This approach requires quite some involvement from the user, including access, installation, and maintenance of the personal assistant software. It also has narrower scope than server-based personalization since it cannot use information about other users with similar interests.

We will limit the rest of our discussion to automatic Web personalization based on *recommender systems*, since they necessitate a minimum or no explicit input from the user. Another advantage is that, being server-based, they benefit from a global view of all users' activities and interests that are used to learn user profiles in order to provide an *intelligent* Web personalization experience, yet they require very little or no explicit input from the user.

Recommender Systems

One of the most powerful modes of personalization comes in the form of *recommender systems* (Nasraoui, 2005). There are several approaches to automatically generate Web recommendations based on user's browsing patterns or explicit ratings (Nasraoui, 2005). Some rely on learning a usage model from Web access data or user ratings. For example, lazy user modeling is used in the most widespread form of collaborative filtering which stores all users' information and then uses *K-Nearest-Neighbors* (*KNN*) to provide recommendations from the previous history of the K most similar users (Schafer et al., 1999). Others ways to form a user model include using data mining, such as by mining *association rules* (of the form: *IF user views page A, THEN user views page B*) (Mobasher, Dai, Luo, & Nakagawa, 2001), or by partitioning a set of user sessions into *clusters* or *groups* of *similar* sessions. The latter groups are called *session clusters* (Mobasher et al., 2000; Nasraoui et al., 1999), or user *profiles* (Mobasher et al., 2000; Nasraoui et al., 1999). A user profile can be represented like a typical session (of the form: *users in this cluster or group are interested in page A, page C, page E*). Association rules and clusters or user profiles can be discovered off-line and then used to build recommendations based on current Web navigation patterns. This latter branch of using data mining techniques to discover user models from Web usage data is referred to as *Web Usage Mining*.

Data Mining Functionality for the E-Learning Domain

Much of what has been investigated so far in the e-learning platform has been based on understating the data generated by activity on the Web server and not about the e-learners' behavior (Monk, 2005). Little has been done about discovering the pattern of their use of different learning styles. Some e-learning systems started to embed multimedia as a way to enhance online course materials, such as Tegrity platform, Camtasia, and so forth. Actually, we have started by a process of transformation from *text*-based material to *multimedia*-based material, and then judged that it was better to give the *option* to students to choose the learning style they prefer. Ideally the same information was supposed to be given to students using *a variety of media* formats to satisfy every learning style. In addition, mining the student's choices and discovering patterns in their choices has the potential of helping educators enhance their course materials.

Recommender System and E-Learning

A recommender system, in an e-learning context, is a software agent that tries to "intelligently" recommend actions to a learner based on the actions of previous learners (Zaiane, 2001). Such recommender system could provide a recommendation to online learning materials or shortcuts. Those recommendations are based on previous learners' activities or on the learning styles of the students that are discovered from their navigation patterns. A previous work on the use of Web mining for developing smart e-learning systems (Zaiane, 2002) integrated Web usage mining, where patterns were automatically discovered from users' *actions* and then fed into a recommender system that could assist learners in their online learning activities by suggesting actions or resources to a user. A similar approach was presented by Zheng et al. (2002) and used hyperlink shortcuts by shortening frequent Web access sequences discovered in the Web log. Another type of data mining in e-learning was performed on *documents rather than on the students' actions*. This type of data mining is more akin to *text* mining (i.e., knowledge discovery from *text* data) than Web usage mining (Hammouda et al., 2005). This approach helps alleviate some of the problems in e-learning that are due to the volume of data that can be overwhelming for a learner. It works by organizing the articles and documents based on the topics and also providing summaries for documents.

Adaptive E-Leaning Tools

Web-Based technology is often the technology of choice for distance learning and the same technology is already being used for e-commerce (Zaiane, 2001). However, while there are already advanced tools developed to understand online customers' behavior, there was very little done to do the same for learners' behavior in online distance learning. Even today, five years after this statement, we notice that little has been done to automatically discover access patterns that help understand learners' behavior.

Cristea and De Mooij (2003) designed MOT (My Online Teacher), a hypermedia tool developed specifically for distance learning. This tool was used at the Eindhoven University of Technology for authoring adaptive hypermedia courses. In this tool, the subject matter of the course to be designed was modelled by means of concept maps. Then, based on these concept maps, lessons were designed. Our concept of adaptation differs from MOT in that we propose an automated personalization approach to adapt the learning materials for online students based on their (and similar users') behavior in previous browsing sessions.

Data-Driven Adaptive E-Learning Platform

System Framework

Our approach is based on a dynamic Web site (see Figure 2) that provides online lectures in three different learning styles: text, audio, and video. Our personalization strategy relies on data that consists of Web site logs of distance learning at Western

Figure 2. Web-based educational platform "© 2008, Leyla Zhuhadar. Used with permission."

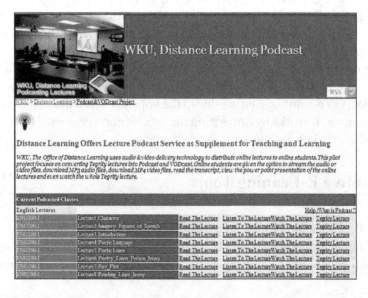

Kentucky University. Web site logs record every user's activity on the Web site. This includes the resources that have been accessed, along with a time stamp, and other information. The preprocessing of Weblogs which includes cleaning them from irrelevant information and transforming them often consumes 80% to 95% of the effort and resources needed for Web usage mining (Edelstein, 2001). In this platform, all the activities of the students were traced, including the sequence of browsing the lectures, and the type of media that has been chosen.

Meaningful information from the Weblogs was extracted to suit the objective of the adaptive system. The Weblogs were cleaned, and their final transformation is shown in Table 2.

We had 931 individual log sessions, with 115 different students from 6 different colleges and 12 different courses. Each student logged to different lectures with a different learning style (Text, Audio, and Video). Table 3 shows the extracted information about each student session, which consists of StudentID, lectures that he/she picked, college name, the day of the week (Weekdays/weekends) time of day (Day time/Night time) and media style (Text/Audio/Video).

The percentages of each learning style for each college were calculated over all the courses, and are shown in Table 4.

Figure 3 shows the distribution of each selected media style in relation to each student, each academic department (or college), the distribution of the Media style

Table 2. Weblog excerpt after cleaning and transforming the data

Student ID	File Name	College	Day of Week	Time	Media Type
Student1	Waters_ENG200_DocLecture1. php	ENGLISH	WEEKEND	DAYTIME	TEXT
Student2	Plummer_Hist119_DocLecture1. php	HISTORY	WEEKEND	DAYTIME	TEXT
Student2	Plummer_Hist119_PodLecture1. php	HISTORY	WEEKEND	DAYTIME	AUDIO
Student3	Plummer_Hist119_Podlecture3. php	HISTORY	WEEKEND	DAYTIME	AUDIO
Student3	Plummer_Hist119_DocLecture3. php	HISTORY	WEEKEND	NIGHT-TIME	TEXT
Student4	Waters_ENG200_DocLecture1. php	ENGLISH	WEEKDAY	NIGHT-TIME	TEXT
...	...	...	...	...	...
...	...	...	...	...	...
...	...	...	...	...	...
Student115	Waters_ENG200_DocLecture1. php	ENGLISH	WEEKDAY	DAYTIME	TEXT

Table 3. Features and attributes of the collected data

# of Students in total	115					
# of College	6 (English, History, Chemistry, Business, Health & Human Services, College of Education)					
# of courses	12					
	English	History	Chemistry	Business	Health & Human Services	College of Education
	Eng200	Hist119	Chm100	BA580	Swrk320	LM22
	Eng200			BA592	CFS111	
				AC450		
				MG333		
				International-al Trade		
Day of Browsing the lecture	(Weekdays, Weekends)					
Time of Browsing the lecture	(Day Time, Night Time)					
Media type of lecture	Text		Audio	Video	Subscribe	

Table 4. Data distribution and the percentages of each learning style for each college

	Text	Audio	Video	Sub-scribe	#of Sessions	#of Students	% Text	% Audio	% Video	% Sub-scribe
English	248	148	17	15	428	40	57%	35%	4%	4%
History	26	22	0	2	50	15	52%	44%	0%	4%
Chemistry	47	27	0	7	81	18	58%	33%	0%	9%
Health & Human Services	16	13	0	7	36	17	44%	36%	0%	20%
Business	170	130	0	10	310	22	55%	42%	0%	3%
College of Education	12	12	0	2	26	3	46%	46%	0%	8%
Total	519	352	17	43	931	115	57%	35%	4%	4%
%	55%	37%	3%	5%						

vs. time, and Media style vs. day of the week. The detailed distribution for each department is shown in Figure 4. The top left Media per student distributions in both Figure 3 and Figure 4 shows that the greatest majority of students do access some text content. However, they also show multimodal interest, that is interest in different media styles (such as text *and* audio). In fact the unimodal student (with interest in only one media style) is rare if not inexistent in most departments. Also as seen in Figure 4, while most students have low affinity to podcast/vodcast styles, there is one exception in the Health & Human services department, showing substantially higher affinity to this subscription based style which is more mobility friendly. Finally, while nontext, that is, *pure Audio* or *Audio/Podcast* style students are rare, we do notice that there are *three such students in the English department* and *one student in the Health & Human services department. One* additional *English* department student has interest in *only audio and video styles*.

The relation between the two factors, Media type and Time of the day is depicted in Figure 5, which shows that regardless of the chosen media style, the majority of students preferred to read/listen to/watch their lectures *during the day*, and most of them preferred to read lectures (text) or listen to podcasted lectures as opposed to watching or subscribing to them.

The relation between the two factors: Media type and Day (shown in Figure 6) indicates that students logged to their lectures during weekdays slightly more than weekends and with a preference to read or listen to podcasted lectures rather than watch it or subscribe to it.

Figure 3. Distribution of media styles per student, lecture, day, and time for all departments "© 2008, Leyla Zhuhadar. Used with permission."

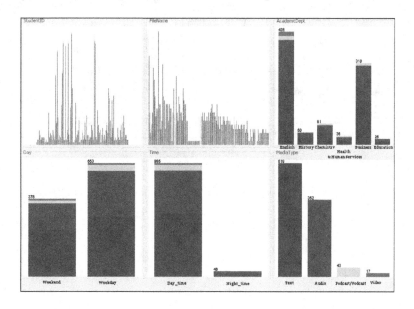

Figure 4. Distribution of Media styles per student, lecture, day, time for each department separately "© 2008, Leyla Zhuhadar. Used with permission."

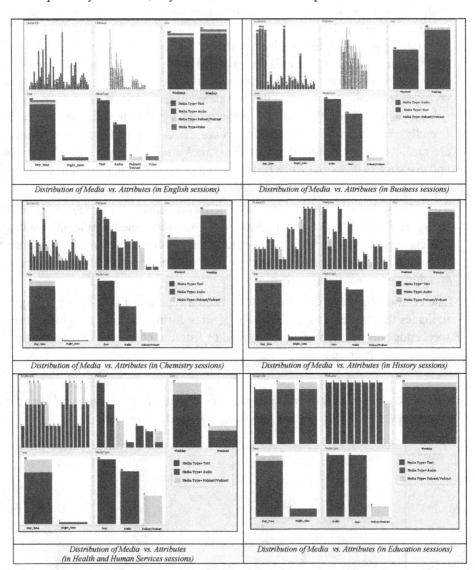

Figure 5. Media type vs. Time "© 2008, Leyla Zhuhadar. Used with permission."

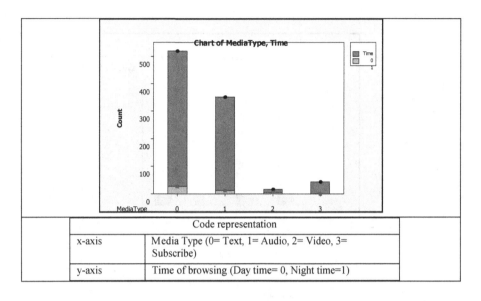

Code representation	
x-axis	Media Type (0= Text, 1= Audio, 2= Video, 3= Subscribe)
y-axis	Time of browsing (Day time= 0, Night time=1)

Figure 6. Media type vs. Date "© 2008, Leyla Zhuhadar. Used with permission."

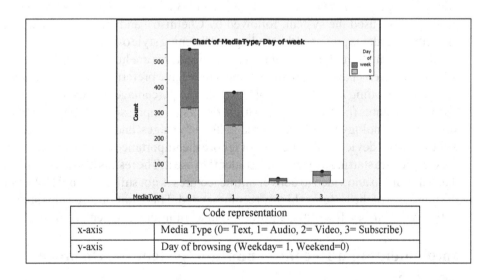

Code representation	
x-axis	Media Type (0= Text, 1= Audio, 2= Video, 3= Subscribe)
y-axis	Day of browsing (Weekday= 1, Weekend=0)

Figure 7. Media type vs. Academic Dept(Colleges) "© 2008, Leyla Zhuhadar. Used with permission."

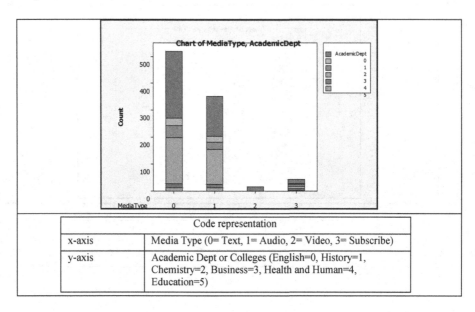

Code representation	
x-axis	Media Type (0= Text, 1= Audio, 2= Video, 3= Subscribe)
y-axis	Academic Dept or Colleges (English=0, History=1, Chemistry=2, Business=3, Health and Human=4, Education=5)

Figure 7 shows the relation between two factors: Media Type and Academic Department (Colleges). It can be seen that English and Business students form the largest group to have used the system, followed by Chemistry and History students. The majority of students preferred the reading and listening style over the visual style. One possible explanation of this result is that video lectures are huge files and streaming them on the Web takes time, hence students may have preferred the less demanding listening or reading (text, power point) style. The percentage of students who subscribed to lectures (podcasting) is not high, but is still impressive compared to Video, since this technology is still considered in its early stages, and not every student can afford an MP3 device. Still, one cannot ignore the importance of this new trend, and universities are starting to encourage students to use it. The results lead us to conclude that using audio and video to deliver online lectures is not sufficient; and that adding the transcript of the lecture is highly recommended. This addition also helps students with certain sensory disabilities and makes our learning environment ADA compliant.

Implementing a Recommendation System for Distance Learning

Our adaptive multimedia Web-based educational platform relies on a recommender system that can recommend lectures to a learner based on their previous navigation or access to lectures, and based on navigation made by other "similar" learners. We have attempted to extract the user models by applying two data mining methodologies: first data clustering and then association rule mining.

The Group User Model (Bollen, 2000) is the collective knowledge of a group of users on a given domain transformed from hyperlink structure. After this group user model (see Figure 8) is formed, it is used to improve and recommend hyperlinks to individual users rather than a group of users. The Web sessions go through data mining. During this stage, user activity models (such as user profiles) were created using either clustering techniques or association rule mining. For example, association rule models can be used to infer the learning technique, learning style, and learning sequence, which could help improve the learning experience of new online students.

The data has been divided into six categories corresponding to the different departments: English, History, Chemistry, Business, Health & Human Services, and College of Education. Then it was analyzed both on a department level, as well as globally. For creating User Models (user profiles), we clustered students based on the similarity between their cumulative access sessions (a record of all lectures viewed by a particular student throughout all their sessions). This would allow us to discover lecture access profiles. Each student's sessions were combined into one long transaction vector with one attribute (or dimension) per lecture, and where the visit to a lecture was represented by a 1 in the corresponding dimension, while a 0 was used for lectures that have not been visited. We used the K-means algorithm (McQueen, 1967) for clustering similar students.

Figure 8. Structure of the e-learning recommendation framework "© 2008, Leyla Zhuhadar. Used with permission."

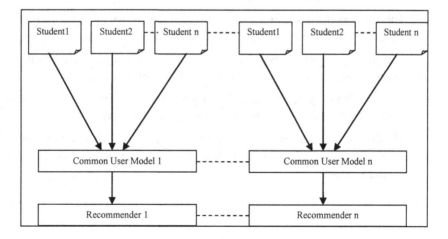

Definition 1: K-Means Clustering Algorithm

K-Means is an algorithm for partitioning or clustering N data points into K disjoint subsets S_j containing N_j data points so as to minimize the sum-of-squared errors criterion

$$J = \sum_{j=1}^{K} \sum_{x_i \in S_j} \left| x_i - c_j \right|^2 , \tag{1}$$

where xi is a vector representing the ith data point and cj is the centroid of the data points in Sj.

Using the Weka open source data mining environment (Witten & Frank, 2000), we applied the K-means algorithm (McQueen, 1967) to cluster the student cumulative sessions into separate clusters, while trying to vary the number of cluster for each college until we obtained the best results. Each cluster contained similar lectures, and similar learning styles selected by the students during their usage of the online system. Those clusters will form a summary of online students' behavior and can form the basis for making future recommendations.

Results of Clustering Student Cumulative Sessions

Clustering was performed on the cumulative student sessions from each department separately. The distribution of student sessions per department is listed below.

a.   **English Weblog sessions:** In English sessions, we had 40 different students logged to 73 different lectures of different media formats.

b.   **Business Weblog sessions:** In business sessions, we had 22 different students logged to 54 different lectures of different media formats.

c.   **Chemistry Weblog sessions:** In chemistry sessions we had 18 different students logged to 9 different lectures of different media formats.

d.   **History Weblog sessions:** In history sessions, we had 15 different students logged to 13 different lectures of different media formats.

e.   **Health & human services Weblog sessions:** In health and human services sessions, we had 17 different students logged to 7 different lectures of different media formats.

f.   **Education Weblog sessions:** In education sessions we had 3 different students logged to 9 different lectures of different media formats.

The numbers of clusters varied from one department to another (English=15, Business=13, History=4, Chemistry=5, Health Human services=2, Education=1). Detailed information about these clusters is shown in Tables 5, 6, 7, 8, 9, and 10. Each cluster centroid is an average of the cumulative sessions assigned to (i.e., closest to) that cluster. The weights are listed in decreasing order. We can see that the cluster centroids summarize the different assortments or combinations of lectures viewed by most students in a particular group of students. Such assortments are interesting because even when interpreted after discovery, the assortments can be seen to reflect intuitive relationships. For example cluster 5 in the English department consists of assortments that combine a lecture on drama (taught by one instructor) with other lectures by a different instructor that are focused on character presentation, reading poetry out loudly, and sonnet rhythms and schemes. This cluster fits a group user profile interested in learning about drama that involves poetry, and in all likelihood certain types of sonnets. What is really interesting about such an output of clustering is that it is automatically discovered by data mining, that is, by a purely data-driven approach, and not inferred by human reasoning. This example illustrates the potential of automated discovery, especially when the data logs and lecture assortments become too large for human reasoning to keep up with. In this case, a simple recommendation strategy would recommend lectures on character presentation and reading poetry out loud, to a student who has just visited the lecture on drama. This kind of recommendation falls within the collaborative filtering family of personalization paradigms, and illustrates the powerful ability of collaborative filtering to transcend simple content matching (which is limited to recommending only similar content) and ability to suggest items that are only subtly related to others, often in an indirect manner, and thus not necessarily even similar (for example: poetry is not directly similar in content to drama). Manually building such recommendation systems for large user bases and large and dynamic item assortments would require extensive amounts of knowledge representation and encoding efforts, and most likely an ability to encode and reason with semantics in a comprehensive manner, a goal that is still considered an open research problem.

Pattern Discovery with Association Rules

In order to discover patterns such as trends and relationships within the Web usage data, we applied association rule mining (see Definition 2). Association rule discovery is a classical data mining problem (Agrawal, 1993) that serves to discover patterns in users' behavior. We used the *Apriori* Association Rule mining algorithm (Agrawal, 1993) with minimum support 5% and confidence 75%.

Table 5. Clusters extracted from the cumulative access sessions of each student in the English

Cluster#	Lecture Name	Centroid Weight	Description
Cluster0	Waters_ENG200_Lecture2.php	1	Fiction: Lecture on fiction.
	Waters_ENG200_Lecture4.php	1	Poetry1:Lecture 1 on poetry
	Waters_ENG200_Lecture5.php	1	Poetry2: Lecture 2 on poetry.
	Waters_ENG200_Lecture6.php	1	Poetry3: Lecture 3 on poetry.
	Waters_ENG200_Lecture3.php	0.875	Love song: Lecture on poem called Love song.
	Waters_ENG200_Lecture7.php	0.875	Poetry: Lecture on poetry.
	Waters_ENG200_Lecture1.php	0.75	Drama: Lecture on Drama.
Cluster1	Waters_ENG200_Lecture2.php	1	Fiction: Lecture on fiction.
	Waters_ENG200_Lecture7.php	1	Poetry: Lecture on poetry.
Cluster2	Waters_ENG200_Lecture1.php	1	Drama: Lecture on Drama.
	Waters_ENG200_Lecture1.php	1	Drama: Lecture on Drama.
	Waters_ENG200_Lecture2.php	1	Fiction: Lecture on fiction.
	Waters_ENG200_Lecture5.php	1	Poetry2: Lecture 2 on poetry.
	Waters_ENG200_Lecture3.php	1	Love song: Lecture on poem called Love song.
	Waters_ENG200_Lecture4.php	0.5	Poetry1:Lecture 1 on poetry
	Waters_ENG200_Lecture7.php	0.5	Poetry: Lecture on poetry.
Cluster3	Waters_ENG200_Lecture2.php	0.25	Fiction: Lecture on fiction.
	Waters_ENG200_Lecture3.php	0.125	Love song: Lecture on poem called Love song.
	Waters_ENG200_Lecture6.php	0.125	Poetry3: Lecture 3 on poetry.
Cluster4	Waters_ENG200_Lecture5.php	1	Poetry2: Lecture 2 on poetry.
	Waters_ENG200_Lecture6.php	1	Poetry3: Lecture 3 on poetry.

continued on following page

Table 5. continued

	Waters_ENG200_Lecture7.php	1	Poetry: Lecture on poetry.
	Waters_ENG200_Lecture2.php	0.5	Fiction: Lecture on fiction.
	Waters_ENG200_Lecture3.php	0.5	Love song: Lecture on poem called Love song.
Cluster5	Waters_ENG200_Lecture1.php	1	Drama: Lecture on Drama.
	Olmsted_ENG200_Lecture1.php	1	Character: Describes 5 methods of character presentation.
	Olmsted_ENG200_Lecture2.php	1	Imaginery_figures_of_speech: Describes the use of language in poetry.
	Olmsted_ENG200_Lecture5.php	1	Poetry_Lines: Describes how to read poems out loud by looking to identify the person.
	Olmsted_ENG200_Lecture9.php	1	Rhyme_Schemes_Sonnets: Lecture on sonnets and rhyme schemes.
Cluster6	Waters_ENG200_Lecture1.php	1	Drama: Lecture on Drama.
	Waters_ENG200_Lecture2.php	1	Fiction: Lecture on fiction.
	Waters_ENG200_Lecture3.php	1	Love song: Lecture on poem called Lovesong.
	Waters_ENG200_Lecture4.php	1	Poetry1: Lecture 1 on poetry
Cluster7	Waters_ENG200_Lecture1.php	1	Drama: Lecture on Drama.
	Waters_ENG200_Lecture2.php	1	Fiction: Lecture on fiction.
	Waters_ENG200_Lecture5.php	1	Poetry2: Lecture 2 on poetry.
	Olmsted_ENG200_Lecture4.php	1	Poetic_Language: Description about poetic language.
Cluster8	Olmsted_ENG200_Lecture1.php	1	Character: Describes 5 methods of character presentation.
	Olmsted_ENG200_Lecture4.php	1	Poetic_Language: Description about poetic language.
	Olmsted_ENG200_Lecture9.php	1	Rhyme_Schemes_Sonnets: Lecture on sonnets and rhyme schemes.
	Olmsted_ENG200_Lecture2.php	0.5	Imaginery_figures_of_speech: Describes the use of language in poetry.
	Olmsted_ENG200_Lecture5.php	0.5	Poetry_Lines: Describes how to read poems out loud by looking to identify the person.
	Olmsted_ENG200_Lecture7.php	0.5	Pov_Plot: Lecture on point of view and plot.

continued on following page

Table 5. continued

Cluster9	Olmsted_ENG200_Lecture3.php	1	Introduction:Welcome lecture on ENG200
	Olmsted_ENG200_Lecture11.php	1	Tone_Style: Lecture on tone and style.
	Olmsted_ENG200_Lecture12.php	1	Visual-cues: Lecture on reading poetry visual cues.
Cluster10	Waters_ENG200_Lecture2.php	1	Fiction: Lecture on fiction.
Cluster11	Waters_ENG200_Lecture1.php	1	Drama: Lecture on Drama.
	Waters_ENG200_Lecture2.php	1	Fiction: Lecture on fiction.
	Waters_ENG200_Lecture5.php	1	Poetry2: Lecture 2 on poetry.
	Olmsted_ENG200_Lecture1.php	1	Character: Describes 5 methods of character presentation.
	Olmsted_ENG200_Lecture2.php	1	Imaginery_figures_of_speech: Describes the use of language in poetry.
Cluster12	Olmsted_ENG200_Lecture1.php	1	Character: Describes 5 methods of character presentation.
	Olmsted_ENG200_Lecture2.php	1	Imaginery_figures_of_speech: Describes the use of language in poetry.
	Olmsted_ENG200_Lecture3.php	1	Introduction: Welcome lecture on ENG200
	Olmsted_ENG200_Lecture4.php	1	Poetic_Language: Description about poetic language.
	Olmsted_ENG200_Lecture5.php	1	Poetry_Lines: Describes how to read poems out loud by looking to identify the person.
	Olmsted_ENG200_Lecture2.php	1	Imaginery_figures_of_speech: Describes the use of language in poetry.
	Olmsted_ENG200_Lecture7.php	1	Pov_Plot: Lecture on point of view and plot.
	Olmsted_ENG200_Lecture8.php	1	Reading_Lines_Irony: Describes how to read lines in the poem and irony.
	Olmsted_ENG200_Lecture9.php	1	Rhyme_Schemes_Sonnets: Lecture on sonnets and rhyme schemes.

continued on following page

Table 5. continued

Cluster 12	Olmsted_ENG200_Lecture11.php	0.8333	Tone_Style: Lecture on tone and style.
	Olmsted_ENG200_Lecture12.php	0.8333	Visual-cues: Lecture on reading poetry visual cues.
	Olmsted_ENG200_Lecture14.php	0.8333	Welcome: Welcome lecture on English 200.
	Olmsted_ENG200_Lecture10.php	0.6667	Setting_Theme: Lecture on setting a theme.
	Olmsted_ENG200_Lecture13.php	0.6667	Visual_cues: Lecture on what visual cues poetry offers to help us understand.
	Waters_ENG200_Lecture2.php	0.5	Fiction: Lecture on fiction.
	Waters_ENG200_Lecture1.php	0.3333	Drama: Lecture on Drama.
	Waters_ENG200_Lecture3.php	0.3333	Love song: Lecture on poem called Lovesong.
	Waters_ENG200_Lecture4.php	0.3333	Poetry1: Lecture 1 on poetry
	Waters_ENG200_Lecture5.php	0.3333	Poetry2: Lecture 2 on poetry.
	Waters_ENG200_Lecture6.php	0.3333	Poetry3: Lecture 3 on poetry.
	Waters_ENG200_Lecture7.php	0.3333	Poetry: Lecture on poetry.
Cluster13	Waters_ENG200_Lecture6.php	1	Poetry3: Lecture 3 on poetry.
Cluster14	Olmsted_ENG200_Lecture4.php	0.3333	Poetic_Language: Description about poetic language.
	Olmsted_ENG200_Lecture10.php	0.3333	Setting_Theme: Lecture on setting a theme.
	Waters_ENG200_Lecture4.php	0.1667	Poetic_Language: Description about poetic language.
	Olmsted_ENG200_Lecture1.php	0.1667	Character: Describes 5 methods of character presentation.
	Olmsted_ENG200_Lecture2.php	0.1667	Imaginery_figures_of_speech: Describes the use of language in poetry.
	Olmsted_ENG200_Lecture5.php	0.1667	Poetry_Lines: Describes how to read poems out loud by looking to identify the person.
	Olmsted_ENG200_Lecture6.php	0.1667	Poetry_Lines_Person_Irony: Describes about irony.
	Olmsted_ENG200_Lecture7.php	0.1667	Pov_Plot: Lecture on point of view and plot.
	Olmsted_ENG200_Lecture8.php	0.1667	Reading_Lines_Irony: Describes how to read lines in the poem and irony.

Table 6. Clusters extracted from the cumulative access sessions of each student in the History

Cluster#	Lecture Name	Centroid weight	Description
Cluster0	Plummer_Hist119_Lecture3.php	1	Old King Egypt: Old and middle kingdom in Egypt
Cluster1	Plummer_Hist119_Lecture1.php	1	Civilization: Western Civilization
	Plummer_Hist119_Lecture3.php	1	Old King Egypt: Old and middle kingdom in Egypt
Cluster2	Plummer_Hist119_Lecture1.php	1	Civilization: Western Civilization
Cluster3	Plummer_Hist119_Lecture1.php	1	Civilization: Western Civilization
	Plummer_Hist119_Lecture4.php	1	New King Egypt: Ancient near eastern culture
	Plummer_Hist119_Lecture3.php	1	Old King Egypt: Old and middle kingdom in Egypt

Table 7. Clusters extracted from the cumulative access sessions of each student in the chemistry

Cluster#	Lecture Name	Centroid weight	Description
Cluster0	LarryByrd_AlgebraicEq_Part2.php	1	Part_2: part 2 of algebraic expressions
	LarryByrd_AlgebraicEq_Part3.php	1	Part_3: part 3 of algebraic equations
Cluster1	LarryByrd_AlgebraicEq_Part1.php	1	Part_1: part one of algebraic equations
	LarryByrd_AlgebraicEq_Part2.php	1	Part_2: part 2 of algebraic expressions
Cluster2	LarryByrd_AlgebraicEq_Part1.php	1	Part_1: part one of algebraic equations
	LarryByrd_AlgebraicEq_Part2.php	1	Part_2: part 2 of algebraic expressions
	LarryByrd_AlgebraicEq_Part3.php	1	Part_3: part 3 of algebraic equations
Cluster3	LarryByrd_AlgebraicEq_Part1.php	1	Part_1: part one of algebraic equations
Cluster4	LarryByrd_AlgebraicEq_Part1.php	1	Part_1: part one of algebraic equations
	LarryByrd_AlgebraicEq_Part3.php	1	Part_3: part 3 of algebraic equations

Table 8. Clusters extracted from the cumulative access sessions of each student in the business

Cluster#	Lecture Name	Centroid weight	Description
Cluster0	Johnson_Lecture1.php	1	Accounting1: Introduction to business processes
	Johnson_Lecture2.php	1	Accounting2: Reporting and sales process
	Johnson_Lecture3.php	1	Accounting3: Customer relationship management
	Johnson_Lecture4.php	1	Managing Non-profits: Welcome lecture on management non-profits course.
Cluster1	Colbert_AC450_Lecture1.php	1	AC450_CH1: Assurance services
	Colbert_AC451_Lecture1.php	1	Intro_Tegrity: Welcome lecture for AC451 course
	Colbert_BA580_Lecture1.php	1	BA580_Intro: Introduction
	Colbert_BA580_Lecture2.php	1	Corporate Governance1: Corporation, legal obligations of directors and organization of the board of directors
	Colbert_BA580_Lecture3.php	1	Corporate Governance2: Board management relationship
	Colbert_BA580_Lecture4.php	1	EA 1of2: How the external auditors operate, what they do and their interaction with board of directors
	Colbert_BA580_Lecture5.php	1	EA 2of2: External auditing and how external auditing relates to the corporate governance.
	Colbert_BA580_Lecture6.php	1	Ethics: What to do in the class regarding ethics.
	Colbert_BA580_Lecture7.php	1	Greetings: Welcome lecture on BA580
	Colbert_BA580_Lecture8.php	1	IntnlCorpGov 1of2: Establishing principles regarding corporate governance.
	Colbert_BA580_Lecture9.php	1	IntnlCorpGov 2of2: How European union promotes international efforts at corporate governance.
	Colbert_BA580_Lecture10.php	1	S-O: This is the first session on Sarbanes-Oxley act
	Colbert_BA580_Lecture11.php	1	S-O 2of2: This is the second session on Sarbanes-Oxley act

continued on following page

Table 8. continued

	Colbert_BA592_Lecture1.php	1	Ethics_CH3: Syllabus and assignments to do for ethics
	Colbert_BA592_Lecture2.php	1	FraudIA: Internal audit standards that deals with fraud.
	Colbert_BA592_Lecture3.php	1	FraudSAS99: Discussion of fraud and standards.
	Colbert_BA592_Lecture4.php	1	IA 1of2: First video about internal auditing.
	Colbert_BA592_Lecture5.php	1	IA 2of2: Second video about internal auditing.
	Colbert_BA592_Lecture6.php	1	Intro: Welcome lecture on corporate governance leadership ethics and values.
	Colbert_BA592_Lecture7.php	1	S_O_MiscNotes: Miscellaneous notes on Sarbanes-Oxley.
Cluster2	InternationalTrade_Lecture1.php	1	Global_Automotive: Welcome lecture Western Kentucky UniversityÕs Global Automotive conference.
	InternationalTrade_Lecture2.php	1	Welcome: Welcome lecture on International Trade course.
Cluster3	Colbert_BA580_Lecture5.php	1	EA 2of2: External auditing and how external auditing relates to the corporate governance.
	Colbert_BA580_Lecture7.php	1	Greetings: Welcome lecture on BA580
	Colbert_BA580_Lecture8.php	1	IntnlCorpGov 1of2: Establishing principles regarding corporate governance.
	Colbert_BA580_Lecture10.php	1	S-O: This is the first session on Sarbanes-Oxley act
	Colbert_BA592_Lecture1.php	1	Ethics_CH3: Syllabus and assignments to do for ethics
	Colbert_BA592_Lecture3.php	1	FraudSAS99: Discussion of fraud and standards.
	Colbert_BA592_Lecture4.php	1	IA 1of2: First video about internal auditing.
	Colbert_BA592_Lecture5.php	1	IA 2of2: Second video about internal auditing.
	Colbert_BA592_Lecture7.php	1	S_O_MiscNotes: Miscellaneous notes on sarbanes-oxley.

continued on following page

Table 8. continued

Cluster4	Colbert_AC451_Lecture1.php	1	Intro_Tegrity: Welcome lecture for AC451 course
	Colbert_BA580_Lecture2.php	1	Corporate Governance1: Corporation, legal obligations of directors and organization of the board of directors
	Colbert_BA580_Lecture4.php	1	EA 1of2: External auditors operate, what they do and their interaction with board of directors
	Colbert_BA580_Lecture5.php	1	EA 2of2: External auditing and how external auditing relates to the corporate governance.
	Colbert_BA580_Lecture6.php	1	Ethics: What to do in the class regarding ethics.
	Colbert_BA580_Lecture7.php	1	Greetings: Welcome lecture on BA580
	Colbert_BA580_Lecture8.php	1	IntnlCorpGov 1of2: Establishing principles regarding corporate governance.
	Colbert_BA580_Lecture9.php	1	IntnlCorpGov 2of2: Describes how European union promotes international efforts at corporate governance.
	Colbert_BA580_Lecture10.php	1	S-O: This is the first session on Sarbanes-Oxley act
	Colbert_BA580_Lecture11.php	1	S-O 2of2: This is the second session on sarbanes-oxley act
	Colbert_BA592_Lecture2.php	1	FraudIA: Internal audit standards that deals with fraud.
	Colbert_BA592_Lecture3.php	1	FraudSAS99: Discussion of fraud and standards.
	Colbert_BA592_Lecture4.php	1	IA 1of2: First video about internal auditing.
	Colbert_BA592_Lecture5.php	1	IA 2of2: Second video about internal auditing.
	Colbert_BA592_Lecture6.php	1	Intro: Welcome lecture on corporate governance leadership ethics and values.
	Colbert_BA592_Lecture7.php	1	S_O_MiscNotes: Miscellaneous notes on sarbanes-oxley.
Cluster5	Colbert_BA580_Lecture2.php	1	Corporate Governance1: Corporation, legal obligations of directors and organization of the board of directors
	Colbert_BA592_Lecture2.php	1	FraudIA: Internal audit standards that deals with fraud.
	Colbert_BA592_Lecture3.php	1	FraudSAS99: Discussion of fraud and standards.

continued on following page

Table 8. continued

Cluster6	Colbert_BA580_Lecture1.php	1	BA580_Intro: Description about the course
	Colbert_BA580_Lecture2.php	1	Corporate Governance1: Corporation, legal obligations of directors and organization of the board of directors
	Colbert_BA580_Lecture5.php	1	EA 2of2: External auditing and how external auditing relates to the corporate governance.
	Colbert_BA580_Lecture11.php	1	S-O 2of2: This is the second session on sarbanes-oxley act
	Colbert_BA592_Lecture7.php	1	S_O_MiscNotes: Miscellaneous notes on sarbanes-oxley.
Cluster7	Colbert_AC450_Lecture1.php	1	AC450_CH1: Describes assurance services
Cluster8	InternationalTrade_Lecture1.php	1	Global_Automotive: Welcome lecture Western Kentucky UniversityÕs Global Automotive conference.
Cluster9	Colbert_AC450_Lecture1.php	1	AC450_CH1: Describes assurance services
	Colbert_BA580_Lecture1.php	1	BA580_Intro: Description about the course
	Colbert_BA580_Lecture7.php	1	Greetings: Welcome lecture on BA580
	Colbert_BA592_Lecture1.php	1	Ethics_CH3: Syllabus and assignments to do for ethics
	Colbert_BA592_Lecture2.php	1	FraudIA: Internal audit standards that deals with fraud.
Cluster10	Colbert_BA592_Lecture1.php	1	Ethics_CH3: Syllabus and assignments to do for ethics
	Colbert_BA592_Lecture5.php	1	IA 2of2: Second video about internal auditing.
Cluster11	Colbert_BA580_Lecture2.php	1	Corporate Governance1: Corporation, legal obligations of directors and organization of the board of directors
	Colbert_BA580_Lecture6.php	1	Ethics: Describes what to do in the class regarding ethics.
	Colbert_BA592_Lecture1.php	1	Ethics_CH3: Syllabus and assignments to do for ethics
Cluster12	Colbert_BA580_Lecture10.php	1	S-O: This is the first session on sarbanes-oxley act
	Colbert_BA592_Lecture2.php	1	FraudIA: Internal audit standards that deals with fraud.

Table 9. Clusters extracted from the cumulative access sessions of each student in the health and human services

Cluster#	Lecture Name	Centroid weight	Description
Cluster0	Kelley_Lecture1.php	1	Welcome: welcome lecture on the Human Nutrition course
Cluster1	Chadha_520_Lecture1.php	1	Video_Instruction: instructions for video taped interview simulation

Table 10. Clusters extracted from the cumulative access sessions of each student in the education.

Cluster#	Lecture Name	Centroid weight	Description
Cluster0	Houston_Lecture1.php	1	Creating PDP: Details about how to create professional growth plan
	Houston_Lecture2.php	1	PDP Process: Details about the professional portfolio process
	Houston_Lecture3.php	1	Standards: Details about the standard movement in education
	Houston_Lecture4.php	1	Welcome: Welcome lecture on LME 512 issues and trends in library media education

Definition 2: Association Rules

Association rules are rules that associate items that frequently appear together within the same transaction or user's choices (Agrawal, 1993). A rule consists of an antecedent, such as (URL1, URL2, URL3), and a consequent, such as (URL5, URL6). In our system, items are either the attribute category types (example: Daytime, Nighttime, Weekday, Weekend, Audio, Text, …, etc.) in case we treat each individual student transaction as one record; or the visited lectures' URLs or identifiers in case we treat each cumulative (long) session as one record. In this latter case, suppose that we have mined a *rule* such as "*(URL1, URL2, URL3)* ➔ *(URL5, URL6)*." In this case, items (URL1, URL2, URL3) appear in the *antecedent* of the rule, while (URL5, URL6) appear in the *consequent* part. Hence, each time that (URL1, URL2, URL3) are visited, it is likely that the items (URL5, URL6) would also be visited by the same student. The *Apriori* algorithm (Agrawal, 1993) constructs a candidate set of frequent itemsets of length k, counts the number of occurrences, keeps only the frequent ones, then constructs a candidate set of itemsets of length $k+1$ from the frequent itemsets of smaller length. It continues iteratively until no larger candidate itemset can be constructed. The heuristic that is used here is that, every subset of a frequent itemset must also be frequent. The rules are then generated from the frequent itemsets with probabilities attached to them indicating the likelihood (called support) that the association occurs. Below, we will describe two association rule experiments that we have performed to extract different kinds of knowledge.

Experiment 1: Mining Association Rules from Single Transaction Rescords with All Attributes

The first experiment was performed on all students' sessions to find association rules that relate all the attributes (such as Day, Time, Media Type, Academic Department). We used a minimum support of 5% and minimum confidence of 75%. The resulting rules are shown in Table 11, where for instance the first rule "*MediaType=Audio 219 ==> AcademicDept=Business 219 conf:(1)*" should be interpreted as follows: of 219 sessions that accessed an Audio lecture, all (thus 219) sessions are from the English department. This in turns results in a confidence of 219/219 which is 1. In this case 219 is the support of the antecedent of the rule "MediaType=Audio," and it is also the support of the rule, that is, the support of the intersection of the antecedent and consequent. On the other hand, rule No. 10 "*Day=weekday MediaType=Text 243 ==> Time=day_time 241 conf:(0.99)*" results in a confidence of 0.99 (or 99%) since the ratio of the support of the rule (241) to the support of the antecedent (243) is 241/243 = 0.99.

From the discovered association rules we may conclude that:

- Media type (Text/Audio) was correlated with day_time: Most of the students Read/Listen to the lectures during the day.
- Weekdays were correlated with Day time: The students who accessed their lectures during the weekdays tended to access them during the day as opposed to the evening hours.
- English courses were more accessed during weekdays, whereas Chemistry courses were more accessed during Weekends.
- Business courses were accessed during weekends more than weekdays and during the day, and with a preference toward Audio lectures (podcast) format.

Experiment 2: Mining Association Rules from Cumulative Session Records with Lecture Attributes

In this experiment, we extracted association rules between lectures, by using as input data, the *cumulative* sessions of each student (into a long binary transaction vector consisting of *all* lectures accessed by the *same* student, as was done in the clustering phase). Consequently, we were able to discover the lecture access patterns that can

Table 11. Association rulesbetween all attributes for all individual sessions

1. MediaType=Audio 219 ==> AcademicDept=Business 219 conf:(1)
2. Time=day_time MediaType=Audio 213 ==> AcademicDept=Business 213 conf:(1)
3. Day=weekday MediaType=Audio 113 ==> AcademicDept=Business 113 conf:(1)
4. Day=weekday Time=day_time MediaType=Audio 107 ==> AcademicDept=Business 107 conf:(1)
5. Day=weekend MediaType=Audio 106 ==> AcademicDept=Business 106 conf:(1)
6. Day=weekend MediaType=Audio 106 ==> Time=day_time 106 conf:(1)
7. Day=weekend Time=day_time MediaType=Audio 106 ==> AcademicDept=Business 106 conf:(1)
8. AcademicDept=Business Day=weekend MediaType=Audio 106 ==> Time=day_time 106 conf:(1)
9. Day=weekend MediaType=Audio 106 ==> AcademicDept=Business Time=day_time 106 conf:(1)
10. Day=weekday MediaType=Text 243 ==> Time=day_time 241 conf:(0.99)
11. AcademicDept=English Day=weekday 207 ==> Time=day_time 205 conf:(0.99)
12. AcademicDept=English Day=weekday MediaType=Text 191 ==> Time=day_time 189 conf:(0.99)
13. AcademicDept=Chemistry 81 ==> Time=day_time 80 conf:(0.99)
14. AcademicDept=Chemistry MediaType=Text 74 ==> Time=day_time 73 conf:(0.99)
15. AcademicDept=Chemistry Day=weekend 53 ==> Time=day_time 52 conf:(0.98)
16. AcademicDept=Chemistry Day=weekend MediaType=Text 48 ==> Time=day_time 47 conf:(0.98)
17. Day=weekday 378 ==> Time=day_time 370 conf:(0.98)
18. MediaType=Audio 219 ==> Time=day_time 213 conf:(0.97)
19. AcademicDept=Business MediaType=Audio 219 ==> Time=day_time 213 conf:(0.97)
20. MediaType=Audio 219 ==> AcademicDept=Business Time=day_time 213 conf:(0.97)
21. AcademicDept=History 50 ==> MediaType=Text 48 conf:(0.96)
22. AcademicDept=English MediaType=Text 396 ==> Time=day_time 380 conf:(0.96)
23. AcademicDept=English 428 ==> Time=day_time 407 conf:(0.95)
24. AcademicDept=Business Day=weekday 122 ==> Time=day_time 116 conf:(0.95)
25. Day=weekday MediaType=Audio 113 ==> Time=day_time 107 conf:(0.95)
26. AcademicDept=Business Day=weekday MediaType=Audio 113 ==> Time=day_time 107 conf:(0.95)
27. Day=weekday MediaType=Audio 113 ==> AcademicDept=Business Time=day_time 107 conf:(0.95)
28. MediaType=Text 652 ==> Time=day_time 617 conf:(0.95)
29. AcademicDept=English Day=weekend Time=day_time 202 ==> MediaType=Text 191 conf:(0.95)
30. AcademicDept=Business 310 ==> Time=day_time 293 conf:(0.95)
31. AcademicDept=Business Day=weekend 188 ==> Time=day_time 177 conf:(0.94)
32. AcademicDept=History 50 ==> Time=day_time 47 conf:(0.94)
33. AcademicDept=English Time=day_time 407 ==> MediaType=Text 380 conf:(0.93)
34. AcademicDept=English Day=weekend MediaType=Text 205 ==> Time=day_time 191 conf:(0.93)
35. Day=weekend 553 ==> Time=day_time 515 conf:(0.93)
36. AcademicDept=English Day=weekend 221 ==> MediaType=Text 205 conf:(0.93)
37. AcademicDept=Business Day=weekday 122 ==> MediaType=Audio 113 conf:(0.93)
38. AcademicDept=English 428 ==> MediaType=Text 396 conf:(0.93)
39. AcademicDept=English Day=weekday 207 ==> MediaType=Text 191 conf:(0.92)
40. AcademicDept=Business Day=weekday Time=day_time 116 ==> MediaType=Audio 107 conf:(0.92)
41. AcademicDept=English Day=weekday Time=day_time 205 ==> MediaType=Text 189 conf:(0.92)
42. Day=weekend MediaType=Text 409 ==> Time=day_time 376 conf:(0.92)
43. AcademicDept=English Day=weekend 221 ==> Time=day_time 202 conf:(0.91)
44. AcademicDept=Chemistry 81 ==> MediaType=Text 74 conf:(0.91)
45. AcademicDept=Business MediaType=Text 81 ==> Day=weekend 74 conf:(0.91)
46. AcademicDept=English Day=weekday 207 ==> Time=day_time MediaType=Text 189 conf:(0.91)
47. AcademicDept=Chemistry Time=day_time 80 ==> MediaType=Text 73 conf:(0.91)
48. AcademicDept=Chemistry Day=weekend 53 ==> MediaType=Text 48 conf:(0.91)
49. AcademicDept=Chemistry Day=weekend Time=day_time 52 ==> MediaType=Text 47 conf:(0.9)
50. AcademicDept=Chemistry 81 ==> Time=day_time MediaType=Text 73 conf:(0.9)
...

be used to compute lecture recommendations for a given student who has accessed certain lectures. We started by dividing our sessions into six separate subsets, one for each department, then mined association rules from each subset.

1.   **English sessions:** The discovered association rules for English sessions are shown in Table 12, with red colored rues explained below.

Analyzing Association Rules

The following relationships illustrate only some of the association rules. Students who visited:

Table 12. Association rules between lectures accessed by the same student for English Sessions

```
1. Pages_31=Waters_ENG200_Lecture1.php Pages_35=Waters_ENG200_Lecture5.php 12 ==> Pages_
32=Waters_ENG200_Lecture2.php 12   conf:(1)
2. Pages_37=Waters_ENG200_Lecture7.php 11 ==> Pages_35=Waters_ENG200_Lecture5.php 11
conf:(1)
3. Pages_33=Waters_ENG200_Lecture3.php Pages_35=Waters_ENG200_Lecture5.php 11 ==> Pages_
32=Waters_ENG200_Lecture2.php 11   conf:(1)
4. Pages_10=Olmsted_ENG200_Lecture4.php 10 ==> Pages_2=Olmsted_ENG200_Lecture10.php 10
conf:(1)
5. Pages_31=Waters_ENG200_Lecture1.php Pages_34=Waters_ENG200_Lecture4.php 10 ==> Pages_
32=Waters_ENG200_Lecture2.php 10   conf:(1)
6. Pages_33=Waters_ENG200_Lecture3.php Pages_34=Waters_ENG200_Lecture4.php 10 ==> Pages_
31=Waters_ENG200_Lecture1.php 10   conf:(1)
7. Pages_31=Waters_ENG200_Lecture1.php Pages_34=Waters_ENG200_Lecture4.php 10 ==> Pages_
33=Waters_ENG200_Lecture3.php 10   conf:(1)
8. Pages_33=Waters_ENG200_Lecture3.php Pages_34=Waters_ENG200_Lecture4.php 10 ==> Pages_
32=Waters_ENG200_Lecture2.php 10   conf:(1)
9. Pages_33=Waters_ENG200_Lecture3.php Pages_37=Waters_ENG200_Lecture7.php 10 ==> Pages_
32=Waters_ENG200_Lecture2.php 10   conf:(1)
10. Pages_32=Waters_ENG200_Lecture2.php Pages_37=Waters_ENG200_Lecture7.php 10 ==> Pages_
33=Waters_ENG200_Lecture3.php 10   conf:(1)
11. Pages_34=Waters_ENG200_Lecture4.php Pages_35=Waters_ENG200_Lecture5.php 10 ==> Pages_
32=Waters_ENG200_Lecture2.php 10   conf:(1)
12. Pages_32=Waters_ENG200_Lecture2.php Pages_36=Waters_ENG200_Lecture6.php 10 ==> Pages_
35=Waters_ENG200_Lecture5.php 10   conf:(1)
13. Pages_32=Waters_ENG200_Lecture2.php Pages_37=Waters_ENG200_Lecture7.php 10 ==> Pages_
35=Waters_ENG200_Lecture5.php 10   conf:(1)
14. Pages_33=Waters_ENG200_Lecture3.php Pages_37=Waters_ENG200_Lecture7.php 10 ==> Pages_
35=Waters_ENG200_Lecture5.php 10   conf:(1)
15. Pages_36=Waters_ENG200_Lecture6.php Pages_37=Waters_ENG200_Lecture7.php 10 ==> Pages_
35=Waters_ENG200_Lecture5.php 10   conf:(1)
```

continued on following page

Table 12. continued

16. Pages_32=Waters_ENG200_Lecture2.php Pages_33=Waters_ENG200_Lecture3.php Pages_34=Waters_ENG200_Lecture4.php 10 ==> Pages_31=Waters_ENG200_Lecture1.php 10   conf:(1)
17. Pages_31=Waters_ENG200_Lecture1.php Pages_33=Waters_ENG200_Lecture3.php Pages_34=Waters_ENG200_Lecture4.php 10 ==> Pages_32=Waters_ENG200_Lecture2.php 10   conf:(1)
18. Pages_31=Waters_ENG200_Lecture1.php Pages_32=Waters_ENG200_Lecture2.php Pages_34=Waters_ENG200_Lecture4.php 10 ==> Pages_33=Waters_ENG200_Lecture3.php 10   conf:(1)
19. Pages_33=Waters_ENG200_Lecture3.php Pages_34=Waters_ENG200_Lecture4.php 10 ==> Pages_31=Waters_ENG200_Lecture1.php Pages_32=Waters_ENG200_Lecture2.php 10   conf:(1)
20. Pages_31=Waters_ENG200_Lecture1.php Pages_34=Waters_ENG200_Lecture4.php 10 ==> Pages_32=Waters_ENG200_Lecture2.php Pages_33=Waters_ENG200_Lecture3.php 10   conf:(1)
21. Pages_31=Waters_ENG200_Lecture1.php Pages_33=Waters_ENG200_Lecture3.php Pages_35=Waters_ENG200_Lecture5.php 10 ==> Pages_32=Waters_ENG200_Lecture2.php 10   conf:(1)
22. Pages_33=Waters_ENG200_Lecture3.php Pages_35=Waters_ENG200_Lecture5.php Pages_37=Waters_ENG200_Lecture7.php 10 ==> Pages_32=Waters_ENG200_Lecture2.php 10   conf:(1)
23. Pages_32=Waters_ENG200_Lecture2.php Pages_35=Waters_ENG200_Lecture5.php Pages_37=Waters_ENG200_Lecture7.php 10 ==> Pages_33=Waters_ENG200_Lecture3.php 10   conf:(1)
24. Pages_32=Waters_ENG200_Lecture2.php Pages_33=Waters_ENG200_Lecture3.php Pages_37=Waters_ENG200_Lecture7.php 10 ==> Pages_35=Waters_ENG200_Lecture5.php 10   conf:(1)
25. Pages_33=Waters_ENG200_Lecture3.php Pages_37=Waters_ENG200_Lecture7.php 10 ==> Pages_32=Waters_ENG200_Lecture2.php Pages_35=Waters_ENG200_Lecture5.php 10   conf:(1)
26. Pages_32=Waters_ENG200_Lecture2.php Pages_37=Waters_ENG200_Lecture7.php 10 ==> Pages_33=Waters_ENG200_Lecture3.php Pages_35=Waters_ENG200_Lecture5.php 10   conf:(1)
27. Pages_35=Waters_ENG200_Lecture5.php 15 ==> Pages_32=Waters_ENG200_Lecture2.php 14 conf:(0.93)
28. Pages_33=Waters_ENG200_Lecture3.php 13 ==> Pages_31=Waters_ENG200_Lecture1.php 12 conf:(0.92)
29. Pages_33=Waters_ENG200_Lecture3.php 13 ==> Pages_32=Waters_ENG200_Lecture2.php 12 conf:(0.92)
30. Pages_34=Waters_ENG200_Lecture4.php 12 ==> Pages_32=Waters_ENG200_Lecture2.php 11 conf:(0.92)
31. Pages_32=Waters_ENG200_Lecture2.php Pages_33=Waters_ENG200_Lecture3.php 12 ==> Pages_31=Waters_ENG200_Lecture1.php 11   conf:(0.92)
32. Pages_31=Waters_ENG200_Lecture1.php Pages_33=Waters_ENG200_Lecture3.php 12 ==> Pages_32=Waters_ENG200_Lecture2.php 11   conf:(0.92)
33. Pages_32=Waters_ENG200_Lecture2.php Pages_33=Waters_ENG200_Lecture3.php 12 ==> Pages_35=Waters_ENG200_Lecture5.php 11   conf:(0.92)
34. Pages_2=Olmsted_ENG200_Lecture10.php 11 ==> Pages_10=Olmsted_ENG200_Lecture4.php 10 conf:(0.91)
35. Pages_11=Olmsted_ENG200_Lecture5.php 11 ==> Pages_2=Olmsted_ENG200_Lecture10.php 10 conf:(0.91)
36. Pages_2=Olmsted_ENG200_Lecture10.php 11 ==> Pages_11=Olmsted_ENG200_Lecture5.php 10 conf:(0.91)
37. Pages_37=Waters_ENG200_Lecture7.php 11 ==> Pages_32=Waters_ENG200_Lecture2.php 10 conf:(0.91)
38. Pages_37=Waters_ENG200_Lecture7.php 11 ==> Pages_33=Waters_ENG200_Lecture3.php 10 conf:(0.91)
39. Pages_37=Waters_ENG200_Lecture7.php 11 ==> Pages_36=Waters_ENG200_Lecture6.php 10 conf:(0.91)
40. Pages_32=Waters_ENG200_Lecture2.php Pages_34=Waters_ENG200_Lecture4.php 11 ==> Pages_31=Waters_ENG200_Lecture1.php 10   conf:(0.91)
41. Pages_33=Waters_ENG200_Lecture3.php Pages_35=Waters_ENG200_Lecture5.php 11 ==> Pages_31=Waters_ENG200_Lecture1.php 10   conf:(0.91)
42. Pages_32=Waters_ENG200_Lecture2.php Pages_34=Waters_ENG200_Lecture4.php 11 ==> Pages_33=Waters_ENG200_Lecture3.php 10   conf:(0.91)

continued on following page

Table 12. continued

43. Pages_37=Waters_ENG200_Lecture7.php 11 ==> Pages_32=Waters_ENG200_Lecture2.php Pages_33=Waters_ENG200_Lecture3.php 10   conf:(0.91)
44. Pages_32=Waters_ENG200_Lecture2.php Pages_34=Waters_ENG200_Lecture4.php 11 ==> Pages_35=Waters_ENG200_Lecture5.php 10   conf:(0.91)
45. Pages_35=Waters_ENG200_Lecture5.php Pages_36=Waters_ENG200_Lecture6.php 11 ==> Pages_32=Waters_ENG200_Lecture2.php 10   conf:(0.91)
46. Pages_35=Waters_ENG200_Lecture5.php Pages_37=Waters_ENG200_Lecture7.php 11 ==> Pages_32=Waters_ENG200_Lecture2.php 10   conf:(0.91)
47. Pages_37=Waters_ENG200_Lecture7.php 11 ==> Pages_32=Waters_ENG200_Lecture2.php Pages_35=Waters_ENG200_Lecture5.php 10   conf:(0.91)
48. Pages_35=Waters_ENG200_Lecture5.php Pages_37=Waters_ENG200_Lecture7.php 11 ==> Pages_33=Waters_ENG200_Lecture3.php 10   conf:(0.91)
49. Pages_33=Waters_ENG200_Lecture3.php Pages_35=Waters_ENG200_Lecture5.php 11 ==> Pages_37=Waters_ENG200_Lecture7.php 10   conf:(0.91)
50. Pages_37=Waters_ENG200_Lecture7.php 11 ==> Pages_33=Waters_ENG200_Lecture3.php Pages_35=Waters_ENG200_Lecture5.php 10   conf:(0.91)
51. Pages_35=Waters_ENG200_Lecture5.php Pages_37=Waters_ENG200_Lecture7.php 11 ==> Pages_36=Waters_ENG200_Lecture6.php 10   conf:(0.91)
52. Pages_35=Waters_ENG200_Lecture5.php Pages_36=Waters_ENG200_Lecture6.php 11 ==> Pages_37=Waters_ENG200_Lecture7.php 10   conf:(0.91)
53. Pages_37=Waters_ENG200_Lecture7.php 11 ==> Pages_35=Waters_ENG200_Lecture5.php Pages_36=Waters_ENG200_Lecture6.php 10   conf:(0.91)
54. Pages_31=Waters_ENG200_Lecture1.php Pages_32=Waters_ENG200_Lecture2.php Pages_33=Waters_ENG200_Lecture3.php 11 ==> Pages_34=Waters_ENG200_Lecture4.php 10   conf:(0.91)
55. Pages_32=Waters_ENG200_Lecture2.php Pages_34=Waters_ENG200_Lecture4.php 11 ==> Pages_31=Waters_ENG200_Lecture1.php Pages_33=Waters_ENG200_Lecture3.php 10   conf:(0.91)
56. Pages_32=Waters_ENG200_Lecture2.php Pages_33=Waters_ENG200_Lecture3.php Pages_35=Waters_ENG200_Lecture5.php 11 ==> Pages_31=Waters_ENG200_Lecture1.php 10   conf:(0.91)
57. Pages_31=Waters_ENG200_Lecture1.php Pages_32=Waters_ENG200_Lecture2.php Pages_33=Waters_ENG200_Lecture3.php 11 ==> Pages_35=Waters_ENG200_Lecture5.php 10   conf:(0.91)
58. Pages_33=Waters_ENG200_Lecture3.php Pages_35=Waters_ENG200_Lecture5.php 11 ==> Pages_31=Waters_ENG200_Lecture1.php Pages_32=Waters_ENG200_Lecture2.php 10   conf:(0.91)
59. Pages_32=Waters_ENG200_Lecture2.php Pages_33=Waters_ENG200_Lecture3.php Pages_35=Waters_ENG200_Lecture5.php 11 ==> Pages_37=Waters_ENG200_Lecture7.php 10   conf:(0.91)
60. Pages_35=Waters_ENG200_Lecture5.php Pages_37=Waters_ENG200_Lecture7.php 11 ==> Pages_32=Waters_ENG200_Lecture2.php Pages_33=Waters_ENG200_Lecture3.php 10   conf:(0.91)
61. Pages_33=Waters_ENG200_Lecture3.php Pages_35=Waters_ENG200_Lecture5.php 11 ==> Pages_32=Waters_ENG200_Lecture2.php Pages_37=Waters_ENG200_Lecture7.php 10   conf:(0.91)
62. Pages_37=Waters_ENG200_Lecture7.php 11 ==> Pages_32=Waters_ENG200_Lecture2.php Pages_33=Waters_ENG200_Lecture3.php Pages_35=Waters_ENG200_Lecture5.php 10   conf:(0.91)
63. Pages_32=Waters_ENG200_Lecture2.php Pages_35=Waters_ENG200_Lecture5.php 14 ==> Pages_31=Waters_ENG200_Lecture1.php 12   conf:(0.86)
64. Pages_31=Waters_ENG200_Lecture1.php Pages_32=Waters_ENG200_Lecture2.php 14 ==> Pages_35=Waters_ENG200_Lecture5.php 12   conf:(0.86)
65. Pages_33=Waters_ENG200_Lecture3.php 13 ==> Pages_35=Waters_ENG200_Lecture5.php 11 conf:(0.85)
66. Pages_33=Waters_ENG200_Lecture3.php 13 ==> Pages_31=Waters_ENG200_Lecture1.php Pages_32=Waters_ENG200_Lecture2.php 11   conf:(0.85)
67. Pages_33=Waters_ENG200_Lecture3.php 13 ==> Pages_32=Waters_ENG200_Lecture2.php Pages_35=Waters_ENG200_Lecture5.php 11   conf:(0.85)
68. Pages_34=Waters_ENG200_Lecture4.php 12 ==> Pages_31=Waters_ENG200_Lecture1.php 10 conf:(0.83)
69. Pages_34=Waters_ENG200_Lecture4.php 12 ==> Pages_33=Waters_ENG200_Lecture3.php 10 conf:(0.83)

continued on following page

Table 12. continued

70. Pages_34=Waters_ENG200_Lecture4.php 12 ==> Pages_35=Waters_ENG200_Lecture5.php 10 conf:(0.83)
71. Pages_34=Waters_ENG200_Lecture4.php 12 ==> Pages_31=Waters_ENG200_Lecture1.php Pages_32=Waters_ENG200_Lecture2.php 10   conf:(0.83)
72. Pages_31=Waters_ENG200_Lecture1.php Pages_33=Waters_ENG200_Lecture3.php 12 ==> Pages_34=Waters_ENG200_Lecture4.php 10   conf:(0.83)
73. Pages_34=Waters_ENG200_Lecture4.php 12 ==> Pages_31=Waters_ENG200_Lecture1.php Pages_33=Waters_ENG200_Lecture3.php 10   conf:(0.83)
74. Pages_31=Waters_ENG200_Lecture1.php Pages_35=Waters_ENG200_Lecture5.php 12 ==> Pages_33=Waters_ENG200_Lecture3.php 10   conf:(0.83)
75. Pages_31=Waters_ENG200_Lecture1.php Pages_33=Waters_ENG200_Lecture3.php 12 ==> Pages_35=Waters_ENG200_Lecture5.php 10   conf:(0.83)
76. Pages_32=Waters_ENG200_Lecture2.php Pages_33=Waters_ENG200_Lecture3.php 12 ==> Pages_34=Waters_ENG200_Lecture4.php 10   conf:(0.83)
77. Pages_34=Waters_ENG200_Lecture4.php 12 ==> Pages_32=Waters_ENG200_Lecture2.php Pages_33=Waters_ENG200_Lecture3.php 10   conf:(0.83)
78. Pages_32=Waters_ENG200_Lecture2.php Pages_33=Waters_ENG200_Lecture3.php 12 ==> Pages_37=Waters_ENG200_Lecture7.php 10   conf:(0.83)
79. Pages_34=Waters_ENG200_Lecture4.php 12 ==> Pages_32=Waters_ENG200_Lecture2.php Pages_35=Waters_ENG200_Lecture5.php 10   conf:(0.83)
80. Pages_32=Waters_ENG200_Lecture2.php Pages_33=Waters_ENG200_Lecture3.php 12 ==> Pages_31=Waters_ENG200_Lecture1.php Pages_34=Waters_ENG200_Lecture4.php 10   conf:(0.83)
81. Pages_31=Waters_ENG200_Lecture1.php Pages_33=Waters_ENG200_Lecture3.php 12 ==> Pages_32=Waters_ENG200_Lecture2.php Pages_34=Waters_ENG200_Lecture4.php 10   conf:(0.83)
82. Pages_34=Waters_ENG200_Lecture4.php 12 ==> Pages_31=Waters_ENG200_Lecture1.php Pages_32=Waters_ENG200_Lecture2.php Pages_33=Waters_ENG200_Lecture3.php 10   conf:(0.83)
83. Pages_31=Waters_ENG200_Lecture1.php Pages_32=Waters_ENG200_Lecture2.php Pages_35=Waters_ENG200_Lecture5.php 12 ==> Pages_33=Waters_ENG200_Lecture3.php 10   conf:(0.83)
84. Pages_32=Waters_ENG200_Lecture2.php Pages_33=Waters_ENG200_Lecture3.php 12 ==> Pages_31=Waters_ENG200_Lecture1.php Pages_35=Waters_ENG200_Lecture5.php 10   conf:(0.83)
85. Pages_31=Waters_ENG200_Lecture1.php Pages_35=Waters_ENG200_Lecture5.php 12 ==> Pages_32=Waters_ENG200_Lecture2.php Pages_33=Waters_ENG200_Lecture3.php 10   conf:(0.83)
86. Pages_31=Waters_ENG200_Lecture1.php Pages_33=Waters_ENG200_Lecture3.php 12 ==> Pages_32=Waters_ENG200_Lecture2.php Pages_35=Waters_ENG200_Lecture5.php 10   conf:(0.83)
87. Pages_32=Waters_ENG200_Lecture2.php Pages_33=Waters_ENG200_Lecture3.php 12 ==> Pages_35=Waters_ENG200_Lecture5.php Pages_37=Waters_ENG200_Lecture7.php 10   conf:(0.83)
88. Pages_35=Waters_ENG200_Lecture5.php 15 ==> Pages_31=Waters_ENG200_Lecture1.php 12 conf:(0.8)
89. Pages_35=Waters_ENG200_Lecture5.php 15 ==> Pages_31=Waters_ENG200_Lecture1.php Pages_32=Waters_ENG200_Lecture2.php 12   conf:(0.8)
90. Pages_36=Waters_ENG200_Lecture6.php 14 ==> Pages_35=Waters_ENG200_Lecture5.php 11 conf:(0.79)
91. Pages_31=Waters_ENG200_Lecture1.php Pages_32=Waters_ENG200_Lecture2.php 14 ==> Pages_33=Waters_ENG200_Lecture3.php 11   conf:(0.79)
92. Pages_32=Waters_ENG200_Lecture2.php Pages_35=Waters_ENG200_Lecture5.php 14 ==> Pages_33=Waters_ENG200_Lecture3.php 11   conf:(0.79)
93. Pages_32=Waters_ENG200_Lecture2.php 18 ==> Pages_31=Waters_ENG200_Lecture1.php 14 conf:(0.78)
94. Pages_32=Waters_ENG200_Lecture2.php 18 ==> Pages_35=Waters_ENG200_Lecture5.php 14 conf:(0.78)
95. Pages_33=Waters_ENG200_Lecture3.php 13 ==> Pages_34=Waters_ENG200_Lecture4.php 10 conf:(0.77)
96. Pages_33=Waters_ENG200_Lecture3.php 13 ==> Pages_36=Waters_ENG200_Lecture6.php 10 conf:(0.77)

continued on following page

Table 12. continued

97. Pages_33=Waters_ENG200_Lecture3.php 13 ==> Pages_37=Waters_ENG200_Lecture7.php 10 conf:(0.77)
98. Pages_33=Waters_ENG200_Lecture3.php 13 ==> Pages_31=Waters_ENG200_Lecture1.php Pages_34=Waters_ENG200_Lecture4.php 10   conf:(0.77)
99. Pages_33=Waters_ENG200_Lecture3.php 13 ==> Pages_31=Waters_ENG200_Lecture1.php Pages_35=Waters_ENG200_Lecture5.php 10   conf:(0.77)
100. Pages_33=Waters_ENG200_Lecture3.php 13 ==> Pages_32=Waters_ENG200_Lecture2.php Pages_34=Waters_ENG200_Lecture4.php 10   conf:(0.77)

- Lecture1= "Drama" & Lecture5="Poetry2", are most likely to visit Lecture2= "Fiction" (rule1)

- Lecture3= "Love song" & Lecture5="Poetry2", are most likely to visit Lecture2= "Fiction" (rule3)

- Lecture2= "Fiction" & Lecture5=" Poetry2" & Lecture7="Compare Poetries " are most likely to visit Lecture3=" Love song" (rule23)

2. **Business sessions:** The discovered association rules for English sessions are shown in Table 13.

Analyzing Association Rules (Some Examples)

Students who visited:

- Lecture5(BA580) = "internal auditing" & Lecture7(BA580) = "intro to international corporate governance", most likely visit Lecture10(BA580) = "Sarbanes Aley Act" (rule30)

Table 13. Association rules for business sessions

1. Pages_7=Colbert_580_Lecture5.php 8 ==> Pages_16=Colbert_592_Lecture5.php 8   conf:(1)
2. Pages_10=Colbert_580_Lecture8.php 7 ==> Pages_2=Colbert_580_Lecture10.php 7   conf:(1)
3. Pages_15=Colbert_592_Lecture4.php 7 ==> Pages_2=Colbert_580_Lecture10.php 7   conf:(1)
4. Pages_18=Colbert_592_Lecture7.php 7 ==> Pages_2=Colbert_580_Lecture10.php 7   conf:(1)
5. Pages_3=Colbert_580_Lecture11.php 7 ==> Pages_4=Colbert_580_Lecture2.php 7   conf:(1)
6. Pages_3=Colbert_580_Lecture11.php 7 ==> Pages_7=Colbert_580_Lecture5.php 7   conf:(1)
7. Pages_3=Colbert_580_Lecture11.php 7 ==> Pages_16=Colbert_592_Lecture5.php 7   conf:(1)
8. Pages_5=Colbert_580_Lecture3.php 7 ==> Pages_4=Colbert_580_Lecture2.php 7   conf:(1)
9. Pages_8=Colbert_580_Lecture6.php 7 ==> Pages_4=Colbert_580_Lecture2.php 7   conf:(1)
10. Pages_5=Colbert_580_Lecture3.php 7 ==> Pages_13=Colbert_592_Lecture2.php 7   conf:(1)
11. Pages_5=Colbert_580_Lecture3.php 7 ==> Pages_14=Colbert_592_Lecture3.php 7   conf:(1)
12. Pages_10=Colbert_580_Lecture8.php 7 ==> Pages_7=Colbert_580_Lecture5.php 7   conf:(1)
13. Pages_15=Colbert_592_Lecture4.php 7 ==> Pages_7=Colbert_580_Lecture5.php 7   conf:(1)
14. Pages_18=Colbert_592_Lecture7.php 7 ==> Pages_7=Colbert_580_Lecture5.php 7   conf:(1)
15. Pages_10=Colbert_580_Lecture8.php 7 ==> Pages_9=Colbert_580_Lecture7.php 7   conf:(1)
16. Pages_15=Colbert_592_Lecture4.php 7 ==> Pages_9=Colbert_580_Lecture7.php 7   conf:(1)
17. Pages_18=Colbert_592_Lecture7.php 7 ==> Pages_9=Colbert_580_Lecture7.php 7   conf:(1)

continued on following page

Table 13. continued

18. Pages_10=Colbert_580_Lecture8.php 7 ==> Pages_14=Colbert_592_Lecture3.php 7	conf:(1)
19. Pages_15=Colbert_592_Lecture4.php 7 ==> Pages_10=Colbert_580_Lecture8.php 7	conf:(1)
20. Pages_10=Colbert_580_Lecture8.php 7 ==> Pages_15=Colbert_592_Lecture4.php 7	conf:(1)
21. Pages_10=Colbert_580_Lecture8.php 7 ==> Pages_16=Colbert_592_Lecture5.php 7	conf:(1)
22. Pages_18=Colbert_592_Lecture7.php 7 ==> Pages_10=Colbert_580_Lecture8.php 7	conf:(1)
23. Pages_10=Colbert_580_Lecture8.php 7 ==> Pages_18=Colbert_592_Lecture7.php 7	conf:(1)
24. Pages_15=Colbert_592_Lecture4.php 7 ==> Pages_14=Colbert_592_Lecture3.php 7	conf:(1)
25. Pages_18=Colbert_592_Lecture7.php 7 ==> Pages_14=Colbert_592_Lecture3.php 7	conf:(1)
26. Pages_15=Colbert_592_Lecture4.php 7 ==> Pages_16=Colbert_592_Lecture5.php 7	conf:(1)
27. Pages_18=Colbert_592_Lecture7.php 7 ==> Pages_15=Colbert_592_Lecture4.php 7	conf:(1)
28. Pages_15=Colbert_592_Lecture4.php 7 ==> Pages_18=Colbert_592_Lecture7.php 7	conf:(1)
29. Pages_18=Colbert_592_Lecture7.php 7 ==> Pages_16=Colbert_592_Lecture5.php 7	conf:(1)

30. Pages_7=Colbert_580_Lecture5.php Pages_9=Colbert_580_Lecture7.php 7 ==> Pages_2=Colbert_580_Lecture10.php 7   conf:(1)

31. Pages_2=Colbert_580_Lecture10.php Pages_9=Colbert_580_Lecture7.php 7 ==> Pages_7=Colbert_580_Lecture5.php 7   conf:(1)

32. Pages_2=Colbert_580_Lecture10.php Pages_7=Colbert_580_Lecture5.php 7 ==> Pages_9=Colbert_580_Lecture7.php 7   conf:(1)

33. Pages_7=Colbert_580_Lecture5.php Pages_10=Colbert_580_Lecture8.php 7 ==> Pages_2=Colbert_580_Lecture10.php 7   conf:(1)

34. Pages_2=Colbert_580_Lecture10.php Pages_10=Colbert_580_Lecture8.php 7 ==> Pages_7=Colbert_580_Lecture5.php 7   conf:(1)

35. Pages_2=Colbert_580_Lecture10.php Pages_7=Colbert_580_Lecture5.php 7 ==> Pages_10=Colbert_580_Lecture8.php 7   conf:(1)

36. Pages_10=Colbert_580_Lecture8.php 7 ==> Pages_2=Colbert_580_Lecture10.php Pages_7=Colbert_580_Lecture5.php 7   conf:(1)

37. Pages_7=Colbert_580_Lecture5.php Pages_14=Colbert_592_Lecture3.php 7 ==> Pages_2=Colbert_580_Lecture10.php 7   conf:(1)

38. Pages_2=Colbert_580_Lecture10.php Pages_14=Colbert_592_Lecture3.php 7 ==> Pages_7=Colbert_580_Lecture5.php 7   conf:(1)

39. Pages_2=Colbert_580_Lecture10.php Pages_7=Colbert_580_Lecture5.php 7 ==> Pages_14=Colbert_592_Lecture3.php 7   conf:(1)

40. Pages_7=Colbert_580_Lecture5.php Pages_15=Colbert_592_Lecture4.php 7 ==> Pages_2=Colbert_580_Lecture10.php 7   conf:(1)

41. Pages_2=Colbert_580_Lecture10.php Pages_15=Colbert_592_Lecture4.php 7 ==> Pages_7=Colbert_580_Lecture5.php 7   conf:(1)

42. Pages_2=Colbert_580_Lecture10.php Pages_7=Colbert_580_Lecture5.php 7 ==> Pages_15=Colbert_592_Lecture4.php 7   conf:(1)

43. Pages_15=Colbert_592_Lecture4.php 7 ==> Pages_2=Colbert_580_Lecture10.php Pages_7=Colbert_580_Lecture5.php 7   conf:(1)

44. Pages_2=Colbert_580_Lecture10.php Pages_16=Colbert_592_Lecture5.php 7 ==> Pages_7=Colbert_580_Lecture5.php 7   conf:(1)

45. Pages_2=Colbert_580_Lecture10.php Pages_7=Colbert_580_Lecture5.php 7 ==> Pages_16=Colbert_592_Lecture5.php 7   conf:(1)

46. Pages_7=Colbert_580_Lecture5.php Pages_18=Colbert_592_Lecture7.php 7 ==> Pages_2=Colbert_580_Lecture10.php 7   conf:(1)

47. Pages_2=Colbert_580_Lecture10.php Pages_18=Colbert_592_Lecture7.php 7 ==> Pages_7=Colbert_580_Lecture5.php 7   conf:(1)

48. Pages_2=Colbert_580_Lecture10.php Pages_7=Colbert_580_Lecture5.php 7 ==> Pages_18=Colbert_592_Lecture7.php 7   conf:(1)

- Lecture5(BA580)= "internal auditing" & Lecture8(BA580) = "international corporate governance2", most likely visit Lecture10(BA580) = "Sarbanes Oxley Act" (rule33)

- Lecture5(BA580)= "internal auditing" & Lecture3(BA580) = "international corporate governance2", most likely visit Lecture10(BA580) = "Sarbanes Oxley Act" (rule37)

- Lecture10(BA580)= "sarbanes oxley act" & Lecture5(BA580) ="intro to international corporate governance internal auditing", most likely visit Lecture7(BA580) = "Sarbanes Oxley Act" (rule48)

- In rules 1, 40, 44, we notice that some students visited lectures from the same professor, but in different course levels (possibly for review purpose, or following the advice from the instructor).

3. **Chemistry sessions:** The discovered association rules for Chemistry sessions are shown in Table 14.

    Analyzing association rules

    Students who visited:

    - Podcast lecture= "algebra equations-all parts" & Lecture2= "algebra equations_part2", most likely visit Lecture3="algebra equations_part3" (rule2). We notice that chemistry students downloaded the entire set of lectures as podcast (*see Note below*), then they started to visit the other formats of the lectures (text/audio).

    - Most of the students visited all the Chemistry lectures.

    Note: Visited pages that *have no lecture name* (such as LarryByrd_3.php in rule 2) are Web pages to subscribe to all the podcasted lectures of this course, and thus allow the student to download all those lectures to his/her MP3 device.

4. **History sessions:** The discovered association rules for History sessions are shown in Table 15.

    Analyzing Association Rules

    Students who visited:

    - Podcasted lectures " Plummer.php ", also visited the other formats (rules: 6,7,8,9,10)

    - Lecture3= "Old King Egypt " & Lecture4= "New King Egypt", most likely visit Lecture1= "Civilization" (rule3)

    - Lecture1= "Civilization" & Lecture4= "New King Egypt", most likely visit Lecture3= "Old King Egypt" (rule4)

Table 14. Association rules for chemistry sessions

1. Pages_0=LarryByrd_3.php 6 ==> Pages_5=LarryByrd_AlgebraicEq_Part3.php 6 conf:(1)
2. Pages_0=LarryByrd_3.php Pages_3=LarryByrd_AlgebraicEq_Part2.php 5 ==> Pages_5=LarryB-yrd_AlgebraicEq_Part3.php 5 conf:(1)
3. Pages_0=LarryByrd_3.php Pages_1=LarryByrd_AlgebraicEq_Part1.php 4 ==> Pages_5=LarryB-yrd_AlgebraicEq_Part3.php 4 conf:(1)
4. Pages_0=LarryByrd_3.php Pages_1=LarryByrd_AlgebraicEq_Part1.php Pages_3=LarryByrd_Alge-braicEq_Part2.php 3 ==> Pages_5=LarryByrd_AlgebraicEq_Part3.php 3 conf:(1)
5. Pages_5=LarryByrd_AlgebraicEq_Part3.php 14 ==> Pages_3=LarryByrd_AlgebraicEq_Part2.php 13 conf:(0.93)
6. Pages_1=LarryByrd_AlgebraicEq_Part1.php Pages_5=LarryByrd_AlgebraicEq_Part3.php 10 ==> Pages_3=LarryByrd_AlgebraicEq_Part2.php 9 conf:(0.9)
7. Pages_1=LarryByrd_AlgebraicEq_Part1.php 14 ==> Pages_3=LarryByrd_AlgebraicEq_Part2.php 12 conf:(0.86)
8. Pages_0=LarryByrd_3.php 6 ==> Pages_3=LarryByrd_AlgebraicEq_Part2.php 5 conf:(0.83)
9. Pages_0=LarryByrd_3.php Pages_5=LarryByrd_AlgebraicEq_Part3.php 6 ==> Pages_3=LarryB-yrd_AlgebraicEq_Part2.php 5 conf:(0.83)
10. Pages_0=LarryByrd_3.php 6 ==> Pages_3=LarryByrd_AlgebraicEq_Part2.php Pages_5=LarryB-yrd_AlgebraicEq_Part3.php 5 conf:(0.83)
11. Pages_3=LarryByrd_AlgebraicEq_Part2.php 16 ==> Pages_5=LarryByrd_AlgebraicEq_Part3.php 13 conf:(0.81)
12. Pages_3=LarryByrd_AlgebraicEq_Part2.php 16 ==> Pages_1=LarryByrd_AlgebraicEq_Part1.php 12 conf:(0.75)
13. Pages_1=LarryByrd_AlgebraicEq_Part1.php Pages_3=LarryByrd_AlgebraicEq_Part2.php 12 ==> Pages_5=LarryByrd_AlgebraicEq_Part3.php 9 conf:(0.75)
14. Pages_0=LarryByrd_3.php Pages_1=LarryByrd_AlgebraicEq_Part1.php 4 ==> Pages_3=LarryB-yrd_AlgebraicEq_Part2.php 3 conf:(0.75)
15. Pages_0=LarryByrd_3.php Pages_1=LarryByrd_AlgebraicEq_Part1.php Pages_5=LarryByrd_Alge-braicEq_Part3.php 4 ==> Pages_3=LarryByrd_AlgebraicEq_Part2.php 3 conf:(0.75)

Table 15. Association rules for history sessions

1. Pages_3=Plummer_Hist119_Lecture4.php 3 ==> Pages_1=Plummer_Hist119_Lecture1.php 3 conf:(1)
2. Pages_3=Plummer_Hist119_Lecture4.php 3 ==> Pages_2=Plummer_Hist119_Lecture3.php 3 conf:(1)
3. Pages_2=Plummer_Hist119_Lecture3.php Pages_3=Plummer_Hist119_Lecture4.php 3 ==> Pages_1=Plummer_Hist119_Lecture1.php 3 conf:(1)
4. Pages_1=Plummer_Hist119_Lecture1.php Pages_3=Plummer_Hist119_Lecture4.php 3 ==> Pages_2=Plummer_Hist119_Lecture3.php 3 conf:(1)
5. Pages_3=Plummer_Hist119_Lecture4.php 3 ==> Pages_1=Plummer_Hist119_Lecture1.php Pages_2=Plummer_Hist119_Lecture3.php 3 conf:(1)
6. Pages_0=Plummer.php 1 ==> Pages_1=Plummer_Hist119_Lecture1.php 1 conf:(1)
7. Pages_0=Plummer.php 1 ==> Pages_2=Plummer_Hist119_Lecture3.php 1 conf:(1)
8. Pages_0=Plummer.php Pages_2=Plummer_Hist119_Lecture3.php 1 ==> Pages_1=Plummer_Hist119_Lecture1.php 1 conf:(1)
9. Pages_0=Plummer.php Pages_1=Plummer_Hist119_Lecture1.php 1 ==> Pages_2=Plummer_Hist119_Lecture3.php 1 conf:(1)
10. Pages_0=Plummer.php 1 ==> Pages_1=Plummer_Hist119_Lecture1.php Pages_2=Plummer_Hist119_Lecture3.php 1 conf:(1)

5. **Health and human services sessions:**

    The discovered association rules for Health and Human Services sessions are shown in Table 16.

    Analyzing Association Rules

    Students who visited:

    - Podcasted lectures "Chadha_3.php" and "Kelley_3.php", also visited some of these lectures in the other formats (rules: 1,2).

    - Lecture1= "Human Nutrition", most likely download all the podcasted lectures (rule3).

    Note: Chadha_3.php (rule1) and Kelley_3.php (rule 2) are Web pages where the students can subscribe to *all the podcasted lectures* of those courses.

6. **Education sessions:** The discovered association rules for Education sessions are shown in Table 17.

    Analyzing association rules

    Students who visited:

    - Lecture1="creating professional growth plan" most likely visit Lecture2= "professional portfolio process" (rule2)

    - Lecture4= "standards movement in education2", most likely visit Lecture3= "standards movement in education" (rule9)

Recommendation in the Adaptive Web-Based Educational Platform

In this section we explain how the results of data mining, as described in the previous sections, can form the basis for automated recommendations. From the association rules that link "all" attributes, we may conclude that different areas of study have different user behavior and different preferences. Moreover, different students have different learning styles, different preferences of time access, and browsing access (Table 11). From the association rules that relate the lectures accessed by the

Table 16. Association rules for health and human services sessions

1. Pages_0=Chadha_3.php 5 ==> Pages_1=Chadha_4520_lecture1.php 5 conf:(1)
2. Pages_2=Kelley_3.php 3 ==> Pages_3=Kelley_Lecture1.php 3 conf:(1)
3. Pages_3=Kelley_Lecture1.php 4 ==> Pages_2=Kelley_3.php 3 conf:(0.75)

Table 17. Association rules for education sessions

1. Pages_2=Houston_Lecture2.php 3 ==> Pages_1=Houston_Lecture1.php 3 conf:(1)
2. Pages_1=Houston_Lecture1.php 3 ==> Pages_2=Houston_Lecture2.php 3 conf:(1)
3. Pages_3=Houston_Lecture3.php 3 ==> Pages_1=Houston_Lecture1.php 3 conf:(1)
4. Pages_1=Houston_Lecture1.php 3 ==> Pages_3=Houston_Lecture3.php 3 conf:(1)
5. Pages_4=Houston_Lecture4.php 3 ==> Pages_1=Houston_Lecture1.php 3 conf:(1)
6. Pages_1=Houston_Lecture1.php 3 ==> Pages_4=Houston_Lecture4.php 3 conf:(1)
7. Pages_3=Houston_Lecture3.php 3 ==> Pages_2=Houston_Lecture2.php 3 conf:(1)
8. Pages_2=Houston_Lecture2.php 3 ==> Pages_3=Houston_Lecture3.php 3 conf:(1)
9. Pages_4=Houston_Lecture4.php 3 ==> Pages_2=Houston_Lecture2.php 3 conf:(1)
10. Pages_2=Houston_Lecture2.php 3 ==> Pages_4=Houston_Lecture4.php 3 conf:(1)

same student, we notice that students follow different paths through the Web site, thus choosing various combinations or assortments of lectures. From the college-based clustering of the cumulative transaction vectors of each student, we notice that students within the same college tend to be divided into several groups based on the combination of lectures that they have chosen, and that this division is not only based on course number or instructor. Rather, it truly shows variability in the menu selections (if we regard a set of chosen lectures as one menu). We can build a recommender system by using any or all of the above models, that is:

a.   Association rules between all attributes (such as Day, Time, Media Type, Academic Department).

b.   Association rules between lectures (accessed by the same student).

c..   Cluster centroids/profiles of lecture assortments that are often chosen by a "group" of similar students in the same college.

Depending on the type of model used, we can form the following types of recommender systems:

a.   *Recommenders of Type A* will tend to recommend a certain *Media Type* based on day, time, or department (or combination thereof) whenever a student session's attributes match the antecedent of any of the rules of model type A. The recommended Media Type corresponds to the one in the consequent part of the matching rules.

b.   *Recommenders of Type B* will recommend a set of lectures to a student if the lectures that were already visited by this student match some the antecedent of the rules in model B. The recommended lectures will be the top ranking lectures of the consequents of the matching rules.

c.   *Recommenders of Type C* will recommend a set of lectures to a student if the lectures that were already visited by this student match some the cluster centroids/profiles in model C. The recommended lectures will be the top ranking lectures when accumulated throughout all the matching and closest profiles.

Cluster-Based Collaborative Filtering Recommendation (Type C)

Table 18 shows the results of clustering English Weblog sessions into 15 clusters; each cell represents the weight of each lecture in the corresponding cluster's centroid.

Using the cosine similarity in (2), which measures the relative amount of overlap between a student's cumulative session A and a cluster centroid B which can be considered as a prototypical cumulative session of a group of users, thus a group profile, and assuming that A_i represents the presence (i.e., a value of 1) or absence (value of 0) of lecture i in session vector A:

$$\cos ine(A, B) = \frac{\sum_{i=1}^{n} A_i B_i}{\sqrt{\sum_{i=1}^{n} A_i^2 \sum_{i=1}^{n} B_i^2}} \tag{2}$$

we were able to map each student to the closest cluster centroids/group profiles. For example, we illustrate the task of recommendation given as input a small *part* of Student 41's session, that is, partial session: *(Waters_ENG200_Lecture1.php, Waters_ENG200_Lecture2.php, Waters_ENG200_Lecture5.php)* by computing the cosine similarity from this student to each cluster's centroid as shown in Table 19.

If we pick the clusters with cosine similarity ≥ 0.6 then the matching clusters should be: 0, 2, 3, 7, 11.

Table 20 shows the lectures (in shaded color) that should be recommended to student41.

Using a threshold >= 0.5, we extracted the following lectures (shown on a dark background in Box 1).

Since student41 already visited the following lectures in the partial session (Box 2).

We must filter out the lectures that have already been visited. Hence, finally the student will be recommended with the following remaining lectures:

Table18. Cluster centroids for the English cumulative sessions (cluster rows were duplicated to accommodate all the lectures)

	Waters_ ENG200_ Lecture1. php	Waters_ ENG200_ Lecture2. php	Waters_ ENG200_ Lecture31. php	Waters_ ENG200_ Lecture4. php	Waters_ ENG200_ Lecture5. php	Waters_ ENG200_ Lecture6. php	Waters_ ENG200_ Lecture7. php
cluster0	0.75	1	0.875	1	1	1	0.875
cluster1	0	1	0	0	0	0	1
cluster2	1	1	1	0.5	1	0	0.5
cluster3	1	0.25	0.125	0	0	0.125	0
cluster4	0	0.5	0.5	0	1	1	1
cluster5	1	0	0	0	0	0	0
cluster6	1	1	1	1	0	0	0
cluster7	1	1	0	0	1	0	0
cluster8	0	0	0	0	0	0	0
cluster9	0	0	0	0	0	0	0
cluster10	0	1	0	0	0	0	0
cluster11	1	1	0	0	1	0	0
cluster12	0.3333	0.5	0.3333	0.3333	0.3333	0.3333	0.3333
cluster13	0	0	0	0	0	1	0
cluster14	0	0	0	0.1667	0	0	0
	Olmsted_ ENG200_ Lecture1. php	Olmsted_ ENG200_ Lecture2. php	Olmsted_ ENG200_ Lecture3.php	Olmsted_ ENG200_ Lecture4. php	Olmsted_ ENG200_ Lecture5. php	Olmsted_ ENG200_ Lecture6. php	Olmsted_ ENG200_ Lecture7. php
cluste0	0	0	0	0	0	0	0
cluste1	0	0	0	0	0	0	0
cluster2	0	0	0	0	0	0	0
cluster3	0	0	0	0	0	0	0
cluster4	0	0	0	0	0	0	0
cluster5	1	1	0	0	1	0	0
cluster6	0	0	0	0	0	0	0
cluster7	0	0	0	0	1	0	0
cluster8	1	0.5	0	1	0.5	0	0.5
cluster9	0	0	1	0	0	0	0
cluster10	0	0	0	0	0	0	0
cluster11	1	1	0	0	0	0	0
cluster12	1	1	1	1	1	1	1

continued on following page

Table 18. continued

clusters	Olmsted_ ENG200_ Lecture8. php	Olmsted_ ENG200_ Lecture9. php	Olmsted_ ENG200_ Lecture10. php	Olmsted_ ENG200_ Lecture11. php	Olmsted_ ENG200_ Lecture12. php	Olmsted_ ENG200_ Lec- ture13. php	Olmsted_ ENG200_ Lecture14. php
cluster13	0	0	0	0	0	0	0
cluster14	0.1667	0.1667	0	0.3333	0.1667	0.1667	0.1667
cluste0	0	0	0	0	0	0	0
cluste1	0	0	0	0	0	0	0
cluster2	0	0	0	0	0	0	0
cluster3	0	0	0	0	0	0	0
cluster4	0	0	0	0	0	0	0
cluster5	0	1	0	0	0	0	0
cluster6	0	0	0	0	0	0	0
cluster7	0	0	0	0	0	0	0
cluster8	0	1	0	0	0	0	0
cluster9	0	0	0	1	1	0	0
cluster10	0	0	0	0	0	0	0
cluster11	0	0	0	0	0	0	0
cluster12	1	1	0.6667	0.8333	0.8333	0.6667	0.8333
cluster13	0	0	0	0	0	0	0
cluster14	0.1667	0	0.3333	0	0	0	0

Table 19.

	Cluster0	Cluster1	Cluster2	Cluster3	Cluster4	Cluster5	Cluster6	
Student41	0.64318	0.40825	0.8165	0.69007	0.46291	0.2582	0.57735	
	Cluster7	Cluster8	Cluster9	Cluster10	Cluster11	Cluster12	Cluster13	Cluster14
Student41	0.86603	0	0	0.57735	0.7746	0.18761	0	0

Table 20. Lectures (in shaded color) that should be recommended to student 41

	Waters_ ENG200_ Lecture1. php	Waters_ ENG200_ Lecture2. php	Waters_ ENG200_ Lecture3. php	Waters_ ENG200_ Lecture4. php	Waters_ ENG200_ Lecture5. php	Waters_ ENG200_ Lecture6. php	Waters_ ENG200_ Lecture7. php
Cluster0	0.75	1	0.875	1	1	1	0.875
Cluster2	1	1	1	0.5	1	0	0.5
Cluster3	1	0.25	0.125	0	0	0.125	0
Cluster7	1	1	0	0	1	0	0
cluster11	1	1	0	0	1	0	0
	Olmsted_ ENG200_ Lecture1. php	Olmsted_ ENG200_ Lecture2. php	Olmsted_ ENG200_ Lecture3. php	Olmsted_ ENG200_ Lecture4. php	Olmsted_ ENG200_ Lecture5. php	Olmsted_ ENG200_ Lecture6. php	Olmsted_ ENG200_ Lecture7. php
Cluster0	0	0	0	0	0	0	0
Cluster2	0	0	0	0	0	0	0
Cluster3	0	0	0	0	0	0	0
Cluster7	0	0	0	0	1	0	0
cluster11	1	1	0	0	0	0	0
	Olmsted_ ENG200_ Lecture8. php	Olmsted_ ENG200_ Lecture9. php	Olmsted_ ENG200_ Lecture10. php	Olmsted_ ENG200_ Lecture11. php	Olmsted_ ENG200_ Lecture12. php	Olmsted_ ENG200_ Lecture13. php	Olmsted_ ENG200_ Lecture14. php
Cluster0	0	0	0	0	0	0	0
Cluster2	0	0	0	0	0	0	0
Cluster3	0	0	0	0	0	0	0
Cluster7	0	0	0	0	0	0	0
cluster11	0	0	0	0	0	0	0

Evaluation

We can evaluate the quality of our recommendation for student41 by computing the recall (1), precision (2), and F-score (3) measures, as shown below, where the true lectures are the lectures that have really been visited by the student, but not including the input lectures in their partial session. Given Student41's *complete* session was *(Waters_ENG200_Lecture1.php, Waters_ENG200_Lecture2.php, Waters_ENG200_Lecture5.php, Olmsted_ENG200_Lecture1.php, Olmsted_ENG200_ Lecture2.php)*, and that his or her *partial* session was: *(Waters_ENG200_Lecture1. php, Waters_ENG200_Lecture2.php, Waters_ENG200_Lecture5.php)*, the *true* lectures (for perfect recommendation) should be *(Olmsted_ENG200_Lecture1.php, Olmsted_ENG200_Lecture2.php)*.

Box 1.

All Recommended Lectures							
Cluster0	Waters_ENG200_Lecture1.php	Waters_ENG200_Lecture2.php	Waters_ENG200_Lecture3.php	Waters_ENG200_Lecture4.php	Waters_ENG200_Lecture5.php	Waters_ENG200_Lecture6.php	Waters_ENG200_Lecture7.php
Cluster2	Waters_ENG200_Lecture1.php	Waters_ENG200_Lecture2.php	Waters_ENG200_Lecture3.php	Waters_ENG200_Lecture5.php			
Cluster3	Waters_ENG200_Lecture1.php						
Cluster7	Waters_ENG200_Lecture1.php	Waters_ENG200_Lecture2.php	Waters_ENG200_Lecture5.php	Olmsted_ENG200_Lecture5.php			
cluster11	Waters_ENG200_Lecture1.php	Waters_ENG200_Lecture2.php	Waters_ENG200_Lecture5.php	Olmsted_ENG200_Lecture1.php	Olmsted_ENG200_Lecture2.php		

Box 2.

Already visited Lectures		
Waters_ENG200_Lecture1.php	Waters_ENG200_Lecture2.php	Waters_ENG200_Lecture5.php

Box 3.

Filtered Recommended Lectures		
Waters_ENG200_Lecture3.php	Waters_ENG200_Lecture4.php	Waters_ENG200_Lecture6.php
Waters_ENG200_Lecture7.php	Olmsted_ENG200_Lecture1.php	Olmsted_ENG200_Lecture2.php
Olmsted_ENG200_Lecture5.php		

Hence

{*true lectures*} = {<u>*Olmsted_ENG200_Lecture1.php, Olmsted_ENG200_Lecture2.php*</u>},

while

{*recommended lectures*} = {*Waters_ENG200_Lecture3.php, Waters_ENG200_Lecture4.php, Waters_ENG200_Lecture6.php, Waters_ENG200_Lecture7.php,* <u>*Olmsted_ENG200_Lecture1.php, Olmsted_ENG200_Lecture2.php,*</u> *Olmsted_ENG200_Lecture5.php*}.

where the underlined lectures are the ones that are *in both the true and the recommended lecture sets.*

Recall

Recall (3) is the proportion of true lectures that are recommended out of all true lectures = 2/2 = 100%

$$recall = \frac{\{recommended \; lectures\} \cap \{true \; lectures\}}{\{true \; lectures\}} \tag{3}$$

Precision

Precision (4) is the proportion of true lectures that are recommended out of all recommended lectures = 2/7 = 28.57%.

$$precision = \frac{\{recommended \; lectures\} \cap \{true \; lectures\}}{\{recommended \; lectures\}} \tag{4}$$

F-measure

The F-score (5) is the weighted harmonic mean of precision and recall, the traditional F-measure or balanced F-score is $F_1 = 2(1)(0.2857)/(1+0.2857) = 0.44$ or 44%

$$F_1 = \frac{2 \cdot precision \cdot recall}{(precision + recall)} \tag{5}$$

Effect of the cluster similarity threshold:

We will illustrate below how the matching threshold affects precision and recall. If we pick the clusters with cosine similarity ≥ 0.7, then the matching clusters are limited to clusters 2, 7, 11. In this case, it is easy to verify that the recommended lectures will be chosen from:

All Recommended Lectures					
Cluster2	Waters_ENG200_Lecture1.php	Waters_ENG200_Lecture2.php	Waters_ENG200_Lecture3.php	Waters_ENG200_Lecture5.php	
Cluster7	Waters_ENG200_Lecture1.php	Waters_ENG200_Lecture2.php	Waters_ENG200_Lecture5.php	Olmsted_ENG200_Lecture5.php	
cluster11	Waters_ENG200_Lecture1.php	Waters_ENG200_Lecture2.php	Waters_ENG200_Lecture5.php	Olmsted_ENG200_Lecture1.php	Olmsted_ENG200_Lecture2.php

This leads to the filtered recommendations:

$\{recommended\ lectures\} = \{Waters\_ENG200\_Lecture3.php, \underline{Olmsted\_ENG200\_Lecture1.php}, \underline{Olmsted\_ENG200\_Lecture2.php}, Olmsted\_ENG200\_Lecture5.php\}$.

Precision now becomes 2/4=50%, while recall remains at 100%. This increases the F_1 to $2(1)(0.5)/(1+0.5) = 0.667$ or 66.7%. What we have just illustrated is a general trend where a more sringent matching threshold can increase the precision. A consequence of this increase is typically a decrease in recall, though, this did not occur at threshold 0.7. Recall would however decrease to 0% (as well as precision) if the cluster matching threshold was increased to 0.8, since only clusters 2 and 7 would match the student session, resulting in:

$\{recommended\ lectures\} = \{Waters\_ENG200\_Lecture3.php, Olmsted\_ENG200\_Lecture5.php\}$.

We summarize the evaluation metrics in Table 21. In this case a cluster similarity threshold of 0.7 seems to yield an optimal tradeoff between precision and recall of recommendations.

Conclusion and Future Work

In order to maximize the usefulness of the online information that a student retrieves from the Web, this information needs to be filtered and adapted to the needs of individual students. Therefore, educational materials need to be tailored to fit the needs, learning styles, and prior knowledge of individual students. Our multimedia Web-based education platform offers several techniques to present the learning material for different types of learners and for different learning styles. We have presented a data driven analysis to find the difference between the students' learning style and its

Table 21. Precision, Recall, and F_1 score for different cluster similarity thresholds

Cluster matching threshold	0.6	0.7	0.8
Precision	28.5%	50%	0%
Recall	100%	100%	0%
F-score	44%	66.7%	0%

Figure 9. Cluster based collaborative filtering recommender system (illustrated for student 41) "© 2008, Leyla Zhuhadar. Used with permission."

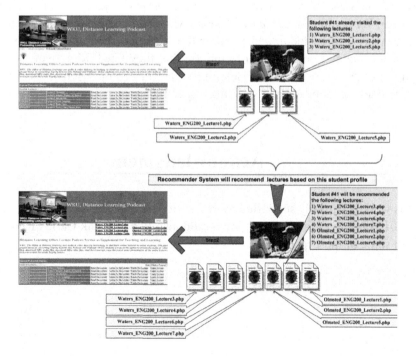

relation to the topic (college), and the time and date of browsing. This information is valuable for the system administrator who maintains the online course material. On the other hand, decisions were made to have the reading learning style not as an option but as a core resource since the majority of students were using it, and this makes our educational platform ADA compliant. Data mining techniques were used to create a recommender system. In particular, we used clustering and association rule mining. User models (user profiles) that were generated by data mining can be used to recommend online students with online lectures that fit their profiles. Of course, the use of Podcasting and Vodcasting was the major difference in this platform as compared to other Web-based educational platforms. The popularity of podcasting is growing very fast and the need to apply it to enhance e-learning can not be ignored. Mining online student activity with respect to the use of Podcasting and Vodcasting can give us an insight into what should be developed to improve an e-learning environment.

The implementation of the proposed Web-based education platform takes students' activity into consideration. The main goal was to create a recommender system which was based on discovering patterns from the online students' behavior, and then comparing these patterns to new learners. While the current recommender system did not allow the educator to be involved in the recommendation process, a future improvement would allow the educator to monitor the recommender system's performance metrics, as well as to modify or expand the discovered patterns used as a substrate for the recommendations. The instructor can thus add some input to improve the recommendations. Moreover, keeping track of selected recommendations by the users can provide a way to evaluate the performance of the recommender system. We could also compare students who followed the recommendations with those who ignored them, and monitor the time that each one of these groups of students spends to reach the information that they need. Moreover, personalized quizzes could be added for each learning style and a comparison between the results could define which learning style fits a specific topic.

Acknowledgment

This work is partially supported by National Science Foundation CAREER Award IIS-0133948 to Olfa Nasraoui. We would also like to thank Carlos Rojas for help with some of the experiments.

References

Agrawal, R., & Swami, A. (1993). Mining association rules between sets of items in large databases. In *Proceedings from 1993 ACM-SIGMOD International Conference. Management of Data*, Washington, DC (pp. 207-216).

Beal, C.R., Qu, L., & Lee, H. (2006). Classifying learner engagement through integration of multiple data sources. In *Proceedings from AAAI 21st National Conference on Artificial Intelligence.*

Bollen, J. (2000). Group user models for personalized hyperlink recommendations. In *Proceedings from International Conference on Adaptive Hypermedia and Adaptive Web-Based Systems, LNCS 1892.*

Brusilovsky, P., & Maybury, M.T. (2002). From adaptive hypermedia to adaptive Web. *Communications of the ACM, The Adaptive Web, 45*(5).

Cristea, A., & De Mooij, A. (2003). Adaptive course authoring: MOT, my online teacher. In *Proceedings from ICT'03, IEEE LTTF International Conference on Telecommunications,* Papeete, French Polynesia.

De Bra, P., Aroyo, L., & Cristea, A. (2004). *Adaptive Web-based educational hypermedia. Web dynamic: Adaptive to change in content, size, topology and use* (pp. 387-410). London: Springer.

Edelstein, H.A. (2001). Pan for gold in the clickstream. *Informationweek.* Retrieved January 8, 2008, from http://www.informationweek.com/828/mining.htm

Hammouda, K., & Kamel, M. (2005). Data mining in e-learning. In S. Pierre (Ed.), *E-learning networked environments and architectures: A knowledge processing perspective.* London: Springer.

Joachims, T. (2002). Optimizing search engines using clickthrough data. In *Proceedings from 8th ACM SIGKDD Conference* (pp. 133-142).

McQueen, J. (1967). Some methods for classification and analysis of multivariate observations. In *Proceedings of 5th Berkeley Symposium on Mathematics, Statistics and Probability* (pp. 281- 298).

Mitrovic, A. (2002). Using evaluation to shape ITS design: Results and experiences with SQL-Tutor. *User Modeling and User-Adapted Interaction, 12*(2-3), 243-279.

Mobasher, B., Cooley, R., & Srivastava, J. (2000). Automatic personalization based on Web usage mining. *Communications of the ACM, 43*(8), 142-151.

Mobasher, B., Dai, H., Luo, T., & Nakagawa, M. (2001). Effective personalization based on association rule discovery from Web usage data. In *ACM Workshop on Web information and data management*, Atlanta, GA.

Monk, D. (2005). Using data mining for e-learning decision making. *The Electronic Journal of E-Learning, 3*(1), 41-54. Retrieved January 8, 2008, from www.ejel.org

Nasraoui, O., Krishnapuram, R., & Joshi, A. (1999). Mining Web access logs using a relational clustering algorithm based on a robust estimator. In *Proceedings from 8th International World Wide Web Conference*, Toronto (pp. 40-41).

Nasraoui, O., Krishnapuram, R., Joshi, A., & Kamdar, T. (2002). Automatic Web user profiling and personalization using robust fuzzy relational clustering. In J. Segovia, P. Szczepaniak & M. Niedzwiedzinski, (Eds.), *E-commerce and intelligent methods in the series studies in fuzziness and soft computing*. London: Springer-Verlag.

Nasraoui, O. World wide Web personalization. In J. Wang (Ed.), *Encyclopedia of data mining and data warehousing*. Idea Group.

Schafer, J.B., Konstan, J., & Reidel, J. (1999). Recommender systems in e-commerce. In *Proceedings from ACM Conference E-commerce,* Denver, CO (pp. 158-166).

Weber, G., & Brusilovsky, P. (2001). ELM-ART: An adaptive versatile system for Web-based instruction. *International Journal of Artificial Intelligence in Education, 12,* 351-38.

Witten, I.H., & Frank, E. (2000). *Data mining: Practical machine learning tools and techniques with Java implementations*. Morgan Kauffman.

Zaiane, O.R. (2001). Web usage mining for a better Web-based learning environment. In *Proceedings from Conference on Advanced Technology for Education*, Banff, Alberta (pp. 60-64).

Zaiane, O.R. (2002). Building a recommender agent for e-learning systems. In *Proceedings from 7th International Conference on Computers in Education (ICCE 2002),* Auckland, New Zealand (pp. 55-59).

Zheng, R.G.T., & Niu, Y. (2002). Webframe: In pursuit of computationally and cognitively efficient Web mining. In *Proceedings from 6th Pacific-Asia Conference on Knowledge Discovery and Data Mining*, Taipei, Taiwan (pp. 264-275).

Further Readings

Taming Evolving, Expanding and Multi-faceted Web Clickstreams. (2005, August 21). (Program and Proceeding), Chicago Illinois. Retrieved January 8, 2008, from http://db.cs.ualberta.ca/Webkdd05/

Web Mining and Web Usage Analysis. (2006, August 20-23). (Program and Proceeding). In *the 12th ACM SIGKDD International Conference on Knowledge Discovery and Data Mining (KDD 2006)*, Philadelphia, Pennsylvania.

Useful URLs

ACM: Ubiquity - The New Challenges of E-learning, http://www.acm.org/ubiquity/interviews/w_graves_2.html

Automatic Personalization Based on Web Usage Mining, http://maya.cs.depaul.edu/~mobasher/personalization/

Building a Recommender Agent for E-Learning Systems, http://www.cs.ualberta.ca/~zaiane/postscript/icce02.pdf

Complete This Puzzle: A Connectionist Approach to Accurate Web Recommendations Based on a Committee of Predictors, http://Webmining.spd.louisville.edu/Web sites/PAPERS/conference/Nasraoui-WebKDD04-NN-final.pdf

Data Mining in E-Learning, http://pami.uwaterloo.ca/pub/hammouda/hammouda-elearning.pdf

E-LEARNING: Challenges and Opportunities for Key Players, http://www.gii.co.jp/english/iu9947_e_leaarning.html

Mining Patterns of Events in Students' Teamwork Data, http://www.cs.ualberta.ca/~zaiane/postscript/edm06.pdf

Pan for Gold in the Clickstream, http://www.informationweek.com/828/mining.htm

Using Data Mining for E-Learning Decision Making, www.ejel.org

Web Personalization, http://Webmining.spd.louisville.edu/Web sites/PAPERS/book_chapter/FINAL-Nasraoui-WWW-Personalization.pdf

Web Usage Mining for a Better Web-Based Learning Environment, http://www.cs.ualberta.ca/~zaiane/postscript/CATE2001.pdf

Appendix

Figure A1.

> **Internet Session: Adaptive Web-Based Educational Platform**
>
> **http://blog.wku.edu/podcasts/** This chapter is based on the implementation of Podcasting and Vodcasting in an adaptive e-learning environment. It uses data mining to track the learning activity of distance learning students. The site can be tested by choosing any lecture offered by the Distance Learning Office as well as a learning style/media. The Recommender *system* has been tested off-line.
>
> **Interaction:**
>
> Choose one of the courses we offer and try different learning styles. See which one in your opinion can fit your learning style the most.

Figure A2.

> **Case Study**
>
> **Adaptive Web-Based Educational Platform**
>
> *The Office of Distance Learning at WKU uses audio and video technology to distribute online lectures to online students. This pilot project focuses on Podcasting and VOD-casting and their use to enhance e-learning. Online students are given the option to stream the audio or video files, download MP3 audio files, download MP4 video files, read the transcript, and even look at the powerpoint presentation of the online lectures. Test this platform by logging to this link: http://blog.wku.edu/podcasts/*
>
> **Questions:**
>
> 1. Which learning styles are preferred the most?
> 2. Did you use the subscription method to download your lectures or did you rather prefer to stream them over the Internet?
> 3. If you tried two different courses from two different colleges, do you think that you would choose the same learning style or could it be different from course to course?

Chapter XI

Towards More Intelligent Assessment Systems

Sonja Radenković, University of Belgrade, Serbia

Nenad Krdžavac, University of Belgrade, Serbia

Vladan Devedžić, University of Belgrade, Serbia

Inside Chapter

This chapter presents a framework for intelligent analysis of the students' knowledge in assessment systems, using description logics (DLs) reasoning techniques. The framework is based on Model Driven Architecture (MDA) software engineering standards. It starts from the IMS Question and Test Interoperability (QTI) standard and includes MDA-based metamodel and model transformations for QTI assessment systems. It also specifies an architecture for QTI assessment systems that is reusable, extensible, and facilitates interoperability between its component systems. An implementation of the QTI metamodel and the relevant example of transformations is provided in order to support developments according to the proposed framework.

Introduction

Many traditional methods of evaluating learners' knowledge by a test depend on their solutions of a series of problems they solve in the corresponding domain. Such methods are hardly suitable for real-time evaluation of learner progress during instruction, because they are time-consuming and limited in their ability to diagnose different levels of expertise. The IMS Question and Test Interoperability (QTI) standard (Lay & Pierre, 2006c) specifies how to represent question (assessmentItem) and test (assessmentTest) data and the corresponding result reports. These items are the smallest exchangeable assessment objects within this specification. An item is more than a "question" in that it contains the question and instructions of how to be presented, the response processing to be applied to the candidate response(s), and the feedback that may be presented (including hints and solutions). According to Lay and Pierre (2006c), there is an exchange of items, assessment, and results between authoring tools, item banks, learning systems, and assessment delivery systems. For interchange *between* these systems, an XMI binding is provided (OMG XMI, 2001).

This chapter proposes a framework and an architecture for development of QTI-based assessment systems (or just QTI systems, for short) and for analysis of students' solutions acquired through the use of such a system. QTI standard does not define such a framework. Thus, to ease system development and deployment, it is necessary to define how to interconnect various components of a QTI system, as well as to provide good response processing.

The chapter is organized as follows. The next section provides definitions and short discussions of the relevant concepts. The section also presents a short literature review important for this research. The following section describes the basic concepts of the QTI standard. We then describe the basic concepts of description logics and reasoning services enabled by description logics and then explain the basic principles of the Model Driven Architecture (MDA) methodology. The final section proposes a framework for intelligent analysis of students' solutions. It also describes the QTI metamodel using the standard unified modeling language (UML) notation. This section explains how description logics (DL) reasoning techniques can be applied in an assessment system and provides an illustrative example.

Background

The concepts defined here are necessary to grasp in order to understand the rest of the chapter. Table 1 summarizes the relevant references.

- **Description Logics (DLs):** Mathematical formalism for knowledge representation. The logics are decidable fragments of first order logic.

- **Tableau:** A tableau is a graph. A DLs formula is transformed in the corresponding tableau in case of checking the satisfiability of DLs concepts. More detailed explanations follow in a later section.

- **Metamodels and Models (Milicev, 2001):** A metamodel is a formal specification of a modeling language. Metamodeling is a process of defining metamodels. A model is a description of a system, constructed in some language. The language is called the modeling language. Modeling is the process of building models.

- **IMS QTI Assessment Standard:** Specification that describes a data model for the representation of question (assessmentItem) and test (assessmentTest) data and their corresponding results reports (Lay & Pierre, 2006c). "QTI" stands for Query and Test Interoperability System.

A Short Survey of the IMS QTI Standard

This section briefly introduces the basic concepts of the IMS Question and Test Interoperability (QTI) standard (Lay & Pierre, 2006c). The IMS QTI specification describes a data model for representation of question (assessmentItem) and test (assessmentTest) data and their corresponding results reports (Lay & Pierre, 2006c).

Table 2 describes the basic modules of a QTI standard, with a short description of the role of each module in an assessment system. According to the QTI standard, there are a few actors relevant to the use cases in a typical assessment system. These

Table 1. A literature review concerning the new research agenda within the e-learning field and description logics

Issue	References	Main contribution
QTI Assessment standard	(Lay & Pierre, 2006c)	IMS Question and Test Interoperability Overview, Version 2.1 Public draft.
	(Lay & Pierre, 2006a)	IMS Question and Test Interoperability Assessment Test, Section, and Item Information.
	(Lay & Pierre, 2006b)	IMS Question and Test Interoperability Implementation Guide.
Description Logics	(Horrocks, 1997)	Optimising Tableaux Decision Procedures for Description Logics.
	(Baader et al., 2003)	The Description Logics Handbook, Theory Application and Implementation.

actors are described in Table 3, with a short description of their roles in assessment systems. The use case actors can be described using UML use case diagrams.

QTI standard is designed to facilitate interoperability between a number of systems (Table 2), in relation to the actors that use them (Table 3). Specifically, QTI is designed to (Lay & Pierre, 2006c):

1.   Provide a well-documented content format for storing and exchanging *items* independent of the authoring tool used to create them;

2.   Support the deployment of item banks across a wide range of learning and assessment delivery systems;

3.   Provide a well-documented content format for storing and exchanging *tests* independent of the test construction tool used to create them;

4.   Support the deployment of items, item banks, and tests from diverse sources in a single learning or assessment delivery system;

5.   Provide systems with the ability to report test results in a consistent manner.

In order to understand the QTI metamodel proposed in this chapter, the understanding of the assessment process as it is defined in the IMS QTI specification is necessary. In this process, the student being assessed—the candidate—is asked questions (represented by *assessmentItem*s) and is required to solve problems presented in tests (represented by *assessmentTest*s) (Table 4). The student enters answers and solutions, and the system scores them. The processes in an assessment system are not independent (Table 4). For example, Outcome processing depends on Assessment (Lay & Pierre, 2006d).

Table 2. Overview of QTI modules (see Lay & Pierre, 2006c)

The name of module	description
ItemBank	A system for collecting and managing collections of assessment items.
testConstruction	A system for assembling tests from individual items
assessmentDeliverySystem	A system for managing the delivery of assessments to candidates.
learningSystem	A system that enables or directs learners in learning activities, possibly coordinated with a tutor.
authoringTool	A system used by an author for creating or modifying an assessment item.

Table 3. Overview of use case actors (see Lay & Pierre, 2006c)

The name of use case actor	description
Author	The author of an assessment item.
itemBankManager	An actor with responsibility for managing a collection of assessment items with an itemBank.
testConstruction	The role of test constructor is to create tests (test forms) from individual items.
Proctor	A person charged with overseeing the delivery of an assessment.
Scorer	A person or external system responsible for assessing the candidate's responses during assessment delivery. In this solution, the scorer is DLs reasoner.
Tutor	Someone involved in managing, directing, or supporting the learning process for a learner but who is not subject to (the same) assessment.
Candidate	The person being assessed by an assessment test or assessment item.

Table 4. Overview of some assessment processes (see Lay & Pierre, 2006d)

The name of assessment process	A short description
FeedBack	The process of presentation material to the candidate. FeedBack includes any material.
Response Processing	The process by which the values of Response Variables are judged (scored) and the values of item Outcomes are assigned. Responses are data provided by the candidate.
Outcome Processing	The process by which the values of item Outcomes (or Responses) are aggregated to make test outcomes. Outcome is the result of an Assessment Test or Item.
Assessment	The process of measuring some aspect of a candidate.

Description Logics

Historically, description logics (DLs) evolved from semantic networks and frame systems, mainly to satisfy the need of giving a formal semantics to these formalisms (Baader, Calvanese, McGinness, Nardi, & Patel-Schneider, 2003). As the name DLs indicates, one characteristic of these languages is that they are equipped with formal logic-based semantics. The basic notions in DLs are *concepts* (unary predicates) and *roles* (binary predicates) (Baader, Calvanese, McGinness, Nardi, & Patel-Schneider, 2003). Complex concepts are developed using atomic ones and using atomic roles. The basic propositionally closed DL is attribute language with complement description logic (ALC DL) (Baader, Calvanese, McGinness, Nardi, & Patel-Schneider, 2003), and some other DLs are extensions of this logic. DLs are logic formalisms used as a basis for the Semantic Web ontology languages (e.g., OWL) (Baader, Horrocks, & Sattler, 2005), and they offer reasoning services (Baader, Calvanese, McGinness, Nardi, & Patel-Schneider, 2003), which can be applied to reasoning with ontologies. Reasoning is important to ensure the quality of ontology (Baader, Horrocks, & Sattler, 2005). Reasoning mechanisms in DLs are mostly based on the tableau algorithm, which is discussed in a laster section.

Example 1: Suppose that the nouns Human and Male are concept names and has-Child is the role name; then the ALC concept (Human $\sqcap \exists$hasChild.$\top$) represents all persons that have a child, whereas the concept Human $\sqcap \forall$hasChild.Male represents all persons that have only male children.

Reasoning in Description Logics

Reasoning services in DLs are based on the *tableau algorithm* (Horrocks, 1997). The tableau algorithm tries to prove the satisfiability of a concept C by demonstrating a model in which C can be satisfied (Horrocks, 1997). A *tableau* is a graph which represents such a model (Figure 1), with nodes corresponding to individuals and edges corresponding to relationships between the individuals. In some cases the tableau is a tree (Figure 1). New nodes are created according to *expansion rules* (Horrocks, 1997). These rules are different in different description logics.

Figure 1. A tree of a tableau

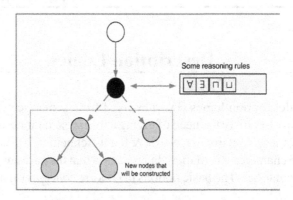

According to Baader, Calvanese, McGinness, Nardi, and Patel-Schneider (2003), basic reasoning services in DLs are: satisfiability subsumption, and instance checking. *Satisfiability* of a concept expression C is a problem of checking whether there exists a model (Horrocks, 1997). This means whether there exists an interpretation I, in which $C^I \neq \emptyset$. In that context, the interpretation I is a model for the concept C. Other reasoning services can be calculated with satisfiability (Horrocks, 1997). The following example demonstrates how to check subsumption of DLs concepts by checking satisfiability.

Example2: Suppose that Person, Male, and Female are atomic concepts, and has-Child is an atomic role. Then the concept:

(Person ⊓ ∀hasChild.Male)...(1)

represents all fathers which have only male children, and the concept

(Person ⊓ ∀hasChild. (Male⊔Female))....................................(2)

represents all fathers which have male or female children. Let us check whether the first concept (1) is subsumed by the second one (2). The problem of concept subsumption:

(Person ⊓ ∀hasChild.Male) ⊑ (Person ⊓ ∀hasChild. (Male ⊔ Female)), can be transformed into the problem of concept satisfiability:

(Person ⊓ ∀hasChild.Male) ⊓ ¬ (Person ⊓ ∀hasChild. (Male ⊔ Female))

Using De Morgan's law, the latter concept is equal to the concept:

(Person ⊓ ∀hasChild.Male) ⊓ (¬Person ⊔ ∃hasChild. (¬Male ⊓ ¬Female))

The above transformations are correct from the semantic point of view. The next step is is to initialize the tree T and create a node "x" labeled with:

L(x)={ (Person ⊓ ∀hasChild.Male) ⊓ (¬Person ⊔ ∃hasChild. (¬Male ⊓ ¬Female))}.

Applying the intersection rule ($\sqcap$) to the last concept, new concepts are added into the set L(x) as follows:

L(x)=L(x) $\cup$ {Person, $\forall$hasChild.Male, ($\neg$Person $\sqcup$ $\exists$hasChild. ($\neg$Male $\sqcap$ $\neg$Female))}.

Applying the union rule ($\sqcup$) to the concept:

($\neg$Person $\sqcup$ $\exists$hasChild. ($\neg$Male $\sqcap$ $\neg$Female))

and saving the tree T, let us try to create L(x) = L(x) $\cup$ {$\neg$Person }. Because of the contradiction {Person, $\neg$Person }, restore tree T and L(x) = L(x) $\cup$ {$\exists$hasChild. ($\neg$Male $\sqcap$ $\neg$Female)}.

Applying the $\exists$-rule, the new node "y" is created, the new edge (x, y) is created, and:

L(y)={$\neg$ Male $\sqcap$ $\neg$ Female}, L((x, y))=hasChild.

If the $\forall$-rule is applied to the concept $\forall$hasChild.Male, and L(x, y))=hasChild, then L(y) = L(y) $\cup$ {Male}. Finally, applying the $\sqcap$-rule to the concept ($\neg$ Male $\sqcap$ $\neg$ Female), we obtain L(y) = L(y) $\cup$ {$\neg$ Male, $\neg$ Female }.

This leads to a contradiction, because {Male, $\neg$ Male } $\subseteq$ L(y). In the end, it can be concluded that the first concept is subsumed by the second one, because the intersection of the first concept and the negation of the second one is non-satisfiable.

Model Driven Architecture

Object Management Group (OMG) (www.omg.org) proposed the unified modeling language (UML) (Heaton, 2001) to be the general language for modeling object-oriented software systems. OMG defined Meta Object Facility (MOF) (http://www.omg.org/mof/) as well, to enable defining other similar languages. UML and MOF are the central parts of the model driven architecture (MDA) (Mukerji & Miler, 2003). The MDA standard emphasizes the model significance in software development. This standard explicitly enunciates that the architecture depends on the models that are used in system development. MDA, Figure 2, enables the interoperability

Figure 2. Four-layer architecture of MDA (Bezivin, 2004)

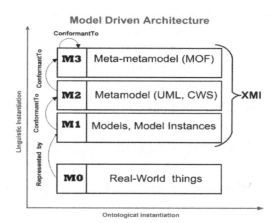

between different platforms using the unified language for metamodel creation. Furthermore, there is the third layer of modeling (M3 layer)—MOF. With MOF in place, new languages can be defined whenever necessary, and existing languages can be extended. Sometimes it can also be advantageous to design new and better ways of doing things that are already possible.

It is possible to define transformations from one model into another if the metamodels of different models are defined in the same language. This language is defined by the XML Meta-Data Interchange (XMI) standard (OMG XMI, 2001). XMI defines how XML tags are used to represent serialized MOF-compliant models in XML. MOF-based metamodels are translated into XML Document Type Definitions (DTDs) and models are translated into XML Documents that are consistent with their corresponding DTDs. Using XMI, it is possible to generate a "middleware" environment automatically, as well as to transform a "middleware" platform into another one.

An important, recently defined MOF-based metamodel is the *Ontology Definition Metamodel* (*ODM*) (Ontology Definition Metamodel, 2004). It covers common concepts of ontological engineering, such as classes, properties, resources, and so forth. To an extent, it is similar to RDF Schema and OWL languages, commonly used for ontology development. However, since it is MDA- and MOF-based, it has an important advantage of enabling the use of graphical modeling capabilities of UML for ontology development. See Ontology Definition Metamodel (2004) for details.

Given that all metamodels can be represented in MOF, a single transformation language for all MOF-based languages (metamodels) can be defined. Mappings to any non-OMG language are also possible if a MOF metamodel for such a language is defined first.

An important framework, closely related to MDA in practical developments, is the Eclipse Modeling Framework (EMF) (Eclipse Modelign Framework, 2006). It is a Java-based open-source framework and code-generation facility for building tools and other applications based on a structured model. While the widely used Eclipse development platform (www.eclipse.org) provides a powerful integration framework at the UI and file levels, EMF enhances this capability to enable fine-grained data sharing among tools and applications.

Query, Views, and Transformations (QVT) standard (Jouault & Kurtev, 2005) is a part of the OMG Meta Object Facility MOF 2.0 specification (Request for Proposal: MOF 2.0, 2005). It supports working with MOF models by enabling:

1.   Queries on MOF and EMF (www.eclipse.org/emf) models;
2.   Views on MOF and EMF models;
3.   Transformations of MOF and EMF models.

Transformations are defined as mappings and a unique transformation language is considered to play a role similar to the role XSLT plays for XML representations. Query determines when and how a transformation (rule) is applicable to a model (or a set of models) and how the result of the transformation will be built. The only difference between a transformation and a view is the underlying implementation. For a transformation, the target extent is independent of the source extent; its objects, links, and values are implemented by storing them. For a view, the target extent remains dependent on the source extent; its objects, links, and values are computed using the source extent. The definition of transformations and views is the same (the specification of source and target models and the relationships between them) (Joualut & Kurtev, 2005).

The Proposed Framework

This section is divided in two subsections. The first subsection describes the main idea underlying the framework and the architecture for development and deployment of QTI systems. The second subsection describes the QTI metamodel in terms of MDA.

An Architecture of QTI Assessment System

Figure 3 shows the main idea underlying the framework and the architecture for development and deployment of QTI systems. The idea is similar to the plug-in approach implemented in the Eclipse (www.eclipse.org) platform for software development. The core part of a QTI system is its *Delivery Engine*, which is a part of assessmentDeliverySystem (Table 3). All other parts can be developed as plug-ins, associated with the core by a corresponding manifest file and the metadata. The manifest must contain a **separate** resource describing the plug-in. The metadata associated with a specific plug-in should conform to the model and XMI binding of the plug-in content.

The Delivery Engine plays the role of a coordinator in the process of analyzing the students' solutions in a QTI system. This means that the assessment items from one subsystem (Figure 3) have to be delivered to the Delivery Engine before transferring them to another subsystem, because every subsystem needs the assessment item in a specific form. This is necessary for the subsystem in order to process the assessment item in its own way, unknown to the Delivery Engine. This form is defined in the metadata of the specific subsystem.

An important part of this system is the *response-processing machine*, as a part of the Delivery Engine. The response-processing machine plays an essential role in the process of creating the questions, as well as in processing the students' answers.

To develop a QTI system using the MDA standard, it is necessary to create QTI models of all system components. QTI models conform to the QTI metamodel. This means that it is possible to exchange the items (transformed from the QTI

Figure 3. The framework for development QTI systems

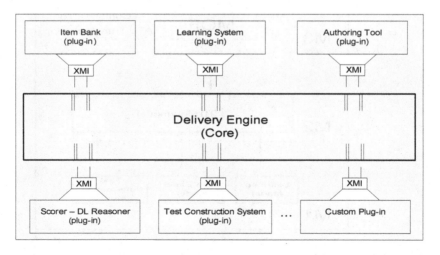

model) between the learning system, item bank, authoring tool, scorer, or some other subsystem.

The essence of QTI system development using MDA standard is the transformation from Platform Independent Model (PIM) to Platform Specific Model (PSM). PIM specifies the system's functionality. PSM is the specification of implementation details in a concrete technical environment. In the case of a QTI system, the PIM is defined as a QTI model and the QTI metamodel. The PSM can be generated using: Java Metadata Interfaces (JMI), Ecore classes of the Eclipse Modeling Framework (Discover the Eclipse Modeling Framework (EMF), 2005), and the QVT standard.

JMI is an implementation of the standard called JSR040 (Dirckze, 2001). The JMI specification (Dirckze, 2001) enables the implementation of a dynamic, platform-independent infrastructure to manage the creation, storage, access, discovery, and exchange of metadata. The main purpose of JMI in the QTI system is to define standard Java interfaces to different modeling components, and thus to enable platform-independent discovery and access of metadata. JMI allows for the discovery, query, access, and manipulation of metadata either at design time or at runtime. The semantics of any modeled system can be completely discovered and manipulated. JMI also provides for metamodel and metadata interchange via XMI.

A MOF-like core metamodel in EMF is called Ecore. Ecore classes can be generated automatically, in the Eclipse Modeling Framework (Eclipse Modeling Framework, 2006), from an Ecore-based metamodel. JMI interfaces and Ecore classes allow users to create, update, and access instances of metamodels using Java.

The transformation from PIM to PSM can be made in the Atlas Transformation Language (ATL) (Jouault & Kurtev, 2005) that is used for model transformation.

Figure 4. A process of analyzing the students' solutions in MDA

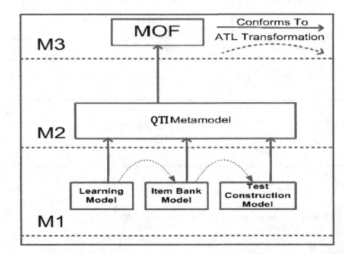

In case of a QTI system, it means that the assessment items will be transferred from the Item Bank model to the Test Construction model (Figure 4), and then the Test Construction Model will be transferred to the DL Reasoning Machine in the process of evaluating a student's answer (see a later section and Figure 13 for details). The DL reasoning machine will check the satisfiability of the answer.

The QTI Metamodel

This section explains the QTI metamodel (Figure 4) (Radenkovic et al., 2007). The metamodel is designed in the Posedion UML tool (www.gentleware.com), according to the IMS QTI standard (Lay & Pierre, 2006c). The metamodel is a UML-based QTI metamodel. The metamodel is divided in four meta-packages, according to the QTI standard described in Table 2. The main packages in the metamodel are: *Item Bank Tool*, *Learning System Tool*, *Test Construction Tool*, and *Description Logics Reasoning Tool*. This section explains the Item Bank Tool and Test Construction Tool.

Item Bank Tool Metapackage

Metaclasses in the *Item Bank Tool* metapackage are divided as follows.

Metaclasses that Represent "Variable Declaration"

Using the QTI standard (Lay & Pierre, 2006a), the following metaclasses may be defined: *ResponseDeclaration*, *TemplateDeclaration*, and *OutcomeDeclaration* (Figure 5 and Figure 6). The metaclasses are derived from the *VariableDeclaration* metaclass (Lay & Pierre, 2006a). The above *declaration* metaclasses have the same attribute called *Identifier.* The *OutcomeDeclaration* metaclass is associated with the *DefaultValue* metaclass (Figure 6).

AssessmentItem Metaclass

The main metaclass in the Item Bank Tool is *AssessmentItem* (Figure 5). The other metaclasses are connected to this metaclass. *Identification* of any assessmentItem model, at the M1 level (Figure 4), is defined using the *identifier* attribute in the metaclass.

ItemBody Metaclass

According to Lay and Pierre (2006a), the *ItemBody* metaclass represents the text, graphics, media objects, and interactions that describe the item's content and in-

Figure 5. Item bank tool's metaclasses

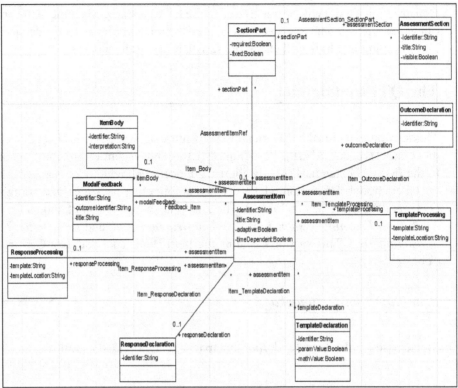

formation about how it is structured. The body is presented by combining it with stylesheet information, either explicitly or implicitly using the default style rules of the delivery or the authoring system (Lay & Pierre, 2006a) (Figure 7). The *ItemBody* metaclass is associated to the *FeedbackBlock* metaclass (Figure 7). The *Feedback-Block* metaclass is important in case of presenting any material to the students.

Processing Metaclasses

The processing metaclasses are *ResponseProcessing, TemplateProcessing,* and *Out-comeProcessing* (Figure 5, Figure 9, Figure 10, and Figure 8). Response processing consists of a sequence of rules that are carried out, in a predefined order, by the response processor (Lay & Pierre, 2006b). The *ResponseProcessing* metaclass has two attributes: *template* and *templateLocation* (Figure 9, Figure 10) (Lay & Pierre, 2006b). *ResponseProcessing* depends on *ResponseConditions* and *ExitResponse* (Figure 9).

Response processing involves the application of a set of *responseRules* including the testing of responseConditions and the evaluation of expressions involving the

Figure 6. The outcomedeclaration metaclass in the QTI metamodel

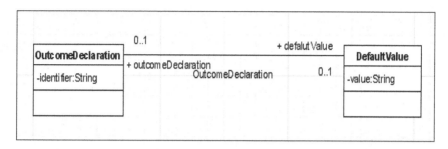

item variables. The *ResponseProcessing* metaclass (Figure 5, Figure 9) represents this involvement. Response processing is the process by which the Delivery Engine (Figure 3) assigns outcomes based on the candidate's responses (Lay & Pierre, 2006a). The OutcomeProcessing metaclass is associated to *OutcomeRules* (Figure 8). The metaclasses *OutcomeCondition* and *ExitTest* extened *OutcomeRule*.

The *feedback* that the QTI system provides to the student (candidate), conditionally includes the material presented. This is based on the result of *responseProcessing*. In other words, the feedback is controlled by the values of outcome variables (Lay & Pierre, 2006b). There are two types of feedback material, modal, and integrated. The *modal feedback* is shown to the student after the response processing has taken place and before any subsequent attempt or review of the item. The *integrated feedback* is embedded in the *itemBody* and is only shown during subsequent attempts or review (Lay & Pierre, 2006b). In the QTI metamodel, feedback is represented with the *FeedBackBlock* metaclass (Figure 7).

Template processing consists of one or more *templateRules* (Figure 10) that are followed by the cloning engine or delivery system in order to assign values to the template variables (Lay & Pierre, 2006a). Template rules are described by the *TemplateRule* metaclass (Figure 10). The *SetTemplateValue* and *SetCorrectResponse* metaclasses extend the *TemplateRule* metaclass.

Test Construction Tool

The central metaclass in the Test Construction Tool metapackage is *AssessmentTest*. This metaclass aggregates the *TestPart* metaclass and the associated *ScoreReport* and *TimeLimits* metaclasses (Figure 11).

The *ItemSession* metaclass is associated with the *ItemVariable* metaclass. The metaclasses *ResponseVariable* and *TemplateVariable* extend *ItemVariable* (Figure 12).

The proposed QTI metamodel is designed using the Poseidon case tool (www. gentleware.com). Then we used the uml2mof.jar tool (http://mdr.netbeans.org/uml-

Figure 7. The ItemBody metaclass in the QTI Metamodel

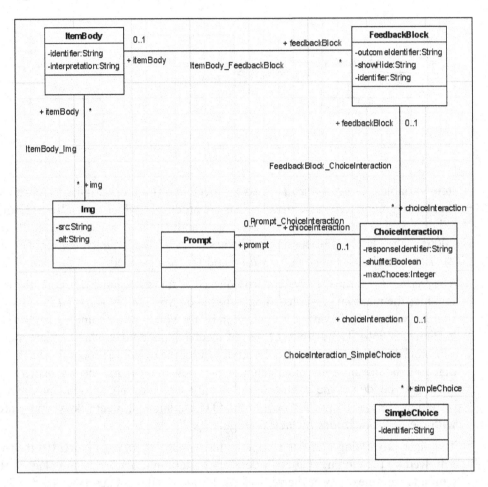

Figure 8. The OutcomeProcessing metaclass in the QTI metamodel

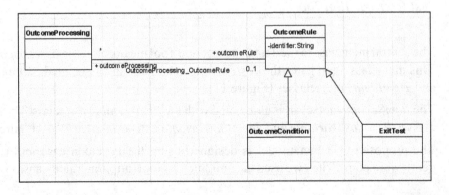

Figure 9. The ResponseProcessing metaclass in the QTI metamodel

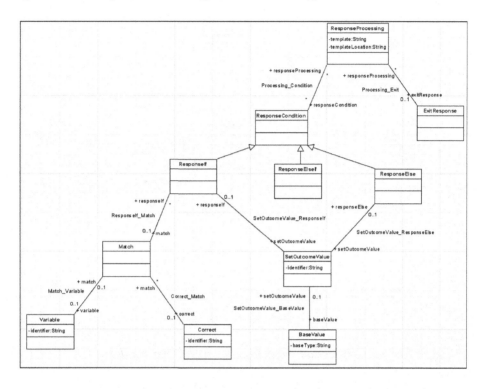

Figure 10. The TemplateProcessing metaclass in the QTI metamodel

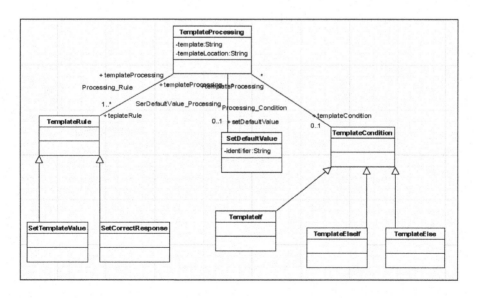

Figure 11. Metaclasses in the test construction tool metapackage

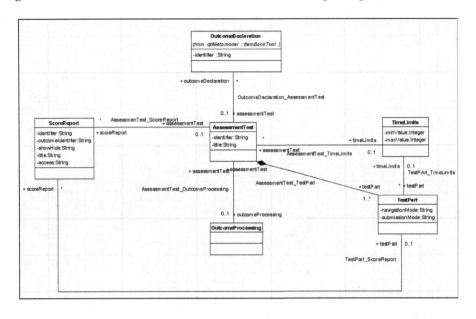

Figure 12. The ItemSession metaclass the in QTI metamodel

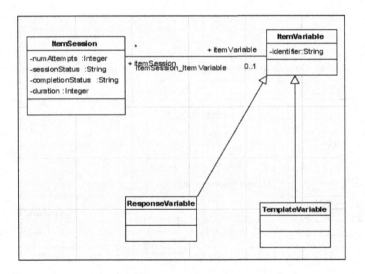

2mof/building.html) to transform the metamodel into the corresponding MOF-based QTI metamodel (Figure 4):

Java –jar uml2mof.jar QTI.xmi QTImof.xmi

After this transformation, we used Eclipse plug-ins (www.eclipse.org/gmt) to transform the metamodel into the equivalent Ecore-based metamodel (EMF repository). The MOF-based QTI metamodel supports the XMI 1.2 standard, and the Ecore-based QTI metamodel (EMF repository) supports the XMI 2.0 standard.

Intelligent Analysis of Students' Solutions

Is it possible to check whether two syntactically different answers, submitted by two students, are both semantically correct? This section explains an application of DL reasoning techniques to this problem. This solution is based on the MDA methodology, that is, on model transformations. We have implemented a prototype assessment system according to the proposed framework to experiment with QTI model transformations. Our DL reasoner is integrated in the prototype system as a plug-in. We explain how to use the reasoner to check the satisfiability (consistency) of students' answers and analyze the answers step by step. This section also discusses some possibilities of applying other kinds of reasoners and theorem provers in this context, such as a modal-logic theorem prover.

DL Reasoning in Intelligent Analysis of the Semantics of Students' Solutions

Many Web-based education environments and adaptive hypermedia systems have an experts' knowledge embedded in their structure. They use different reasoning techniques to help the authors make improvements in the course design (e.g., case-based reasoning techniques explained in (Ferrario & Smyth, 2001), or for intelligent analysis of the students' solutions. For example, Simic (Simic, 2004) used an XML format to represent the domain knowledge and generate a CLIPS file (*.clp) before using the reasoning mechanism. The Jess expert system shell's inference engine was used as the reasoning mechanism. However, some problems are difficult for Jess to solve:

1. Reasoning about the course material subsumed by another one (i.e., classification of learning material);

2. Reasoning about a student's answer which is a model of domain knowledge (in the sense the term "model" is used in DLs);

3. Intelligent analysis of the semantics of students' solutions.

Intelligent analysis of students' solutions using a DL reasoner may fulfill the following requirements:

1. Check whether the student's answer is consistent w.r.t. the question;
2. Find the student's mistakes (semantic inconsistencies) in the answer;
3. Find if the student's answer can be described with an uncertainty, rather than just as a true/false answer;
4. Use different pedagogical strategies in the analysis of students' solutions, according to a hierarchy of answers.

These requirements may be satisfied using DL reasoning services like classification (subsumption) and consistency.

According to (Horrocks, 1997), consistency and subsumption can be calculated with satisfiability of concept terms. Clasification is usefull in cases of chekcing the hierachy of students' answers or teaching courses. A question submitted to the student may imply a few different answers, and all of the answers may be true. In case of a few true answers, the reasoner may find the most common answer and give positive (but different) marks to the student. The answer hierarchy can be calculated using the DL subsumption reasoning technique. This classification cannot be applied in cases when there exists only one answer to the question.

Consistency reasoning is a very important technique in such an analysis. The benefit of applying it is the capability of finding (with a DL reasoner) logical mistakes in the students' answers.

Existing YES/NO DL reasoners may not fulfill the above requirements. The problem is in their architectures. For example, the FACT reasoner (Horrocks, 1997), implemented in LISP, is difficult to integrate with Intelligent Web-based Education Systems (IWBESs). FACT may check the consistency of some students' answers (if they are submitted as an ontology), but cannot discover inconsistencies precisely. Moreover, it is difficult to do it using a DL reasoner, especially if the reasoner should be integrated with an IWBES as a plug-in.

A DL Reasoner in Intelligent Analysis of Students' Solutions

For intelligent analysis of the semantics of the students' solutions, to fulfill the above mentioned requirements we propose a DL reasoner that uses MDA model transformations. We assume that the students' answers are submitted to the resoning machine as QTI models—Test Construction Models (Figure 4). The meaning of the term "concept model" in MDA is different than that in mathematical logics. A test

Figure 13. Analysis of students' solutions in MDA using a DL reasoning machine

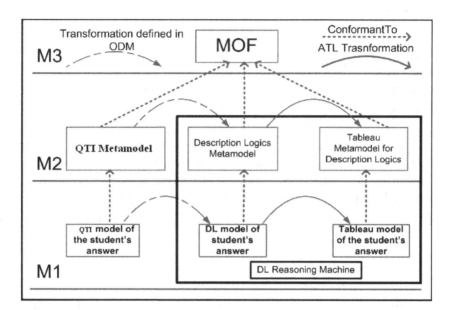

construction model conforms to the QTI metamodel. The reasoner takes a student answer as a DL model, transformed from the QTI model (Figure 13).

Our DL reasoner transforms the DL model of the student's solution into the tableau model (conformant to the tableau metamodel) (Krdzavac, Devedzic, 2006). The tableau model can be described using XMI. XMI has a tree-like structure—every tableau model is a tree (Horrocks, 1997). Using the interfaces generated for the tableau metamodel (JMI interfaces and Ecore classes), we can analyze such a tableau model, that is, the reasoner can find the student's mistakes and return them to the Assessment Delivery System (see Table 3).

To transform DL models of students' solutions to the corresponding tableau models, we used the Atlas Transformation Language (ATL) (Jouault, & Kurtev, 2005). The ATL language satisfies OMG's QVT RFP standard (Request for Proposal: MOF 2.0, 2002).

DL reasoning mechanisms (classification, satisfiability, etc.) can be, also, used in IWBES (Intelligent Web-based Education Systems), where the teaching materials are based on ontologies. It is also possible to use other formalisms to support reasoning, such as First Order Logic (FOL) or conceptual graphs. DL reasoners are useful only in cases of classification or consistency. A good alternative is a modal logic theorem prover implemented using the MDA methodology. A modal logics formula has different truth-values in different worlds (Multiple Worlds) (Feys, 1965). These characteristics may help in intelligent analysis of students' solutions, that is, for implementation of different pedagogical strategies during the QTI process.

An Example of Applying a DL Reasoner in an Assessment System

This section gives and example of applying a DL reasoner in an assessment system. The solution is based on model transformations from the TestConstraction model to the reasoning machine. The target model is the tableau model of a student's answer.

The Scorer is a person or an external system responsible for assessing the candidate's responses during the assessment delivery. Scorers are optional; for example, many assessment items can be scored automatically using response processing rules defined in the item itself (Lay & Pierre, 2006c). The reasoning machine is the scorer (see Table 2) in intelligent analysis of a student's answers.

The process of intelligent analysis of a student's solutions is divided in two parts:

1.   Generating the tableau model from a student's answer and returning it to the Assessment Delivery Engine (Figure 3);
2.   Analysis of the tableau model of the student's answer using a graphical user interface (GUI).

Suppose that after transforming a test construction model into a DL model (Figure 4), the DL model represents the intersection of two atomic concepts—Student and Professor (Figure 14).

The representation of this model in DLs notation is (Professor ⊓ Student). The main role of the reasoner in this example is to check whether the student's answer is satisfiable. Other requirements listed in another section of the chapter (for example, checking the consistency of the student's answer), can be calculated using concept satisfiability. The DL model (Figure 14) conforms to the DLs metamodel, defined in the Ontology Definition Metamodel (Ontology Definition Metamodel, 2004). The model is saved in the EMF repository (Discover the Eclipse Modeling Framework, 2006), that is, in the Ecore base XML file. The XML representation of the model is shown in Figure 15.

The reasoning is done during the transformation from the DL model to the tableau model. In this example, the reasoning machine applies the rule for intersection of two concepts (Horrocks, 1997), and creates a constraint as follows:

$L(x) = \{$Professor ⊓ Student, Student, Professor$\}$

At this point of analyzing the student's answer, the DL reasoning machine creates the tableau model and saves it in an XML file. The tableau model conforms to the

Figure 14. Intersection of two atomic concepts, Professor and Student

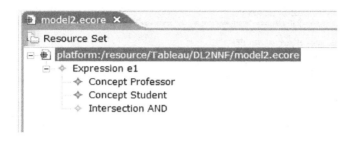

Figure 15. XML representation of the model from Figure 14

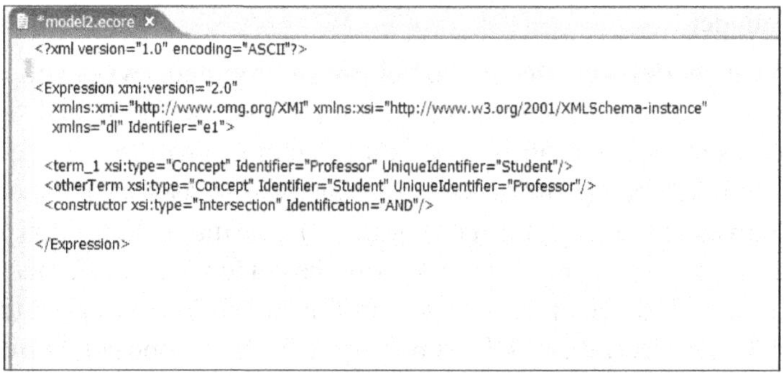

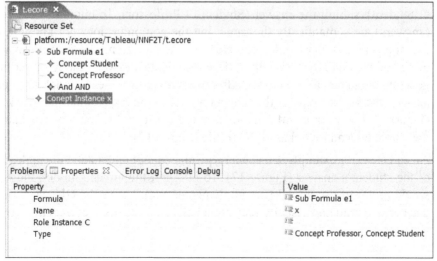

Figure 16. Tableau model of the concept (Professor ⊓ Studenr)

Figure 17. XML representation of the tableau model

```
<?xml version="1.0" encoding="ISO-8859-1"?>
<xmi:XMI xmi:version="2.0" xmlns:xmi="http://www.omg.org/XMI" xmlns:xsi="http://www.w3.org/2001/XMLSchema-instance" xmlns="tableau">

  <SubFormula name="e1" conceptInstanceSF="/1">
   <otherTerm xsi:type="Concept" name="Student" member="/1"/>
   <left xsi:type="Concept" name="Professor" member="/1"/>
   <constructor xsi:type="And" Identification="AND"/>
  </SubFormula>

  <ConeptInstance name="x" formula="/0" type="/0/@left /0/@otherTerm"/>

</xmi:XMI>
```

tableau metamodel (Figure 13). Figure 16 shows the tableau model created from the DL model.

The tableau model is created in the Eclipse environment (www.eclipse.org) and using the Ecore editor. Appliying the reasoning rules, an individual "x" is connected to the concepts Student, Professor, and Student ⊓ Professor in the tableau model (Figure 17). All changes in the process of analysis (reasoning) of the student's solution are saved in the XML format (Figure 17). The main idea of this methodology is to create a graph (tableau), Figure 1, from the student's answer, then save the graph in XML, and find semantic mistakes in the student's answer using an intelligent graphical user interface (GUI) as a plug-in for the proposed architecture (Figure 3). Thus the generated tabeau model can convey the information that the student's answer is (or is not) satisfiable.

In case of syntactically different answers, submitted by two students, the reasoner can check if the answers are both semantically correct, using satisfiability and instance checking. In this example, another student may, instead of answering (Professor ⊓ Student), submit the answer (Student ⊓ Professor). To humans, both concepts (answers) are semantically the same, but the computer does not know it. In this example, the reasoner would generate the same tableau model for both answers. In more complex and syntactically different students' answers, the reasoner may not generate the same tableau model. After generating the tableau model for a student's answer, the system returns the tableau model to the Assessment Delivery Engine (Figure 3). The returned information is not just "satisfiable" or "nonsatisfiable," but the whole tableau model as an XML file (Figure 17).

An end user (for example, a teacher) typically cannot understand the tableau model of the student's answer (Figure 17). To interpret the tableau model, the end user would prefer to use a GUI (not implemented yet). Using the GUI, a student or a teacher will read and visually understand all semantically incorrect answers in the test report.

Conclusion and Future Trends

The development of assessment software must harmonize pliability and standardization with improvement. Application Model Driven Architecture (MDA) methodology in development such software may satisfy some of above conditions, but not all. According to our practical experience, MDA allows us to develop flexible assessment software with high productivity, but with strongly satisfiability of standards (for example QTI, Lay & Pierre, 2006c). The second benefit is increasing the level of abstraction and less coding written by hand, for example JMI interfaces generated from QTI metamodel. Application design patterns in MDA-based development of assessment software increases the quality of productivity and allows us to incorporate best practices.

The framework presented in this chapter provides reusability of QTI systems. It is possible to improve a specified subsystem individually, without changing other subsystems. Also, it will be possible in the future to extend the system with new plug-ins (for example, the GUI plug-in). Of course, using a DL reasoner is a big advantage here, because with a DL reasoner one can analyze the semantics of students' answers.

Our future work will be focused on integration of the IMS QTI standard (IMS QTI) (Lay & Pierre, 2006c) and other logic-based reasoning techniques. The integration will be specified using the UML 2.0 language. The ultimate idea is to develop a UML Profile for E-Learning and a UML-Profile for Theorem Provers.

References

Dirckze, R. (2002). *Java Metadata Interface (JMI) API Specification version. 1.0.* Retrieved January 10, 2008, from http://jcp.org/aboutJava/communityprocess/final/jsr040/

Discover the Eclipse Modeling Framework (EMF) and Its Dynamic Capabilities. (2005). Retrieved January 10, 2008, from http://www.devx.com/Java/Article/29093

Mukerji, J., & Miler, J. (2003, June). *MDA guide version. 1.0.1.* Retrieved January 10, 2008, from http://www.omg.org/docs/omg/03-06-01.pdf

Heaton, L. (2001, September). *OMG unified modeling language specification.* Retrieved January 10, 2008, from http://www.omg.org/docs/formal/01-09-67.pdf

Lay, S., & Pierre, G. (2006a, June). IMS global learning consortium. *IMS Question and Test Interoperability Assessment Test, Section, and Item Information*

Model. Retrieved January 10, 2008, from http://www.imsglobal.org/question/qtiv2p1pd2/imsqti_infov2p1pd2.html

Lay, S., & Pierre, G. (2006b, June). IMS global learning consortium. *IMS Question and Test Interoperability Implementation Guide,* Retrieved January 10, 2008, from http://www.imsglobal.org/question/qtiv2p1pd2/imsqti_implv2p1pd2.html

Lay, S., & Pierre, G. (2006c, June). IMS global larning consortium. *IMS Question and Test Interoperability Overview, Version 2.1 Public draft*. Retrieved January 10, 2008, from http://www.imsglobal.org/question/qtiv2p1pd2/imsqti_oviewv2p1pd2.html

Lay, S., & Pierre, G. (2006d, June). IMS global learning consortium. *IMS Question and Test Interoperability Assessment Test, Section, and Item Information Model*. Retrieved January 10, 2008, from http://www.imsglobal.org/question/qtiv2p1pd2/imsqti_infov2p1pd2.html

OMG XMI Specification, version 1.2. (2001). OMG Document Formal/02-01-01, 2002. Retrieved January 10, 2008, from http://www.omg.org/cgi-bin/doc?formal/2002-01-01.pdf

Ontology Definition Metamodel. (2004). Preliminary Revised Submission to OMG RFP ad/2003-03-40 1. Retrieved January 10, 2008, from http://codip.grci.com/odm/draft

Radenković, S., Krdžavac, N., & Devedžić V. (2007, October 15-17). *A QTI Metamodel*. International Multiconference on Computer Science and Information Technology. Wisla, Poland.

Request for Proposal: MOF 2.0 Query/Views/Transformations RFP. (2002). OMG Document: ad/2002-04-10. Retrieved January 10, 2008, from http://www.omg.org/docs/ad/02-04-10.pdf

UML (2004). *Unified modeling language (UML) Specification: Infrastructure, version 2.0*. Finalized Convenience Document. Available at http:// http://www.omg.org/docs/ptc/04-10-14.pdf

Further Readings

Baader, F., Calvanese, D., McGinness, D., Nardi, D., & Patel-Schneider, P. (2003). *The description logics handbook, theory application and implementation*. Cambridge: Cambridge University Press.

Baader, F., Horrocks, I., & Sattler, U. (2005). Description logics as ontology languages for the Semantic Web. In D. Hutter & W. Stephan (Eds.), *Mechanizing mathematical reasoning: Essays in honor of Jörg Siekmann on the occasion of his 60th birthday (LNAI 2605, pp. 228-248). Berlin, Germany:* Springer.

Bezivin, J. (2004). In search of basic principles for model driven architecture. *The European Journal for the Informatics Professional, 5*(2).

Ferrario, M., & Smyth, B. (2001). Collaborative knowledge management & maintenance. In *Proceedings of German Workshop of Case Based Reasoning,* Germany (pp. 14-15).

Feys, R. (1965). *Modal logics (collection de logique mathematique).* Paris: Gauthier-Villars.

Horrocks, I. (1997). Optimising tableaux decision procedures for description logics, Doctoral dissertation, University of Manchester. *Dissertation Abstract International, 47.*

Jouault, F., & Kurtev, I. (2005). Transforming models with ATL. In *Proceedings of the Model Transformations in Practice Workshop at MoDELS,* Montego Bay, Jamaica.

Krdzavac, N., & Devedzic, V. (2006). A tableau metamodel for description logics. In *Proceedings of 13th Workshop on Automated Reasoning, Bridging the Gap Between Theory and Practice,* Bristol, England (pp. 7-9).

Lay, S., & Pierre, G. (Eds.). (2006, June). *IMS question and test interoperability assessment test, section, and item information model, ver. 2.1.* Retrieved from http://www.imsglobal.org/question/index.cfm

Milićev, D. (2001). *Automatic transformation models in software systems for modeling tools.* Ph.D. Thesis, Faculty of Electrical Engineering, University of Belgrade

Simic, G. (2004). *The multi-cources tutoring system design,* vol. 1, no.1. ComSIS. Retrieved from http://www.comsis.fon.bg.ac.yu/ComSIS/Volume01/Papers/GoranSimic.htm

Chapter XII

Can Person-Centered Technology Enhanced Learning Contribute to Develop Project Management Soft Skills in an Academic Context?[1]

Renate Motschnig-Pitrik, University of Vienna, Austria

Michael Derntl, University of Vienna, Austria

Inside Chapter

In the preceding years we employed active technology enhanced learning in a course on project management soft skills that was particularly well received by students. This chapter presents the underlying philosophy, the current course design, students' reactions, and our experiences and lessons learned. Concurrently, we confirm the applicability of participatory action research as a methodological framework suited for improving course design, specific interventions, and theory building. We propose to complement that framework by qualitative and quantitative methods in order to deal with specific research questions. Results indicate that students consider their active involvement in the course, both face-to face and online, the top factor from which they benefit. Furthermore, the majority of students felt that it was easier for them to work in teams and to establish social relationships. The primary goal of the chapter is to provide a pool of inspiration for other educators in practice and research.

Introduction

Authors from constructivist, learner-centered, and person-centered traditions have argued that learning is most effective if it includes the whole person. This means that for meaningful, deep and persistent learning, not only the intellect but also feelings, meanings, ideas, skills, attitudes, and so forth, need to be included. Recently, this has also been voiced in the European Association for the Education of Adults' (2004) strategic statement of core competencies in our society. But how can these principles and strategies be put into practice?

Recent research indicates that technology enhanced learning settings, that is, settings that mix face-to-face and online learning, offer the required flexibility (Garrison & Kanuka, 2004; Reichelmayr, 2005) in which resourceful persons can foster experiential, whole person learning that addresses the learner at the level of intellect, social skills, and attitudes/dispositions (Holzinger & Motschnig-Pitrik, 2005). In this chapter, we aim to share the whole cycle of experience involved in designing, conduction, and evaluating a course that is aimed at addressing students at all three levels with an emphasis on soft skills. In other words, what can we do to allow students to become better communicators, negotiators, and constructive teammates in cooperative tasks?

Within the design, we focus on the process, that is, the nature and sequence of activities and the aspect of blending face-to-face and online elements within the course design. Furthermore, the chapter raises some methodological questions regarding research design. It illustrates the inadequacy of any single research paradigm to answer the multitude of research questions the investigators are interested in. Examples of such questions are: Have the learning targets been met? Which aspects of the course design, learning platform, interventions, and so forth, could be improved? In which respects, in particular, do students benefit? Is the blending optimal for the intended learning outcome? From these considerations we suggest a research procedure that integrates qualitative and quantitative methods under a participatory action research framework (Figl, Derntl, & Motschnig, 2005). As a kind of proof of concept, we present and discuss initial research results on the effects of the course on social relationships, teamwork, the degree of students' engagement, and aspects from which students tend to benefit. In the spirit of participatory action research, we share some personal thoughts on the course experience and its meaning for continued action and research.

Rather than fixing and closing up concepts, the chapter aims to inspire further research as well as practice along the paths initiated by our endeavors in the research lab for educational technologies at the University of Vienna. This is intended to confirm or inspire readers in facilitating deep, meaningful learning in technology-enhanced environments and thereby provide a basis for effective personal and knowledge development.

The key background concepts, and the contributions made by the chapter, are given in Figure 1.

The chapter is structured as follows. The next section provides a concise introduction into the didactical baseline underlying our approach to blended learning. The following section is central in so far as it introduces the research methods chosen and applies it to the course on project management soft skills (PM-SS). We trace a whole action research cycle encompassing the analysis of the situation, the planning, action taking, evaluation, and specification of learning including personal experiences that other educators may find useful. The final section summarizes the chapter and identifies challenges and questions for further research.

Figure 1. Concepts and contributions of the chapter

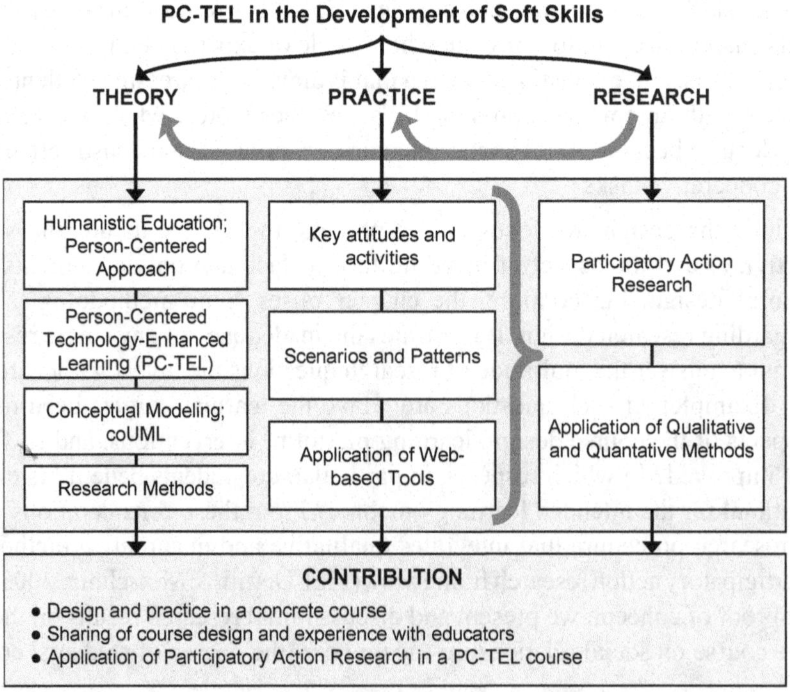

PC-TEL in the Development of Soft Skills

THEORY   PRACTICE   RESEARCH

Humanistic Education; Person-Centered Approach	Key attitudes and activities	Participatory Action Research
Person-Centered Technology-Enhanced Learning (PC-TEL)	Scenarios and Patterns	
Conceptual Modeling; coUML	Application of Web-based Tools	Application of Qualitative and Quantative Methods
Research Methods		

CONTRIBUTION
- Design and practice in a concrete course
- Sharing of course design and experience with educators
- Application of Participatory Action Research in a PC-TEL course

Underlying Philosophy and Didactic Approach

Our approach to blended learning, that is, combined face-to-face and online learning, builds upon humanistic educational principles as realized in the person-centered approach (PCA) by Carl Rogers (Rogers, 1961, 1983). Person-Centered learning is a personally significant kind of learning that integrates new elements, knowledge, or insights to the current repertoire of the learner's own resources such that he or she moves to an advanced constellation of meaning and resourcefulness (Barrett-Lennard, 1998). It can be characterized by active participation of students, a climate of trust provided by the facilitator, building upon authentic problems, and raising the awareness of meaningful ways of inquiry (Rogers, 1983).

Research in the PCA has proved (Aspy, 1972; Cornelius-White, Hoey, Cornelius-White, Motschnig-Pitrik, & Figl, 2004; Rogers, 1961) that students achieve superior results along with higher self-confidence, creativity, openness to experience, and respect if they learn in a climate in which the facilitator (instructor, teacher, etc.) holds three core attitudinal conditions and if the learners perceive them, at least to some degree. The core conditions are realness or congruence of the facilitator, acceptance or respect towards the student, and empathic understanding of the students and their feelings. The way in which these core conditions can be expressed in blended learning situations in general is discussed in more detail in Motschnig-Pitrik and Mallich (2004). The current chapter shares a course design that provides space for the core conditions to be expressed. To fill the space, however, instructors personally need to be sufficiently open to experience, real and transparent in their communication, yet respectful and acceptant, and endeavoring to understand students' inner worlds: their meanings, feelings, potentials as well constraints.

Action Research Applied to the Course on Project Management Soft Skills

Action Research is gaining recognition in accompanying the introduction of new media into innovative teaching styles (Baskerville, 1999). This can be understood from the fact that pioneering teachers/facilitators aim to enrich their courses by introducing new media and are likely to combine research with practice in acting as reflective practitioners in their own courses. This blend has become known as participatory action research (PAR) (Ottosson, 2003). In this chapter we take up Susman and Evered's (1978) proposal that suggests that action research typically proceeds in cycles (here each course instance forms one cycle) that consist of five phases: diagnosing, action planning, action taking, evaluation, and specifying learning. In the following section, we discuss selected issues of one action research

Table 1. Main issues as well as references and their contributions as addressed in the chapter

Issue	References	Contribution
Person-Centered Approach (PCA)	(Rogers, 1961, 1983; Barrett-Lennard, 1998)	Humanistic educational approach based on facilitative attitudes (acceptance, realness, empathic understanding) and learner-centered settings
	(Aspy, 1972; Cornelius-White et al., 2004; Rogers, 1961)	Evidence of the effect of PCA's facilitative attitudes on learning outcome
	(Motschnig-Pitrik & Mallich, 2004)	PCA in a blended learning environment
Active Learning Active Learning	(Garrison & Kanuka, 2004; Reichelmayr, 2005)	Technology enhanced (blended) learning as a flexible teaching and learning approach
	(Holzinger & Motschnig-Pitrik, 2005).	Whole-person learning based on the PCA in technology-enhanced courses
	(Bull, 1998; European Association for the Education of Adults, 2004; Motschnig-Pitrik, 2002)	Studies indicating the need for a more holistic educational approach addressing the levels intellect, skills, and dispositions to facilitate the development of key competencies for work
	(Derntl & Motschnig-Pitrik, 2005)	Evidence of positive effects of the PCA in a blended learning environment
Action Research (AR)	(Baskerville, 1999)	AR as an effective research approach in socio-technical environments
	(Ottosson, 2003)	Active involvement of researcher and integration of research and practice in "Participatory AR"
	(Susman & Evered, 1978)	Action research as a cyclic approach with five phases in each cycle
	(Motschnig-Pitrik, 2004)	AR framework for assessing blended learning scenarios
	(Kock, 2004)	Discussion of the primary threats to be dealt with in an AR based research context
	(Figl et al., 2005)	Thoughtful integration of qualitative and quantitative evaluation methods ("method mix")
Scenario Modeling	(Rumbaugh, Jacobson, & Booch, 1999)	Unified Modeling Language (UML) reference manual
	(Derntl & Motschnig-Pitrik, n.d.)	coUML approach to visual modeling of cooperative, technology-enhanced learning environments
	(Derntl, 2006)	Pattern repository of blended learning settings based on the PCA
	(Derntl & Motschnig-Pitrik, 2004)	Conceptual integration of learning and technology in TEL through a layered model of blended learning systems
	(Motschnig-Pitrik & Derntl, 2005)	Modeling approach for blended learning scenarios based on UML

cycle, more precisely the third, of the course on project management soft skills. As mentioned above, however, pure action research needs to be extended to allow one to deal systematically with particular research questions or variables.

Diagnosing

Currently, most academic courses tend to emphasize the level of knowledge or intellect. However, several sources indicate that this focus is questionable and that deep, persistent learning needs to include attitudes and skills as well. Arguments in favor of whole person learning come from various sources, such as the following:

- In a recent study (Motschnig-Pitrik, 2002) managers of ICT enterprises were asked about the required qualifications of business informatics graduates. The items "social skills" and "ability to work in teams" headed the list.
- When considering the major causes of project failure, experts agree that people issues clearly dominate technology issues. For example, in the Bull survey (Bull, 1998), the item "bad communications between relevant parties" heads the list of reasons for project failure.
- Within the EU, the strategic statement on key competencies clearly states that within the new curriculum skills and attitudes shall be addressed aside of knowledge (European Association for the Education of Adults, 2004).

Clearly, industry and educational strategies call for the development of skills and attitudes aside from knowledge. A key question is whether academic, blended learning courses are proper settings to achieve this goal and, if so, what are the most important factors that enable whole person learning. A closely related question is how development at the skills and attitudes level can be assessed. Our challenge has been to approach the needs voiced above and to examine, as objectively as possible, the direction we decided to choose.

Action Planning

The course is aimed at addressing students at all three levels of competence or learning, knowledge, skills, and attitudes, with a clear emphasis on experientially developing soft skills such as active listening, effective communication and negotiation, moderation, team development, and so forth.

Based on experiences from preceding terms, we started with explicitly formulating course goals and assigning them to the three levels of learning. Since we consider this activity as central for the following discussion, the course goal structure is given below:

General goal:

Acquire personal experiences and skills in project situations such as presentations, teamwork, meetings, consultation, and so forth

Goals on the level of knowledge and intellect:

Theory of interpersonal communication, conflict management, group processes, negotiations, presentation, moderation, and rhetoric

Goals on the skills and capabilities level:

To perceive the potentials and limitations of exercises that are aimed at improving communication

To improve teamwork

To moderate meetings

To gain active listening skills

To experience the interactive presentation, moderation, and discussion of a theme

To increase one's problem solving capability and creative approach to tasks

To gather and reflect experience in the application of computer-mediated communication

Goals on the attitudes, awareness level:

To view learning as a personal project and take co-responsibility for it

To gain self-experience in expressing own intentions

To live the group process

To gain openness to experience

To experience the meaning of active listening and develop one's own attitude towards it

To perceive the creative influence and self-organization through the open design of a topical unit

To perceive a constructive working climate and offer it to the group.

The next step was to design the course scenario, specify individual activities and to allocate activities to face-to-face and online phases. The scenario blends face-to-face and Web-supported learning such that the strengths of both settings, mediate and immediate, can be exploited and the learning process can proceed closer to the intentions and needs of individuals.

Action Taking

In order to provide room for active interaction in class, fundamental material, links, and a list with references to further literature are supplied by the instructor over the learning platform at the time of course initialization. Also, key data on the course such as time, location, goals, brief description, and so forth, are provided such that students have initial information before enrolling in the course. The initial meeting is used to discuss the innovative course style, requirements, and learning methods, as well as to introduce the learning platform and to finalize the list of participants. Then students are asked to fill out an online questionnaire aimed at capturing their initial motivation, attitudes towards learning, ways they tend to profit from academic courses, and so forth. Furthermore, students are asked to assign themselves to small teams of about three to four students for cooperative work.

As shown in Figure 2, the face-to-face thread of the course consists of ten moderated workshops, 4 hours each, where individual topics within the gross framework of "soft-skills in project management" are elaborated following a strongly interactive style. The first three workshops are moderated by the instructor who practically introduces students to elements of the moderation technique. This is done by conducting team discussions on selected aspects of the course, collecting expectations on a flip chart, using moderation cards to reflect on attitudes of good listeners, drawing mind maps, having students prepare a flipchart on frequent barriers in communication, and so forth. Accompanying descriptions of these techniques and more theoretical background on their application is provided via the learning platform and can be inspected on demand. The remaining seven workshops are prepared by teams of students on topics we agree upon during the initial sessions. Preparation of a workshop includes the provision of e-content regarding the selected topic. Preparation also encompasses consultation with the instructor with regard to the moderation sequence and elements. After each workshop, students submit online reaction sheets that can be read by all participants and are aimed at providing multiperspective feedback to the team that moderated the workshop. At any time, students have access to the basic material provided on the platform. Concurrently, they are expected to briefly document their learning activities in a personal diary that shall support them in writing their self-evaluation in the end of the course. Furthermore, a discussion forum is available for communication with the instructor, Web master, and fellow students on all course relevant issues.

At the end of the course students evaluate themselves online. This is accomplished by responding to questions such as: What did I contribute? What could I take with

Figure 2. Course scenario for project management soft skills (PM-SS) specified using UML (Rumbaugh et al., 1999) and including Web-based (W), blended (B) and face to face (P) elements (Motschnig-Pitrik & Derntl, 2005)

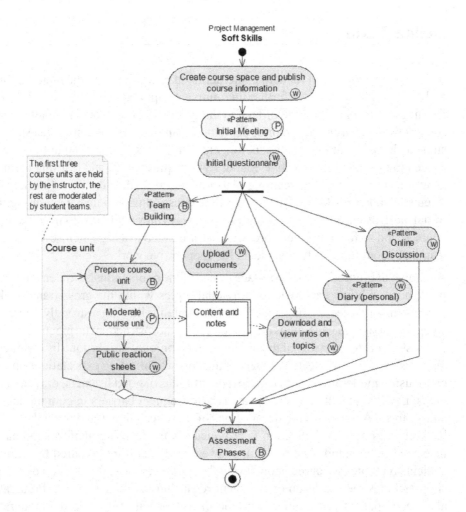

me from the course? How intensive was my contribution with respect to my team mates? In addition, an online peer-evaluation in conducted in which each team evaluates all other teams in terms of their moderated workshop and the e-content they provided. Furthermore, students fill out a final online questionnaire that is used to evaluate the course on a more objective level. This kind of mixed evaluation scenario at the end of the course follows the "Blended Evaluation" pattern as proposed in (Derntl, 2006) and depicted in Figure 3. The rationale behind the use of this pattern is that the self- and peer-evaluations are used by the instructor in his or her grading, thus complementing the grading process by an individual- and

Figure 3. The "blended evaluation" pattern

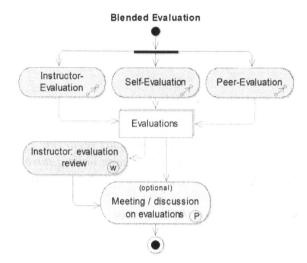

a group perspective reflecting the participative, person-centered didactic strategy inherent in course conception and design.

A first look reveals that the scenario has multiple threads and didactic elements. In our view, however, this additional complexity adds significant value to the learning process, such as:

- More self-directed learning with more responsibilities of the learners and the group;
- Learning on the intellectual level, due to the elaboration of literature, as well as learning on the social and personal level due to intensive teamwork and moderation of a course unit;
- More active participation and communication of students and instructor in face-to-face as well as online phases;
- More authenticity of the problems to be tackled can be achieved, since students can select problems and material and raise questions they find worth considering;
- More perspectives on the content/theories can be discussed;
- Students take on more roles. Besides being authors, moderators, presenters, and listeners, they are peers and comment on the work of others;
- More group orientation and cooperation.

- • Explicit consideration and integration of qualitative and quantitative means of quality assurance allowing for participative, formative evaluation and improvement of the course.

Evaluation

Below we share excerpts from student's self-evaluations.

One student writes:

I hope I have contributed with my own inputs regarding the topic of negotiation and through active participation in all course units. I have learned to apply new moderation techniques and have acquired a balanced overview of soft skills… In addition I could, for sure, gain maximum benefit through frequently posing my own questions and thereby framing the discussions. A key experience was the workshop we held on our own: Despite intensive preparation I have realized ways of improvement that were shown up by the feedback we received.

Another student reports:

I have participated actively and have often volunteered to take part in exercises since I have seen that it is impossible to moderate a good workshop without the support of the whole group. I have delivered detailed reaction sheets since I believe that honest and specific feedback of the group can be truly facilitative.

A more quiet student mentions:

I had the opportunity to contribute my experience/view. Usually I am quite hesitant and rather shy in this respect. However, through the support of the facilitator and the positive resonance it was easier for me to jump over my shadow and contribute actively. Now I find it easier to present my viewpoint in meetings.

The only criticism some students voiced was that sometimes the units had lasted too long and they would have preferred to have more breaks. Some suggested that the course be placed earlier in the curriculum such that they could profit more for their studies.

In the end of the self-evaluation students were asked to rate how much they contributed to the course and how much they benefited from it. As shown in Table 2, the students' rating on both dimensions was very positive, with benefit still above contribution. When compared with other courses conducted by the same instructor following the same person-centered philosophy but a different course design, the ratings for students' contribution and benefit tended to be slightly though not sig-

Table 2. Students' ratings of their perception how much they contributed to and benefited from the course on project management soft skills; scale from 1 standing for "not at all," to 11 meaning "very much"; n = 20

	average value	min value	max value
I contributed to the course	9.00	5	11
I benefited from the course	9.95	7	11

nificantly lower than in project management soft skills. Also, the ratings slightly (by about 0.5) improved over the last 2 years indicating the influence of experience.

Regarding learning/development on the levels of knowledge/intellect, skills, and personality, we were interested, whether students' perceptions matched the course goals. Therefore, in the final online questionnaire, we included the question: "Please indicate, how much you benefited on the individual levels of learning." On a scale where 1 indicated very little and 5 meant very much, the level of skills received the highest rating of 4.71, followed by the personality level rated with 4.45 and the knowledge/intellect rated with 3.76. This can be seen as a confirmation of the course goals in so far, as emphasis has been given to development at the level of soft skills. Figure 4 illustrates these results and compares them with students' estimates on how much they benefit on the respective levels in conventional courses. Students perceive that in conventional courses they tend to benefit slightly more on the level of intellect. However, in the course on project management soft skills they indicate to benefit significantly more on the level of skills and attitudes. Consequently, in the students' view, PC-TEL courses significantly differ from conventional courses in developing soft skills. We note that these are initial results and more research is needed to determine the essential factors for the development of soft skills in technology enhanced environments.

Interestingly, all students (n = 21) responded to the online questionnaire, although it had been sent out after the grades were given. We consider this fact noteworthy, since to us it reflects the students' dedication, engagement, and thankfulness in response to the active and personal style of facilitating/learning.

In the final questionnaire, two further questions were included in order to find out whether students found it easier or more difficult to work in teams and to establish positive interpersonal relationships in PM-SS when compared with other courses of their studies. As shown in Figure 5, most students felt that in the course on PM-SS it was somewhat easier to work in teams and easier to establish positive interactions. Some students felt it was about the same. They tended to argue that this was due to the fact that they already knew their teammates from previous courses. From this we conclude that care must be taken in interpreting the results, since several factors

Figure 4. Learning on three levels in the course on project management soft skills as perceived by students in relationship with other courses (n = 21)

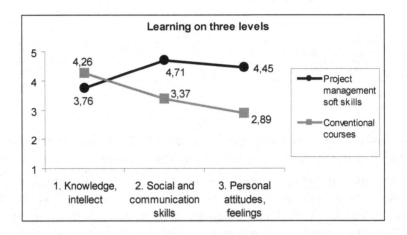

Figure 5. Students ratings on teamwork and interactions in PMSS when compared with other courses in their studies. Scales from 1.. "more difficult" to 5.. "easier"; n = 21.

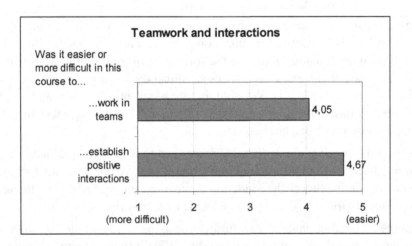

aside of the course style and atmosphere may be co-responsible for the students' perceptions on teamwork and relationships. Nevertheless, the reaction sheets and self-evaluations give further qualitative evidence that the positive atmosphere in the course and the open discussions contributed to highly constructive cooperation and interaction.

When asked for the reasons, one student responded: "Because of the intensive contacts between us. The work in small teams, the moderation of the course, but also the sitting arrangement in a circle significantly supported the interactions and building of positive relationships." Regarding teamwork a student comments: "I knew my colleagues already from other courses, hence I knew what to expect. At the same time, the course offered sufficient inputs and space to coordinate team work well."

Finally we were interested to find out from which aspects of the course students benefited most. For this reason we included 25 features in the online questionnaire and asked students to indicate to what degree they benefited from each of them. On a scale from 1 meaning "not at all" to 5 standing for "very much" the top five features and their average values were:

- Practical exercises during the lab hours (4.71)
- Active participation during the course (4.67)
- Exchange and discussion with colleagues (4.62)
- Cooperation with peers (4.57)
- Exchange and discussion with the instructor (4.52)

Interestingly, the feature: "Support by a Web based platform" came in place 9 with an average value of 4.14, along with the feature "Considering situations from different points of view." This illustrates that although support by new media clearly is considered helpful, students do not view it as one of the primary features for their learning in the context of PM-SS.

Specifying Learning

When I first conducted the course 3 years ago as a supplement to the more technical aspects of ICT project management, I realized how important and often overlooked the human aspect was in academic contexts. Equally, it was the first time I experienced how motivated, creative, and productive students are if given space to contribute to themes they themselves consider important in ways they are largely free to choose. I also realized how much the course experience changed me. I started valuing flexibility and process above large amounts of content and a rigid structure to be imposed on the students. Personally, I believe that the person centered courses I facilitated along with my participation in person centered encounter groups made me more open to fresh experience and a better facilitator.

Regarding the structure of the course, it appears effective that the first three units are conducted by the instructor/facilitator following a person centered style. In this phase students can grow together as a group and perceive a constructive working climate. Moreover, they experience moderation elements as "consumers" and participate in constructive dialogue and negotiation in class. A continuation with a lead by the instructor, however, in my view would be far less potent than having teams of students take over the moderation. Some of the reasons for sharing the responsibility with student teams are:

- All participants are exposed to a larger repertoire of styles and ideas. Collectively, these contribute to a particularly rich and versatile experience.

- Students actively engage in designing and organizing their unit. Thereby they not only acquire knowledge but also negotiate topics, divide their work, coordinate meetings, cooperate as a team both face-to-face and online, make decisions on what exercises to choose and how to moderate them, and so forth.

- Initial moderators are hardly ever perfect. Learning from "mistakes" or better from personally feeling that some aspects could be improved tends to be a strong force in learning if the communicative culture in the group acknowledges the impact of such learning.

- Students experience multiple roles: they are (at least) participants, moderators, contributors, listeners, team mates, authors, and reviewers.

- Students leave the course with the feeling of cooperatively having accomplished something that they feel is important for their future job.

One student reflects on what he gained from preparing and moderating a course unit:

The design of the unit undoubtedly was a challenging task. It took me much effort to decide which topics to select for presentation and which just to refer to. I needed some time for reading, getting an overview, and making my own picture. Once I had overlooked the theme I considered everything important and necessary in order to capture the whole context. It was a real challenge to moderate the theme over a period of time I never experienced before, but equally it was a highly interesting and valuable experience. Tackling a task of this dimension shows how one manages to integrate oneself into a team and goes about solving problems in that team. In my view, our team did grow together quite intensively in the preparation phase. ... I think the constructive criticism of the group was more than justified in order to learn from it.

However, it has proved more effective to limit the students' moderation sequences to about 2 to 2.5 hours from each 4 hour unit in order to leave time for reflection, spontaneously upcoming issues, and for living a group process that underlies the topical contributions. This is because "real" issues such as conflicts, specific needs, sudden problems, or special interests and opportunities have the potential to significantly increase learning on the attitudes and skills side if there is space to include them.

It has proved practical to offer a repository of relevant materials (book summaries, links, slides) on the learning platform but equally to encourage students to include their own sources/materials. Furthermore, I have experienced that discussing the concept students make for their moderation unit has often led to valuable insight and, as confirmed by the students, to a smoother unit design. It has also given me the opportunity to exclude dubious exercises, that is, exercises of which I was not sure that the dynamics they might cause would be helpful.

Conclusion and Further Work

Retrospectively, the course was born out of the coincidence of three influential factors. First, a survey among managers directed my attention to the soft skills aspect. Second, blending face-to-face and online learning allowed me to emphasize active learning by including students into the versatile activities described, and by providing Web space for materials and more intellectual content. Last but not least, my active engagement in person centered encounter groups and workshops changed me personally so as to become more open to new experience, to perceive the importance of processes and interaction, and to strive for better understanding of peoples' meanings, directions, intentions, and so forth. Personally I am convinced that the educator's or better facilitator's attitudes, skills, and experiences in project- or group situations can serve as an essential input for students' experiential learning. Participatory Action Research, complemented by qualitative and quantitative methods, has proved helpful for investigating learning scenarios.

Whereas the lead in effective learning still stays with persons, their capabilities, and social- and interpersonal values, thoughtfully designed scenarios, customized Web services, and easily accessible content have the potential to significantly support persons in their striving to support learning by new technology. If we succeed in reducing the time for lecturing and administrative issues, we can invest it in an exciting and more meaningful way of learning for all persons involved in the process. Clearly, this requires not only highly usable tools but also personal skills and a high degree of transparency, openness, acceptance, flexibility, and understanding from the facilitators. To develop these appears to be a most challenging task for institutions that propagate technology *enhanced* learning (Kerres, Euler, Seufert, Hasanbegovic, & Voss, 2005; Motschnig-Pitrik, 2005). A subsequent task will be the development regarding creative means of how to evaluate personal and social competence and growth, which are sought to be promoted in any deep learning experience.

Acknowledgment

The authors sincerely thank their colleague Kathrin Figl for her support regarding the course evaluation and Jürgen Mangler and Klaus Spiegl for their platform support.

References

Aspy, D. N. (1972). *Toward a technology for humanizing education*. Champaign, IL: Research Press Company.

Barrett-Lennard, G. T. (1998). *Carl Rogers' helping system - journey and substance*. London: Sage Publications.

Baskerville, R. L. (1999). Investigating information systems with action research. *Communications of the Association for Information Systems, 2*. Retrieved January 11, 2008, from http://cais.isworld.org/articles/2-19/

Bull. (1998). *Bull survey on project failure statistics*. Retrieved January 11, 2008, from http://www.it-cortex.com/Stat_Failure_Cause.htm

Cornelius-White, J. H. D., Hoey, A., Cornelius-White, C., Motschnig-Pitrik, R., & Figl, K. (2004). Person-centered education: A meta-analysis of care in progress. *Journal of Border Educational Research, 3*(1), 81-87.

Derntl, M. (2006). *Patterns for person-centered e-learning*. Berlin, Germany: Aka Verlag.

Derntl, M., & Motschnig-Pitrik, R. (2004, June 30 – July 2). BLESS - a layered blended learning systems structure. In *Proceedings of 4th International Conference on Knowledge Management (I-KNOW '04)*, Graz, Austria (pp. 592-599).

Derntl, M., & Motschnig-Pitrik, R. (2005). The role of structure, patterns, and people in blended learning. *The Internet and Higher Education, 8*(2), 111-130.

Derntl, M., & Motschnig-Pitrik, R. (2008). coUML—A visual language for modeling cooperative environments. In L. Botturi & T. Stubbs (Eds.), *Handbook of visual languages for instructional design: Theories and practices*, 155-184. Hershey, PA: Idea Group, Inc.

European Association for the Education of Adults. (2004). *Strategic statement on key competencies.* Retrieved January 11, 2008, from http://www.eaea.org/doc/Strategic_document_2004.doc

Figl, K., Derntl, M., & Motschnig, R. (2005). Assessing the added value of blended learning: An experience-based survey of research paradigms. In *Proceedings of Interactive Computer Aided Learning,* Villach, Austria.

Garrison, D. R., & Kanuka, H. (2004). Blended learning: Uncovering its transformative potential in higher education. *The Internet and Higher Education, 7*(2), 95-105.

Holzinger, A., & Motschnig-Pitrik, R. (2005). Considering the human in multimedia: Learner-centered design (LCD) & person-centered e-learning (PCeL). In P. Micheuz, P. K. Antonitsch & R. Mittermeir (Eds.), *Innovative concepts for teaching informatics* (pp. 102-112). Vienna, Austria: Carl Ueberreuter.

Kerres, M., Euler, D., Seufert, S., Hasanbegovic, J., & Voss, B. (2005). *Lehrkompetenz für eLearning-Innovationen in der Hochschule: Ergebnisse einer explorativen Studie zu Massnahmen der Entwicklung von eLehrkompetenz.* (SCIL-Arbeitsbericht 6, October 2005). St. Gallen: University of St. Gallen.

Kock, N. (2004). The three threats of action research: A discussion of methodological antidotes in the context of an information systems study. *Decision Support Systems, 37*(2), 265-286.

Motschnig-Pitrik, R. (2002). getProfile: Anforderungsanalyse an Wirschaftsinformatiker(innen) aus der Sicht der Wirtschaft. *OCG Journal, 1,* 8-11. Retrieved January 11, 2008, from http://almighty.pri.univie.ac.at/~getprofile

Motschnig-Pitrik, R. (2004, June 21-26). An action research-based framework for assessing blended learning scenarios. In *Proceedings of ED-MEDIA 2004: World Conference on Educational Multimedia, Hypermedia & Telecommunications,* Lugano, Switzerland (pp. 3976-3981).

Motschnig-Pitrik, R. (2005). Person-centered e-learning in action: Can technology help to manifest person-centered values in academic environments? *Journal of Humanistic Psychology, 45*(4), 503-530.

Motschnig-Pitrik, R., & Derntl, M. (2005). *Learning process models as mediators between didactical practice and Web support.* In *Proceedings of Conceptual Modeling - ER 2005: 24th International Conference on Conceptual Modeling,* Klagenfurt, Austria (pp. 112-127).

Motschnig-Pitrik, R., & Mallich, K. (2004). Effects of person-centered attitudes on professional and social competence in a blended learning paradigm. *Journal of Educational Technology & Society, 7*(4), 176-192.

Ottosson, S. (2003). Participation action research - a key to improved knowledge of management. *Technovation, 23,* 87-94.

Reichelmayr, T. (2005). Enhancing the student team experience with blended learning techniques. In *Proceedings of 35th ASEE/IEEE Frontiers in Education Conference*, Indianapolis, IN.

Rogers, C. R. (1961). *On becoming a person - a psychotherapists view of psychotherapy*. London: Constable.

Rogers, C. R. (1983). *Freedom to learn for the 80's*. Columbus, OH: Charles E. Merrill Publishing Company.

Rumbaugh, J., Jacobson, I., & Booch, G. (1999). *The unified modeling language reference mManual*. Reading, MA: Addison Wesley.

Susman, G. I., & Evered, R. D. (1978). An assessment of the scientific merits of action research. *Administrative Science Quarterly, 23*(4), 582-603.

Further Readings

Baskerville, R. L. (1999). Investigating information systems with action research. *Communications of the Association for Information Systems, 2,* Retrieved January 11, 2008, from http://cais.isworld.org/articles/2-19/

Derntl, M., & Motschnig-Pitrik, R. (2004, June 30 – July 2). BLESS - a layered blended learning systems structure. In *Proceedings of 4th International Conference on Knowledge Management (I-KNOW'04),* Graz, Austria (pp. 592-599).

Derntl, M., & Motschnig-Pitrik, R. (2005). The role of structure, patterns, and people in blended learning. *The Internet and Higher Education, 8*(2), 111-130.

Derntl, M., & Motschnig-Pitrik, R. (n.d.). coUML - a visual language for modeling cooperative environments. In L. Botturi & T. Stubbs (Eds.), *Handbook of visual languages for instructional design: Theories and practices.* Hershey, PA: Idea Group, Inc.

Kock, N. (2004). The three threats of action research: A discussion of methodological antidotes in the context of an information systems study. *Decision Support Systems, 37*(2), 265-286.

Motschnig-Pitrik, R. (2004, June 21-26). An action research-based framework for assessing blended learning scenarios. In *Proceedings of ED-MEDIA 2004: World Conference on Educational Multimedia, Hypermedia & Telecommunications,* Lugano, Switzerland (pp. 3976-3981).

Motschnig-Pitrik, R. (2005). Person-centered e-learning in action: Can technology help to manifest person-centered values in academic environments? *Journal of Humanistic Psychology, 45*(4), 503-530.

Useful URLs

PC-TEL Pattern Web: http://elearn.pri.univie.ac.at/patterns

Publications of the Research Lab for Eduational Technologies, University of Vienna: http://www.cs.univie.ac.at/publications.php?oid=34

Online proceedings of the 2006 Frontiers in Education Conference: http://fie.engrng.pitt.edu/fie2006/

The Person-Centered Approach in Higher Education: http://elaern.pri.univie.ac.at/pca; http://en.wikipedia.org/wiki/Carl_Rogers

Derntl, M., & Motschnig, R. The role of structure, patterns, and people in blended learning: http://www.pri.univie.ac.at/Publications/2005/iheduc05-derntl.pdf

McCombs, B. The learner-centered framework on teaching and learning. as a foundation for electronically networked communities and cultures: http://pt3.altec.org/technology/html/mccombs.html

Baskerville, R. Investigating information systems with action research: http://cais.isworld.org/articles/2-19/

Endnote

[1]   This chapter is based on "Participatory Action Research in a Blended Learning Course on Project Management Soft Skills" by Renate Motschnig-Pitrik, which appeared in the proceedings of the 36th ASEE/IEEE Frontiers in Education Conference 2006, © 2006 IEEE.

Appendix

Figure A1.

> **Case Study**
>
> Title: My Active, Technology Enhanced Course
>
> Basically any course is appropriate as a case to consider here. Take any course in your professional teaching and ask yourself the following questions:
>
> **Questions:**
>
> 1. What are the learning goals at the three levels?
>
> 2. What are the curricular requirements; where can I grant freedom to students?
>
> 3. What authentic problems could be solved?
>
> 4. What can I do to improve the contact and communication between students and students and educators?

Chapter XIII

Military Applications of Adaptive Training Technology

James E. McCarthy, Sonalysts, Inc., USA

Inside Chapter

This chapter provides an overview of the use of adaptive training technology within the military domain. Throughout the chapter, we will discuss the use of intelligent tutoring, adaptive interactive multimedia instruction, and their combination to form closed-loop adaptive training. Frequently, the discussion of a particular approach will be illustrated with one or more case-studies. Moreover, we will explore impediments to widespread adoption of these interventions throughout the military, methods to overcome these impediments, and the migration of this technology into other domains. We will conclude by summarizing trends that are likely to characterize on-going development. Rather than providing a comprehensive review of technology-enhanced learning in the military, which is likely to be outdated before it is published, the author hopes that this illustrative review will open new avenues of thought for researchers, developers, and purchasers of these systems.

Introduction

The challenges facing military trainers are manifold. Among the most vexing are:

1. The need to take large numbers of individuals from very heterogeneous backgrounds and train them to uniformly high standards of performance, and
2. The need to do so under extremely tight financial constraints.

The use of adaptive training technologies is a very powerful way of addressing these two, seemingly conflicting, objectives. Adaptive training technologies consider the current state of a learner on one hand, and the goals of the course on the other hand, to craft an individualized training plan (ITP) for each learner. The creation and management of this plan addresses the first of the noted challenges. Moreover, adaptive training approaches are often quite well suited to address the students near the center of the "bell curve" without the need of much instructor intervention. This frees the instructional staff to address the needs of the students at either end of the performance spectrum through remediation or enrichment. Moreover, focusing the staff on these more targeted interactions allows a given number of instructors to manage a larger number of students without sacrificing instructional quality. In other words, adaptive training technologies allow training commands to leverage instructional resources to cope with the second challenge, small and shrinking budgets.

In this chapter we offer an abbreviated survey of the application of adaptive training technology in military settings. We will begin by reviewing three classes of adaptive training technology. Adaptive multimedia training technology is generally used to achieve knowledge outcomes, intelligent tutoring systems are generally used to achieve skill outcomes, and closed-loop systems are used to dynamically achieve both classes of outcomes. For each category of training technology, we will briefly review the technology itself and then examine ways in which that technology has been applied in a military training context.

In the second section, we will discuss some impediments to further adoption of intelligent tutoring technology. We will review some of the cost pressures that limit adoption and then suggest ways in which a convincing business case may be produced. We will then briefly review some of the technology challenges limiting adoption and offer some suggestions on how they may be overcome.

In the third section, we will explore the ways in which this technology can transfer from the military domain to the public sector. We will first consider classroom applications of this technology. This includes typical K-12 applications as well as applications in higher education settings such as community colleges and universities. Second, we will discuss industrial applications of this technology.

Adaptive Training Technologies

Many researchers (see, for example, Anderson, 1993; Anderson & Schunn, 2000) draw a distinction between declarative and procedural knowledge. Declarative knowledge is often defined as factual knowledge that an individual can describe in words and is not goal related (e.g., knowing the fact, "a shape that has three sides is a triangle"). In Anderson's scheme, declarative knowledge is stored in declarative memory as units, or pieces, of information, which are referred to as chunks (Anderson, 1993). Chunks are schema-like structures that comprise elemental pieces of information (attributes) to form a single piece of information (Anderson, Matessa, & Lebiere, 1997). Procedural knowledge is knowledge of how to do something (e.g., a skill, an ability to use the declarative knowledge "a shape that has three sides is a triangle" to determine that a yield traffic sign is a triangle) and is represented in Anderson's framework as production rules (Anderson, 1993).

Different instructional approaches are thought to be more or less effective in developing mastery of these different types of knowledge. Consequently, different adaptive training technologies have been developed to support these different approaches. In this section, we will review these technologies. We will begin with a consideration of adaptive training technologies tailored to achieving declarative knowledge outcomes. Later, we will review those dedicated to skill development.

Adaptive Multimedia Training

Within the military training community, constructivist techniques (see, for example, Laurillard, 1987) have yet to gain much of a foothold. These more active models are characterized by student influence on both the *content to be covered* and the *method of instruction* and are said to be most appropriate when the student's goal is to construct a representation of some domain that is similar, but not necessarily identical, to that of any one expert in the field (Carlson & Falk, 1990). Rather, more didactic approaches are the norm. Within these approaches, "instruction flows into a reactive learner. The learner absorbs the instructional content but does not influence either the content or style of its presentation" (Carlson & Falk, 1990). Given this chapter's focus on military training, we will devote ourselves to adaptive training techniques that support didactic instruction.

Any Web search on computer- and Web-based instruction will quickly yield a significant list of vendors touting "adaptive" learning solutions. In many cases, a closer examination shows that such solutions simply collect learner preferences in advance of a training session in order to provide a somewhat personalized presentation of the material. This intuitively attractive approach echoes Laurillard's (1987) suggestion that the student himself knows how he learns most efficiently, and thus we should allow the student to choose the format in which the knowledge is presented. Unfortunately, Laurillard's assumption is unproved, and in fact is contradicted by a number of studies that indicate that learners often do not know how to guide their own cognitive processing to optimize learning (e.g., Chipman, Segal, & Glaser, 1985; Ghatala, 1986). We will not discuss "adaptation as personalization" techniques in this chapter.

Another technique frequently labeled as "adaptive" is to preselect the particular learning pathways to be made available to the learner (for example, those based on differing roles). Within this model, operators receive one version of a curriculum, managers a second, and salespersons a third. One could argue that these differences really reflect differences in learning objectives and thus are truly adaptive. We will not discuss "role adaptation" techniques in this chapter.

Instead, in this chapter we will adopt a more "active" definition of adaptive instruction. We will reserve the term "adaptive" for those training technologies that:

- Gather data about learners,
- Use those data to create an individualized training plan (ITP) for *each* user that addresses a common set of learning objectives *across* users, and
- Monitor and update the training plan in real time as additional learner data is captured.

InTrain™

To appreciate adaptive multimedia training, it is helpful to contrast it with traditional didactic delivery approaches. Conventional training delivery strategies are often based on a textbook metaphor. An instructional designer begins with an understanding of the topics to be covered (often captured as performance-based learning objectives, and determines the "best way" to teach that material to an "average student." Usually, this process results in some form of a storyboard. Media specialists then produce the media (e.g., graphics, animations, videos) required by the storyboard and an author/programmer assembles them to a final sequence (usually using a "flowchart" metaphor). For the most part, all students taking the resultant course share in a common experience.

Even within a conventional training architecture, steps can be taken to relax the "one size fits all" style of conventional interactive multimedia instruction (IMI). For example, depending on factors such as authoring skill and budget, conditional branching can be used to route students down various predefined pathways. Thus, a student's previous actions can dictate their future training experience. In a sense, this provides some minimal level of "adaptivity." IMI authoring tools provide a range of tools to support this function and the sequencing and navigation logic in

SCORM 2004 (Advanced Distributed Learning, 2004) is another way to accomplish this end in a more transportable fashion. However, care must be exercised in this regard. The more branching that is added, the more complicated and costly the courseware becomes and the more difficult it is to maintain.

The InTrain tutoring engine manifests a different approach. Developed as a complement to the ExpertTrain™ intelligent tutoring system (discussed later), InTrain uses a tutoring (rather than a textbook) metaphor to deliver IMI. A human tutor considers the learning objectives that must be addressed as well as what the student already knows. Together, this tells the tutor what he or she must teach the student. Next, the tutor uses what he or she knows about the student to select some instructional activities that are likely to be effective. After working through the instruction, the tutor presents some assessment activities that are tailored to the student and to the content of instruction. If the student does well, the tutor can move on to new content. If not, then the tutor can select other ways of teaching the material and assessing mastery. This can continue until the student has mastered all of the required learning objectives.

InTrain attempts to simulate this tailoring of instruction. That is, InTrain is used to automatically create and deliver an ITP at run-time, based on the student's mastery of defined learning objectives, available content objects that support those learning objectives, course/instructional definition data, and instructional history (see, for example, McCarthy, 1996; McCarthy, Johnston, & Paris, 1998).

Two concepts are central to InTrain's functioning. The first is the notion that instructional content can be captured as a set of addressable objects and the second is the notion of a learner model.

Inspired by the rise of object-oriented programming techniques and the practical need to re-use and repurpose content, the idea of content-objects has become increasingly influential. For example, the Content Aggregation model within SCORM 2004 defines a hierarchy of content objects and a vocabulary of metadata that can be used to describe their contents. Intuitively, these content objects can be thought of as reusable boxes of content and the metadata as labels that describe the contents of each box. When a given type of content is needed, it can be located via the metadata and plugged into place using standard interfaces.

Although InTrain itself predates SCORM, much of its approach is consistent with, in fact hinges on, this object-based vision of instruction. Within InTrain, each learning objective is associated with one or more methods of teaching the content associated with the objective. Each of these instructional methods is captured as a separate instructional object (see Figure 1). In a similar vein, each learning objective is associated with one or more methods of assessing mastery of the objective. In fact, in some cases, smaller objects (such as question stems or response options) can be combined at run-time to dynamically create new assessment items.

The second critical aspect of the InTrain approach is the use of a multidimensional learner model. InTrain's learner model is essentially a database of information about individual learners. Each learner has his/her own learner model and it is updated in real-time as the student interacts with the system.

Ohlsson (1986) describes several approaches to student modeling. *Performance models* describe the student in terms of how successfully he solves problems in the knowledge domain. A shortcoming of this approach is that performance models often tell the system how much the student knows, but not what the student knows. *Overlay models* depict student knowledge as a subset of expert knowledge. The overlay indicates which bits of expert knowledge the student has acquired and which he has not. The primary difficulty with the student model is that experts not only (and not always) know more than novices, but they know differently. Experts organize problems and solutions in a fundamentally different way than novices. Overlays do not capture the misconceptions and gaps that are characteristic of novice performance. *Error descriptions* compare the performance of a student to a pre-established error catalog and from the performance attempt to deduce the gaps in the student's understanding. The weakness of the error description approach is that it presupposes a single representation of the subject domain. An alternative representation would invalidate the meaningfulness of the errors. *Generative student models* attempt to form runnable simulations of student behaviors that will lead to the pattern of accurate and inaccurate performance that the student has generated. Misconceptions and gaps are described implicitly in the model. Generative student models are weakened because they tend to focus on the surface features of student behavior (Laurillard, 1987) and because they are inextricably tied to certain theoretical assumptions (Anderson, Boyle, & Reiser, 1985; Ohlsson, 1986; Scandura, 1988).

InTrain uses an overlay approach described by Murray (1991), known as endorsement-based modeling (EBM). One of the key benefits of the Murray approach is that it provides a mechanism to meaningfully combine evaluative information from sources that vary greatly in reliability. Using EBM, the system collects evidence for and against the proposition that the student knows a given concept. Evidence may be directly observed (e.g., answers to test questions) or inferred from the objective's place in the hierarchy (e.g., if a parent concept is mastered, there is some evidence that all of its children will be mastered as well).

The arguments are partitioned according to the presumed reliability of the evidence source. Within each reliability level, evidence for and against mastery is compared. In this way, each reliability level contributes a "view" of whether or not the student has mastered the concept. Beginning with the most reliable evidence, InTrain looks for "unbalanced" evidence (i.e., the presence of more positive evidence than negative evidence, or the converse). At the first unbalanced reliability level, the polarity of the comparison is taken as indication of mastery. That is, if the most reliable unbalanced reliability category has more positive than negative evidence, the learning objective is said to be mastered. Conversely, if the most reliable unbalanced reliability category has more negative evidence than positive evidence, the learning objective is said to be unmastered.

InTrain augments this endorsement-based mastery profile with data about the student's instructional history (i.e., which instruction or assessment objects have been presented) and a demographic profile (e.g., to what subpopulation does the student belong). Together, these three elements (mastery profile, instructional history, learner characteristics) form the learner model for each student.

InTrain uses these learner model data, as well as information about course goals stored as course data, to create an ITP for each learner that utilizes available objects. It then executes the ITP by providing content, practice, and assessment activities until mastery of the requisite learning objective(s) is attained. The on-going ITP is updated as these activities are presented to the student and he/she responds.

Two independent evaluations of InTrain's instructional effectiveness have been performed. In the Perrin, Dargue, and Banks (2003) study, an existing course was rehosted using four instructional models. Two control conditions were used. The Computer Control Condition largely replicated the original course by presenting students with a fixed linear instructional sequence. In addition, the Classroom Control Condition replicated this course in a "standup" format. The Perrin et al. (2003) study explored a number of experimental conditions. Two of these are shown in Figure 2. The Mastery Learning condition implemented a fairly typical InTrain sequence in which initial instruction is followed by assessment and adaptive remediation. Training in the Adaptive Remediation condition "was similar to Mastery Learning, except that mastery of previously tested objectives could be retracted. This occurred when previously mastered declarative knowledge was overlooked or used incorrectly in a problem-solving exercise." After receiving training on one of these conditions, participants took a post-test.

The results of the post-test were used to create a "learning performance" measure. The study authors noted that, "the learning performance score had two components—accuracy on the problem-solving test and speed of completion. Speed is a

Figure 1. Adaptive IMI Instruction (© 2007, Sonalysts, Inc. and James E. McCarthy, PhD. Used with permission)

Figure 2. Boeing evaluation results (© 2007, Sonalysts, Inc. and James E. McCarthy, PhD. Used with permission)

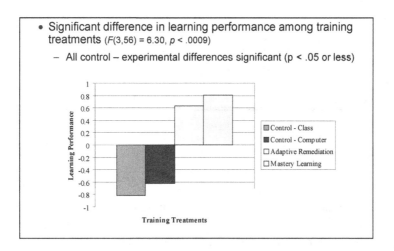

common measure of the *strength* of knowledge and reflects its resistance to forgetting" (Anderson, 2001). To form a stable estimate, we converted speed and accuracy to z scores and then averaged them to form a combined learning performance score. Figure 2 illustrates the findings.

These results were echoed in a study performed by the U.S. Navy's Naval Submarine School (NAVSUBSCOL) (Birchard, Dye, & Gordon, 2002). NAVSUBSCOL is the "Center of Excellence" for Submarine Warfare Training. Traditionally, training for the NAVSUBSCOL has taken place in instructor-led classrooms. To test the effectiveness of the InTrain model, NAVSUBSCOL re-authored 8.5 hours of the Sonar Fundamentals curriculum taught during the 10-week Submarine Officer Basic Course (SOBC). Submarine School staff instructors, working with guidance from instructional designers and subject matter experts (SMEs), developed the required adaptive IMI course. The content then was delivered to a class of 21 students during two 4-hour dedicated periods.

Following the training, students were given a paper based mastery test. For comparison purposes, the same test was given to two other groups of students (taught using conventional classroom methods) and all tests were graded by the same set of instructors. In addition, historical performance levels for this material were assessed. Table 1 summarizes the comparison.

In both the Perrin et al. (2003) and NAVSUBSCOL studies, student post-test performance in the adaptive IMI conditions approached ceiling levels. As such, the reported results may underestimate the potential gains.

Table 1. NAVSUBSCOL evaluation results (© 2007, Sonalysts, Inc. and James E. McCarthy, PhD. Used with permission)

	InTrain Students (One class)	Instructor-Led Group (Last 2 classes of students)	Historical[1] (Instructor-Led Group)
Population	21	75	≥ 300
Student Mean[2]	95%	88.5%	84.5%
No. of Exam Failures[3]	0	3	N/A

REDEEM

Two of the impediments to widespread adoption of adaptive multimedia training are the large body of legacy instructional material (i.e., "if we adopt an adaptive approach, we will have to abandon our legacy investment") and the lack of generally usable authoring tools. In developing the Reusable Educational Design Environment and Engineering Methodology (REDEEM), Ainsworth and her colleagues addressed both concerns (Ainsworth & Grimshaw, 2004). REDEEM provides tools to overlay conventional computer-baed training CBT content developed in HTML or with the tool ToolBook with features of adaptive training. Moreover, whereas the authoring tools developed for InTrain presumed use by instructional systems development (ISD) professionals, REDEEM was developed with classroom teachers in mind.

The REDEEM architecture has four major components (Ainsworth et al., 2003):

- Courseware catalog
- Authoring tools
- ITS shell
- Student model

Addressing the need to reuse existing content, a key component of the REDEEM architecture is a courseware catalog. This catalog consists of a collection of individual ToolBook or HTML pages. The authoring tools allow teachers to describe and augment content as we will describe later. The ITS shell interprets the teachers' authoring inputs and adaptively presents the course to the student. The student model uses an overlay methodology to capture the student's current standing in the course.

The REDEEM authoring approach can be summarized as comprising three primary steps:

- Characterizing content
- Characterizing students
- Associating strategies

Typically, the teacher's first authoring step is to characterize the content of instruction. Using the authoring tools, the teacher aggregates pages of content in the courseware catalog into sections and then associates metadata with each of the pages and sections. Using relatively simple widgets, the teacher "scores" each page/section on its familiarity, difficulty, and so forth. It is important to note that it is also at this stage that the teacher can add interactive activities (e.g., practice questions) to the course. As we discuss later, this is especially important in that there is evidence that this increase in interactivity leads to improved learning performance.

Next, the teacher is guided through a process of defining categories of students and assigning students to those categories. The teacher can define as many, or as few, categories as deemed appropriate. In some settings, for example, a K-12 classroom, this may be very powerful (Ainsworth & Grimshaw, 2004). However, in many military training contexts, it may be more problematic (Ainsworth, Williams, & Wood, 2001).

The definition of student categories is critically related to the last primary authoring step—defining strategies. At this stage of development, the teacher defines instructional strategies and associates a given strategy with each student category. This technique, labeled as "macro-adaptation" (Ainsworth & Grimshaw, 2004), presents each student with a content sequence unique to the category to which the student belongs. Strategy definition reflects decisions on nine instructional parameters (e.g., who controls the content to be delivered, what is the balance between presentation of content and testing of knowledge, should content begin with or build up to the presentation of general concepts). In addition, as part of each strategy, the teacher must indicate the type (e.g., multiple-choice, true/false) and difficulty (easy, medium, hard) of test questions to intersperse with the content (the timing and behavior of the testing account for several of the nine instructional parameters that the teacher must set). In addition, during a process called "strategy refinement" teachers are asked a series of multiple choice questions that help the teacher identify when certain aspects of a given strategy should be changed (e.g., when should question difficulty be increased or when should a different style be adopted).

When a student takes the course, the ITS shell presents the sections and pages of content in a sequence determined by the strategy associated with that student's category. Periodically, as dictated by the strategy, practice questions will be presented to the student. If need be, the student can ask for one of five levels of hints provided by the teacher. When they answer, they will be presented with teacher-developed feedback. It does not appear that remedial instruction is provided if the student struggles on a given section.

Ainsworth and her colleagues have evaluated both the usability of the authoring environment and the effectiveness of the resultant training. In both military and civilian environments, the authoring tools have proven themselves to be quite usable. Minimal training is required (an hour or two) and authors are able to be quite productive.

A somewhat more murky answer emerges when one considers whether authoring tools are useful; that is, do they provide precisely the functions that teachers want to use to add adaptivity to their courses (Ainsworth et al., 2003). In the civilian sector, REDEEM seemed to provide a good set of functionality in that teachers used multiple student categories and developed a range of strategies to address those categories. It is worth noting, however, that within content domains, there were significant interauthor differences with respect to a number of decisions throughout the authoring process (e.g., the definition of content sections, student categories, and instructional strategies). A positive reflection on this matter would be that it shows that the tools provide needed functionality; that is, they allowed the instructors to craft courses tailored to their pedagogical preferences. A more negative view might be that the teachers lacked the background to make the most efficacious decisions. We will return to this point shortly.

In the military domain, the differentiation features of the tool were found to be less useful. This is hardly surprising given that military trainers often work with their students for only a short period of time and do not have the detailed knowledge required for useful categorization. Where differentiation was used, it often had more to do with the purpose to which the content would be applied (e.g., initial training, refresher training, just-in-time training, classroom aid) than it did with the students who would take the course.

Clearly, the critical issue was the degree to which REDEEM improved student learning performance. After all, the usability of the authoring tool is only of issue if it produces content of superior quality.

A pair of Ainsworth and Grimshaw (2004) studies examined this issue in a K-12 setting using a course on genetics. In both studies, the genetics syllabus was divided into two courses. Half of the students received the REDEEMed version of the first course (part one of the curriculum) and the normal CBT version of the second course (part two of the curriculum). The other half took the normal CBT version of the first course and the REDEEMed version of the second course. In the first study, conducted by bringing students from their normal school setting to the university, the authors found that both the conventional and REDEEMed version of the course improved performance, but that REDEEM did not lead to more learning (i.e., the difference in improvement scores was not significantly different). For the second study, the students were allowed to remain in their school. A second teacher re-authored the course using REDEEM to reflect both differences in the curriculum taught at that school and differences in his preferred instructional style. Here, the authors found that REDEEM did improve performance more than conventional CBT, but only for the group that received REDEEM first. For the group that received REDEEM second, the improvement scores were not significantly different from the CBT condition.

Ainsworth and her colleagues also examined the efficacy of REDEEM in a set of studies conducted in a military environment (Ainsworth & Fleming, 2004; Ainsworth et al., 2001). For these studies the content addressed issues in information technology (IT) and the participants were drawn from the British Royal Navy, an undergraduate population, or the British Royal Air Force. The same cross-over design described earlier was used for these studies. In the Navy study, Naval instructors developed the courses and no REDEEM advantage was reported. In the undergraduate and RAF studies, the results indicated that REDEEM did lead to greater gains than conventional CBT. Further analysis of the results indicated that, as in the case of the genetics studies, the gains were largely attributable to increases in interactivity rather than to the macro-adaptation features of REDEEM.

Other Approaches

Throughout the years, a number of other approaches have been used. Most of these have not been used in military settings and here we will only offer a sampling. Mc-Combs and McDaniel (1981) adapted instruction to individual differences by applying multiple regression procedures to identify the individual characteristics (e.g., low reading ability or high anxiety level) that were interfering with performance on a given lesson segment. The given lesson segment was then rewritten to be tolerant of the individual characteristics. McCombs and McDaniel (1981) demonstrated improved performance with their approach. Given the breadth of content that must be produced and the heterogeneous nature of the student population, this approach, while effective, may not be practical in military communities.

Dillenbourg (1989) used a machine learning approach to identify which instructional tactics were effective in a given situation. Dillenbourg (1989) first identified a number of tactics appropriate for his concept formation task. His system attempted to teach a concept with one of the tactics. If it was unsuccessful, another tactic was used. Those tactics that were successful were separated from those that were not. A separate program analyzed the successful and unsuccessful tactics and generated rules for their use. Examples of the rules that were developed include: Tactic 1 is successful if it is the fourth strategy after a test; Tactic 2 is successful if it follows Tactic 1. Dillenbourg (1989) did not find a statistically significant increase in performance based on these rules. Furthermore, they are composite rules that do not reflect individual learning styles.

More recently, some developers have begun to develop courses that exploit the Sequencing and Navigation capabilities afforded by SCORM 2004. These developers have been able to achieve a degree of learner sensitivity by tracking the status of "objective" information for a Sharable Content Object (SCO) and using this information in a prescribed rule set to perform inter-SCO sequencing evaluations.

Summary

The two most developed adaptive multimedia systems reviewed here, InTrain and REDEEM, share many features. For example, both tools have adopted some form of an overlay student model and both make decisions about what to instruct and how to instruct it. However, there are also significant differences in their approaches. REDEEM was developed with classroom teachers in mind and it has extensive functionality to define unlimited categories of students and a large number (10,000) of instructional strategies (Ainsworth & Grimshaw, 2004). On the other hand, accommodating different instructional purposes and remediating identified student deficiencies are not central to the REDEEM framework. InTrain accommodates exactly three student populations and only four instructional sequencing strategies. On the other hand, InTrain has more functionality to develop instructional sequences for differing instructional purposes and includes remedial training as one of its core functions.

Both REDEEM and InTrain have demonstrated improved learning performance relative to conventional CBT. Within the REDEEM studies, the effect is variable and largely attributable to increased interactivity. The data from the InTrain studies does not allow a comprehensive examination of this issue. However, the Perrin et al. (2003) study does offer some hints.

Before considering this study further, it is important to note that InTrain supports two types of adaptivity. First, InTrain adapts by, optionally, providing remedial training when a student's assessment performance indicates that some concepts are not mastered. When enabled, this leads to the creation of an ITP focused on those unmastered learning objectives. Second, InTrain adapts by accommodating differences in student population. Unlike REDEEM, InTrain supports a fixed number of student populations.[1] The instructional designer is left to his or her own devices to create content objects tailored to each population. For example, a designer might choose to use different language, examples, or analogies to teach the same content to different populations.

Table 2 demonstrates this process. The designer might define any number of content objectives for a given population. These objects can be further discriminated according to the level of detail contained within them. At delivery time, InTrain attempts to present the student with an object from the closest population and level of detail category. Traditionally, the level of detail starts at "low" and is increased at each remediation attempt. If no object is available in the best cell, internal logic selects the next best match (including re-using content as a last resort).

Table 2. Content categories (© 2007, Sonalysts, Inc. and James E. McCarthy, PhD. Used with permission)

		Population		
		A	B	C
Level of Detail	High	1		2
	Medium	1	2	
	Low	1		1

In the Perrin et al. (2003) study, one of the control conditions was the normal In-Train course with remediation disabled. That is, in that condition, students received instruction and assessment activities, but the results of instruction were not used to generate remedial instruction/assessment using an alternative instructional strategy (i.e., moving up a column in Table 1). Perrin et al. (2003) noted that the "mastery" condition that enabled the remedial training (i.e., allowed level of detail to increase on subsequent retraining efforts) produced a significant advantage relative to the control condition. An interpretation of the Perrin et al. (2003) study that is consistent with the REDEEM studies is that the mastery condition led to more and more focused interactions. To date, no InTrain research has explored the value of adapting to student population.

In short, the research to date indicates that adaptive multimedia training improves performance relative to both classroom instruction and CBT. The mechanism of this improvement may be tied to increases in student interactivity. Enforcing interactivity, especially through remedial training, seems to improve the consistency of the results.

Intelligent Tutoring Systems

Now let us turn our attention to the development of skills. Recall that the thinking here is that the best (perhaps only) way to achieve mastery of procedural knowledge is to practice deploying that knowledge to address authentic problems (Hannafin, Hill, & McCarthy, 2002). Applying adaptive training technology to this problem leads to the development of intelligent tutoring systems. These systems place the students into an authentic environment and ask them to perform the tasks required by that environment (e.g., solve problems, operate equipment). The performance of the student is then monitored and some form of coaching is provided.

Intelligent tutoring systems generally consist of four components. The first is the environment in which students are asked to perform. Problems of some sort are presented to the students and they are asked to use the interface provided by the environment to solve those problems. The second is the student model. As we have discussed earlier, the student model is the system's representation for who each student is and what he or she knows. The third component is the instruction expert. This is a software component that embodies the rules by which instructional will be delivered. For example, the instructional expert might choose the problems to present to the student, decide what feedback to provide, and decide on the form that that feedback might take. The fourth component is frequently referred to as the domain expert. This software component is designed to assess the student's problem-solving performance.

Two forms of intelligent tutoring dominate the military domain—process-based tutors and case-based tutors. These two approaches differ in their approach to the domain expert portion of an ITS. Process-based tutors capture domain expertise in a more- or less-detailed cognitive model (often reflecting underlying assumptions about the nature of cognition). Presented with world data, the process-based tutors "think" about the situation in a way that is purportedly human-like and reach a conclusion about the most advisable course of action. For these types of ITSs, the unit of analysis is often fine-grained and the knowledge engineering requirements can be extensive. The model must be populated with all the data that experts consider, as well as the data that describe the processing methods that are employed. Other intelligent tutoring systems employ case-based logic. For this class of tutor, knowledge engineering consists of identifying cases that span the likely problem space.

In this section, we will explore both of these approaches. Our goal is not to offer a comprehensive review, but rather to offer some insights into approaches that are used throughout the military today.

Process-Based Systems

Some of the earliest intelligent tutoring systems were developed under military sponsorship (Fletcher, 1988). For example, both SOPHIE (Brown, Burton, & Newell, 1982) and STEAMER (Hollan, Hutchins, & Weitzman, 1984) were developed in the early 1980s with funding from the military. SOPHIE used simulation and natural language processing to teach students about troubleshooting electronic systems. STEAMER trained naval officers in the operation of steam propulsion systems.

Later in that decade, additional systems emerged to continue the military's leadership in intelligent tutoring system development. For example, Massey, Kerland, Tenney, de Bruin, and Quayle (1986) describe the Maintenance Aid Computer for HAWK – Intelligent Institutional Instructor (MACH – III) that is used to train students to maintain the illuminating radar on the U.S. Army's HAWK air defense system.

Moreover, application of intelligent tutoring was not limited to maintenance. The Intelligent Conduct of Fire Trainer (INCOFT) is used to train U.S. Army personnel to operate the engagement control station of the PATRIOT air defense system (Feurzeig, Massey, Downes-Martin, & Ritter, 1986).

Perhaps one of the most thoroughly researched intelligent tutoring systems in the military domain is SHERLOCK, developed near the beginning of the 1990s (Katz & Lesgold, 1993; Lesgold, Lajoie, Bunzo, & Eggan, 1992). Like SOPHIE and MACH-III, SHERLOCK was developed to improve troubleshooting skills, this time in conjunction with the F-15 Avionics Test Station. The original SHERLOCK research demonstrated that about 25 hours of practice in that environment had an impact on post-test performance equal to about 4 years of on-the-job experiences (Corbett & Koedinger, 1997). Gott, Kane, and Lesgold (1995) followed up with a report that reviewed five separate evaluations of SHERLOCK. That review showed an overall effect size of about 1.05 standard deviations.

ExpertTrain tutoring engine provides a fairly prototypical model of a process-based tutor in use today (see, for example, McCarthy, Pacheco, Banta, Wayne, & Coleman, 1994; McCarthy, Stretton, & Hontz, 1995). Like most tutoring systems, ExpertTrain comprises the following components:

- **Domain expert:** A software module that represents the knowledge of an expert in the subject matter domain and assesses the student's performance.

- **Learner model:** A data repository that reflects the student's mastery with respect to course learning objectives and the coaching that the learner has received.

- **Instructional expert:** A software module that produces instructional decisions. Considering inputs from the learner model and the domain expert, the instructional expert determines whether to intervene in the student's activity, what issue to address if an intervention is warranted, and which type of intervention to employ.

- **Learner-device interface:** The medium of communication between the student and the ITS. The learner-device interface creates the learning environment by presenting the student with engaging stimulus events and by providing the student with the ability to respond to those events.

A description of how these components interact during a simulation-based education session is presented in Figure 3.

Using these components, the student is placed in a situated learning environment. Scenario events within this environment invoke expectations in a domain expert. The domain expert monitors the student's response to scenario events and assesses whether expectations were met or violated. These assessments are then passed to the instructional expert and used to update the learner model. The instructional expert, using the input from the domain expert and information from the learner model, determines the appropriate instructional feedback and provides it dynamically. This cycle of stimulus event, student action, assessment, and feedback continues throughout the exercise.

Within ExpertTrain, learning objectives are the fundamental organizing construct. A cognitive task analysis (CTA) is used to first identify these objectives at an appropriate level of detail and then to identify two classes of information for each learning objective. One class of information describes the environmental conditions associated with a learning objective; that is, under what conditions does a particular learning objective come into play? Depending on the tutor, these conditions might specify the state of the simulation and/or simulated entities or some set of real-world conditions.

The second set of information describes the expected student actions associated with each learning objective; that is, for a given learning objective, what is the expected student performance? By extension, this allows ExpertTrain to answer the question, "Given observed conditions, what do I expect of the student?" Notice that the learning objective infrastructure serves as a linking function between observed conditions and expected actions. Also notice that the "expectations" can be both positive and negative; that is, in addition to specifying good performance (referred to as "target"

Figure 3. ExpertTrain cycle of operation (© 2007, Sonalysts, Inc. and James E. McCarthy, PhD. Used with permission)

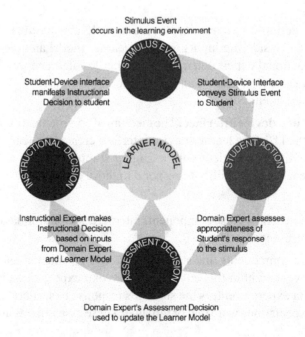

behaviors or states), ExpertTrain also monitors student performance for likely or prototypical errors (referred to as "bugs"). The expected actions (targets and bugs) are described in terms of observed student behaviors or effects (e.g., student control actions or changes within the modeled world).

Figure 4 illustrates how this process is implemented within the ExpertTrain tutoring engine. Beginning at the bottom of the figure, the results of the CTA are used to define certain aspects of world data that are instructionally appropriate. Software engineers then develop a set of data-driven "sensors" or "demons" that are sensitive to those data.

Continuing up through the figure, the CTA also reveals how certain combinations of world data can be combined to form the basis for generating expectations. In a manner similar to a semantic network or a production system, ExpertTrain recognizes certain combinations of events, links them to expectations, and prioritizes those expectations.

A similar process examines the student's performance. Separate sensors examine the states or changes in system controls or other data the CTA revealed as important. The sensor findings are combined to indicate the presence/absence of critical student actions (e.g., taking a certain operational or troubleshooting action).

Assessment decisions are the result of the comparison process indicated in the center of the figure. Each action that is recognized in the top of the figure is "offered" to each of the expectations originating from the bottom. In turn, the expectations can "claim" an action as matching a target expectation or matching a known bug associated with that expectation. As additional actions are recognized, expectations

Figure 4. ExpertTrain assessment process (© 2007, Sonalysts, Inc. and James E. McCarthy, PhD. Used with permission)

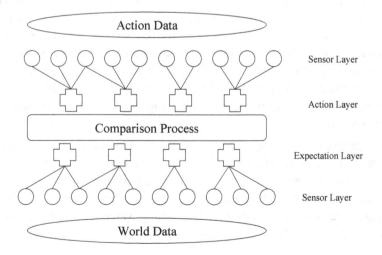

(targets or bugs) may become "completed." When an expectation has been completed, a positive (for targets) or negative (for bugs) assessment decision is rendered and appropriate coaching is provided.

ExpertTrain was introduced in 1992. Since that time, it has been used to produce a wide range of intelligent tutoring systems for the U.S. Navy, Army, and Air Force, including:

- Radar system controller intelligent training aid (RSC ITA)
- Nuclear power intelligent training aid (NITA)
- Photonics mast intelligent training aid (PITA)
- Advanced embedded training system (AETS) - Embedded AAW team training system
- Tactical control program intelligent training aid (TCP ITA)
- Multiple launch rocket system virtual sand table (MLRS VST)
- Artillery targeting officer intelligent training aid (ATO ITA)
- Armor virtual sand table
- Wheeled vehicle virtual sand table
- Integrated satellite operations trainer (ISOT)
- ASTAC intelligent training aid (AITA)
- Virtual observer/controller (VOC)

In the U.S. Navy, an informal evaluation of the RSC ITA was conducted. Students with varying levels of expertise and experience were asked whether they believed that the RSC ITA improved their general ability to operate the radar system. They were also asked whether the RSC ITA improved their ability to respond to clutter, jamming, and chaff (notoriously troublesome operational and training factors). Finally, the students were asked whether they would recommend the continued inclusion of the RSC ITA as part of the RSC curriculum. Between 80% and 90% of the students responded positively to each question (McCarthy et al., 1995). In addition, the introduction of the RSC ITA allowed the schoolhouse to dramatically increase their throughput without increasing the number of instructors that had to be employed.

A comprehensive evaluation of the MLRS VST was conducted by the U.S. Army Research Institute (ARI). The MLRS is a rocket system that provides counterfire, suppression of enemy air defenses, and destruction of light material and personnel targets. The MLRS delivers large volumes of firepower in a short time against critical time sensitive targets (Wisher, Banta, Macpherson, Abramson, Thornton, & Dees, 2001; Wisher, Macpherson, Abramson, Thornton, & Dees, 2001). The

MLRS VST was used to train U.S. Army captains to make decisions regarding reconnaissance, selection, and occupation of position (RSOP) for emplacement of an MLRS. Wisher and his colleagues compared the training effectiveness of the MLRS VST with conventional training approaches. In their study, the MLRS VST demonstrated an effect size of 1.05. That translates to a 35% increase in learning effectiveness. Although not specifically addressed in the report, the MLRS VST capability to deliver training over standard Internet portends obvious (though not quantified) savings in training travel expenses (see our later discussion on removing impediments to wide-scale adoption).

Another contemporary approach is adopted within the COGNET family of intelligent tutoring applications. COGNET is a theoretical framework of human information processing and decision-making that has been applied as a cognitive modeling and implementation tool for simulating the performance of a skilled operator working within a human-machine environment. COGNET has been used to develop entities for computer-generated forces (e.g., LeMentec, Glenn, Zachary, & Eilbert, 1999), support investigations of human-computer interaction (e.g., Zachary & Ross, 1991), and as a mechanism for developing intelligent tutoring systems (e.g., Ryder, Santarelli, Scolaro, Hicinbothom, & Zachary, 2000).

The COGNET architecture is based on two theories: (1) the Model Human Processor (MHP) (Card, Moran, & Newell, 1983) and (2) blackboard system methodology. MHP is a cognitive science theory that describes human performance as being composed of three processes: (1) perceptual, (2) cognitive, and (3) motor. Consequently, the COGNET framework describes information processing as three parallel processing mechanisms: (1) perception, (2) cognition, and (3) motor activity and is composed of four architectural components: (1) perception, (2) cognition, (3) extended working memory, and (4) motor activity (LeMentec et al., 1999). These processes describe a cyclical system of human performance in which the perceptual process receives information from the environment, stores the information in working memory, and the cognitive process interprets the information stored in working memory and chooses an appropriate action that is executed by the motor process.

COGNET uses a Goals, Operators, Methods, and Selection Rules (GOMS)-like notation (Card et al., 1983), which is augmented with attention triggers and a priority formula (Zachary, Le Mentec, & Ryder, 1996), to define cognitive tasks. The cognitive task notation comprises two parts: (1) a procedural body, which utilizes the GOMS notation to express the goal and operations associated with a specific task, and (2) a metacognitive tag, which contains the attention trigger and priority notation.

Blackboard system methodology (Nii, 1986) evolved as an approach to replicate group problem solving. The blackboard is a global database that contains a hierarchy of abstractions that represent the task and its environment. Declarative knowledge is posted to, or manipulated (e.g., reorganized) on, the blackboard by the perceptual and cognitive processes dynamically as the situation changes (Zachary, Cannon-Bowers, Bilazarian, Krecker, Lardieri, & Burns, 1999). Perceptual demons either post (add declarative chunks) or reorganize the contents of the blackboard. Cognitive tasks manipulate (reorganize, post/unpost, suspend, or subrogate) knowledge on the blackboard based on inferences made by the procedural knowledge in the cognitive component (LeMentec et al., 1999).

Cognitive tasks comprise procedural knowledge chunks (procedural knowledge units) that describe how a specific task to achieve a specific goal is performed, and the cognitive tasks are stored in COGNET's procedural memory (LeMentec et al., 1999). Activation of a cognitive task results in either manipulation of declarative knowledge that is stored in extended working memory (LeMentec et al., 1999) or an action that is executed by the motor component. Only one cognitive task may be executed at a given time due to the limitations of an operator's attentional resources.

Metacognitive knowledge is used to manage the competition for attentional resources and to determine when the conditions associated with a particular cognitive task are present. Additionally, cognitive tasks also possess formulas to determine their relative priorities (Zachary et al., 1996). The priority formula uses the current pattern of facts and knowledge elements on the blackboard to determine the priority level. The priority level of the cognitive tasks enables the associated perceptual knowledge units on the blackboard (extended working memory) to demand attentional resources.

COGNET cognitive models have been used to support various components of intelligent tutoring systems (Ryder et al., 2000). Specifically, COGNET cognitive models have been used as the domain expert component to support a model-tracing intelligent tutoring application and as instructional agents to perform the functions of three intelligent tutoring system modules (student model, domain expert, instructional model). Ryder et al. (2000) suggest that the difference between a domain expert and an instructional agent is that an expert model uses model-tracing to enable a separate instructional component to diagnose and provide remediation, while an instructional agent uses a model-tracing procedure to evaluate, diagnose, and provide tailored instruction within a single component.

Domain Expert Approach. COGNET models of expert performance (Ryder et al., 2000) were developed to serve as a model-tracing mechanism for the AETS ITS, which was developed to support team training in an Aegis-based Combat Training System for the U.S. Navy. Performance evaluation, diagnosis, and instruction were focused on high-level tasks, called high-level actions (HLAs), which encapsulate several lower-level actions (e.g., button presses, keystroke sequences, eye movements). Consequently, the expert models of operator performance were built at the HLA unit level (Zachary et al., 1999). Feedback was provided at the level of the HLAs to reduce the amount of feedback the trainee received while performing the task in an effort to prevent the feedback from disrupting the trainee's performance. Additionally, an automated assessment system and a human instructor performed evaluation, diagnosis, and feedback functions.

The COGNET expert models interfaced with an automated assessment and diagnosis component (Zachary et al., 1999) that dynamically compared the student's actions with the domain expert's expectation of the trainee's actions, which is essentially a model-tracing procedure. The automated data capture component enabled the domain expert to identify the HLAs that the student performed. After the expected HLAs were identified, the domain expert identified the knowledge and skill elements that corresponded to the HLAs. Real-time, automated feedback was provided based on the lapsed time since the student last received feedback and the priority of the training objective, and a corresponding feedback template was selected, which varied according to the information content and directiveness of the feedback.

Instructional Agents. COGNET instructional agents are designed to provide instruction through guided practice (Ryder et al., 2000) for dynamic tasks, such as ship handling and flying. With this approach, the COGNET models serve as the domain expert and instructional expert simultaneously. Student performance is dynamically assessed through a model tracing procedure in which the student's actions are compared to the scenario-specific expectations and performance metrics. Students are diagnosed based on how their actions related to the actions predicted by the instructional agent model. If the student's performance deviates from the model's expectations of performance, the instructional model reports the desired actions and the steps required to perform the desired action to the student. If the student's performance does not deviate from the model's expectation of performance, the student is considered to be performing optimally.

A specific example is the plan for developing an instructional agent for the Virtual Environment Training Technology (VETT) (Ryder et al., 2000). A cognitive model was proposed to evaluate student performance by: (1) building a mental model of the student's performance, (2) relating discrete performance metrics to overall metrics, (3) predicting the kinematic effects of the student's actions, and (4) categorizing the student's performance by strategy type. It was proposed that the instructional model would identify the strategy the student was using based on the student's actions (e.g., gaze, commands issued), the ship's dynamics (e.g., speed, heading), and declarative ship handling knowledge specific to the UNREP task. COGNET was also used to develop a similar instructional agent for the Electronically Assisted Ground-Based Learning Environment (EAGLE) to monitor and evaluate the student. The agent evaluates the student's performance against preclassification of performance deviation.

Case-Based Systems

Process-based tutors provide a very powerful solution to the development of intelligent tutoring systems. Once the cognitive model underlying the domain expert has been developed, an essentially limitless number of scenarios within that domain can be added to the curriculum at no extra cost. Moreover, when paired with natural-language systems, the cognitive model provides the foundation for powerful dialog-based coaching interactions.

However, there are domains in which developing a formal cognitive model of performance expertise is impossible, or at least impractical. In domains like these, case-based ITSs provide a viable solution. In these systems, rather than developing a cognitive model that can respond to a limitless number of scenarios, each scenario is associated with a specific assessment strategy and associated training material.

In addition to enabling the development of an ITS in domains where it would otherwise be impractical, case-based tutors also enable more direct involvement of SMEs. With process-based tutors, skilled analysts interact with SMEs to perform a CTA, the results of which are used to produce the required cognitive model. This opacity between the SME and the resultant coaching can cause difficulty in getting the ITS to respond precisely as the SME would. Case-based systems generally remove the opacity of the "CTA-and-Translation" process. Often, SMEs are asked to directly develop scenarios, assessment strategies, and so forth for each case (Stottler & Vinkavich, 2000).

This scenario-by-scenario development strategy also enables the development of authoring tools that are quite useful and usable. As we discussed in conjunction with REDEEM, the availability of these tools can have a tremendous impact on community acceptance and cost. Authoring tools can certainly be developed for process-based ITSs and, as we discuss later in this chapter, significant progress is being made. However, it remains true that authoring case-based ITSs is likely to remain considerably easier than authoring process-based tutors for the foreseeable future.

Clearly, central to the development of these tutors is the definition of the cases themselves. Rather than developing an extensive case library and then matching a new problem to an exemplar in the library, most case-based tutors simply define self-contained instructional cases. These cases frequently contain a definition of the problem-solving scenario, a description of the expected behavior within this particular scenario (we will discuss this in greater detail shortly), and training/explanatory material associated with the expected behavior (see, for example, Stottler & Ramachandran, 1999).

Definition of the expected behavior within each scenario includes describing the target behavior itself (perhaps in reference to underlying principles) as well as describing the mechanism through which that behavior will be recognized. There are three conventional mechanisms by which this evaluation takes place. The first is to identify specific time-based outcomes (Stottler & Ramachandran, 1999). Within this mechanism, the case author defines the states that the student must have achieved, or the actions that he or she must have completed by certain critical time-points. Failure to achieve these outcomes in a timely fashion is taken as evidence that the student lacks mastery of the associated skills/principles.

A problem with this approach is that it assumes that the scenario will unfold following the same time course during each run. For certain static scenarios this may be a plausible assumption. For others, though, it is clearly untrue. In most evolving scenarios, a student's actions, or lack thereof, have a pronounced effect on which behaviors may be expected at any given time point. To solve these problems, one option available to the case author is to define how to recognize appropriate/inappropriate behaviors, as opposed to correct/incorrect (Stottler & Ramachandran, 1999). To make these "good enough" determinations, Stottler, Fu, Ramachandran, and Jackson (2001a) suggested using Finite State Machines (FSMs). The FSMs provide relatively simple conditional logic needed to determine whether certain desired outcomes have been achieved. However, Stottler et al. (2001a) also noted that the FSMs were limited in their ability to support more complex assessments that involved complicated analysis of patterns of conditions and outcomes. To address this weakness, Jensen, Tasoluk, Sanders, and Marsall (2005) extended the FSM notion by introducing the concept of Behavior Transition Networks (BTNs). BTNs are arbitrarily complex bits of logic that can come to life when their defined conditions are satisfied. Once activated, they examine the state of the world to determine if the student's actions should be deemed appropriate or not.

By introducing notions such as FSMs/BTNs, case-based tutors come to look much more like process-based tutors than they might ordinarily. The primary difference becomes the generality of the resultant assessment widgets. For case-based tutors, assessment routines such as FSMs/BTNs are explicitly tied to scenarios. For process-based tutors, the mapping is more general; applicable to most any scenario within the specified domain. The choice thus comes down to a balance between ease of development which favors the case-based approach and generality which favors more process-oriented approaches.

The student's experience in interacting with a case-based tutor is not much different than when interacting with a process-based tutor. Initially, the student may be asked some bootstrapping questions to identify instructional principles on which to focus (Stottler & Pike, 2002). Case-based tutors, like process-based tutors, assume declarative instruction has been provided by some source. If classroom instruction does not accompany the tutor, then the system might provide some instruction on the principles to be addressed (Stottler et al., 2001b). When it is time to present a scenario, a prebrief is usually given to provide the context for the problem and to briefly describe the goals/expected performance. Students then work through the problem-solving scenario and have their performance evaluated.

An interesting issue concerns *when* students receive feedback. In early examples of this form of tutoring, feedback was almost always reserved for a debrief session at the end of the scenario (Stottler & Pike, 2002; Stottler & Vinkavich, 2000). However, later versions included the notion of real-time feedback (Jensen et al., 2005). In fact, Jensen et al. (2005) indicated that the different feedback approaches differentially improved retention of certain types of knowledge. Immediate feedback significantly reduced procedural errors, while feedback presented during a debrief promoted the retention of conceptual knowledge. What was not clear from the report of Jensen et al. (2005) was whether this difference should be attributed to the time of the feedback (perhaps owing to the differential availability of cognitive resources in the two settings) or to its content.

Case-based tutors have been used across the various branches of military service. For example, tutors have been developed to train U.S. Navy tactical action officers (TAOs) in both the schoolhouse (Stottler & Vinkavich, 2000) and aboard ships (Stottler, Fu, Ramachandran, & Jackson, 2001b). In general, the tutors have been well-received. Stottler & Vinkavich (2000) report on a 12-student survey that demonstrated a favorable reaction to the tutor. Stottler et al. (2001b) offered a similar appraisal of the shipboard version, albeit with the caveat that some users were concerned that the TAO ITS did not evaluate all incorrect actions that a student could take.

In the U.S. Army, these tutors have been applied to train personnel on the proper application of Command and Control systems such as the FBCB2 (Stottler & Pike, 2002) and Future Combat System Command and Control Vehicle (Jensen et al., 2005). These systems allow the students to practice planning and conducting missions with the systems and are roughly parallel to the MLRS VST described in conjunction with our discussion of process-based tutors. As noted earlier, the Jensen et al. (2005) study looked at the differential impact of immediate and delayed feedback, but did not examine the absolute advantage provided by tutoring.

In the air domain, case-based tutors have been developed to support training the Weapon Director on board the U.S. Air Force's Airborne Warning and Control System (AWACS; (Stottler & Ramachandran, 1999) and the pilots flying F/A-18 (Stottler et al., 2001a).

Closed-Loop Systems

Given the observations that different instructional techniques are useful for developing mastery of declarative and procedural knowledge, and the efficacy that adaptive training technologies have shown in both of these environments, one might wonder whether any systems have been developed to address both of these issues within a common domain. This is the goal of closed-loop adaptive systems.

Closed-loop adaptive education is an emerging concept that integrates object/objective-based adaptive IMI, an ITS, and modeling and simulation technologies. The result is an inherently learner-focused approach that manages mastery of knowledge and skill learning objectives dynamically (McCarthy, Wayne, & Morris, 2001).

McCarthy et al. (2001) are developing such a system by merging the InTrain and ExpertTrain technology discussed earlier. At the core of this approach is a common Learner Model. The Learner Model contains current mastery information for all covered learning objectives (both declarative and procedural) and is able to accept endorsement data from a range of performance environments (e.g., test performance in the adaptive IMI environment and task performance from the ITS). As was the case with the component training engines, the learner model also includes data relating to learner characteristics, instructional history, and feedback history. The Learner Model sends and receives data from a family of domain and instructional expert software that guides the learner's instructional experience. In addition to considering the state of the learner (captured in the Learner Model), the experts consider the goals of instruction (captured as course data). Armed with current and historical information on the learner and the goals of the course, an adaptive learning system can employ IMI or simulation-based learning and assessment activities that are linked to specific learning objectives.

Combining the fully automated IMI and simulation-based adaptive learning approaches results in a true, automated closed-loop education system that supports individual education (McCarthy, Morris, & Castro, 2000; Morris, McCarthy, Pacheco, Bowdler, & Bennett, 2000). For example, suppose that a student has problems with some specific procedure during a simulation-based refresher education assessment exercise conducted on a personal computer. This deficiency would be noted and his/her Learner Model would be updated to reflect lack of mastery for the associated learning objective(s). The Instructional Expert, using the Learner Model as input, would create an ITP that uses IMI to address the particular learning objective(s). The student then works through the IMI until he/she masters the learning objective(s). This mastery can then be confirmed in another simulation-based assessment exercise using a scenario tailored to stimulate demonstration of mastery of the required learning objective(s). This paradigm can be accomplished without human intervention.

Although our discussion has focused on individual education, the power of the closed-loop approach can also be applied to team development. The team setting provides opportunities for assessing different types of learning objectives and supports different types of instructional approaches, but the essential framework remains constant: mastery of learning objectives (individual/team) is monitored in media and simulation-based learning environments and leads to the construction and execution of tailored instructional plans.

Varying degrees of automation can be applied to the above model where necessary; however, *the core component remains the Learner Model*. It is the Learner Model that provides the glue for the adaptive education approach by providing the data to the human and/or machine that specifies the degree of mastery for all required knowledge and skill learning objectives for every student.

Closed-loop adaptive education represents an exciting evolution in the realm of interactive learning that has broad applications within the educational community. Closed-loop systems are beginning to be used for military training. For example, in the U.S. Navy, a closed-loop system is being developed to train tactical air controllers and the U.S. Air Force is investigating using this same technology to train satellite operators. Within a closed-loop system, students can learn new concepts, practice associated skills, and be assessed on their mastery of the requisite knowledge and skills, all under the supervision of the Domain and Instructional Experts that interact with the integrated Learner Model. Because the Learner Model is endorsed in real-time and contains in-depth information regarding student mastery of required learning objectives and instructional history, the human instructor can target his/her efforts to those students requiring additional help or greater challenges.

Impediments to Adoption

In the preceding discussion, we presented evidence that adaptive training technology can produce significant increases in performance. Despite this proven track record, the application of this technology to military domains (and, as we will see in the next section, to other appropriate domains) is considerably less than might be expected. In this section, we will examine a few of the reasons for this. We will conclude this section with a discussion of steps that are being taken to remove the impediments that we describe.

In many cases, cost is cited as the reason that adaptive training technology is not adopted at rates commensurate with its performance. In military domains, training activities are chronically under-funded. Moreover, when funds must be redirected to support other priorities (e.g., when hostilities occur or construction costs increase), training funds are often among the first targeted.

Into this context comes adaptive training technology. These interventions often present a larger upfront cost than their conventional counterparts. Consider adaptive IMI as an example. To produce this material, a needs analysis must be performed followed by design, development, and implementation. Ideally, evaluation activities will be performed throughout this process with the results informing each step. Each of these activities has an associated cost, and the total bill must be paid before the first student is trained. Compare this to a conventional classroom training model in which a subject-matter expert (SME) is brought in and told to teach a 10-week course on a given topic. Here the cost might not begin until the SME reports for duty.

A closely related issue is that, often the parties responsible for paying for the technological intervention are not those that reap the reward. That is, in the example that we just introduced, a given commanding officer might decide to "bite the bullet" and use precious resources to purchase adaptive training technology. Committing those funds immediately puts his command in a financial bind. Moreover, given the nature of the contracting process and the length of the development cycle, the seeds that are planted might not bear fruit for 2 or more years. About that time, the commanding officer might be preparing to move on to another command. Similarly, in a new construction environment, those responsible for purchasing the equipment (and the training that goes with it) are not responsible for operating or maintaining it. Their goal is to complete the construction effort as cheaply as possible. If that means increasing life-cycle costs—well, that is often someone else's problem.

If this is a problem for adaptive IMI where the cost differential between adaptive and conventional approaches is relatively small (related mostly to the need to design and develop additional content objects to support adaptation decisions), one can imagine the situation facing developers of intelligent tutoring systems and their correspondingly larger costs. For these systems, development of the cognitive model, the performance environment, the instructional support, and other related elements can quickly become quite expensive. Again, the bill for these efforts comes due long before the benefits of improved student performance can be realized.

Given this context, it is hardly surprising that it is the rare commander who will take the long view and invest in the development of adaptive training technology.

On the technological front, adaptive training technology must fit within the always shifting military infrastructure. For example, in many military circles (as well as within the civilian community), there is increased emphasis on delivering content via the Internet in general and the World Wide Web in particular. Web-based training presents a number of advantages to the military. First and foremost, it allows warriors to "train in place." That is, they do not have to travel to remote schools to train, but can train at their primary duty station. In this way a range of costs are reduced (we will return to this point shortly in our discussion of return-on-investment). Moreover, Web-based training provides a means to support central management of content and student records. This eases maintenance burdens (if the central course is updated, all students immediately see the new course) and simplifies record keeping (a single Learning Management System can track student progress and status).

In fact, the maintenance issue is another important one within the military community. Often military content is fairly volatile. That is, it undergoes frequent changes to reflect changes in missions, equipment, tactics, and so forth. The military recognizes this fact and is understandably reluctant to invest in a training solution that either is not flexible enough to accommodate these changes or inextricably ties the military to a particular vendor for the life of a given course.

Fortunately, progress is being made on these fronts and as the impediments to adoption are removed, we anticipate seeing the rate of progress increase. For example, adaptive training technologies are often burdened by a lack of effective development tools (e.g., authoring systems). These tools are important because they directly address two of the impediments noted earlier, namely the cost of initial development and the ease with which developed courseware can be maintained.

The adaptive IMI domain has a good start in the development of authoring tools. For example, as noted earlier, both InTrain and REDEEM provide authoring tools that allow developers to more easily produce and maintain the adaptive courseware provided by these systems. Others, such as Retalis and Papasalouros (2005) and Mödritscher, García-Barrios, and Gütl (2004) are adding valuable contributions to this area as well.

While the problem facing developers of intelligent tutoring systems is considerably more complex, and therefore, useful and useable tools are harder to produce, progress is being made on this front too. For example, Anderson and his colleagues are developing a suite of authoring tools to ease the production of process-based tutors (Aleven, Sewall, McLaren, & Koedinger, 2006). Similarly, Ramachandran, Remolina, and Fu (2004) are producing tools to support the development of case-based tutors. Meanwhile, the tools produced by Towne and Munroe (1990) are aiding the development of maintenance tutors. Tools such as these will drive down development costs and ease courseware maintenance. As such, they will produce a competitive advantage for their developers and increase the penetration of adaptive training technology within the affected markets.

Similar advances are being made in the area of Web-based delivery. InTrain and REDEEM courses are available, to some extent, on the Web. For example, in the Birchard et al. (2002) study described earlier, the courseware in question was delivered via a Web-based client/server architecture. Intelligent tutoring systems are beginning to make the transition as well (Alpert, Singley, & Fairweather, 1999). Although the process is beginning, significant hurdles remain. Developers must contend with bandwidth limitations and the ability to reliably handle a large number of simultaneous users. Similarly, the technical solutions that are developed must integrate smoothly with a range of learning management systems, content management systems, server architectures, and client environments.

Although the presence of authoring tools can reduce costs and ease maintenance burdens, they do not fundamentally change the basic equation—purchasers must still be convinced that their large upfront expenditure will produce a significant return on investment (ROI).

Part of the required ROI can come from content re-use. Whether adaptive or non-adaptive techniques are used, content that can be re-used or repurposed is almost always less expensive than content that must be created "from scratch."

Moreover, there are several ways that adaptive training technology can "pay for itself." First, adaptive training technology can, in some cases, reduce the time to train. Every day removed from the training pipeline is associated with real monetary savings as personnel are returned to their "real jobs."

Second, adaptive training technology can pay for itself by improving student performance. Tools such as REDEEM have been shown to improve student performance by approximately 0.5 standard deviations and, as we discussed in earlier sections, tools such as InTrain have shown even greater results. When intelligent tutoring systems are considered, the effect size can increase to one standard deviation or more. The most direct cost savings of improved performance is through decreased attrition. When students attrite from a course of instruction, the entire investment made in them up to that point is, in some sense, wasted. If adaptive training technology can improve performance and thereby decrease attrition, these "bad investments" can be reduced. A less direct medium of cost reduction is through the effects of improved performance. Poor performance can result in unsuccessful missions, property damage, loss of life, and so forth. Each of these has a significant associated cost. However, it is quite difficult to estimate beforehand the level of reduction that can be anticipated and equally difficult to apportion observed reductions to the performance of a training system.

Third, adaptive training technology can pay for itself by improving instructor effectiveness while maintaining or increasing student achievement (performance). Within this technological framework, the adaptive training technology can perform most of the instructional tasks for a larger portion of the students in the middle of the bell curve; freeing instructors to address the needs of students at either extreme. Just as a cost could be associated with each student, a greater cost can be associated with each instructor. With each billet that is eliminated or avoided, more savings accrue.

The fourth means by which adaptive training technology can pay for itself is by allowing students to "train in place." In doing so, we can eliminate a whole range of costs (travel, lodging, *per diem*, lost productivity, instructors, training infrastructure, etc.).

By combining these arguments, developers can form a compelling business case analysis for the development of adaptive training systems. However, it must be kept in mind that those who pay for training development often are not those that get credit for its superior performance (or must live with its inferior performance). The business case can keep developers in this area "in the game," but may not always be enough to allow them to bring home the win.

Tutoring in Other Domains

Clearly, adaptive training technology can be applied in nonmilitary domains. Some of the most promising transfer domains are to support standard classroom education, educate physicians, and train industrial workers. Our goal here is not to provide a comprehensive review of the work performed in this domain, but merely to introduce it and draw parallels between these efforts and those found in military circles.

Adaptive Training Technology in Educational Settings

Anderson and his colleagues have produced some of the most successful intelligent tutors to be applied in conventional educational domains. These process-based tutors have been developed based on the ACT-R cognitive modeling structure. Originally developed more to learn about skill acquisition and to test the ACT-R theory itself than to provide training benefit, these tutors are called "cognitive tutors" and seek to develop "cognitive skills" in their users.

Although there have been several approaches to developing ACT-R cognitive tutoring systems, the tutor's architecture typically consists of the same components. These components (Anderson, Corbett, Koedinger, & Pelletier, 1995) are a cognitive model of an ideal student, which serves as the domain expert model, the student interface, and the curriculum for the application.

The heart of the cognitive tutors is the underlying cognitive model (for consistency with the preceding discussion, we will use the term domain expert). The domain experts within cognitive tutors are simplified versions of ACT-R cognitive models.

The domain expert assesses student performance through a process called "model tracing." Given the current state of the problem (reflected in various declarative knowledge chunks), the domain expert is capable of generating a set of production sequences that represent correct or buggy solutions to the problem. The student's actions are then compared to these anticipated states. If the student action is consistent with one of the correct paths, a positive assessment decision is reached. If the action is not consistent with a correct path, a negative assessment decision is reached. In either case, the processing proceeds along two paths: providing feedback and updating the student model.

When the student's action is incorrect, cognitive tutors provide error feedback. Error feedback informs the student of his specific error and provides an explanation of why the action is wrong. Error feedback is developed during the cognitive tutor development and associated with each of the buggy productions in the cognitive model. In order to tame the potential for combinatorial explosion, earlier tutors also required the student to immediately return to a correct solution path. More recent tutors have relaxed this constraint.

The second processing path involves updating the student model to reflect the student's recent performance; that is, based on performance, the system must update the probability that the student knows a given production. This process is known as "knowledge tracing" and is based on a family of Bayesian calculations. Student mastery is achieved when "the learning probability of each production rule has reached .95" (Corbett & Anderson, 1993).

In addition to error feedback, students can request help at any time. Help messages provide the student with hints regarding the correct action, or set of actions, required to correctly solve the problem in a text format. Templates are written to describe the correct productions, and the help messages are assembled from the templates associated with each of the production rules that would have been fired up to the point at which the help message is provided. The selection of hints is based on model tracing (where is the student along the solution path and what needs to be done next), as well as the broader problem-solving context (e.g., the tools and interface objects that are active). The hints are layered to provide just enough scaffolding for struggling students (Koedinger & Anderson, 1998). Depending on the hint layer, the student might be provided with: "(1) a description of the current goal, (2) an explanation of how to achieve the goal, and (3) a description of the exact action to perform" (Corbett & Anderson, 1993).

Performance assessment and knowledge tracing are used to advance the student through the curriculum. Classes of problems that require the same productions are grouped together in sections. As students are developing the productions required to solve that class of problem, they remain in that section. Once knowledge tracing reveals that they have achieved mastery of those productions, they are advanced to a new section that requires new (presumably related) productions. Similarly, subtle changes to the interface may automate tasks that were previously accomplished manually. This is done to focus the student's cognitive resources on mastering the new material.

An interesting aspect of cognitive tutor development is the relationship between the student-device interface and CTA. Cognitive Tutors are said to provide instruction for solving problems for a specific task *using a particular interface*. Consequently, the production rules that comprise the task will be governed by the interface and cannot be identified until the interface has been identified. The student interface is provided in a Windows format and typically comprises the following types of windows (Corbett & Anderson, 1993): (1) problem statement; (2) student solution entry (e.g., space to type an equation or program code, a graphing area, or a table to complete); (3) a skill meter, which provides the student with a graphical display of the knowledge that he has acquired thus far; and (4) tools (e.g., calculator, list of computer programming expressions, etc.).

This interface dependence creates some interesting transfer issues, and in some cases, failure transfer was attributed to a mismatch between the requirements of the learning environment and the requirements of the transfer environment (Anderson et al., 1995).

Most cognitive tutors belong to one of three families:

- Programming
- Geometry
- Algebra

The programming family of cognitive tutors began with the LISP Tutor (Anderson et al., 1995; Corbett & Anderson, 1993) in 1983. The curriculum of the LISP tutor comprises problems that are solved by applying a specific LISP programming skill. The cognitive tutor presents the problem to the student and the student solves the problem by typing LISP code which is assessed on a symbol by symbol basis. The LISP tutor uses the model-tracing procedure to match each of the student's steps with a production rule in the cognitive model. If the student is on a viable path, the LISP tutor functions as standard programming environment. However, if the student makes an error, the tutor provides immediate feedback. If the student appears to be stuck or explicitly requests help, the tutor can provide one of a hierarchically structured series of hints.

In the original LISP evaluation, students attended standard lectures and then completed a set of programming problems in either a standard programming environment or in the LISP tutor. Anderson et al. (1995) reported that, "students using the tutor completed the exercises 30% faster and performed 43% better on a posttest. Similar results were found in a second study designed to assess the effectiveness of the tutor in a self-paced environment. In this study, lectures were replaced with a text that students had to read prior to completing the programming problems. In this study, students using the tutor completed the exercises 64% faster and performed 30% better on the posttest.

On the strength of these results, the original LISP Tutor has been expanded to become the ACT programming tutor (APT). The APT provides programming students with a self-paced environment for developing LISP, Prolog, and Pascal programming skills.

Work on the Geometry Tutor began at essentially the same time as the LISP Tutor (Anderson, Boyle, & Yost, 1986). Using a structure very similar to the LISP Tutor, the Geometry Tutor was designed to help students master the development of geometric proofs. To evaluate the tutor, Anderson and his colleagues formed two groups of students. Both groups had the same instructor, but only one had access to the tutor. In some cases, each student had access to the student's own Geometry

Tutor system. In other cases, logistic constraints mandated that two students share a single system. When students had solitary access to a Geometry Tutor system, their performance on the final examination was improved by more than one standard deviation and one letter grade. When students had to share a system, the tutoring advantage evaporated (Anderson et al., 1995).

In the early 1990s, a second-generation tutor for geometric deduction, called ANGLE, was produced (Koedinger & Anderson, 1993b). The goal of ANGLE was to make explicit one strategy for solving geometric proofs (induction of possible proof paths followed by deductive construction of proofs) and to develop student mastery of that strategy. The classroom evaluation of ANGLE revealed an interesting pattern. The evaluation made use of three teachers, one of whom had been actively involved with the development of the trainer. Each teacher taught at least one class with ANGLE and at least one without. Overall, ANGLE did not produce a significant performance advantage. However, the researchers noted that the "involved" teacher's ANGLE classes did much better than those in the other groups. In fact, that group's post-test performance was more than one standard deviation better than the performance of the other groups. More generally, Anderson et al. (1995) report that it often takes classroom teachers considerable time to learn how best to leverage the advantages provided by the tutors. They report that their data indicate achievement gains are higher in the second year that teachers work with a tutor. We will return to this notion shortly.

By far, the most widely used tutor in the ACT-R family is the Algebra Tutor. Initially introduced into schools in 1992, the original tutor was developed in conjunction with the Pittsburgh Urban Math Project (PUMP) and became known as the PUMP Algebra Tutor or PAT. PUMP in general, and PAT in particular, arose in response to the National Council of Teachers of Mathematics (NCTM) call for bringing mathematics into the lives of all students through an emphasis on mathematical reasoning and the solving of problems of practical interest.

By any standard PAT has been a tremendous success. Students who use the Algebra Tutor score twice as high on post-tests that assess mastery of the learning objectives on which the tutor is based. Similarly, these students score 15% higher on standardized assessment tests (Corbett, Koedinger, & Anderson, 1997). Perhaps more striking is the rate of adoption of the tutor. In 1992, 1 school used the tutor; in 1993, 3 schools adopted the tutor, in 1995, the total was up to 6 schools. By 2004, the tutor was used in approximately 2,000 United States high schools (Koedinger & Corbett, 2006).

The Anderson's group experience with fielding practical tutors in the school generated a range of lessons learned (Anderson et al., 1995; Koedinger & Corbett, 2006). Here, we will only touch on a few of the most salient. A primary theme that is relevant both to the military application of adaptive training technology and its application to civilian classrooms is the urgent need to include classroom teachers in the development process. Koedinger and Corbett (2006) emphasize the inclusion of instructional staff as one of their key metadesign principles. They correctly point out that including teachers on the design team simultaneously serves as a source of subject-matter expertise, enables the developed system to better fit with the existing curriculum, and provides a built-in advocate for the system when it is introduced. Experience in the military domain only reinforces these points.

A related point is the need to "train-the-trainers." That is, to maximize the effectiveness of the tutoring system (in both military and civilian sectors) it is critical to develop a training program that provides teachers with the knowledge, skills, and (perhaps most importantly) attitudes required to maximize their efficacy in the presence of the new system. Typically, there is some level of resistance to introducing new technology. In addition to this, the role of the teacher can undergo radical changes with the introduction of the new technology. For example, considerably less time is spent delivering lectures to a group and considerably more time is spent surgically intervening with individuals/groups at either extreme of the typical bell-shaped performance curve (Koedinger & Corbett, 2006). All these changes can lead to, at best, diminished performance (Anderson et al., 1995; Koedinger & Anderson, 1993b) and at worst, outright rejection of the technological innovation.

A third theme that emerges from the classroom work on cognitive tutors is the need to provide solid declarative instruction to complement the procedural training provided in the tutoring environment (Anderson et al., 1995). In some cases, the classroom instruction is provided in a relatively unperturbed way. In others, a complete set of curriculum material (e.g., text books, lecture notes, classroom activities) is developed to complement the tutoring (Koedinger & Anderson, 1993b; Koedinger & Corbett, 2006). However it is provided, aligning the declarative and procedural instruction is a key design task in every environment. Note that this is precisely the goal of the closed-loop adaptive training approach summarized earlier.

The last issue to be discussed is the role that external factors can play in determining the success of a given tutoring intervention. The Geometry Tutor provides an excellent demonstration of this. By many measures, the Geometry Tutors were among the least successful of the cognitive tutors. One primary factor in this was the shift of the text book to be used away from one that emphasized geometric proof to one that, in keeping with NCTM standards that were emerging at the time, de-emphasized deduction. The Geometry Tutors were focused on this particular skill and thus lost their *raison d'être*. Such shifting currents can affect military training to an even greater degree than civilian training. Programmatically, one can guard against it by involving stakeholders from a wide community to increase the likelihood of recognizing sea changes early enough to be proactive. Tactically, one can decide, like the cognitive tutor team, to develop turn-key solutions that limit the external linkages (e.g., third-party text books) that can complicate the introduction process.

Before concluding this chapter, we will touch on two other application domains in which application of adaptive training technology is less widespread, but within which this technology holds great promise. The first is the area of medical training.

Medical applications of intelligent tutoring technology can be traced to the introduction of the GUIDON tutor (Clancy, 1983). GUIDON, in turn, is based on MYCIN, a consultation program designed to assist physicians in the diagnosis and treatment of certain bacterial infections. Students using GUIDON were presented with diagnostic problems and had to ask various questions to determine the nature of the infection. When they deviated from the logic path laid out in MYCIN, feedback was provided.

Although GUIDON suffered from a range of instructional problems, it clearly showed a path forward for medical training. Today, a wide variety of medical tutors have been developed in areas such as circulatory physiology (e.g., CIRCSIM: Nakhook et al., 1989), radiology (e.g., MR Tutor: Sharples, Jeffery, de Boulay, Teather, Teather, & du Boulay, 2000; RadTutor: Azevedo & Lajoie, 1998; VIA-RAD: Rogers, 1995), and pathology (e.g., SlideTutor: Crowley, Medvedeva, & Jukic, 2003). Although most of these systems maintain the model of individualized tutoring, some systems, such as COMET, are attempting to apply this technology to the popular area of problem-based learning with small groups (Suebnukarn & Haddawy, 2004).

Despite these mostly positive cases, the field of medical tutoring has yet to "explode" like one might imagine. After all, in a field in which one significant limitation to mastery is experience, intelligent tutoring systems seem an ideal means to artificially expand the experience base of would-be physicians. From an outside perspective the limiting factors seem to revolve around two significant issues: the complexity of the underlying knowledge base and the difficulty of establishing natural interfaces.

The importance of the complexity dimension cannot be overlooked. Crowley et al. (2003) estimated that a relatively isolated area of pathology, diagnosing inflammatory diseases of the skin, might require a cognitive model with one million steps. In addition to the upfront complexity of gathering and representing these rules, one must also consider the burden imposed by testing the response of each rule and difficulty associated with maintaining such a complex knowledge base.

The nature of the interface also impacts both the educational power of the tools and the willingness of the community to accept them. In considering the first of these issues, consider the earlier discussion of the impact of interface design on transfer (Anderson et al., 1995). Moreover, the nature of the interface can often lead to a particular cognitive organization of the instructional content. Indeed, this is an explicit goal in the design of Cognitive Tutors (Anderson et al., 1995). In domains such as military operations or mathematics, this might not be much of an issue and in fact could be used advantageously to promote leaning. However, there is a concern that unnatural interfaces in medical tutors could lead to inert knowledge that does not transfer to the application environment. This is one reason why natural language interfaces are increasingly popular in medical trainers (Evens et al., 2001). In addition to the educational effects of interfaces, they also have a tremendous effect on technology adoption. Without a natural interface, devices such as these often lack the face validity required to allow stakeholders to introduce something new.

Even more surprising than the relative lack of tutors in medicine is the dearth of industrial tutoring systems. The lack of tutors in the area is even more surprising when one considers that some of the ground-breaking work in intelligent tutoring was done in engineering domains. Recall that some of the earliest tutoring work done within the military domain (e.g., SOPHIE and SHERLOCK) addressed troubleshooting skills that would be directly applicable to an industrial setting. Moreover, in this same domain, contributions from the Intelligent Maintenance Training System family of tutoring systems developed by Towne and Munroe (1988, 1990) further increased the ease of technology transfer.

Moreover, the value proposition of intelligent tutoring systems would be quite high in many industrial settings. In environments such as power plant operations, petrochemical processing, and high throughput manufacturing, small errors in operations or maintenance operations can lead to huge costs in terms of facility damage, lost productivity, and regulatory fines. Despite the potential savings and the demonstrated power of intelligent tutoring systems to provide an ROI, the examples of tutoring systems developed for use in industrial settings are few and far between. One is left to assume that the same, or similar, factors that limit adoption within the military are also operating here.

Conclusion

In this chapter we have reviewed the application of adaptive training technology within military circles. We have noted that for both declarative and procedural outcomes, adaptive solutions exist and have proven their effectiveness. Further, we have summarized a few of the impediments to further adoption of these technologies and suggested methods through which those barriers can be removed.

As these technologies continue to advance, it seems likely that progress will center on three themes:

- **Authoring tool development:** The creation of more flexible, powerful, and useable tools will increasingly reduce development costs, reducing a significant impediment to wide-scale adoption. Further, tools such as these will make adaptive technology more practical for extremely complex and/or volatile domains.

- **Distributed operation:** In addition to driving the technology to more Web-based architectures, current trends are leading to the interoperability of separate components. For example, a simulation developed by one team may need to interface with a domain expert developed by a second. The domain expert might share data with an adaptive multimedia system developed by another team via a student model whose origins are unknown. Efforts are underway to standardize the communication pathways that will facilitate this type of interoperability.

- **Natural interfaces:** Although much work has been done, much remains to allow adaptive technology to provide effective instruction in a natural way. Mixed initiative tutorial dialogs for both declarative and procedural training will continue to advance over the foreseeable future.

As these trends continue to emerge, the application of adaptive training technologies is likely to become more common both within the military domain and in the civilian sector.

Note

InTrain, ExpertTrain, and CLAT are trademarks of Sonalysts, Inc. All other trademarks are the property of their respective owners.

References

Advanced Distributed Learning. (2004). *Sharable content object reference model (SCORM) 2004* (3rd ed). Retrieved January 12, 2008, from www.adlnet.org

Ainsworth, S.E., & Fleming, P.F. (2004). Teachers as instructional designers: Does involving a classroom teacher in the design of computer-based learning environments improve their effectiveness? In P. Gerjets, P.A Kirschner, J. Elen, & R. Joiner (Eds.), *Instructional design for effective and enjoyable computer- supported learning,* Proceedings of the first joint meeting of the EARLI SIGs Instructional Design and Learning and Instruction with Computers (pp. 283-291).

Ainsworth, S.E., & Grimshaw, S.K. (2004). Evaluating the REDEEM authoring tool: Can teachers create effective learning environments? *International Journal of Artificial Intelligence in Education, 14*(3/4), 279-312.

Ainsworth, S.E., Major, N., Grimshaw, S.K., Hayes, M., Underwood, J.D., Williams, B. et al. (2003). REDEEM: Simple intelligent tutoring systems from usable tools. In T. Murray, S. Blessing & S.E. Ainsworth (Eds.), *Advanced tools for advanced technology learning environments* (pp. 205-232). Amsterdam: Kluwer Academic Publishers.

Ainsworth, S.E., Williams, B.C., & Wood, D.J. (2001). Using the REDEEM ITS authoring environment in naval training. *IEEE International Conference on Advanced Learning Technologies*.

Aleven, V., Sewall, J., McLaren, B. M., & Koedinger, K. R. (2006). Rapid authoring of intelligent tutors for real-world and experimental use. In R. Kinshuk, P. Koper, P. Kommers, D. Kirschner, G. Sampson & W. Didderen (Eds.), *Proceedings of the 6th IEEE International Conference on Advanced Learning Technologies (ICALT 2006)* (pp. 847-851). Los Alamitos, CA: IEEE Computer Society.

Alpert, S.R., Singley, M.K., & Fairweather, P.G. (1999). Deploying intelligent tutors on the Web: An architecture and an dxample. *International Journal of Artificial Intelligence in Education, 10*(2), 183-197.

Anderson, J.R. (1993). *Rules of the mind.* Hillsdale, NJ: Erlbaum.

Anderson, J.R., Boyle, C.F., & Reiser, B.J. (1985). Intelligent tutoring systems. *Science, 228*(4698), 456-462.

Anderson, J.R., Boyle, C.F., & Yost, G. (1986). The geometry tutor. *The Journal of Mathematical Behavior*, 5-20.

Anderson, J.R., Corbett, A.T., Koedinger, K., & Pelletier, R. (1995). Cognitive tutors: Lessons learned. *The Journal of Learning Sciences, 4,* 167-207.

Anderson, J.R., Matessa, M., & Lebiere, C. (1997). ACT-R: A theory of higher level cognition and its relation to visual attention. *Human-Computer Interaction, 12,* 439-462.

Anderson, J.R., & Schunn, C.D. (2000). Implications of the ACT-R learning theory: No magic bullets. In R. Glaser (Ed.), *Advances in instructional psychology* (Vol. 5). Mahwah, NJ: Erlbaum.

Azevedo, R., & Lajoie, S.P. (1998). The cognitive basis for the design of a mammography interpretation tutor. *International Journal of Artificial Intelligence in Education. 9,* 32-44.

Birchard, M., Dye, C., & Gordon, J. (2002). An empirical evaluation of sonar courseware developed with intelligent tutoring software (InTrain™) at naval submarine school. In *Proceedings of the 24th Interservice/Industry Training Systems and Education Conference*, Orlando, FL.

Brown, J.S., Burton, R.R., & de Kleer, J. (1982). Pedagogical, natural language and knowledge engineering techniques in Sophie I, II and III. In D. Sleeman & J.S. Brown (Eds.), *Intelligent tutoring systems*. London, UK: Academic Press.

Card, S., Moran, T., & Newell, A. (1983). *The psychology of human-computer interaction.* Hillsdale, NJ: Erlbaum.

Carlson, H.L., & Falk, D.R. (1990). Interactive learning models using videodiscs in college and inservice instruction. *Computers in Human Services, 7*(3-4), 277-293.

Chipman, S.F., Segal, J.W., & Glaser, R. (Eds.). (1985). *Thinking and learning skills: Volume 1, relating instruction to research.* Hillsdale, NJ: Lawrence Erlbaum Associates.

Clancy, W.J. (1983). Guidon. *Journal of Computer-based Instruction, 10.*

Corbett, A.T., & Anderson, J.R. (1993). Student modeling in an intelligent programming tutor. In E. Lemut, B. du Boulay & G. Dettori (Eds.), *Cognitive models and intelligent environments for learning programmin.* New York: Springer-Verlag.

Corbett, A.T., Koedinger, K.R., & Anderson, J.R. (1997). Intelligent tutoring systems. In M.G. Helander, T.K. Landauer & P.V. Prabhu (Eds.), *Handbook of human-computer interaction.* Amsterdam, The Netherlands: Elsevier Science B. V.

Crowley, R.S., Medvedeva, O., & Jukic, D. (2003). Slide tutor – a model-tracing intelligent tutoring system for teaching microscopic diagnosis. In *Proceedings of the 11th International Conference on Artificial Intelligence in Education.* Sydney: Australia.

Dillenbourg, P. (1989). Designing a self-improving tutor: PROTO-TEG. *Instructional Science, 18*(3), 193-216.

Evens, M., Brandle, S., Chang, R., Freedman, R., Glass, M., Lee, Y. et al. (2001). CIRCSIM-tutor: An intelligent tutoring system using natural language dialogue. In *Proceedings of the 12th Midwest AI and Cognitive Science Conference (MAICS 2001).* Oxford, OH.

Feurzeig, W., Massey, L.D., Downes-Martin, S., & Ritter, F. (1986). *TRIO to INCOFT adaptation study.* BBN Report No. 6194. Cambridge, MA: BBN Laboratories.

Fletcher, J.D. (1988). Intelligent training systems in the military. In S.J. Andriole & G.W. Hopple (Eds.), *Defense applications of artificial intelligence: Progress and prospects.* Lexington, KY: Lexington Books.

Ghatala, E.S. (1986). Strategy-monitoring training enables young learners to select effective strategies. *Educational Psychologist, 21,* 43-54.

Gott, S.P., Kane, R.S., & Lesgold, A. (1995). *Tutoring for transfer of technical competence.* Air Force Technical Report: AL/HR-TP-1995-0002. Brooks AFB, TX: Armstrong Laboratory, Human Resources Directorate.

Hannafin, M.J., Hill, J.R., & McCarthy, J.E. (2002). Designing resource-based learning and performance support systems. In D.A. Wiley (Ed.), *The instruc-*

tional use of learning objects (pp. 99-129). Bloomington, IN: Agency for Instructional Technology and Association for Educational Communications & Technology.

Hollan, J.D., Hutchins, E.L., & Weitzman, L. (1984). STEAMER: An interactive inspectable simulation-based training system. *Artificial Intelligence Magazine, 5*, 15-27

Jensen, R., Tasoluk, C., Sanders, M., & Marsall, H. (2005). FCS intelligent structured training – experimental results and future applications. In *Proceedings of the 25th Interservice/Industry Training Systems and Education Conference,* Orlando, FL.

Katz, S., & Lesgold, A. (1993). The role of the tutor in computer-based collaborative learning situations. In S.P. Lajoie & S.J. Derry (Eds.), *Computers as cognitive tools.* Hillsdale, NJ: Erlbaum.

Koedinger, K.R., & Anderson, J.R. (1993a). Reifying implicit planning in geometry: Guidelines for model-based intelligent tutoring system design. In S.P. Lajoie & S.J. Derry (Eds.), *Computers as cognitive tools.* Hillsdale, NJ: Erlbaum.

Koedinger, K.R., & Anderson, J.R. (1993b). Effective use of intelligent software in high school math classrooms. In *Proceedings of the World Conference on Artificial Intelligence in Education.* Charlottesville, VA: AACE.

Koedinger, K.R. (2001). Cognitive tutors as modeling tool and instructional model. In K. D. Forbus & P. J Feltovich (Eds.), *Smart machines in education: The coming revolution in educational technology* (pp. 145-168). Menlo Park, CA: AAAI/MIT Press.

Koedinger, K.R., & Corbett, A.T. (2006). Cognitive tutors: Technology bringing learning science to the classroom. In K. Sawyer (Ed.), *The Cambridge handbook of the learning sciences.* Cambridge University Press.

Laurillard, D. (1987). Computers and the emancipation of students: Giving control to the learner. *Instructional Science, 16*(1), 3-18.

LeMentec, J.C., Glenn, F., Zachary, W., & Eilbert, J. (1999). Representing human sensory and motor action behavior in a cognitive modeling architecture. In *Proceedings of the Eighth Conference on Computer Generated Forces and Behavioral Representation,* Orlando, FL.

Lesgold, A., Lajoie, S., Bunzo, M., & Eggan, G. (1992). SHERLOCK: A coached practice environment for an electronics troubleshooting job. In J. Larkin & R. Chabay (Eds.), *Computer-assisted instruction and intelligent tutoring systems: Shared goals and complementary approaches.* Hillsdale, NJ: Lawrence Erlbaum Associates.

Massey, L.D., Kerland, L., Tenney, Y., de Bruin, J., & Quayle, K.C. (1986). *HAWK MACH-III intelligent maintenance tutor design development report.* BBN Report No. 6315. Cambridge, MA: BBN Laboratories.

McCarthy, J.E. (1996, February). *The InTrain™ system: Past and future*. Talk presented to the Conference on Cognitive Approaches to Work Behavior, Pennsylvania State University, State College, PA.

McCarthy, J.E., Johnston, J., & Paris, C. (1998, November). Toward development of a tactical decision making under stress integrated trainer. In *Proceedings of the 20th Interservice/Industry Training Systems and Education Conference*, Orlando, FL.

McCarthy, J.E., Morris, J.J., & Castro, K. (2000). *Emerging technologies in training development* (Tech. Rep. AFRL-VS-TR-2000-1032).

McCarthy, J.E., Pacheco, S., Banta, H.G., Wayne, J.L., & Coleman, D.S. (1994, November). The radar system controller intelligent training Aid. In *Proceedings of the 16th Interservice/Industry Training Systems and Education Conference*, Orlando, FL.

McCarthy, J.E., Stretton, M.L., & Hontz, E.B. (1995). A classroom evaluation of an intelligent training aid. In *Proceedings of the 39th Annual Meeting of the Human Factors and Ergonomics Society*, San Diego, CA.

McCarthy, J.E., Wayne, J.L., & Morris, J.J. (2001). Closed-loop adaptive instruction. In *The Proceedings of ED-MEDIA 2001, World Conference on Educational Multimedia, Hypermedia, and Telecommunications*, Tampere, Finland.

McCombs, B.L., & McDaniel, M.A. (1981). On the design of adaptive treatments for individualized instruction systems. *Educational Psychologist, 16*(1), 11-22.

Mödritscher, F., García-Barrios, V.M., & Gütl, C. (2004). Enhancement of SCORM to support adaptive e-learning within the scope of the research project AdeLE. In *Proceedings of E-Learn* (pp. 2499-2505). Washington, DC.

Morris, J.J., McCarthy, J.E., Pacheco, S.P., Bowdler, D.L., & Bennett, W. (2000). Closed-loop adaptive training – applications for satellite operator training. In *Proceedings of the 22nd Interservice/Industry Training Systems and Education Conference*, Orlando, FL.

Murray, W.R. (1991). *An endorsement-based approach to student modeling for planner-controlled intelligent tutoring systems*. Technical Paper AL-TP-1991-0030. Prepared for the Human Resources Directorate Technical Training Research Division, Brooks Air Force Base, TX.

Nii, P.H. (1986). Blackboard systems: The blackboard model of problem solving and the evolution of blackboard architectures (Part One). *AI Magazine, 7*(2), 38-53.

Ohlsson, S. (1986). Some principle of intelligent tutoring [Special issue: Artificial intelligence and education]. *Instructional Science, 14*(3-4), 293-326.

Perrin, B. M., Dargue, B. W., & Banks, F.Z. (2003). Dynamically adapting content delivery: An effectiveness study and lessons learned. In *Proceedings of the 25th Interservice/Industry Training Systems and Education Conference,* Orlando, FL.

Ramachandran, S., Remolina, E., & Fu, D. (2004). FlexiTrainer: A visual authoring framework for case-based intelligent tutoring systems. *Intelligent Tutoring Systems 2004,* 848-850.

Retalis, R., & Papasalouros, A. (2005). Designing and generating educational adaptive hypermedia applications. *Educational Technology & Society, 8*(3), 26-35.

Rogers, E. (1995). VIA-RAD: A blackboard-based system for diagnostic radiology. *Artificial Intelligence in Medicine, 7,* 343-360.

Ryder, J., Santarelli, T., Scolaro, J., Hicinbothom, J., & Zachary, W. (2000). Comparison of cognitive model uses in intelligent training systems. In *Proceedings of IEA2000 / HFES2000.*

Scandura, J.M. (1988). Role of relativistic knowledge in intelligent tutoring [Special issue: Dialog on the relationship of learning theory to instructional theory]. *Computers in Human Behavior, 4*(1), 53-64.

Sharples, M., Jeffery, N.P., du Boulay, B., Teather, B.A., Teather, D., & du Boulay, G.H. (2000). Structured computer-based training in the interpretation of neuroradiological images. *International Journal of Medical Informatics, 60,* 263-280.

Stottler, R.H., Fu, D., Ramachandran, S., & Jackson, T. (2001a). Applying a generic intelligent tutoring system (ITS) authoring tool to specific military domains. In *Proceedings of the 23rd Interservice/Industry Training Systems and Education Conference,* Orlando, FL.

Stottler, R.H., Fu, D., Ramachandran, S., & Jackson, T. (2001b). Transitioning an ITS developed for schoolhouse use to the fleet: TAO ITS, a case study. In *Proceedings of the 23rd Interservice/Industry Training Systems and Education Conference,* Orlando, FL.

Stottler, R.H., & Pike, B. (2002). An embedded training solution: FBCB2/tactical decision making intelligent tutoring system. In *Proceedings of the 24th Interservice/Industry Training Systems and Education Conference,* Orlando, FL.

Stottler, R.H., & Ramachandran, S. (1999). A case-based reasoning approach to Internet intelligent tutoring systems (ITS) and ITS authoring. In *Proceedings of the 21st Interservice/Industry Training Systems and Education Conference,* Orlando, FL.

Stottler, R.H., & Vinkavinch, M. (2000). Tactical action officer intelligent tutoring system (TAO ITS). In *Proceedings of the 22th Interservice/Industry Training Systems and Education Conference,* Orlando, FL.

Suebnukarn, S., & Haddawy, P. (2004). A collaborative intelligent tutoring system for medical problem-based learning. In *Proceedings of the 9th International Conference on Intelligent User Interfaces,* Madeira, Portugal.

Towne, D. M., & Munro, A. (1988). Intelligent maintenance training system. In J. Psotka, L.D. Massey & S.A. Mutter (Eds.), *Intelligent tutoring systems: Lessons learned*. Hillsdale, NJ: Lawrence Erlbaum Associates.

Towne, D.M., & Munro, A. (1990). Model-building tools for simulation based training. *Interactive Learning Environments*, *1*, 33-50.

Wisher, R.A., Macpherson, D.H., Abramson, L.J., Thornton, D.M., & Dees, J.J. (2001). *The virtual sandtable: Intelligent tutoring for field artillery training*. Research Report 1768. U.S. Army Research Institute for the Behavioral and Social Sciences.

Wisher, R.A., Banta, H.G., Macpherson, D.H., Abramson, L.J., Thornton, D.M., & Dees, J.J. (2001). The adaptation and evaluation of an intelligent tutoring system for the multiple launch rocket system. In *Proceedings of the 23rd Interservice/Industry Training Systems and Education Conference*, Orlando, FL.

Zachary, W., Cannon-Bowers, J., Bilazarian, P., Krecker, D., Lardieri, P., & Burns, J. (1999). The advanced embedded training system (AETS): An intelligent embedded tutoring system for tactical team training. *Journal of Artificial Intelligence in Education, 10*, 257-277.

Zachary, W., Le Mentec, J.C., & Ryder, J. (1996). Interfact agents in complex systems. In C. Ntuen & E.H. Park (Eds.), *Human interaction with complex systems: Conceptual principles and design practice* (pp. 35-52). Norwell, MA: Kluwer Academic Publishers.

Zachary, W., & Ross, L. (1991). Enhancing human-computer interaction through the use of embedded COGNET models. In *the Proceedings of the Human Factors Society 35th Annual Meeting*. Santa Monica, CA: Human Factors Society.

Endnotes

[1]   Historical averages are based on exam results from the previous year.

[2]   The written examination included two topics that were not developed into CBT but were presented to the students in traditional lecture format. The average for those two questions was 79%. A corrected average for performance on just the InTrain instructed material was 96.2%. Removal of these two topics from the other tests did not change the historical or last four class means in any significant fashion ($\pm$ 0.2%).

[3]   Exam failures are counted in the student mean as 70%. Remediation and re-exam are conducted upon exam failure.

Chapter XIV

The Future of Technology Enhanced Active Learning:
A Roadmap

Claus Pahl, Dublin City University, Ireland

Claire Kenny, Dublin City University, Ireland

Inside Chapter

The notion of active learning refers to the active involvement of learner in the learning process, capturing ideas of learning-by-doing and the fact that active participation and knowledge construction leads to deeper and more sustained learning. Interactivity, in particular learner-content interaction, is a central aspect of technology-enhanced active learning. In this roadmap, the pedagogical background is discussed, the essential dimensions of technology-enhanced active learning systems are outlined, and the factors that are expected to influence these systems currently and in the future are identified. A central aim is to address this promising field from a best practices perspective, clarifying central issues and formulating an agenda for future developments in the form of a roadmap.

Introduction

Activity and interaction are central in learning processes. Technology-enhanced learning (TEL) software can act as a mediator between the learner and the learner's environment, that is, content, peers, and instructors. Engaging the learner to actively learn is a central objective towards deeper and lasting learning experiences. With recent technology advances, for example in multimedia and Web technologies, a shift from purely knowledge-based learning towards activity-based learning and training can be observed. Interactive Web and multimedia technologies are enablers of skills-oriented training in technology-enhanced learning environments. In a wide range of areas from technical and scientific applications to language learning, training of activities and skills is of paramount importance.

The overall aim of this chapter is to address emerging technologies for new-generation TEL and challenges for the future. This investigation targets a specific form of learning—active learning and training—and its technology support. A reflective analysis of existing technology-enhanced active learning (TEAL) environments shall establish the state-of-the-art and best practice. Based on major dimensions of these environments, external factors are identified that are likely to have an impact on their development and deployment in the future. Their impact on active learning support is examined and emerging trends, challenges, and possible solutions are discussed. The aim is to identify a realistic roadmap scenario for future technology-enhanced active learning.

Based on an analysis of the state-of-the-art, dimensions of technology-enhanced active learning environments and external factors that influence these are identified (Figure 1). The factors can be categorised along the dimensions as follows: (a) modelling, architecture, and development, (b) interoperability, delivery, and standards, (c) learning and systems evaluation, and (d) evolution. A discussion of the pedagogical context of activity-based learning and training and an analysis of some sample systems complements the discussion of the four dimensions. The dimensions are relevant in terms of best practices considerations:

- Pedagogy addresses the skills training perspective necessary for a wide range of subjects.

- Development addresses the effective and efficient development of TEAL environments.

- Change and evolution capture the mid- to long-term perspective on TEAL deployment.

- Examples for analysis are relevant for both development and deployment.

- Implementation addresses exchanges and reuse through interoperability.

- Evaluation focuses on the effectiveness of approach and environment.

Affected practically by these factors and dimensions are both learners and instructors, through content and instruction, and the administrators, through infrastructure aspects. Our discussion shall provide answers to some questions:

- How to support activity-oriented topics that require the learner to acquire skills and experience,
- How to provide such an environment in terms of developing new material and infrastructure and also in terms of reusing and integrating existing artefacts,
- How to manage such an environment on a long-term basis based on regular evaluation and continuous evolution.

A number of technologies enable the support of active learning and training, including devices, media, architecture, and semantics. These enablers are discussed in the context of the factors to highlight characteristics of current and future technology-enhanced active learning environments.

In terms of best practices, this chapter serves two purposes. First, TEAL is promoted in terms of best practices in the TEL context by illustrating its benefits through a case study. Second, a roadmap in form of an agenda for the future of this still underdeveloped field is discussed in order to enhance current best practice.

A case study—the Interactive Database Learning Environment (IDLE), which is a Web-based learning and training system for database modelling and programming—is used to illustrate concepts and to discuss current state-of-the-art and challenges. IDLE has been used since 1996 in a blended learning context for an

Figure 1. Dimensions of technology-enhanced active learning (TEAL)

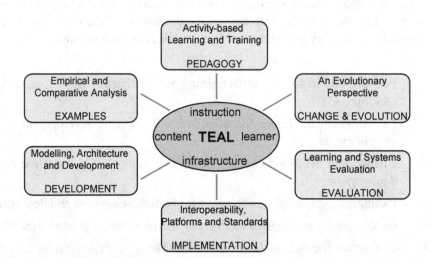

undergraduate computing degree (Kenny & Pahl, 2005). IDLE is based on the virtual apprenticeship model, which emphasises skills-oriented learning activities. The system acts as a mediator between a learner and interactive content in a realistic training environment.

Activity-Based Learning and Training

This section introduces active learning and training as a pedagogical framework:

- Active learning and training is a conceptual framework that captures the current trend towards skills and training as opposed to classical knowledge learning.
- Pedagogical frameworks such as activity theory and scaffolding, which explain the role of technology in technology-enhanced learning, are introduced.
- Specific forms such as the virtual apprenticeship framework, which has been developed to address active learning and training, are also looked at.

This section aims to clarify the role of activity for a deeper understanding and more successful learning experience.

Interactivity and Learning Activities

Northrup (2001) emphasises learning as an active process in which interactivity is central. Moore (1992) distinguishes three learning interactivity types: learner-learner, learner-instructor, and learner-content interactions. Among these types, content has a more central function in TEL than interaction with peers or instructors (Ohl, 2001; Sims, 1997). Ohl's (2001) definition of interaction as an internal dialogue of reflective thought that occurs between learner and the content supports this perspective. As part of the interactions between learner and content, the following learning and training activities can be facilitated by TEL systems:

- The aim of declarative knowledge acquisition activities is the acquisition of declarative knowledge in order to reason about it.
- The aim of procedural knowledge acquisition activities is the acquisition of procedural knowledge in order to reason about it.

- Skills acquisition activities aim at the acquisition of procedural knowledge and experience in order to perform the instructions.

The style of the interaction and activity execution is constrained by the degree of involvement and influence of the learner. Different types of interaction ranging from system-controlled to learner-controlled environments can be distinguished:

- Observation is a form of knowledge acquisition with no influence on the environment activities by a passive learner.
- Controlling is a form of knowledge acquisition mixed with knowledge production, based on observational elements, but allowing the learner to influence the environment activities to control their ordering.
- Creation is a form of activity where knowledge or skills are created by producing some form of artefact that can be processed by the learning environment.

Declarative knowledge is often acquired through observation, procedural knowledge for reasoning purposes through controllable animations, and skills through knowledge or artefact creation and processing. The targets of this investigation are TEL environments more geared towards skills acquisition and creation.

Active Learning and Training

The learning-by-doing idea is part of the active learning and training approach focussing on procedural knowledge and skills acquisition. It captures the interplay of knowledge acquisition and knowledge creation in an interactive process with the learning environment.

This focus is for instance displayed in IDLE by considering knowledge acquisition on the one hand and skills and experience acquisition on the other hand as dual sides of learning and training. One of the skills acquisition activities in the IDLE system is SQL (i.e., database) programming. A student works through guided material covering a range of individual problems while being directly connected to a database system. Each problem is based on a submission and execution cycle with a high degree of involvement of the learner through knowledge creation. Each solution—content-specific knowledge that is created by the learner—is analysed and, based on an individual activity history and integrated assessments, personalised feedback is given by the system. An important aspect of the design of a system like IDLE is the design of the learner activities within the framework of an underlying pedagogical model.

Pedagogical Models

Various models and theories have been proposed to capture and explain the ideas of active learning.

- Activity theory is a conceptual framework that can describe the structure, development, and context of computer supported activities (Nardi, 1997). Activity theory explains the principle of tool mediation in an online environment—here multimedia tools handle the student's interaction with the learning content. The emphasis on the interaction between learners and their environment explains the principle of tool mediation. Tools shape the way humans interact with reality. Educational tools reflect experiences learners and instructors have made in trying to solve particular problems.

- The cognitive apprenticeship model captures the relationship between an apprentice and a master (Collins, Brown, & Holum, 1991). An apprentice is a learner who is coached by a master (an instructor) to self-reliantly perform a specific task. The model applies this relationship notion and adopts it to the cognitive processes of knowledge learning.

- Scaffolding is a support technique that can substitute the master in the apprenticeship model in the virtual world (McLoughlin, Winnips, & Oliver, 2000). Scaffolding uses an analogy to construction where a temporary framework supports the learner in becoming self-reliant and in obtaining skills and competency. Scaffolding features in practice offer the learner support only as long as necessary, withdrawing this support as the learner becomes more and more self-reliant.

An overall constructivist style of education should be facilitated, allowing the learner to construct knowledge and obtain experience through active participation in a course. The learner should be engaged in solving meaningful problems in an activity-based, realistic setting.

Another, more targeted example of a pedagogical model is the virtual apprenticeship model (Murray, Ryan, & Pahl, 2003), which is a pedagogical theory based on the cognitive apprenticeship model that defines an activity-based and skills-oriented learning and training framework. In a TEL environment, the master's role is often replaced by an intelligent software tool. Tools reflect the experience people, such as the apprentice's master or the instructor, have made in trying to solve a particular problem. The apprenticeship model determines a number of aspects including the activity purpose and the degree of involvement, interaction styles (e.g., the organisation of learning into sessions and cycles), and the interconnectedness of activities and features. The virtual apprenticeship model puts an emphasis on skills-oriented activities with a high degree of involvement of the learner.

Discussion

Active learning and training plays an important role in recent instructional design approaches. Learning is seen as a process in which learners actively construct knowledge and acquire skills. In the context of technology-enhanced active learning and training environments, the role of the computer environment needs to be defined through pedagogical models. The TEAL environment is a tool that mediates the interaction between learner and content at the centre, but also between learners and their instructors and peers. While appropriate theories exist, they have mainly, with the exception of the virtual apprenticeship, been applied to knowledge learning.

Empirical and Comparative Analysis

Active learning is central in recent approaches to instructional design where learners actively construct knowledge and acquire skills.

- An empirical analysis of IDLE as a situated, authentic active learning and training environment forms the core of this section.

- A range of other learning tools and environments including intelligent tutoring systems and virtual instruments used in science, engineering, and medicine and simulators are also considered.

The section aims to reflect examples of best practice in active learning and looks at current state-of-the-art and recent challenges.

Evaluation Criteria

Based on the key characteristics of pedagogical theories that support active learning and training, the instructional aspects that TEAL systems need to support can be summarised as follows:

- The active participation of the learner through knowledge and artefact creation is highly beneficial.

- Active construction of knowledge and skills results in an increased ownership of the learner in the learning process.

- Meaningful projects allow learners to acquire skills and, importantly, also experience.

- A realistic setting improves the learning experience and demonstrates the applicability of knowledge and skills.

- Guidance and feedback provide instructional support in the environment.

These aspects can service as an evaluation guideline for TEAL systems.

Activities for the learner, such as programming in IDLE, are at the centre of technology-enhanced active learning and training environments. However, supporting the learner through scaffolding is also essential from the instructional perspective (Guzdial & Kehoe, 1998). In addition to just mediating between student and tools, the environment must fulfil functions of the instructor. The environment replaces the instructor in form of a virtual master that guides a learner through exercises and that provides immediate feedback on activities. Each activity needs to be complemented by conceptual and procedural knowledge in the form of, for instance, virtual lectures and animated tutorials that are relevant and problem-related for the activity in question.

IDLE Analysis

An interactive SQL learning and training environment is embedded into IDLE (Pahl, Barrett, & Kenny, 2004). The SQL part forms a central part of IDLE as database programming is one of its core learning objectives. Programming (i.e., defining, updating, and querying database tables) is a skill. Programming skills need to be trained. Moreover, this course is also an introduction to database engineering. Therefore, understanding and mastering the overall development process of a database application is equally important.

The system provides coherent integration of different learning and training activities relevant in the context of database development and programming:

- Conceptual knowledge is presented in a virtual lecture system.
- Procedural knowledge is presented in an animated tutorial system. SQL and parts of its underlying data model are about the execution of instructions.

- Programming skills acquisition is the core activity, supported by an interactive tutorial that guides the student through exercises to be worked on within the system. The tutorial guides a student through a sequence of exercises with increasing difficulty. Syntactic and semantic feedback is available.

- Development skills are equally central, which supported by an integrated lab environment with modelling, programming, and analysis features. The student is provided with a workspace in which the student can create and store a data model. An integrated, realistic lab environment that resembles features of database development environments is the central feature.

The pedagogical frameworks list a number of best practice-related success criteria for TEAL environments that are addressed in IDLE:

- Realistic setting and meaningful problems. A realistic setting with meaningful problems is a crucial aspect, required by for instance activity theory, which IDLE supports through database application development. The IDLE system creates a realistic setting by integrating tools of a real database development environment into a learning and training environment. These features are enhanced by the inclusion of instructional functionality such as guidance and feedback.

- Tool mediation. In particular, the tutorial and lab support features are mediating tools in the activity theory sense, sharing the experience of developers and instructors with learners. They support modelling and programming problems, that is, the developer's perspective, but they also incorporate the instructor's experience in teaching the topic over several years.

Active Learning Environments

Intelligent tutoring systems (ITS) are examples of systems where knowledge-level input is processed by the system. Like IDLE, the SQL Tutor (Mitrovic & Ohlsen, 1999) is an example of this category in the same subject domain. The aims are to allow students to practice and to get feedback. An emphasis has been on providing students with feedback as it would be given by an expert in the domain. The constraint-based reasoning that is applied to analyse student input had to provide only pedagogically useful and constructive responses, that is, should only respond if the response can actually be understood by the learner and used to improve the previous input. This system highlights the difficulty that a correction feature itself is not sufficient. The virtual master or mediating tool in the environment needs to understand the student, which in some form has to be captured in terms of learner model.

A virtual instrument (VI) is a multimedia tool that can be used to present information on an experiment prior to and during students performing it (Brabazon, McLoughlin, & Smyth, 2006). Evaluation of student performance has shown improved and indicates a greater degree of student interaction with the instrumented experiments. For example, a VI might present an animation of how the experiment should be performed, a real time graph of the experimental data, or interactive equations to be used to calculate the experimental results. Animations, images, and video clips can virtualise the experiment. This engages students and allows them to relate theoretical concepts to real world examples. This allows students to obtain the hands-on benefit of the laboratory whilst gaining a greater understanding of the concepts being presented to them. Simulators allow learners to train specific activities that might otherwise be difficult to provide or dangerous.

Authentic and situated learning environments require learners to actively engage in real-world problem solving that reflects both the context and complexity of the practical situations in which the need for learning was created (Herrington & Oliver, 2000). Language learning is a classical example where the immersion in the cultural context is more effective than textbook-based learning. TEL systems can provide virtual environments in which learning can take place, where for instance learners can move through and communicate in virtual organisations to achieve a particular learning goal. The importance of the context or environment in which an activity takes place is emphasised in this approach to learning and training.

Problem-based learning is another direction that is captured by the term active learning (Barrows, 2000). Specific, meaningful problems that usually require the interaction between learner and content, but also between the learner and both instructors and peers, form the basis of the learning experience. While in this context the construction and processing of knowledge is not always an issue, the collaboration of groups of learners is.

Discussion

The analyses have emphasised the practice-oriented success factors for current TEAL environments. What can be clearly seen from this evaluation are the challenges that TEAL brings.

- The use of interactive educational multimedia needs to go beyond the use of for instance Web technologies today, which are mainly text and image oriented. An interaction in terms of the concepts and objects of the subject domain (such as programs or graphical models for databases) is a challenge.

- Integration and interoperability of tools and components is a necessity to complement each individual learning activity, such as skills training activities with declarative and procedural learning activities. Education-specific standards and agreed interfaces are required.

- Collaboration emerges as a central of interaction. Real problems can often only be solved in groups, possibly involving different roles. A TEL system for this context needs to facilitate collaboration in terms of interaction/communication and shared workspaces.

Beyond these individual aspects, one general observation summarises an essential requirement. Ravenscroft, Tait, and Hughes (1998) highlight the importance of the appropriate level of student interaction with learning content. Often, a distinction is made between content aimed at developing conceptual knowledge on one hand and content aiming at skills development on the other (Weston & Barker, 2001). The learner motivation in TEAL environments is the acquisition of skills and good performance in practical coursework and examinations. Consequently, the form of interaction with content supporting active learning of skills is different from knowledge-based learning. IDLE is an example for the importance of the appropriateness of content interaction, in the IDLE case the implementation of skills-level interactions such as interactive programming and modelling.

Modelling, Architecture, and Development

The previous section has looked at full TEAL systems and now the content at their core shall be investigated. The learning object notion as a reusable and sharable unit is becoming more and more important. This section:

- Introduces learning objects for active learning, their modelling, and their reuse
- Focuses specifically on modelling the assembly of these learning objects
- Discusses the automated generation of content objects from models, possibly enriched to semantical, knowledge-based models

Modelling, architecture, and semantics emerge as technical notions that will impact the practical aspects of content authoring. These have the potential to bring together the requirements from technology enablers with the requirements from the active learning perspective.

Learning Objects

Learning objects are reusable, digital representations of learning content. Learning content is expensive to develop, in particular if advanced features such as IDLE's interactive programming feedback system or graphical modelling tools are considered. In order to facilitate the content development process and to allow content to be reused, the representation of content in the form of individual, identifiable, and sharable learning objects is a solution. Two reasons motivate a notion of learning objects:

- First, the clear separation of content and the infrastructure that controls its storage, delivery, and presentation. A learning object is a notion that reflects this separation and allows content units to be clearly identified in these infrastructure environments.

- Second, learning objects are content units of a small to medium size, which allow their reuse and flexible combination in different instructional contexts.

Content in the form of learning objects does not exist on its own. Learning objects need to be supported by a software infrastructure—which makes the joint discussion of learning objects and the architecture that process them necessary. Some IDLE learning objects are software components in their own right, which interact with other infrastructure components

Architectures

The architecture of a technology-enhanced learning system is the description of its structural and abstract behavioural characteristics. It describes the learning object storage, processing, and delivery. The different stages of the content lifecycle provide the starting point to understand the functional architecture of a TEL system. Three learning object development stages are:

- Creation and maintenance of learning objects based on ontologies and models,

- Making learning objects accessible through navigation infrastructures and adaptive delivery, including assets such as multimedia objects, references, and links,

- Packaging and assembling content to form interoperable ready-to-use units of study.

An essential aspect of architectures is their role in facilitating learning object design and deployment. Each of the above stages requires specific infrastructure support. If, for instance, existing active learning objects are imported to compose larger units of study, their interaction interfaces need to be supported by the infrastructure.

The Web Services architecture aims to enable interoperability for software using the Web platform. The principle of software services, provided at certain locations on the Web that can be used by other software applications, is the basis. Service-oriented TEL systems are the application of this principle in the educational context (Devedžić, 2004). This architecture platform blurs the distinction between content and infrastructure system. Content will be provided through services, as will standard functions of a learning technology system such as user management or evaluation support. From the perspective of instructors and learners, it requires to see learning content as dynamic, interactive objects encapsulated as services that can support active learning.

Semantics, Ontologies, and Modelling

Learning objects and supporting architectures also need to be looked at in the context of another development in learning technology—the use of explicit knowledge representation and semantics through ontologies and models (Aroyo, Dicheva, & Cristea, 2004; Mizoguchi & Bourdeau, 2000; Wilson, 2004). Knowledge plays a central, though often implicit role in the creation, management, and delivery of learning content. Ontologies are explicit representations of knowledge structures of a particular domain. Ontologies can support the modelling and creation of learning objects, add flexibility to the abstract model-based management and organisation of learning objects, and improve the guided delivery of learning objects (Devedžić, 2006; Pahl & Holohan, 2004).

Ontologies and learning objects can act as the central information objects of an information model for the creation and maintenance subsystem of an architecture. Ontologies consist of concepts, relationships, and instances. Learning objects can, for example, be lessons or tests. The content of a lesson usually consists of text and images, which can both be related to concepts or instances of the ontology. Similarly, tests consist of a question, possible answers, and the correct solution, where the answers and solutions are again directly based on concepts and instances.

Support for ontology-based authoring and delivery is still in its infancy and currently limited to static content. Providing this support for active learning objects requires specific ontologies and models for their description and generation that go beyond standard domain ontologies, which focus on static concepts rather than procedures and activities. In order to enable an explicit and more effective use of knowledge in learning object development and deployment, an adequate architecture of learning content management systems (LCMS) for authoring and storage and learner management systems (LMS) for delivery to support these activities is then also needed.

Discussion

Reusable active learning objects cause problems across all aspects discussed in this section, such as available and sharable ontologies and models and also architecture standards and interfaces (which are addressed in more detail in the next section). In addition, the practical aspects of the development of reusable active learning objects is not well understood either. The development of learning objects and infrastructure architecture for knowledge-based learning objects need to be looked at from two perspectives:

- The functional (or structural) view on architectures is the classical view on software architectures, focusing on the system components and their assembly.
- The development (or process-oriented) view focuses on the development and authoring activities of learning objects in these architectures.

The process model underlying the development view captures the learning object authoring process and, therefore, determines central aspects of the functional architecture.

Interoperability, Platforms, and Standards

Learning technology enablers, such as devices, media, architectures, or semantics, are central for the delivery. In this section, the previous focus on content shall be moved to infrastructure, discussing the potential of arising new platforms (e.g., iPod or mobile phones) and their impact on new forms of active learning and training, and the standards—current and in progress—in relation to the delivery of active learning and their shortcomings. The challenges arising from the limitations of the new platforms for active learning are discussed.

Interoperability and Platform Requirements

Technology-enhanced learning is a central aspect of education today. In particular, the Web as the platform for development and delivery has impacted TEL. While initially mainly static resources were provided, the focus has shifted to more effective learning through engaging learning content objects. Active learning objects (ALOs) that support active and engaging learning and architectural frameworks for ALO development and deployment to enable reuse and interoperability of ALOs are currently being investigated.

- Their development can be supported by a description and discovery technique that allows learners to find and select suitable ALOs. The infrastructure aim is to support abstract description in particular in terms of interactions and activities and to facilitate discovery.

- Their deployment can be supported by container-based component or service architectures. The core problem is interaction between learning objects and learner and also infrastructure services. Questions concern the level of interaction in terms of concepts and activities of the subject and the support of standard learning services.

Another central aspect is learner-centricity, that is, pursuing an infrastructure that enables a learner to control the selection, integration, and consumption of content, motivated by current trends in mobile gaming and music; an issue that can be expected to become more important in the near future with changes in learner behaviour and expectations. The emerging support for portable devices such as mobile phones and iPods has already greatly impacted music and entertainment.

What these observations show is the need for standards and platforms supporting the interoperability of active learning objects and architecture components and services. The proliferation of TEAL is currently hampered by high development costs and the lack of reusability and interoperability technology. Two facets characterise the current developments in this area:

- ALO Engineering. ALOs are currently investigated from an instructional design perspective, but the systematic engineering of these objects as reusable entities has not been considered. A systematic approach is, however, necessary to develop the quality for reusable and interoperable, well-documented and annotated learning objects.

- Interoperability and Architecture. Currently, standardisation efforts and learner management systems focus on static learning objects, providing only a minimal interaction interface for learning objects. There is a need to advance interoperability to include a higher degree of knowledge/skills-level interaction, but also to consider a wider range of technology platforms.

A number of technologies affect these developments, both in terms of active learning and also proliferation of technology platforms and devices. Current standards provide a minimalist standard for learning objects integration. Java applets provide mobile code technology. Enterprise Java Beans, the Java component technology, for instance, is based on containers that provide a standardised set of common functions and in which reusable components are executed. Web services provide a higher degree of interoperability and a possibility to package learning objects in a uniform way. Learning object integration needs to be progressed further for ALOs using mobile component and container technologies to provide a platform for learner-centric active learning on the Web platform comprising an engineering solution and infrastructure support.

Standards Overview

A number of standards relating to learning objects and supporting infrastructure and architectures shall briefly be discussed:

- The SCORM suite of standards is implemented by most LMS and LCMS for the exporting and importing of learning content and sequencing instructions (ADL, 2004). The standards that come together can be grouped into three groups. They are the Content Aggregation Model (CAM), the Sequencing and Navigation (SN), and the Run-Time Environment (RTE). CAM is used for the packaging and description of learning content. RTE describes how a package is to be managed and utilised at runtime. The RTE allows the learning resources within packages to be platform- and LMS-independent. SN describes how learning content contained within a package can be sequenced according to learner actions and preferences.

- IMS Learning Design (LD) is a standard addressing the development of composite learning activities (IMS, 2003). Instructional knowledge is needed to give structure to educational resources. Education-specific markup languages, such as Learning Design LD, can form a notational system for content development and representation.

- The IEEE Learning Object Metadata standard (LOM) provides a basic metadata framework for the facetted description and classification of learning objects (IEEE, 2002). LOM defines the attributes required to fully describe a learning object. It classifies attributes into nine categories addressing for example general, technical, educational, and lifecycle aspects.

- The IEEE Learning Technology System Architecture (LTSA) is a functional architecture based on the software components of a learning technology system (IEEE, 2002). This architecture is geared towards a software developer.

Discussion

Although standardisation is in progress, these have been addressing static learning objects and approaches to learning and training. These standards are currently lowest common denominators of available technology and consequently do not support best practice concerns adequately. Their extension to embrace active learning and training is therefore of paramount importance. Without reusability and standardisation, the high costs of development of TEAL might turn out to be prohibitive. The focus has so far also been on PC-based environments, leaving mobile devices until very recently largely unexplored.

Learning and Systems Evaluation

Novel platforms, as just discussed, and new types of technology utilisation for any learning type raise questions about the acceptance and usage of technology by learners. Evaluation of their behaviour in these systems is therefore paramount. This section looks at how to capture changing learner attitudes and behaviour. It addresses how to implement constant monitoring and formative evaluation. Specific approaches, such as for instance data mining techniques, that consider the higher level and the complexity of interactions for the targeted active learning context are investigated.

Evaluation of Interaction and Learning Activities

So far, the development and deployment of active learning content and infrastructure has been discussed. This lifecycle is not complete without an evaluation stage. Novel methods that combine classical survey methods with computational techniques for data mining and analysis are needed to address the evaluation needs for interaction and activity in TEAL environments. On the technical level, interaction is a reflection of learning activities and strategies. The evaluation of learning and training behaviour needs to be based on the analysis of content interaction in TEAL environments. Learning behaviour in learning and training environments particularly with a high degree of activity ad knowledge-level interaction, however, is currently not well understood. In contrast to traditional classroom-based learning and training, the learning strategies and behaviour are more determined by the learner's own decisions how to organise learning and training (Northrup, 2001). Additionally, often several educational features are available at the same time, allowing competent learners to choose their own approach of combining resources and features. Consequently, the analysis and evaluation of learning and training behaviour is of central importance

(Oliver, 2000). A general understanding of effective and preferred learning styles and behaviour is required for authors and instructional designers to improve the design of learning content. Instructors require feedback on usage to improve the delivery of educational resources.

Learner Behaviour

The behaviour of learners in computer-based teaching and learning environments is influenced by the motivation to use the system and the acceptance of the approach. These two more abstract aspects relate concrete learning behaviour with the objectives and state-of-mind that have led to that behaviour. A learning activity is an engagement towards a learning objective. Two aspects of the student's concrete behaviour can be distinguished, which defines the learning activity. First, the learning organisation addresses the study habits and captures how students organise their studies over a longer period of time. This includes how they plan to learn and work on coursework, and how they prepare for exams. Second, the usage of the system captures single learning activities and embraces how the student works with and behaves in the system in a single study session. Overall, four aspects of learning behaviour can be identified:

- Motivation, the reason to do something, causes the learner to act in some planned and organised way, giving the activities a purpose.

- Acceptance, to follow the learning approach and use the system willingly, is crucial for the introduction of new educational technology.

- Organisation, the way the learning activities are planned and put into logical order, reflects the study habits and is guided by the purpose.

- Usage, the way the tool is actually used, reflects the actual learning activities.

Both the pedagogical framework and the TEAL system need to support the objectives that form the students' motivation in order to be accepted. The organisation is determined by the motivation—the objectives determine how activities are organised and executed. The usage follows the organisational plan to achieve the objectives. Motivation and acceptance are necessary to interpret organisation and usage.

Instruments for Behaviour Evaluation

Traditionally, direct observation and surveys are used to determine the learning behaviour in classroom-based learning and training, but with the emergence of computer-supported, and in particular Web-supported learning and training environments, there is now another option. Learners leave traces of their activities and behaviour in TEAL systems. In Web-based systems, access logs are automatically generated by Web servers that handle user requests.

Behaviour in learner-controlled environments is determined by the four aspects identified above. Consequently, the instruments for the behaviour analysis include two instrument types: survey methods to address motivation and acceptance and data mining techniques (Pahl, 2006a) to capture organisation and usage directly from records of learner activity in the environment. This combination provides a more complete and accurate picture than surveys and student observation alone or student tracking features available in various learning technology systems. Formative evaluations of behaviour are vital for identifying key design issues and for improving the understanding of pedagogical issues and the design of effective types of learning environments (Kinshuk, Patel, & Russell, 2000). A framework for the analysis and evaluation of active learning and training behaviour and interaction needs to support a variety of techniques:

- The detection and discovery of learning and training interaction from sources such as access logs,

- The explicit capture and representation of interaction behaviour abstracted from the interaction and access requests recorded in the logs,

- The analysis and interpretation of behaviour within the educational context using an analytic model of activities.

Current standardisation efforts, for example in the SCORM context, address functionality to track and store learner behaviour in LMS.

Behaviour and Usage Mining

Data mining (Chang, Healey, McHugh, & Wang, 2001; Scime, 2004), in the application to behaviour in Web-based environments called Web usage mining, can be used to make implicit, latent knowledge in activity logs explicit. Data mining is about the discovery, extraction, and analysis of data from large databases. Web usage mining aims to extract behaviour in Web sites from access logs. To derive learning activities from navigation and interaction in Web-based systems is not always straightforward. Web log data can give a precise and objective account of low-level activities. Web logs record accesses to resources, which then have to be associated to learning activities. Web usage mining is an observation-oriented evaluation technique suitable for learning behaviour analysis (Ventura & Romero,

2006). Despite some limitations, it offers a nonintrusive form of observation that is useable at all times and that can contribute substantially to reliable and accurate evaluation results for TEL.

In addition to classical Web usage statistics such as number of hits in a period of time, usage mining allows a more targeted analysis of Web log data for educational purposes (Ventura & Romero, 2001). TEL-specific analyses can be supported based on two mining techniques developed for the educational context (Pahl, 2006b):

- Session classification. An access log is a chronologically ordered list of resource requests. The first task is to identify learning sessions, which are defined as periods of uninterrupted usage of an individual user. The classification tries to identify purposes or activities of a session, for example interactive learning, attending a virtual lecture, or downloading resources.

- Behavioural pattern discovery. The access log provides a sequential list of learner requests representing the learner activities in the system. The first task is to find sequential patterns (i.e., recurring sequences of requests). The second step is the identification of behavioural patterns such as repetition or the parallel use of features in these sequences and sequential patterns.

These two techniques allow the interpretation of low-level activities and interactions in terms of the broader learning activities.

Discussion

In practice, evaluation is a key instrument to address the effectiveness of teaching and learning. Overall, complementary evaluation instruments—student surveys and observation-based Web usage mining—can be combined in evaluations to address the different aspects of behaviour. Adding Web usage mining gives instructors an improved interpretative strength over classical methods for behaviour analysis. A benefit of the combination is the validation of behaviour-specific survey results and addition of preciseness through usage mining.

While for static content, navigation behaviour is already indicative of the learner's activities, the evaluation of active learning and training behaviour requires also the identification and interpretation of knowledge-level interactions. The reliability of these interpretations is crucial, since design decisions are meant to be based on them, but have proven so far to be difficult to capture in a generic tool.

An Evolutionary Perspective

Technology-enhanced learning is subject to constant evolution. Change needs to be embraced from the outset.

- Factors of change, like infrastructure, content, organisation, and pedagogy, are identified and their impact discussed.
- Solutions for the active learning context such as specific approaches modularity and standards are outlined.

This section brings some of the earlier aspects into a more long-term perspective.

The Impact of Change and Evolution

The IDLE system is a good example for the impact of evolution and change. IDLE has grown substantially since its first deployment in 1996 (Pahl et al., 2004). In addition to the continuing development and extension, the maintenance of the existing content and functionality has become a problem. Changes that were made to the content and the system can be captured in a model, which reflects the different change facets of a TEL system and also the different stakeholders involved.

- **Content:** The subject-oriented perspective. The learner works with the content for a subject, which is, however, created by the instructor.
- **Format:** The organisational perspective. The organisation determines aspects such as syllabus, stakeholders, or aspects of the environment.
- **Infrastructure:** The technical perspective. Both organisation and developer are responsible for determining the infrastructure technology.
- **Pedagogy:** The educational perspective. The instructor is the key factor in determining the pedagogy.

While properly designed learning objects themselves should not be affected by for instance change in a course format, in reality these aspects are often not clearly separated and changes in format, infrastructure, or pedagogy will impact content. IDLE has been subject to changes in all facets, resulting in simple and cost-effective changes to the sometimes necessary discontinuation of features.

Design for Change

The IDLE experience calls for a more systematic approach to active learning objects and infrastructure development that embraces change from the outset. Change and evolution are factors that accompany content in any form and require appropriate management support (Pahl, 2003). A number of factors need to be kept in mind when learning objects—on which shall be focused here—are designed.

- **Reusability.** Reuse is a necessity to keep development and maintenance costs under control. Reuse requires learning objects to be developed for this purpose. Reusable learning objects need to be internally coherent. Reusable objects tend to be small in scale in order to enable their modular composition to courses in different contexts. Reusable objects need to be described to allow potential users to determine for instance the infrastructure requirements the object might have. This type of knowledge about dependencies helps to determine the change impact and carry out modifications.

- **Standards.** Standards enable interoperability. For static learning objects this refers to the format in which the objects are represented. For dynamic, interactive learning objects, their integration into a delivery environment is more challenging. These objects are executable software artefacts that have to be invoked by the delivery systems they are integrated in. This invocation interface needs to be standardised. The composition of learning objects—often referred to as sequencing—is equally important. Standards-compliant representation of content and interfaces guarantee a certain degree of stability and also control over the impact of changes.

- **Maintainability.** Similar to reusability, maintainability requires an adequate design. Internal coherence and small scale are factors that tend to reduce change impacts. Changes cause by the environment will occur. The main issue is to predict the impact of changes and the costs to deal with them and to limit them. The four facets can act as a TEL-specific guideline to assess the implications of change.

Discussion

Overall, the separation of concerns is one the central rules for the design of maintainable learning objects and TEL systems. In practice, maintainability is a crucial but often neglected aspect. Content needs to be separated from its configuration into courses, from adaptivity and personalisation in the delivery, and from any scaffolding added to support the learner. Change and evolution are, however, inevitable and need to be catered for from the beginning by limiting the change impact and allowing this impact to be determined easily. The novelty of TEAL means that major evolutions in pedagogy and technology that have been outlined will take place.

Conclusion

The use of technology-enhanced learning and training environments to enhance or replace traditional forms of learning and training has increased over the past years. In particular, the World-Wide Web has gained the status as the predominant platform for these environments. First generation Web-based educational environments succeeded due to their advantage of easy access to educational resources. Recently, the focus has been on supporting a wider range of educational activities, thus enhancing the learning experience for the learner through improved interactivity and engagement. Traditional knowledge-based learning is complemented by skills-oriented active learning and training. The combined facilitation of interaction between learners and content supporting knowledge acquisition and skills training is central.

While the benefits of active learning are widely recognised, a range of problems remain concerning best practices. Pedagogical frameworks exist and some successful prototypes have been developed. These have highlighted the limitations in terms of standards and interoperability, in actually making implicit knowledge of different types explicit, and, last but not least, understanding the learner's behaviour in these environments. Practical aspects such as development and maintenance problems limit the full exploitation of the potential. The development, or rather the overall lifecycle of active learning content and infrastructure, needs to be supported by a comprehensive engineering framework. The development of TEL environments is a participative effort of instructors, learners, and software specialists that requires an adequate methodological framework. In particular, the maintenance and evolution of these systems as a consequence of formative evaluations and technological changes in the deployment context need to be embraced from the outset. These aspects are hampered by the fact that active learning and training on the one hand and current technology development (e.g., devices) and pedagogy trends (e.g., collaborative learning) on the other hand, however, often have opposing requirements. Pedagogy, examples, development, implementation, evaluation, and change and evolution are the aspects of the presented roadmap that summarise the main technical, pedagogical and administrative challenges of TEAL as an approach.

As technology-enhanced active learning is still in its infancy, a two-stage evolutionary process is likely to address the issues arising from this roadmap discussion.

- In a first phase, active learning and training with current media and architecture technology still need more best practice results for authoring and delivery to try to understand how learners work best in these environments.

- In a second phase, these results can be adapted to new contexts such as emerging delivery platforms and devices, integrating some of the advanced aspects such as ontologies that have been discussed here.

Ultimately, due to the recognition of constructive and active learning as beneficial, these will be implemented in technology-enhanced learning environments but require a period of further learning for developers and instructors and also technology development before this can take place.

References

ADL. (2004). *Sharable content object reference model (SCORM) – content aggregation model (CAM), run-time environment (RTE), sequencing and navigation (SN)*. Retrieved January 13, 2008, from http://www.adlnet.org/index.cfm?fuseaction=scormabt

Aroyo, L., Dicheva, D., & Cristea, A. (2002). Ontological support for Web courseware authoring. In *Proceedings Conference on Intelligent Tutoring Systems ITS'02* (pp. 270-280). Springer-Verlag.

Barrows, H. (2000). Foreword. In D. Evenson & C. Hmelo (Eds.), *Problem-based learning: A research perspective on learning interaction* (pp. vii-ix). New Jersey: Lawrence Erlbaum Associates.

Brabazon, D., McLoughlin, E., & Smyth, P. (2006). Virtual instruments - visualising and logging science and engineering experiments. *Assocation for Learning Technology Online Newsletter*, 5. Retrieved February 20, 2008, from http://newsletter.alt.ac.uk/e_article000613246.cfm?x=b11,0,w

Chang, G., Healey, M.J., McHugh, J.A.M., & Wang, J.T.L. (2001). *Mining the World Wide Web - an information search approach*. Boston: Kluwer Academic Publishers.

Collins, A., Brown, J.S., & Holum, A. (1991, Winter). Cognitive apprenticeship: Making thinking visible. *American Educator*, 6(11), 38-46.

Devedžić, V. (2004). Web intelligence and artificial intelligence in education. *Educational Technology & Society*, 7(4), 29-39.

Devedžić, V. (2006). *Semantic Web and education*. Springer-Verlag.

Guzdial, M., & Kehoe, C. (1998). Apprenticeship-based learning environments: A principled approach to providing software-realized scaffolding through hypermedia. *Journal of Interactive Learning Research, 9*(3/4), 289-336.

Herrington, J., & Oliver, R. (2000). An instructional design framework for authentic learning environments. *Educational Technology Research and Development, 48*(3), 23-48.

IEEE Learning Technology Standards Committee LTSC. (2002). Draft standard for learning object metadata (LOM). *IEEE Computer Society*. IEEE P1484.12/D4.0. Retrieved February 20, 2008, from http://ltsc.ieee.org/wg12/materials.html

IEEE Learning Technology Standards Committee LTSC. (2003). Draft standard for learning technology systems architecture (LTSA). *IEEE Computer Society*. IEEE P1484.1/D11. Retrieved February 20, 2008, from http://ltsc.ieee.org/wg1/materials.html

IMS Global Learning Consortium. (2003). *IMS learning design (LD) standard*. Retrieved January 13, 2008, from http://www.imsglobal.org/learningdesign/

Kenny, C., & Pahl, C. (2005). An automated tutor for a training environment for database programming. In *ACM SIGCSE Computer Science Education Symposium 2005* (pp. 58-64). ACM Press.

Kinshuk, P.A., & Russell, D. (2000). A multi-institutional evaluation of intelligent tutoring tools in numeric disciplines. *Educational Technology & Society, 3*(4).

McLoughlin, C., Winnips, J.C., & Oliver, R. (2000). Supporting constructivist learning through learner support online. In *World Conference on Educational Multimedia, Hypermedia and Telecommunications EDMEDIA'2000* (pp. 674-680).

Mitrovic, A., & Ohlsen, S (1999). Evaluation of a constraint-based tutor for a database language. *International Journal of Artificial Intelligence in Education, 10,* 238-256.

Mizoguchi, R., & Bourdeau, J. (2000). Using ontological engineering to overcome common AI-ED problems. *International Journal of Artificial Intelligence in Education, 11,* 107-121.

Moore, M.G. (1992). Three types of interaction. *The American Journal of Distance Education, 3*(2), 1-6.

Murray, S., Ryan, J., & Pahl, C. (2003). A tool-mediated cognitive apprenticeship approach for a computer engineering course. In *IEEE International Conference on Advanced Learning Technologies ICALT'03* (pp. 2-6).

Nardi, B. (Ed.). (1997). *Educational context and consciousness: Activity theory and human-computer interaction*. MIT Press.

Northrup, P. (2001). A framework for designing interactivity into Web-based instruction. *Educational Technology, 41*(2), 31-39.

Ohl, T.M. (2001). An interaction-centric learning model. *Journal of Educational Multimedia and Hypermedia, 10*(4), 311-332.

Oliver, M. (Ed.). (2000). Special issue on evaluation of learning technology. *Educational Technology & Society, 3*(4).

Pahl, C. (2003). Evolution and change in Web-based teaching and learning environments. *Computers & Education, 40*(1), 99-114.

Pahl, C. (2006a). Behaviour analysis for Web-mediated active learning. *International Journal of Web-Based Learning and Teaching Technologies, 1*(3), 45-55. Idea Group Publishers.

Pahl, C. (2006b). Data mining for the analysis of content interaction in Web-based learning and training systems. In S. Ventura & C. Romero (Eds.), *Data mining in e-learning* (pp. 41-56). WIT Press.

Pahl, C., Barrett, R., & Kenny, C. (2004). Supporting active database learning and training through interactive multimedia. In *International Conference on Innovation and Technology in Computer Science Education ITiCSE'04* (pp. 58-62). ACM Press.

Pahl, C., & Holohan, E. (2004). Ontology technology for the development and deployment of learning technology systems – a survey. In *International Conference on Educational Hyper- and Multimedia EdMedia'04* (pp. 2077-2084). AACE.

Ravenscroft, A., Tait, K., & Hughes, I. (1998). Beyond the media: Knowledge level interaction and guided integration for CBL systems. *Computers & Education, 30*(1/2), 49-56.

Scime, A. (2004). *Web mining: Applications and techniques.* Hershey, PA: Idea Group Inc.

Sims, R. (1997). Interactive learning as emerging technology: A reassessment of interactive and instructional design strategies. *Australian Journal of Educational Technology, 13*(1), 68-84.

Ventura, S., & Romero, C. (Eds.). (2006). *Data mining in e-learning.* WIT Press.

Weston, T.J., & Barker, L. (2001). Designing, implementing, and evaluating Web-based learning modules for university students. *Educational Technology, 41*(4), 15-22.

Wilson, R. (2004). The role of ontologies in teaching and learning. In *JISC Joint Information Systems Committee – Technology and Standards Watch Report TSW0402.* Retrieved January 13, 2008, from http://www.jisc.ac.uk/uploaded_documents/tsw_04_02.pdf

Further Readings

Boyle, T. (2003). Design principles for authoring dynamic, reusable learning objects, *Australian Journal of Educational Technology, 19*(1), 46-58.

Karampiperis, P., & Sampson, D. (2005). Designing learning services: From content-based to activity-based learning systems. In *Proceedings of the 14th International World Wide Web Conference WWW2005* (pp. 1110-1111).

Yang, S.J.H., Lan, B.C.W., Chen, I.Y.L., Wu, B.J.D., & Chang, A.C.N. (2005). Context aware service oriented architecture for Web-based learning. *Advanced Technologies for Learning, 2*(4).

Ohl, T.M. (2001). An interaction-centric learning model. *Journal of Educational Multimedia and Hypermedia, 10*(4), 311-332.

Okamoto, T., Cristea, A., & Kayama, M. (2001). Future integrated learning environments with multimedia. *Journal of Computer Assisted Learning, 17*, 4-12.

Moore, M.G. (1992). Three types of interaction. *The American Journal of Distance Education, 3*(2), 1-6.

Useful URLs

Kaleidoscope, European research network: http://www.noe-kaleidoscope.org/pub/

European Learning Grid Infrastructure (ELeGI): http://www.elegi.org/

Ontologies for Education Portal: http://iiscs.wssu.edu/o4e/

Activity Theory Resources: http://carbon.cudenver.edu/~mryder/itc_data/activity.html

Active Learning Site: http://www.active-learning-site.com/

Learning Technology Standards Observatory: http://www.cen-ltso.net/Users/main.aspx

Data Mining: http://www.the-data-mine.com/

Instructional Design Models: http://carbon.cudenver.edu/~mryder/itc_data/id-models.html

Learning Management System - An evaluation of LMS solutions, software and services: http://dir.wolfram.org/learning_management_systems.html

IMS Global Learning Consortium: http://www.imsglobal.org/

Knowledge and Learning Management Systems: http://www.educause.edu/content.asp?page_id=2607&bhcp=1

Appendix

Figure A1.

> **Internet Session:**
>
> Although not interactive, the Kaleidoscope project Web site (http://www.noe-kaleidoscope.org/pub/) is a useful address to find out about current research issues in technology-enhanced learning. It demonstrates some state-of-the-art case studies, outlines current research objectives in the area, and gives pointers to active research across a number of organisations and researchers.

Figure A2.

> **Case Study:**
>
> Develop a system design for an active technology-enhanced learning system for a subject that required active, knowledge- and skills-level interactions if supported by software applications.
>
> Specify the system architecture. Develop scenarios that illustrate how knowledge engineering can support the authoring and delivery of active content for this subject. Discuss how different multimedia and hypermedia technologies can support the implementation of such a system.

About the Contributors

Miltiadis D. Lytras is an assistant professor in the Computer Engineering and Informatics Department-CEID (University of Patras). His research focuses on Semantic Web, knowledge management, and e-learning, with more than 100 publications in these areas. He has co-edited/co-edits 25 special issues in International Journals (e.g., *IEEE Transaction on Knowledge and Data Engineering, IEEE Internet Computing, IEEE Transactions on Education, Computers in Human Behaviour,* etc.) and has authored/co-edited 12 books (e.g., *Open Source for Knowledge and Learning management, Ubiquitous and Pervasive Knowledge Management, Intelligent Learning Infrastructures for Knowledge Intensive Organizations, Semantic Based Information systems).* He is the founder and officer of the Semantic Web and Information Systems Special Interest Group in the Association for Information Systems (http://www.sigsemis.org). He serves as the co-editor in chief of 12 international journals (e.g., *International Journal of Knowledge and Learning, International Journal of Technology Enhanced Learning, International Journal on Social and Humanistic Computing, International Journal on Semantic Web and Information Systems, International Journal on Digital Culture and Electronic Tourism, International Journal of Electronic Democracy, International Journal of Electronic Banking, International Journal of Electronic Trade)* while he is associate editor or editorial board member in 7 more.

Dragan Gašević is an assistant professor at the School of Computing and Information Systems at Athabasca University and is an adjunct professor at the School of Interactive Arts and Technology at Simon Fraser University Surrey in Canada. His current research interests are in the area of the Semantic Web, Model Driven Engineering (MDE), technology enhanced learning, and service-oriented architectures. So far, he has authored/co-authored more than 170 research papers and book chapters, and 2 books. He is the lead author of the book Model Driven Architecture and Ontology Development published by Springer in 2006. He has been severing on the editorial board of the Interactive Learning Environments, International Journal of Learning Technology, and International Journal of Technology Enhanced Learning and he has been a reviewer or guest editor of several international journals (e.g., IET Software and IEEE Transactions on Software Engineering). He has also been an organizer/program committee member/reviewer of several international conferences/workshops.

Patricia Ordóñez de Pablos is professor in the Department of Business Administration and Accountability, at the Faculty of Economics of the University of Oviedo (Spain). Her teaching and research interests focus on the areas of strategic management, knowledge management, intellectual capital measuring and reporting, organizational learning, and human resources management. She is executive editor of the *International Journal of Learning and Intellectual* and the *International Journal of Strategic Change Management.*

Weihong Huang is a senior lecturer at the Faculty of Computing, Information Systems and Mathematics at Kingston University London, U.K. His current research interests include Context-Aware Computing, Semantic Web Technologies, Intelligent Mobile Agents, Multimedia and Intelligent e-Services (e.g. e-Learning, e- Commerce, e-Healthcare). He has served as editor/co-editor for a number of journals and programme committee member for various international conferences in related fields. Dr. Huang is a member of ACM and IEEE Computer Society.

* * *

Martin Beer is a principal lecturer in the Information Technology Programme Area of the Faculty of Arts, Computing, Engineering and Science at Sheffield Hallam University, where he leads the Web & Multi-Agents Research Group. His current research interests include the use of multi-agent systems to assist in the delivery of community and clinical care and the delivery of mobile collaborative learning environments. He was technical director of the OTIS (Occupational Therapy Internet School) project, and managed the Sheffield Hallam contribution to the MOBIlearn and AgentCities projects. He has published over a hundred research papers.

Giuseppe Chiazzese is a researcher at the Institute for Educational Technologies of the Italian National Research Council. His research interests concern the study, design, and application of distance learning environments; defining new methodologies and technologies for implement teaching and learning processes. At the moment, his research activity concern the field of distance education with particular interest to the Web-based systems to support metacognitive process for Web learning.

Antonella Chifari is a psychologists and since 2001 has been a researcher at the Institute for Educational Technology in Palermo. Her main research interests concern the use of the use of Information Technology to define new learning methodologies and to design environments to support different aspects of learning.

Paul Crowther is a principal lecturer in charge of the Information Systems subject group at Sheffield Hallam University. His research interests are in knowledge base systems and knowledge management. His most recent work has been associated with the European Union funded MOBIlearn project where he was involved in requirements analysis.

Jacqueline (Jay) Dempster is deputy director (and Head of Educational Development and E-Learning) in the Centre for Academic Practice at the University of Warwick. She has over 15 years experience in educational development in higher education both at institutional and national levels. She has been involved in various national organisations since 1993. Jay has been an active proponent in establishing national professional development opportunities for staff interested or active in using technology in teaching and the support of learning. She chaired the project steering group for the national accreditation scheme, Certified Membership of the Association for Learning Technology (CMALT), and leads Masters-level programmes in e-learning at Warwick. Jay's interests focus on developing professional practice and research-based learning at curriculum, departmental and institutional levels. Over the years, she has developed a number of innovative learning technology projects. Her research has focused on the management of change in higher education, in particular, exploring institutional structures and processes and staff development needs in introducing technology into teaching practices.

Michael Derntl is researcher and lecturer at the Research Lab for Educational Technologies at the University of Vienna, where he is also serving as Vice-Head. From 2001 to 2005 he was Research Assistant and PhD candidate at the Research Lab for Educational Technologies. His PhD research and thesis were on patterns for blended learning. He is currently employed as postdoctoral researcher in the "Technology-Enhanced Learning" project. His current research interests include technology enhanced learning, design patterns, conceptual modeling, and social aspects of information technology. You can get more information at http://www. cs.univie.ac.at/michael.derntl

Vladan Devedzic is a professor of Computer Science and Head of the Department of Software Engineering of the FON—School of Business Administration at the University of Belgrade. He received his BSc, MSc, and PhD from the University of Belgrade. His long-term professional goal is to bring close together the ideas from the broad fields of intelligent systems and software engineering. His current professional and scientific interests include knowledge modeling, ontologies, intelligent reasoning techniques, Semantic Web, software engineering, and application of artificial intelligence to education and medicine. He has written more than 260 papers (more than 30 of them have been published in internationally recognized journals by publishers such as *ACM, IEEE, Pergamon Press,* etc.), three books on intelligent systems, and several chapters in books on intelligent systems and software engineering edited by distinguished scientists.

Karen García has vast experience in the development of organizations and community programs across the nited States, Puerto Rico, and internationally. She earned her BA, MA, and EdD at the University of Puerto Rico, San Francisco State University, and at the University of Massachusetts, respectively. Her expertise in social science research methods, general systems theory, and participatory educational methods makes her a unique practitioner and change facilitator. Karen centers her practice on issues of economic parity, ethnic relations, gender equity, and mental health and is committed to the development of a Latino presence online. Her current interest is the widespread use of technology within learning environments and its associated cultural transformation.

Timothy Hall is director of EMRC-Educational Media Research Centre, and Technical Director of PUII – Programme for University Industry Interface, University of Limerick, Ireland. His research interests are: TEL, TEL support for PBL-Problem Based Learning, online access to real experimental equipment, collaborative and self-organised learning, and the integration of these techniques into a complete and supportive learning environments, e-learning pedagogy, curriculum design, personalisation, reusability, and interoperability. For many years Tim has been active in EU collaborative programmes in education and training and maintains links in most EU countries, Central and Eastern Europe, and beyond in China and Malaysia

Axel Hunger studied Electrical Engineering at the RWTH Aachen and was awarded his PhD in 1982. Between 1979 and 1987, he was the leader of a Test and Simulation of Digital Circuits research group at the RWTH Aachen before being appointed Professor for Computer Engineering in the Faculty of Electrical Engineering at the University in Duisburg in 1988. His areas of research include the development of multimedia tools for teaching and learning platforms, curriculum development for international degree programmes, and engineering training in an international context.

Kevin Johnson has a degree in Electronic Engineering and an MEng in Computer Engineering from the University of Limerick, graduating with a PhD in 2004 after working on the Encompass Project. To date, he has worked on a number of projects with the EMRC using LAMP technologies. He has worked on the Consortium for Open Source in the Public Administration (COSPA) project, funded under the EU's Sixth Framework Programme (FP6). Currently he is working within the Programme for Universty Industry Interface (PUII) in the University of Limerick on several projects looking to better the links between Industry and University and the graduates therein.

Claire Kenny is a research assistant at Dublin City University, currently involved in an EU-supported learning technology project on learning object development and reuse. Claire has recently completed her MSc by research on a topic in intelligent tutoring systems. Claire has been involved in the development of content and supporting infrastructure for technology-enhanced active learning, including the IDLE system, for several years.

Nenad Krdzavac received his BSc from the Department of Mathematics and Informatics of the Faculty of Science at the University of Kragujevac in Serbia in 1998. He received his MSc from the Faculty of Electrical Engineering of the University of Belgrade in Serbia in 2007. Currently, he is a PhD student at FON—School of Business Administration of the University of Belgrade. So far, he has authored several research papers. He is a member of the GOOD OLD AI research group. His research interest is description logics.

Bogdan Marin received his MSc in Computer Science in 2002, at the University of Craiova—Romania. Since 2003, he has been researching on artificial intelligence with a focus on agent-based intelligent (Teaching-) Tutoring Systems within the framework of his doctoral dissertation at the University of Duisburg-Essen. Results of his research activities are first of all implemented in the synchronous groupware PASSENGER and analysed in real test scenarios.

James E. McCarthy. After receiving his bachelor's degree in Mathematics Education from Winona State University in 1986, McCarthy entered the Applied Experimental Psychology program at Miami University. There his studies focused on human factors and ergonomics, cognitive psychology, as well as sensation and perception. While attending Miami University, Jim participated in a 1-year research fellowship at Honeywell's System Research Center. After receiving his PhD in 1992, Jim completed a post-doctoral fellowship at McGill University in Montreal. Following the fellowship, Jim accepted a position with Sonalysts, Inc. in Waterford, CT.

Elevated to Vice President, Instructional Systems, Jim continues to lead Sonalysts' research and development efforts as they pertain to advanced training technology. He has led the development of systems that delivery adaptive multimedia training and intelligent tutoring. He has also developed a suite of authoring and delivery tools that allow subject-matter experts to produce an integrated set of high-quality interactive electronic technical manuals (IETMs), training, and performance support material. Jim continues to be active in the human systems integration (HSI) community as well. He is currently participating in the design of a next-generation destroyer for the U.S. Navy.

Gianluca Merlo graduated with a degree in Psychology at the University of Palermo in 2003. Since then, he has collaborated with the Institute for Educational Technology in Palermo. His research interests concern the use of metacognition in educational environement as a way to improve both awareness and performance of students.

Leonel Morgado is assistant professor at the University of Trás-os-Montes e Alto Douro, in Portugal, where he lectures on the use of computers in early childhood education. His main research interest is the use of computer programming as a tool for learning, particularly within the context of preschool education. Before pursuing an academic career, he was a terminologist for an MS Office 97 localization team, a manager of Web-development and software-deployment teams, and a programmer.

Renate Motschnig is professor of computer science at the University of Vienna and heads the Research Lab for Educational Technologies at the Faculty of Computer Science. Her research goals center in the discovery of principles and the development of methods and techniques to improve the development, effectiveness, and the quality of socio-technical systems. Her current research interests include conceptual modeling, humanistic education, process models, group and team processes, technology enhanced learning, motivation, development of metacognitive competence, cognitions and emotions in learning, the Person Centered Approach, communication, and new media. Most recently, Renate Motschnig has focused on exploring the potentials of the Person-Centered Approach in the fields of knowledge, learning, and management.

Tom Myers studied physics in Bogotá, Colombia and Buenos Aires before his BA in the Great Books program of St. John's College of Santa Fe (1975) and PhD in computer science from the University of Pennsylvania (1980). He taught computer science (at the University of Delaware and at Colgate University) until 1990. His books go from *Equations, Models, and Programs: A Mathematical Introduction to Computer Science* (Prentice-Hall, 1988) to *Google, Amazon and Beyond: Creating* *and Consuming Web Services* (with A. Nakhimovsky; Apress, 2004). He has also written articles and computer programs, mostly involving Java, JSP, Javascript, XML, and XSLT. His recent work has mostly been in collaboration with Alexander Nakhimovsky of Colgate.

Alexander Nakhimovsky (PhD Cornell 1979) is associate professor of Computer Science at Colgate University. Major interests include international science education, especially in developing countries; collaborative Internet Technologies, and the impact of technology on Linguistics and Education. Recent publications include a book on Web Services (Apress 2003), and papers on semantic information processing. He recently taught courses including Introduction to Linguistics (2005) and a First-Year seminar on globalization (2003).

Olfa Nasraoui is the Endowed Chair of E-Commerce and the director of the Knowledge Discovery and Web Mining Lab in the department of Computer Science and Engineering at the University of Louisville. She received her PhD in Computer Engineering and Computer Science from the University of Missouri-Columbia in 1999. From 2000 to 2005, she was an assistant professor at the University of Memphis. Her research activities include data mining, in particular, Web mining and mining evolving data streams, Web personalization, and computational intelligence. She has served on the organizing and program committees of several conferences and workshops, including the leading series of workshops in the Web Mining and Web Usage Analysis area: WebKDD 2004, WebKDD 2005, and WebKDD 2006. She is the recipient of the National Science Foundation CAREER Award for research in Web usage mining. Her research is funded mainly by NSF and by NASA. She is a member of IEEE and ACM.

Emma O'Brien is a postdoctoral researcher at the University of Limerick where she is actively involved in the Programme for University Industry Interface. She received a primary degree in Business Computing and a Masters Degree in Computing in Education from Limerick institute of technology in 2000 and 2003 respectively. In 2005 she graduated with a PhD from the University of Limerick. Emma has previously worked on many EU funded projects. Areas of research include e-learning, training models for SMEs, and open and distance learning.

Simona Ottaviano is a psychologists and since 2001 has been a researcher at the Institute for Educational Technology in Palermo. Her main research interests concern the use of the use of Information Technology to define new learning methodologies and to design environments to support different aspects of learning.

Claus Pahl is a senior lecturer and the leader of the Web and Software Engineering research group at Dublin City University, which focuses on Web technologies and e-learning applications in particular. Claus has published more than 125 papers including a wide range of journal articles, book chapters, and conference contributions on e-learning. He is on the editorial board of the *International Journal on E-Learning* and the *International Journal of Technology-Enhanced Learning* and is a regular reviewer for journals and conferences in the area of software, Web, and learning technologies and their applications. He has extensive experience in educational technologies, both as an instructor using technology-supported teaching and learning at undergraduate and postgraduate level and as a researcher in Web-based learning technology. The IDLE environment, developed by him and his students, is in use in undergraduate teaching since 1999.

Sonja Radenkovic received her BSc in Information Systems from the Department of Information Systems and Technologies of the FON—School of Business Administration at the University of Belgrade in Serbia in 2004. She is a master's student at the FON of the University of Belgrade. In 2002, she was awarded the Norwegian scholarship as the best student during the studies. Her research interest is in the area of e-learning systems. She has authored several research papers. She is member of the GOOD OLD AI research group.

Luciano Seta is a researcher at the Institute for Educational Technologies of the Italian National Research Council. He holds a degree in Physics and PhD in Applied Mathematics from Palermo University. His research interests concern mathematical modelling in different aspects of real life phenomena originating in physics biology, economy, and social science

Goran Shimic is a teacher of applied computer science at the Military Academy, University of Belgrade, Serbia. He became master of computer science at School of Business Administration, University of Belgrade (MS, 2004). The mastering thesis was named Multitutor – Intelligent tutoring system. Currently, he is working on his doctorial thesis, Intelligent E-Learning Management. His main research interests include software engineering, intelligent systems, knowledge representation, ontologies, intelligent reasoning, applications, artificial intelligence techniques to education, and Web tehnologies. He has developed several practical intelligent systems (Multitutor, MTutor), and actively participates as a consultant to several ongoing projects in education (ProLearn, Ariadne, IFIP TC AI). He is a member of GOOD OLD AI group (http://goodoldai.org.yu).

Renata Suzuki is an Oxford graduate with 20 years' experience in Japan as an EFL teacher/lecturer. Her expertise is in EFL, curriculum development, and environmental education. She has designed courses combining environmental awareness with English education, and published a free book of environmental songs for kids available at http://www.onegreenleaf.net. Renata has extensive experience working with all levels and ages of English teaching in Japan and Europe. Presently she is involved in professional development at the University of Birmingham. Her current research interest centers on the use of blogs in teacher development. Visit and comment at her blog at http://grankageva.blogspot.com/

Tetyana Sydorenko (MA Linguistics Eastern Michigan University 2006) is a PhD student in the Second Language Studies program at Michigan State University. Her major interests are applications of technology to foreign language learning, materials development for language instruction, and cognitive processing in language learning. She has recently presented on software design for language learning (MITESOL 2005). She has taught English as a second language and a course on TOEFL preparation (2005-2006).

Elizabeth Uruchurtu is an associate lecturer in the ACES Faculty at Sheffield Hallam University, where she collaborates with the e-learning group in the dissemination of best practices. She is also completing her PhD (Heriot-Watt University, Scotland). Her research focuses on the design of adaptive interfaces for the personalisation of Web-based learning materials. Previously she received an MSc in Interactive Multimedia from Heriot-Watt University.

Robert Wyatt is an assistant professor of Biology and the director of Distance Learning at Western Kentucky University. He received a BS with Honours in Biology from Indiana University and a PhD in Molecular Biology from the University of Georgia. He has taught courses at a distance since 1992, starting via compressed video (ITV) between the islands of St. Thomas and St. Croix while at the University of the Virgin Islands, later adding Web components to the courses, and finally a totally online course in 1996.

Leyla Zhuhadar is a doctoral candidate in the Department of Computer Engineering and Computer Science at the University of Louisville. After receiving her master's degree in Computer Science from Western Kentucky University in 2004, Ms. Zhuhadar started her doctoral program under the supervision of Dr. Olfa Nasraoui at the University of Louisville. For the past 3 years, Ms. Zhuhadar has been working as an Instructional Designer and Web Mining Consultant at the Distance Learning Office at Western Kentucky University under the guidance of Dr. Robert Wyatt. She has been involved in developing and introducing several cutting-edge instructional technology processes for distance education, such as Web mining, Podcasting, and VODcasting. Ms. Zhuhadar's research interests include Web mining, Web personalization, recommender systems, and distance education. Her dissertation focuses on the use of Web mining and Web personalization in distance education.

Index